ethics
of eros

ethics
of eros

IRIGARAY'S
REWRITING
OF THE
PHILOSOPHERS

Tina Chanter

ROUTLEDGE   NEW YORK • LONDON

Published in 1995 by

Routledge
29 West 35th Street
New York, NY 10001

Published in Great Britain by

Routledge
11 New Fetter Lane
London EC4P 4EE

Library of Congress Cataloging-in-Publication Data

    Chanter, Tina.
    Ethics of Eros : Irigaray's rewriting of the philosophers / Tina Chanter.
    p.   cm.
    Includes bibliographical references and index.
    ISBN 0-415-90522-2—ISBN 0-415-90523-0 (pbk.)
    1. Irigaray, Luce. I. Title.
B2430.I74C47   1994   93-44311
194—dc20   CIP

British Library Cataloguing-in-Publication Data also available

for Jane and Miglena
in friendship,
past and future

The very word "erotic" comes from the Greek word eros,
*the personification of love in all its aspects—born of Chaos—and personifying
creative power and harmony. When I speak of the erotic, then, I speak of it as
an assertion of the life force of women; of that creative energy empowered, the
knowledge and use of which we are now reclaiming in our language, our
history, our dancing, our loving, our work, our lives.*

—Audre Lorde

contents

acknowledgments

A FEW YEARS AGO I DID NOT FULLY APPRECIATE THE POINT of the acknowledgments and dedications that authors write at the beginning of their books. Not until I tried to write a book of my own did I begin to understand what a major undertaking it was and how it could not help but affect in some way at some time everyone I knew well.

I am indebted to Robert Bernasconi, who has been exemplary in so many ways—as a teacher, as a scholar, and most of all as a friend. It was Robert who first introduced me to the work of Derrida, Hegel, Heidegger, and Levinas, and whose readings of these thinkers have had an abiding influence on my own understanding not only of these central figures but of philosophy as a whole. I am grateful for his comments on early drafts of the material on Levinas and Irigaray. Noreen O'Connor's influence can also be felt throughout this book in more ways than one. Noreen's work on Levinas has been important for me, but far more important is the impact she has had on my development as a feminist. From the time I first met Noreen she encouraged me not only to take feminism seriously, but, in doing so, to take myself seriously. Her influence has had a profound and lasting effect on me, and her personal example is a continual source of inspiration to me, even across the water.

At crucial points during this project Jill Robbins offered her support, comments, encouragement, and enthusiasm. Her response to the book was characteristically generous. Margaret Whitford offered detailed, constructive, and informed criticisms and advice from which I have learned, and which I have followed as far as I am able. I want to thank both of them for their time and effort in reading the entire manuscript. The critical feedback and support I received from Michelle Massé and Idee Winfield, both of whom also read most of the manuscript, was invaluable during the final stages of writing. It helped me to clarify my ideas, clean up my prose, and refine the project as a whole. I cannot thank them enough. Michelle has been more than supportive not only as a reader but also in her role as director of Women's and Gender Studies at Louisiana

State University. She manages to represent so many of the things that feminism, at its best, can be.

Portions of this book have been written at numerous desks, tables, and computers, in many different libraries, cafés, and houses, in a number of different states, and in a few different countries, and many of the chapters are reminiscent for me of particular times, places, events, and friends. In particular, I want to thank Erin Rice and Kay Parkhurst for their friendship and hospitality in Massachusetts during the summers of 1990 and 1991, and Ann Stokes for the use of her studio in Vermont in the summer of 1990.

A postdoctoral fellowship at the University of Virginia Commonwealth Center for Literary and Cultural Change from 1990 to 1991 provided me with the opportunity to make substantial headway with the book. I gratefully acknowledge the support of Ralph Cohen, director of the center. I would also like to thank Louisiana State University for their partial support of me during 1990–1991, and during the summer of 1990. In the summer of 1992, as the recipient of the Charles Manship Fellowship, I was able to write chapter four, and to edit several other chapters. A grant from the Center for French and Francophone Studies at Louisiana State University in the summer of 1993 enabled me to put the finishing touches to the book. I am grateful to Edouard Glissant, the director, for this award.

Some of the material in chapter one was first conceived in a paper that Rodolphe Gasché invited me to present to the Comparative Literature Program in the Eugenio Donato Lecture Series in 1992 at the State University of New York at Buffalo. The paper, "Kristeva's Politics of Change: Tracking Essentialism with the Help of a Sex/Gender Map," is published in *Ethics, Politics, and Difference in Julia Kristeva's Writings* (ed. Kelly Oliver [Routledge, 1993]). Judith Butler was kind enough to comment on an earlier version of this article, and I am indebted to her for her helpful response. Chapter two has appeared in another version in *Ellipsis* (1[2] [1991]: 225–75). It originated in a presentation I gave in July 1990 at the Collegium Phaenomenologicum in Perugia, Italy, in the context of the theme "Phenomenology, Ethics, Politics: The Question of Difference/Unity." I would like to express my gratitude to Guiseppina Moneta, to other faculty and students present, and in particular to Peg Birmingham who directed the Collegium, and who made it possible to engage in a philosophical inquiry of feminism in a way that proved fruitful for many of the participants. I also extend my thanks to Toril Moi and Elizabeth Spelman for their comments on early drafts of this chapter.

Chapter three is based on a paper I presented at the Collegium Phaenomenologicum in July 1991, under the title "The Imperialism of the

Same: Irigaray, Hegel, and Women." The theme of the collegium that year was "On the Tragic: Hegel, Hölderlin, Nietzsche, Heidegger," and I thank Dennis Schmidt for inviting me to contribute to it, and the students and faculty who made the occasion possible. I also gratefully acknowledge Adelaide Russo's comments on earlier versions of this chapter.

I presented an early version of chapter five at a Department of Philosophy Colloquium at the University of Virginia in 1990. Chapters four and six include some material, in a reworked form, from "Metaphysical Presence: Heidegger on Time and Eternity," in *Ethics and Danger: Currents in Continental Thought*, Selected Studies in Phenomenology and Existential Philosophy (eds. C. Scott and A. Dallery [Albany: State University of New York Press, 1992], pp. 125–38), and "Derrida and Heidegger: The Interlacing of Texts," *The Textual Sublime: Deconstruction and its Differences* (eds. H. Silverman and G. Aylesworth [Albany: State University of New York Press, 1990], pp. 61–68). A different version of Chapter five is to appear under the title "Beyond Eros: Metaphysical Desire in Levinas's Philosophy," in *Philosophy and the Discourses of Desire* (Continental Philosophy Series VII, ed. H. Silverman). Some material in the afterword is appearing in a forthcoming issue of *The Southern Journal of Philosophy*. Conversations with Charles Shepherdson helped me think through the project as a whole.

While this book bears only a very tangential relation to my Ph.D. thesis, I owe a debt to the professors and students at the State University of New York, Stony Brook. I want to thank in particular David Allison, whose painstaking attention to the stylistic travesties I committed in my Ph.D. thesis helped me to begin to learn how to write. I am grateful too for the continuing support of Edward Casey, Donn Welton, and Hugh Silverman.

Among my colleagues at L.S.U., Greg Schufreider helped to smooth the transition I had to make in moving from England to the United States in innumerable ways, while members of the Women's and Gender Studies faculty provided a community within which I have been able to pursue my work. Charles Bigger read and commented on chapter four of the book, and I am grateful for his collegiality and support.

In the background of this book are all the people who taught me as a student at the University of Essex, and who welcomed me back as a colleague. My colleagues at Thames Polytechnic and at the University of London helped me in a variety of ways. I want to acknowledge most of all Alison Assiter's friendship and encouragement. I also want to acknowledge the support and help offered me over the years by David Wood of Vanderbilt University. In the final stages of putting together the manuscript, the Department of Philosophy at the University of Memphis provided me with a friendly and stimulating atmosphere within which to work. I am very appreciative of Mary Bloodsworth's meticulous and efficient help with copyediting, a task she undertook with good humor and conscientiousness. I would also like to thank Marias Cimitele, John Drabinski, Claire Katz, and Philip Maloney for their help with proofreading.

Less tangible, but no less important to the completion of this project, is the friendship of Jill Bambury, Anne Boudreau, Kate Blacklock, and Lori Waselchuk. I also want to thank my parents and family for their continual support. Finally, Maureen MacGrogan seemed to know when to leave me alone to write, and when to press me to let go of the manuscript. She allowed me to discover what book I wanted to write, and trusted me when I changed directions.

abbreviations

IRIGARAY

OTHER AUTHORS

AROO Woolf, *A Room of One's Own* (1981)

ASD Beauvoir, *All Said and Done*, trans. Patrick O'Brian (1984)

AV Derrida, "At This Very Moment In This Work Here I Am," trans. R. Berezdevin, in *Re-Reading Levinas* (1991)

BN Sartre, *Being and Nothingness*, trans. Hazel E. Barnes (1956)

BT Heidegger, *Being and Time*, trans. John Macquarrie and E. Robinson (1980)

BW Heidegger, *Martin Heidegger: Basic Writings*, ed. David F. Krell (1978)

C Derrida, "Choreographies," interview with Christie V. McDonald (1982)

DC Levinas, interview in *Dialogues with Contemporary Continental Thinkers*, ed. Richard Kearney (1984)

DF Levinas, *Difficult Freedom: Essays on Judaism*, trans. Seán Hand (1990)

EE Levinas, *Existence and Existents*, trans. Alphonso Lingis (1978)

EI Levinas, *Ethics and Infinity* (1985)

FOC Beauvoir, *The Force of Circumstance*, trans. Richard Howard (1985)

G Derrida, *Glas*, trans. John P. Leavey Jr. and Richard Rand (1986)

M Descartes, "Meditations on First Philosophy," *The Philosophical Works of Descartes*, vol. 1, trans. Elizabeth S. Haldane and G. R. T. Ross (1979)

OB Levinas, *Otherwise than Being or Beyond Essence*, trans. Alphonso Lingis (1981)

OG Derrida, "*Ousia* and *Grammē*" in *Margins of Philosophy*, trans. A. Bass (1982)

OGr Derrida, *Of Grammatology*, trans. Gayatri Spivak (1976)

OWA Heidegger, "The Origin of the Work of Art" in *Poetry, Language, Thought*, trans. Albert Hofstadter (1975)

P Aristotle, *Physics*, vol. 1, trans. Philip H. Wicksteed and F. M. Cornford (1980)

PC Derrida, *The Post Card: From Socrates to Freud and Beyond* (1987)

PhS Hegel, *Phenomenology of Spirit*, trans. A.V. Miller (1979)

PI Heidegger, "The Principle of Identity," in *Identity and Difference*, trans. Joan Stambaugh (1974)

PL Beauvoir, *The Prime of Life*, trans. Peter Green (1984)

PLT Heidegger, *Poetry, Language, Thought*, trans. Albert Hofstadter (1975)

PS Derrida, *Positions*, trans. Alan Bass (1981)

QCT Heidegger, *The Question Concerning Technology and Other Essays* (1977)

RP Levinas, "Reflections on the Philosophy of Hitlerism," trans. Seán Hand (1990)

S Derrida, *Spurs*, trans. Barbara Harlow (1979)

SE Freud, *Standard Edition of the Complete Works of Freud*, trans. James Strachey

Sem I Lacan, *The Seminar of Jacques Lacan*, Book I, ed. Jacques-Alain Miller, trans. John Forrester (1991)

Si Levinas, "Signature," trans. Adriaan Peperzak (1978)

SS Beauvoir, *The Second Sex*, 2 vols. (1954)

TB Heidegger, *On Time and Being*, trans. Joan Stambaugh (1969)

TI   Levinas, *Totality and Infinity,* trans. Alphonso Lingis (1979)

TO   Levinas, *Time and the Other,* trans. Richard Cohen (1987)

TP   Derrida, *The Truth in Painting,* trans. Geoff Bennington and Ian McLeod (1987)

WB   Derrida, "Women in the Beehive," (1987)

WD   Derrida, "Violence and Metaphysics: An Essay on the Thought of Emmanuel Levinas," in *Writing and Difference,* trans. Alan Bass (1978)

JOURNALS

FS   *Feminist Studies* 6 (2) (Summer 1980)

YFS   *Yale French Studies* 72 (1986)

FOREIGN LANGUAGE TEXTS

AE   Levinas, *Autrement qu'être ou au-delà de l'essence* (1978)

CP   Derrida, *La carte postale: de Socrate à Freud et au-delà* (1980)

DE   Levinas, *De l'existence à l'existant* (1984)

DG   Derrida, *De la Grammatologie* (1967)

DL   Levinas, *Difficile liberté* (1976)

DS   Beauvoir, *Le deuxième sexe,* 2 vols. (1949). References are to volume 1, for example DS: 13, unless preceded by the number 2, for example, DS 2: 13

EC   Levinas, "Et Dieu créa la femme" in *Du sacré au saint, cinq nouvelles lectures talmudiques* (1977)

ED   Derrida, "Violence et métaphysique: Essai sur la pensée d'Emmanuel Levinas," in *L'écriture et la différence* (1967)

EeI   Levinas, *Éthique et infini* (1982)

EM   Derrida, "En ce moment même dans cet ouvrage me voici," in *Textes pour Emmanuel Levinas* (1980)

EN   Sartre, *L'être et le néant* (1943)

FA   Beauvoir, *La force de l'âge* (1960)

FDC   Beauvoir, *La force des choses* (1963)

GI   Derrida, *Glas* (1974)

H   *Holzwege* (1957)

ID   Heidegger, *Identität und Differenz* (1957)

OGe   Derrida, "*Ousia* et *Grammē*," in *Marges de la philosophie* (1972)

PhG   Hegel, *Phänomenologie des Geistes* (1952)

PT   Derrida, *Positions* (1972)

R   Derrida, "Restitutions de la vérité en pointure" (1978)

SD   Heidegger, *Zur Sache des Denkens* (1969)

SZ   Heidegger, *Sein und Zeit* (1984)

TA   Levinas, *Le temps et l'autre* (1979)

TCF   Beauvoir, *Tout compte faite* (1972)

TeI   Levinas, *Totalité et infini* (1980)

TH   Levinas, "Transcendance et hauteur" (1962)

VA   Heidegger, *Vorträge und Aufsätze* (1978)

preface

ONE OF THE MOST POWERFUL CATEGORIES OF ANALYSIS that has served the needs of feminism in recent years is that of gender.[1] To the extent that the discourse of sexual difference puts into question some of the assumptions that are typically made in gender analyses, sexual difference is regarded with suspicion. Feminists committed to maintaining gender as the center of feminist analyses object to the discourse of sexual difference on the grounds that it is ahistorical, that it conceives of the relationship between male and female in universal terms, and that it does not leave any room for social change. The latter objection is often couched in terms of the idea that to take psychoanalytic theory seriously is to give up any hope of improving women's situation, an idea which in turn is sometimes expressed as a misgiving about the priority that psychoanalysis accords to language. To privilege language—the implication is—is to deprive feminism of its potential to effect change through social protest. Thus Elaine Showalter—who stands momentarily as a representative[2] of feminists whose understanding of psychoanalysis leads them to suspect it of inhibiting the activist edge of feminism—writes that

> Critics working under the rubric of "sexual difference" make use of Freudian and post-Freudian accounts of the construction of gendered subjectivities, relying heavily on the work of Jacques Lacan. They believe that gender is primarily constructed through the acquisition of language, rather than through social ascription or cultural practice (Showalter, 1989: 3).[3]

The disjunction betokened by Showalter's phrase "rather than" implies that if one is concerned with language, one cannot also be concerned with social change.[4]

The suggestion that the discourse of sexual difference construes the relations that currently exist between men and women as inevitable and incapable of improvement, because they are seemingly universal and static, is indeed a cause for concern. The question is whether critics are justified in their belief that the psychoanalytic discourse of sexual difference reifies sexual relations in a way that renders hope for social change an impossible dream.[5] One task of the discussion that follows is to suggest that the discourse of sexual difference need not invoke the current social configurations between men and women as either inevitable or universal, and that Luce Irigaray's does not. Irigaray's interrogation of sexual difference is, I suggest, at the same time a concern with the possibilities for social change.

Suspicions that Irigaray's position militates against social change are perpetuated by the misrepresentation of the structuralist or post-structuralist beliefs that are attributed to her. Critics misrepresent the uses to which the discourse of post-structuralism puts Saussurian linguistics partly because they have an inadequate understanding of the more traditional metaphysical conceptions of language that thinkers such as Irigaray, Derrida, and Lacan attempt to overcome. Thus Eve Tavor Bannet writes that "For Lacan, language is a self-referential system which coincides only tangentially with the experienced reality of things."[6] Such a reading misconstrues Saussure's arbitrariness of the signifier as if it amounted to a quasi-empiricism. That is, it assumes the independence of reality from language, rather than seeing language as constitutive of reality. The result is that Lacan seems to conceive of language as somehow misrepresenting the true nature of reality, where "reality" is understood as outside of, and beyond the reach of, language. In fact this conception of language has more in common with the empiricist model from which structuralism sought an escape, than it does with Lacan, Irigaray, or Derrida. The empiricist view of language involves a subject vainly trying to represent an objective world that stands over against it. Here, language is considered an inadequate tool for getting at the truth, insofar as it can merely produce inferior copies or images of a forever inaccessible and transcendent world. To concede that an already constituted reality exists, independently of a community of language users, returns us to metaphysical assumptions that can be traced back to a dualistic metaphysics, in which subjects are cut off from a world to which they unsuccessfully try to gain access through language. Catherine Zuckert mistakenly aligns Derrida with such an empiricist view of language when she says,

> According to earlier modern philosophers like Locke, Hume, and Kant, the world as we experience it is actually not composed of "things." All we know or experience are the impressions these things make on us. We do not, as Kant argued, ever know the "things in themselves."

> If this is true, Derrida suggests, the "things in the world" are rather like the marks a writer leaves on a page—traces of a cause, source, or author who or which is never present (Zuckert, 1991: 340).

The assumption of a pre-existent reality, prior to language, is precisely what Irigaray and Lacan, influenced in this respect by Hegel and Heidegger, want to overcome.

Insofar as the idea that Irigaray endorses currently prevailing social configurations rests upon a failure to distinguish her view of language from naively metaphysical accounts, it seems to me to be emblematic of a more general problem that plagues the reception of feminists who take seriously the continental tradition of philosophy. There is a conspicuous lack of close readings and textual analyses of their work, and, in Irigaray's case, a neglect of both the philosophical texts that she discusses at length and the history of philosophy. In place of careful or detailed readings, we are offered general (and often faulty) statements about the inadequacy of post-structuralist tenets, and then asked to use these to judge the value of feminists who are assumed to adhere to them. It is hard to imagine two more divergent views of language than those endorsed by post-structuralism on the one hand, and those of empiricism on the other hand—yet these are hastily lumped together as if one explains the other. By elaborating the phenomenological and post-phenomenological background out of which Irigaray's thought arises, I hope to correct some of the more blatant misconceptions as to what her "post-structuralist" views amount to.

If inadequate comprehension of the history of philosophy is in part responsible for the poor press Irigaray has received, the problems do not stop there. A screen has been erected between the writings of Irigaray and the political activism that is such a vital aspect of feminism. There are those who are fascinated by the images on the screen—the art critics, the film theorists, and the psychoanalysts.[7] And then there are those who see the screen as nothing more than a barrier of mystification, barring access to the "real" issues with which feminism should concern itself. Representing two extreme attitudes toward French feminism, these two audiences of Irigaray—those who applaud her radicality and those who denounce her as reactionary—have little to say to one another. The image Irigaray presents to those who champion her as a French feminist, embracing the free play of signifiers, and as such explicitly repudiating essentialism, is hardly recognizable by those who are convinced that French feminism is implicated in biological determinism.

Irigaray's call to interrogate sexual difference has been interpreted as a danger signal by many feminists who are wary of essentialism.[8] Mary Poovey criticizes Irigaray's alleged biological essentialism when she says, "Luce Irigaray . . . authorizes th[e] return to biology and essentialism in her creation of a myth of female desire and in basing 'feminine' language on the physical properties of female genitalia" (Poovey, 1988: 55). Lynne Segal and Toril Moi point out that to insist that particular traits of women's nature are biologically determined involves essentialist assumptions.[9] Insofar as it claims for women a fixed nature, essentialism does indeed constitute a danger for feminism. If women's subordinate and inferior position in society is predetermined by their biological makeup, then there is no hope of improving their situation, short of interfering with biology. It is clear that essentialism is to be guarded against. It is far from clear, however, whether the charge of essentialism is justified in Irigaray's case. Diana Fuss, despite her largely sympathetic reading of Irigaray, still labels her a "materialist essentialist."[10] Iris Marion Young says,

> French theorists explicitly criticize feminist tendencies toward essentialism [but they] nevertheless share some of the essentialist tendencies of gynocentric feminism in the U.S. They rely on an opposition between the masculine and the feminine, even where, as in Kristeva, they do not necessarily associate these with men and women. Though these theories explicitly question Western dichotomous thinking, their use of the opposition of masculinity and femininity retains its traditional dichotomous terms, in revaluated form: the masculine is power, discursive rationality, calculation, abstraction, while the feminine is desire, sensuality, poetic language, the immediacy of contact with nature. Like their counterparts across the ocean, these French theorists tend to reduce women's specificity to reproductive biology and the function of mothering (Young, 1985: 181).

Young refers to Domna A. Stanton, who, while she does not want "to deny the importance of an initial counter-valorization of the maternal-feminine as a negation/subversion of paternal hierarchies, a heuristic tool for reworking images and meanings, above all, an enabling mythology," nonetheless warns that "the moment the maternal emerges as a new dominance, it must be put into question before it congeals as a feminine essence, as unchanging in-difference" (Stanton, 1989: 170).

If Young and Stanton criticize French feminists for the biological essentialism they think is entailed by their interest in the maternal, others see

Irigaray's work as psychologically reifying. Janet Sayers says of Irigaray that she "claims that women's femininity is given in essence by their biology. Women, she says, have a distinctive psychology and desire given by the nature of their sexual organs" (Sayers, 1986: 42). While the maternal function and the body are the site of many essentialist critiques of French feminism, Irigaray has been found guilty of endorsing "social" essentialism too. Henry Louis Gates writes that he is "concerned about her implicit *social* essentialism, which is entailed by her conception of the patriarchal order as wall-to-wall, all-pervasive; as another name for totality" (Gates, 1988: 621–22).

My suggestion is that the essentialist charge originates from a well-meaning but outmoded idea of what feminism should be. To use the language of the essentialist debate—language from which I want to move away—one might say that the essentialist dismissal of Irigaray rests upon an essentialist definition of feminism—namely, the idea that feminism can only consist in playing down sexual difference.[11] Underplaying sexual difference, in this feminist scenario, is the corollary of emphasizing gender construction, which appeals not to sexual difference but to the commonalities between the sexes. To emphasize gender rather than sex has been an important motif in the struggle to achieve equality of opportunities and rights between men and women. The strategy of stipulating social roles as the most decisive influence on women's lives has served as an effective way of acknowledging and facilitating the possibility of changing the most restrictive aspects of those roles. It is hard to overestimate the importance of this strategy in securing equality for women to date, but the success of playing off gender against sex should not obscure the need for feminism to move with the times, to redefine its goals, and to adapt to changing circumstances. A crucial part of this re-evaluation of feminist goals should be to reassess how useful it is to emphasize gender to the extent of obliterating the significance of sexual difference. Do we have to neglect sexual difference in order to emphatically reject gender-role stereotyping? Can we find a way out of the impasse that has been generated for feminists who are afraid that if we admit to significant differences between the sexes we risk losing the ground that feminism has fought so hard to win? Is there a way of consolidating the successes of feminism without retreating from the urgent task of critically evaluating our fundamental aims, strategies, and assumptions?

I suggest that both those who impatiently dismiss French feminists as essentialist, and those who uncompromisingly defend them against such charges, tend to appeal to a distinction that has played a fundamental role in feminism, but which depends upon a variety of dichotomies that need to be questioned. The dichotomies that are associated with the distinction between sex and gender include biology versus society, and nature versus culture. Supported by these tenuous oppositions, the essentialism/anti-essentialism distinction itself is in need of demystification. If we are to understand the issues Irigaray raises, we need first to clean the various lenses through which her various readers view her. I argue that Irigaray's interest in the question of sexual difference does not preclude consideration of the issues at stake in gender analyses, but rather requires their inclusion. While it is true that the relations between sex and gender are subjected to a rethinking in Irigaray's interrogation of sexual difference, the realignment of these categories does not militate against social change—far from it.

Although some have tried to clean up the image of French feminism, the taint of essentialism remains, residues of biological reductionism seem to linger on, and hostile suspicion of reactionary elitism persists. If you see the free play of signifiers as an open invitation to any and all interpretations of feminism, including those that, however unwittingly, fall back on traditional stereotypical views of femininity, it is hard to appreciate the significance of this free play, whatever radicality post-structuralist theorists might claim for it.

To confront fundamental questions about what feminism should be doing and how it should conceive of itself need not be a matter of forcing feminism into a single mold by over-generalizing about the movement as a whole. To ask far-reaching questions about the nature of feminism is to accede to the need to formulate feminist positions carefully and to be reflective about our goals. In the wake of heated debates over multiculturalism, feminists are becoming increasingly aware of the need to redefine their relations to race. At the same time, socio-economic problems, such as unemployment, are bringing into focus still more forcefully issues of class. The more scarce jobs become, the less sympathy there is likely to be for practices that have become an established part of feminist agendas, such as preferential hiring practices designed to benefit women and minorities.

Many men, who have traditionally been the breadwinners, are having difficulty in successfully maintaining that role in the current economic climate. To the extent that feminism forces them to compete with a wider range of applicants, some of whom may be viewed more favorably than traditional breadwinners, it is not surprising that feminism is perceived as a threat, particularly by would-be workers who occupy the ranks of the lower-income brackets and who typically lack alternative resources to improve their situations. Those who are—or at least perceive themselves to be—most directly affected by and who therefore have the most to fear from feminist successes in the job market, are precisely those who, in more favorable economic circumstances, might have been allies of feminists.

Tensions arising from the current economic climate thus put working-class politics at odds with feminist politics, rather than fostering the potential for cooperation between groups that share the problems of the disadvantaged in common. In short, feminism is undergoing a crisis of identity, a crisis that is neither far removed from, nor incidental to the economic and political crises that the Western industrialized capitalist world is undergoing, at both the global and individual levels. Feminism cannot afford to neglect basic questions either about the nature of feminist struggles, or about the relations of feminism to other political struggles.

Irigaray maintains that while it remains important to continue to lobby for equal rights, it is a mistake to restrict feminism to such a goal. To do so is to neglect even more fundamental questions about whether or not the equality with men for which feminists strive is worthy of attainment. Irigaray is not merely concerned with equal rights for women, but with a critique of what passes for success according to patriarchal standards. bell hooks makes a similar point when she says,

> It is difficult to involve women in new processes of feminist politicization because so many of us think that identifying men as the enemy, resisting male domination, gaining equal access to power and privilege are the end of any feminist movement. Not only is it not the end, it is not even the place we want revitalized feminist movement to begin. We want to begin as women seriously addressing ourselves, not solely in relation to men, but in relation to an entire structure of domination of which patriarchy is one part (hooks, 1990: 191).

While it may be necessary for women to work within the confines of the current political and social structures in order to achieve equality of rights and opportunities, these efforts should not be allowed to obscure the problems inherent in such structures. Irigaray acknowledges the necessity of establishing "an equitable legal system for both sexes" (JTN: 82; JT: 102), but she also stipulates that the strategy of equality "should always aim to get differences recognized" (JTN: 84; JT: 105). Insofar as women's struggle for equality with men accepts the terms of classical liberal theory it not only makes certain assumptions about the value of individualism and competition in a free-market economy, but it also assumes the neutrality of the social order. Irigaray's point is that "the current social order . . . is not neutral when viewed in terms of the difference of the sexes. Working conditions and production techniques are not equally designed nor equally applied with respect to sexual difference" (JTN: 84; JT: 105). To the extent that feminism rehearses the rhetoric of a tradition that is built on the exclusion of women, it needs to be self-conscious and self-critical of the assumptions it makes in doing so. In order to confront the writing out of women from history, Irigaray reopens the most basic questions about love and knowledge, representation and writing, and space and time. To this end Irigaray reinterrogates the philosophical tradition from the Greeks on, challenging the very language in terms of which our political inheritance and social ideals are expressed.

The essentialist reading of Irigaray—that she falsely constructs the group "women" as if it were a homogeneous, white, middle-class group—is based on the misconception that, by emphasizing sexual difference, Irigaray ignores all other differences. In fact, Irigaray's questioning of sexual difference, rather than precluding serious consideration of other differences, requires that they be taken into account.[12] She warns that in narrowly construing demands for equality between the sexes we are in danger of neglecting human rights at a more fundamental—global—level. Irigaray points to the ambiguity of foreign intervention by imperialist powers, strategies that may be presented as providing aid to poorer or less developed countries, but which are perhaps employed in order to preserve the balance of power in the global economy. Irigaray suggests that "the reestablishment of a pseudo-order is sought through the restoration of order to another country by nations incapable of managing their own problems" (JTN: 82; JT: 102). In her view, the failure of ostensibly democratic societies to acknowledge sexual difference in their attempt to legislate sexual equality cannot be divorced from questions of foreign aid, which is perhaps, she suggests, less a matter of disinterested altruism and "more a question of apparently generous alibis in order to remain masters of the situation" (JTN: 82; JT: 102). In order to adequately confront diversity among women, in addition to the differences between women and men, it is necessary, according to Irigaray's view, to rethink basic assumptions about sameness and difference, justice and equality, rationality and subjectivity, the whole and its parts, potentiality and actuality, form and matter, space and time.

This book is not merely directed against essentialist critiques of Irigaray. It is intended to account for the proliferation of these critiques by providing the context in which they arose, and by uncovering the assumptions that motivated them. If the view that Irigaray is "guilty" of essentialism is in need of critical scrutiny, if we need some distance from the categories in terms of which essentialist accusations are wielded, this does not mean that we can simply ignore the charge of essentialism. The concerns that are aired in the debate over essentialism demand our attention. Legitimate concerns include the fear that in drawing attention to the differences between the sexes, differences between women are glossed over; that the discourse of sexual difference risks reducing cultural differences to biological or innate psychological explanations, and that in doing so it distracts feminism from the urgent task of continuing its social struggle for equality. So long as women are explained in terms of their biological or innate capacities, there is little room for transforming their social roles or potential.

We have seen, in the last few years, the appearance of a few books that resist earlier tendencies to over-generalize about "French feminism" and, in the process, oversimplify Irigaray's work, most notably Margaret Whitford's important study *Luce Irigaray: Philosophy in the Feminine*.[13] Anyone concerned with a serious study of Irigaray is indebted to Whitford's clear, balanced, and scholarly discussion. Despite its title, Whitford's approach focuses more on the psychoanalytic aspects of Irigaray's work than the philosophical elements.[14] The present study is an attempt not so much to challenge as to supplement and build upon that approach, by providing what has so far been largely neglected—namely, the philosophical import of Irigaray's rereading of both philosophy and feminism. At the same time, I hope that the current work, by discussing the philosophical context and importance of Irigaray's work, will promote debate and further clarification of major issues in feminist theory. This is not intended to be an exhaustive study of all aspects of Irigaray's work, nor even an exhaustive study of all its philosophical implications. Rather, it is an attempt to situate Irigaray as a feminist theorist in the tradition of post-phenomenological thinking to which she belongs and against which, insofar as it remains a male tradition, she reacts. In restricting myself to a consideration of Irigaray's work as it relates to major figures of this tradition, particularly Hegel, Heidegger, Derrida, and Levinas, I hope to have gone some way toward filling one of the lacunae that has punctuated the reception of Irigaray's work in the English-speaking world to date. I think that if feminists become more aware of the philosophical background that much of Irigaray's work both assumes and plays off, her contribution to feminism will be clearer and, perhaps, better appreciated.

I am aware of the fact—and my awareness has been heightened by perceptive readers of earlier drafts of this book—that Irigaray's name sometimes functions in my text in a way that extends beyond what Irigaray may say. It is emblematic of the influence that both she and the continental philosophers she reads have had on my attempt to think about feminism. In writing and rewriting this book I have tried not to refuse responsibility for thoughts that could be said to be my own, but I know that at times the inspiration not only of Irigaray, but also of Derrida, Heidegger, and Levinas is discernible in my text in ways that are inseparable from what "I" say. It may be possible to detect in the role that I hereby attribute to Irigaray an uncertainty about what I am willing to say in my own voice, but perhaps this hesitation should not be read so much as a lack of confidence on my part as the impossibility of precisely distinguishing my voice from the texts I have been reading for years.[15]

Another way of expressing this ambivalence that no doubt remains, despite my attempts to use precision in claiming my own voice where I see it as my own, is to narrate a change in approach that marks the development of my work. The transition that has occurred, and is still taking place in my work, is gradual, and probably less transparent to me than it is to others. I find myself writing less "textually," less as an explicator of texts, less in the tradition of hermeneutics, and more as a feminist philosopher who has thoughts of her own to articulate, thoughts that bear a relation to the texts Irigaray reads, but which are not reducible to the insights of those texts. I would characterize the direction of my thinking no longer in terms of a philosopher whose interest lies in examining feminist texts and questions, which may have described my earlier position, but more as a feminist who is interested in philosophical texts and questions. While this neither means that I have entirely moved beyond my earlier position—I still think close textual analysis is important—nor, I hope, does it entail a less philosophical approach, it does signal a more overt commitment to articulating my own position as a feminist philosopher.

For all the empirical inaccuracies that we commit when we employ the label "French feminists" to designate the divergent approaches represented by Irigaray (Belgian), Kristeva (Bulgarian), and Cixous (Algerian), what remains undeniable is the ideological impact of the bifurcation of feminism along the politically powerful divide separating the so-called French feminists from their "Anglo-American" counterparts.[16] I characterize the diverse reactions to French feminism in these admittedly reductive terms in order to point to a pervasive tendency that is shared not only by critics of French feminism, but also by many of its supporters. If, in these preliminary statements, I retain the image of a polemical divide between "French feminists" and their "Anglo-American" readers, it is not in the interests of perpetuating that ideological and somewhat artificial division. Let me add that while I have felt it necessary to provide examples of feminists who have argued at certain points in their work that, for example, Irigaray is essentialist, I mean neither to dismiss their work as a whole, nor to diminish it. In many cases I have learned a considerable amount from those critics whose positions I nevertheless wish to distinguish from my own, and my intention is not to reduce them to what they have said at a particular point in their histories, texts, and thinking. I want to be able to articulate my position as distinct from that of others, without allowing my criticism of others to degenerate into what bell hooks calls "excessive trashing" (hooks, 1991: 31).

The cultural and political climate in which Irigaray writes is permeated with an intellectual history that blends phenomenology with psychoanalysis and post-structuralism. If we fail to make some attempt to appropriate this heritage in reading Irigaray's texts, we will also fail to understand a considerable amount of their significance and meaning. Those who acknowledge the theoretical context of French feminism often do so in derisory terms. The theoretical frameworks of French feminists tend to be viewed with suspicion in and of themselves. Their preoccupation with theories to which many feminists do not have access makes their language inaccessible and esoteric, and their concerns seem irrelevant to women outside the academy—and even to some women schooled in the academy. Barbara Christian's criticism of "the race for theory" that she sees as characteristic of contemporary feminism includes a powerful condemnation of the French feminists for their exclusionary politics. Christian is critical of the authority French feminism has accrued for itself as a theoretical discourse that she sees as "monologic" (1989: 233). At the same time she is wary of what she sees as the essentialist tendencies of French feminist theorists. She says,

> They concentrate on the female body as the means to creating a female language, since language, they say, is male and necessarily conceives of woman as other. . . . By positing the body as the source of everything French feminists return to the old myth that biology determines everything and ignore the fact that gender is a social rather than a biological construct (Christian, 1989: 233).

However much one disagrees with the interpretation implied by these comments, the concerns that motivate Christian are far from trivial. While they may not be the central motivating concerns for Irigaray, I do not think she ignores them completely. Irigaray insists upon the need to construe the relation between I and other in terms of radical alterity, thereby pushing to the limits the question of what it means to inhabit the role of the other. She thereby questions the adequacy of relying solely on the category of equality to formulate questions not only about the sexes but also about races (see SG: vi; SP: 7–8).

I have tried to write what follows in a way that is accessible to feminists (and nonfeminists) who are not necessarily sympathetic to the work of Irigaray or familiar with the philosophers she discusses. Although my language is by no means free of academic jargon, I have done what I can to use it in such a way that those largely unfamiliar with the conceptual apparatus of philosophy will not feel excluded, but I am aware that there are points at which the density of the texts I discuss (I am thinking of Hegel in particular) prohibit easy access. I have also made an effort not to assume the rituals of feminist criticism to the extent of alienating readers not well-versed in it, in the hope that nonfeminist philosophers, and others who are not necessarily sympathetic to feminism, might find something of interest to them. I think it is important not to exacerbate the exclusivity that characterizes theory, but I think it is equally important, as a feminist, not to simply avoid theory, leaving it to its more traditional purveyors.

French feminism, along with other theories and feminisms, has indeed functioned in ways that exclude not only women of color, but any woman who is distanced from a debate that has largely been carried on within the confines of the academy. I want to break down some barriers between academic language and the contradictions facing contemporary women. While Irigaray cannot provide all the answers—no single theorist can—her questioning of sexual difference can perhaps provide some resources not only to move beyond the labels "French" and "Anglo-American" feminism, but also to demystify the debate over essentialism.[17]

In the first chapter, "Tracking Essentialism," I argue the case for the need to rethink a distinction that has become canonical for feminists—namely, the difference between sex and gender—introducing my discussion by referring to the debate over what it means to read as a woman. I pay particular attention to the dialogue between Miller and Kamuf. By briefly reviewing the recent history of feminism I provide the cultural and intellectual background to the debate over essentialism in order to show why Irigaray and her contemporaries have been widely misread as essentialist in recent years. I argue that the feminist ideology that privileges gender over sex has had the effect, in the last twenty years or so, of casting suspicion on any discourse about the body, sexual difference, or biology. The bracketing of sexual difference was strategically important because it allowed feminists to bypass whatever empirical differences there are between the sexes in order to concentrate on changing socially constructed gender roles. Concentrating upon gender roles allowed women to be single-minded in challenging the restrictions imposed on them by the ideals of femininity, without the distraction of trying to account for sexual difference.

Despite the various challenges that confront the continuing ascendancy of the sex/gender distinction as the foundational motif of feminism, the distinction has lost surprisingly little ground. By elaborating two interlocking paradigms—one produced by the sex/gender distinction and the other by the essentialism/anti-essentialism debate—I read the theoretical exclusion of the body as a feminist taboo on sex. I point to a subterranean ethic that is produced by the intersection of the sex/gender distinction with the more recent essence/anti-essence schema. Both motifs are supported by a shared substructure that operates at a more or less subterranean level, one that consists of a metaphysic of being and becoming, and a supporting ethical schema pitting evil against good.

In chapter two, "The Legacy of Simone de Beauvoir," I argue that, while Beauvoir goes some way toward making the issue of sexual difference central, she deprives herself—or perhaps she suffers from the fact that she wrote in the early stages of twentieth-century feminism—of the resources that she needs in order to complete the project. Inaugurating the project of thinking through the otherness of women, I show that, if in some ways Beauvoir paves the way for Irigaray's rethinking of woman as other, in other ways she falls short of it.[18] *The Second Sex* sets out to explore the specificity of women's situation, but it remains limited both by the intellectual legacy Beauvoir inherits from her philosophical mentors, and by her refusal, or inability, to fully inhabit the role of a woman. Throughout her work—both theoretical and autobiographical—we see Beauvoir's reluctance to embrace her womanhood. What starts out as an interrogation of women's situation from a woman's point of view is transformed into an analysis of other women's lives from the standpoint of existentialist ethics. Beauvoir explores women's situation by fusing together the philosophical perspectives of Sartre and Hegel in an account that never quite manages to overcome the problems that such a marriage of minds produces. On the one hand, by taking the Hegelian master-slave dialectic as her paradigm for the male/female relationship (however approximate it may be as a model), Beauvoir assumes, rather than demonstrates, that human relationships are fundamentally conflictual and that they must be thought in terms of an oppressor and an oppressed. On the other hand, following Sartre's belief in the absolute freedom of the individual to make of one's life what one will, Beauvoir is committed to the view that however disadvantaged an individual may be by the circumstances of her life, she can overcome discrimination by realizing the full potential of her ability to act as an autonomous human being. According to this view, adversity can be transcended, given the appropriate exertion of willpower.

For the existentialist, to remain locked into a situation is due to bad faith, or to one's inability to commit oneself to changing adverse circumstances. Oppression is thereby explained not in terms of social discrimination, but in terms of refusing to actualize one's true potential as a human being by failing to take responsibility for one's life. Oppression appears to be more chimerical than it is real, more a matter of a lack of willpower on the part of individuals than it is a matter of systemic disenfranchisement of a group's rights. The emphasis on the individual's capacity to triumph over adversity is underscored by Beauvoir's tendency to see herself as the exception to the rule, as one of those rare individuals who has managed to gain an education and to thereby escape the confines of traditional femininity.

To say that Beauvoir sees herself as a token man overstates the point. Suffice it to say that, while her stance was a radical one in her time, feminism is now able to risk what Beauvoir could not manage—to resolutely endorse the position of being a woman with all the contradictions that involves. Intellectually, Beauvoir's refusal of the position of woman plays itself out in her adherence to a philosophical tradition that made very little room for women. I am not so much suggesting that she would have done better to draw on other philosophers—it is hard to think of any who would have been any more suited to her attempt to analyze women's situation. Beauvoir herself was one of the first modern women philosophers, and perhaps she paid the price of being one of philosophy's earliest female investigators, even as she laid the foundations for further philosophical inquiry into feminism. I am reminded of Woolf's call to women, in 1929, "to write all kinds of books," a call that does not hesitate to include philosophy in its orbit (AROO: 109). For, as Woolf says, in her perfectly pitched understatement, "books have a way of influencing each other" (AROO: 109). Beauvoir's *The Second Sex* answered Woolf's call, and made it possible to refine and build upon the ideas she began to elaborate.

The tension between Hegel and Sartre never gets resolved in Beauvoir's application of their philosophies to the situation of women. At times Beauvoir sees women as complicitous, while at other times she exonerates them from any responsibility for being the "second sex." Her successors are left to attend to the complex dynamics of acknowledging the reality and pervasiveness of history's representation of women as other, without acquiescing to the victim mentality that this might lead to.

In chapter three, "Looking at Hegel's Antigone through Irigaray's Speculum," I examine the complexity of woman's role as other. My central reference point is Irigaray's reading of Hegel's Antigone. Hegelian philosophy serves as Irigaray's paradigm of the system that carves woman out of the public sphere, and imprisons her in a private one. Antigone is granted leave to die a slow death, in an enclosure where she is allowed only to commune with nature. If Creon literally sends Antigone to such a fate, Hegel accomplishes the same task figuratively when he refuses to recognize in Antigone's ethical consciousness anything but a natural harmony with divine spirits. Hegel's refusal is supported by a systematic bifurcation of male and female that adumbrates male as rational, universal, political, and actual, while allocating to the female the irrational, the particular, the familial, and the potential. The architect of this rift intends Antigone no harm. On the contrary, Hegel honors her, exalting in her tragic fate. She is, for this great scholar of the classics (as he likes to boast), the supreme tragic hero. More tragic than Oedipus or Creon, more of a woman than Aeschylus' Clytemnestra, she is all that a man could want in a tragic heroine. Why? Because she never once wavers or falters in her undeviating course toward her own death, destruction, internment? Because she wants to die—would rather die than live and be deprived of the only action that is rightfully hers? The reason that Antigone is so precious to Hegel is that she is ethical through and through. She knows, according to Hegel, her place as a woman: she knows her duty and she sticks to it. But this "knowledge" is an intuitive knowledge. Antigone may be steadfast, and for this Hegel can honor her, but she is limited in her ethical vision, and for this Hegel criticizes her. Her knowledge is unmediated, improper knowledge. For she is only a woman and, as such, she cannot reflect, negate, or mediate—not according to a system that sends men to war and keeps women at home, that gives men reason and women babies, that provides men with access to the universal and limits women to the particular. This system is the ethical operation of sexual difference à la Hegel. This system is why Irigaray finds it not only necessary but imperative to write another ethic of sexual difference.

In chapter four, "Irigaray, Heidegger, and the Greeks," I develop the parallel relationship between Heidegger's questioning of Being and Irigaray's questioning of sexual difference. By referring to Irigaray's readings of Aristotle and Plato, this chapter extends the parallel between Heidegger's questioning of Being and Irigaray's questioning of sexual difference to their mutual interest in returning to the Greeks. Like Heidegger's question of Being, which he thinks is forgotten by the Western tradition of metaphysics, Irigaray's questioning of sexual difference has been covered over, not least by the efforts of feminism itself. According to Heidegger the philosophical tradition, from the Greeks on, obscured the ontological difference, that is, the difference between Being and beings. For Irigaray, the central issue philosophy evades is sexual difference, or the difference between men and women. In both cases, the evasion of the question is not accidental to the very conception of philosophy. According to Heidegger, metaphysics is governed by its inability to construe the problematic relation between Being and time. At the heart of philosophical discourse lies concealed a blindness about the nature of the philosophical inquiry itself. Philosophy has always assumed, without properly thinking through this assumption, the priority of the present. In doing so, it has inadvertently but systematically understood existence in terms of the present. Heidegger seeks to demonstrate that the metaphysical priority of presence hides the question of the meaning of Being. The history of Western philosophy is a history in which the true nature of Being gets distorted, since it is always represented as present, instead of being situated in terms of a past out of which it emerges, and a future toward which it portends. Not merely is Being thereby obfuscated, but the very question of its meaning is concealed. The task of raising the question of the meaning of Being thus involves first of all gaining access to the question for a philosophical tradition that has rendered the question meaningless, unintelligible, illogical. Similarly, for Irigaray, the question of sexual difference has been put out of bounds—and not merely by the philosophical tradition itself, but even by feminism. If, in the tradition of Western philosophy, the question of sexual difference was an invisible one, it was because men talked, thought, and wrote philosophy. If feminists, in construing feminism in terms of equality, sought to detract from sexual differences, it was because any differences appeared to threaten their project, which consisted of playing down the differences in order to emphasize the similarities between the sexes. For Irigaray, the question of sexual difference is in danger of being put to rest as illegitimate before it has ever been properly thought through.

The chapter ends with a brief discussion of Irigaray's reading of Nietzsche, a reading that betrays the influence of Derrida's discussion of Nietzsche on women in *Spurs*. Like Heidegger, Nietzsche regards Greek philosophy as something of a high point in the philosophical tradition of the West. Irigaray's interest in both Heidegger and Nietzsche extends to their return to the Greeks, particularly their relation to the Pre-Socratics' reflections on the elements. Irigaray's attempt to rehabilitate the elemental— earth, fire, air and water—is indebted to Heidegger and Nietzsche.

In chapters five and six, I argue that Levinas' reconception of the other has significantly influenced Irigaray, in part by way of Derrida's elaboration of Levinas' conception of the feminine. Chapter five, "Levinas and the Question of the Other," provides an overview of Levinas' philosophy, which, I assume, will be less familiar to readers than the work of Heidegger and Derrida. Accordingly my account of Levinas is more detailed. I think that Levinas' rethinking of the other has a particular importance for Irigaray's attempt to reread the history of philosophy as a history that has excluded women as other. Levinas' attempt to rethink the other has also had a significant impact on Derrida's attempt to think difference, and has thus influenced Irigaray both directly and indirectly (through Derrida). By raising the question of whether it is possible to take account of the radically other without either reducing that otherness to categories of the same, or rendering philosophical an experience that is extra-philosophical, Levinas gives new impetus to Irigaray's interrogation of what it means for women to be cast as other, to somehow occupy the position of the other while at the same time challenging that designation.

Levinas asks if it is possible to avoid the hegemony of the same. He is concerned with what it means to find ourselves in a culture that operates by means of thematizing rules and regulations that treat individuals as if they were identical to one another. Levinas nowhere disputes the need for social organization, formalized codes of conduct, or the institutionalization of ethics. He acknowledges its necessity, but sees it as a need to which we as individuals do not have to adhere blindly. To the extent that the reduction of humans to numerical statistics is inevitable, and no doubt endemic to large-scale bureaucratic agencies, Levinas accepts the uniformity to which any systematic ethics must appeal, but argues that the leveling of differences entailed in the discourse of equality rests on a prior recognition of original alterity. In suggesting that ethics gains its impetus not from the fundamental similarity, symmetry, or commonality between human beings but rather from an original difference, asymmetry, or otherness, he is fully aware that even this gesture, this pointing out of difference, already embraces a sameness in its very attempt to point out difference. Perhaps we can learn from Levinas' attempt to keep alive the possibility of thinking radical difference— even if in the very thought that thinks it, difference disappears, becomes a trace of itself, even if difference cannot be thought in itself. Perhaps the tension in feminism between the need for solidarity, unity, togetherness among women, and the need to leave room for difference, otherness, alterity, can be addressed through Levinas' constant vigilance about the danger of collapsing difference into the familiar categories of the same.[19]

Levinas' philosophy can be seen as an attempt to correct phenomenology's neglect of ethics, a neglect that Levinas attributes to its failure to pay enough attention to the other. For Levinas, Heidegger's philosophy, for all its radicality in departing from the metaphysical tradition, remains steeped in a philosophy that understands others on the model of the self. It is Levinas' attempt to focus on the absolute alterity of the other that marks the originality of his philosophy. The ethical relation *par excellence*, a relation that Levinas calls "face to face," consists not in the equality of its terms, but in an essential dissymetry. The other presents herself or himself not as my equal, but by challenging my very identity, by bringing into question who I am.

Derrida argues that a significant shift takes place in Levinas' work. He thinks that, despite Levinas' early attempts to emphasize the heterogeneity of the self's relation to itself in texts such as *Time and the Other* and *Existence and Existents* (1947), Levinas cannot sustain these attempts in his later philosophy. Levinas' earlier insistence on finding differences within the interiority of the self becomes, on Derrida's reading of his later work, a "false heterology" (WD: 94; ED: 140). While agreeing with Derrida that a significant shift occurs in Levinas' thinking between 1947 and 1961, I emphasize different reasons for this shift, namely the progressive eclipse of eros from his work, and with it the subordination of the feminine to the masculine.

The feminine figure served as a model for Levinas' re-thinking of the absolutely other, particularly in his early work. In his later work the feminine, which is at first understood in the context of eros, is restricted to the idea of the maternal. Levinas' attitude toward the feminine is at best ambiguous. While on the one hand, he singles out the feminine as the paradigm of the other, on the other hand, insofar as the feminine is thought in tandem with the erotic—if not *as* the erotic—Levinas is suspicious of femininity. Since, according to Levinas, the erotic falls short of the genuine alterity of the face-to-face relation in that it involves what Levinas calls a "return to self," the erotic relation is less than ethical. As Levinas' philosophy becomes progressively absorbed in the investigation of the ethical relation, so his interest in eros—and thus in the feminine—appears to decrease. The feminine is only addressed obliquely in his later work. It begins to look as if Levinas capitulates to the most traditional of tropes by sanitizing the feminine of its earlier erotic connotations and substituting the traditionally acceptable motif of femininity in the guise of motherhood. Even if this is true, it remains the case that, in thinking through the alterity of the other, Levinas raises the question of otherness to a new level, one which allows Irigaray to reinterpret the history of philosophy with a radicality hitherto prohibited, with the result that, perhaps for the first time, the question of sexual difference receives the thorough treatment it deserves.

Reading Irigaray's critique of Levinas, I suggest that, despite the distance Irigaray takes from Levinas, she also profits from Levinas' rethinking of the other. If Levinas' challenge to the Judeo-Christian philosophical tradition takes the form of rethinking the other in the context of ethics, Irigaray puts Levinas' insights to work in the context of sexual difference. Levinas may fail to do justice to feminism, but his insistence upon the need to recognize in otherness or difference a radicality hitherto unacknowledged inspires Irigaray's attempt to rethink sexual difference. Just as Levinas' understanding of the absolutely other is premised upon a recognition of alterity within subjectivity, Irigaray's reflections on sexual difference are not limited to endorsing the heteronomous relation between multiple subjects, but extend to an affirmation of plurality within subjectivity and among different members of the same sex.

Chapter six is devoted to a discussion of Derrida's relation to feminism and to Irigaray. While I have no interest in arguing that Derrida is a feminist—this is a position that he himself clearly denies—his influence, via Levinas, on Irigaray's thought, is crucial. Derrida's work has proved controversial for many feminists. Here I argue for Derrida's importance for feminism, and I suggest that his reflections on the position of women can be seen as a development of Levinas' conception of the feminine as other— although, as we shall see, Derrida goes beyond Levinas in an important respect. The texts where this is most evident include Christie McDonald's interview with Derrida, "Choreographies," and Derrida's second essay on Levinas, "At This Very Moment in This Text Here I Am." At issue in these texts is the question of women's marginality, the question of how to mark women's differences from men without capitulating to the exclusions that historically have determined those differences, and without marking them as if they were mere deficiencies. How can women maintain their multiple differences from men productively, how can we use those differences to challenge the systematic power imbalances that still define women's relation to men, and how can we articulate sexual difference such that differences between women are not obliterated?

Themes that organize my treatment of these questions include the text as property and as gift, the question of debt and restoration, and the place of woman both as dissimulating and as dissimulated by a tradition that can only misrepresent her. In order to pursue these themes, in addition to Derrida's discussion of femininity in Levinas' texts, I consider briefly "Restitutions" (1987b), *Geschlecht*, and *Spurs,* before turning to Irigaray's articles on Derrida, "*Le v(i)ol de la lettre*," and "Belief Itself." The latter, which I discuss in my Afterword, takes Derrida's discussion of the *fort-da* game in *The Post Card* as its point of departure. My analysis of this text allows me to discuss, albeit in a cursory manner, some of the psycho-analytic issues raised by Irigaray.[20]

Teresa de Lauretis suggests that in the history of feminism, there are

> two concurrent drives, impulses or mechanisms . . . at work in the production of its self-representation: *an erotic, narcissistic drive* that enhances images of feminism as difference, rebellion, daring, excess, subversion, disloyalty, agency, empowerment, pleasure and danger, and rejects all images of powerlessness, victimization, subjection, acquiescence, passivity, conformism, femininity; and *an ethical drive* that works toward community, accountability, entrustment, sisterhood, bonding, belonging to a common world of women or sharing what Adrienne Rich has poignantly called "the dream of a common language." Together, often in mutual contradiction, the erotic and the ethical drives have fueled not only the various polarizations and the construction of oppositions but also the invention or conceptual imaging of a "continuum" of experience, a global feminism, a "house of difference," or a separate space where "safe words" can be trusted and "consent" given uncoerced. . . . I suggest . . . an erotic and an ethical drive may be seen to underlie and sustain at once the possibility of, and the difficulties involved in, the project of articulating a female symbolic (1990: 266).

I find this characterization of feminism both compelling and provocative. While I titled this book "Ethics of Eros," I could have called it just as easily "Eros of Ethics."[21] The territory it explores includes both the conjunction and the disjunction between the erotic and the ethical tensions that struc-ture and invade the various fields of feminist discourse. The ethical impetus behind feminist responses to fundamental questions about how to act together as women, how to communicate with one another in ways that respect the differences between us, and how to remain a politically viable movement cannot help but intersect, and conflict, with questions about how we love and live, what we want for ourselves and for those closest to us, and how we envision, endorse, and enact our friendships with others.

one TRACKING ESSENTIALISM WITH THE HELP OF A SEX/GENDER MAP

Within feminism and within some other discourses, essentialism seems to be a kind of blind spot that won't go away. It hasn't, by and large, been historicized or related to the history of high philosophical essentialisms, but has been invoked to distance and disallow certain kinds of discourses.

—ROONEY

Essentialism is a loose tongue. In the house of philosophy, it's not taken seriously. You know, it's used by non-philosophers simply to mean all kinds of things when they don't know what other word to use.

—SPIVAK

Anthropology, and descriptions of kinship systems, do not explain the mechanisms by which children are engraved with the conventions of sex and gender. Psychoanalysis, on the other hand, is a theory about the reproduction of kinship. Psychoanalysis describes the residue left within individuals by their confrontation with the rules and regulations of sexuality of the societies to which they are born.

—RUBIN

TWO DOMINANT FEMINIST MOTIFS

POLITICAL MOVEMENTS SUCH AS FEMINISM GENERATE conceptual schemata around which they organize and motivate support. Certain motifs emerge as dominant, and become symbolic of the various forces directed toward improving women's lives. These motifs are utilized to mobilize people, to change situations, to communicate agendas. Some of these motifs are so successful that it becomes difficult to differentiate between feminism as an ongoing and developing discourse, and the slogans that arise to address particular needs, to express sentiments specific to a given era, and to instantiate the feelings of significant numbers of feminists during that period.

In recent years, the oppositional grid created by the distinction between sex and gender has become an organizing motif to the extent of becoming almost synonymous with feminism itself. To qualify as feminine is not the same thing as to be a member of the female sex. The set of meanings associated with being gendered feminine derive from social values about sex, which are defined locally, and which are specific to cultures and historical periods. In contrast, one's categorization as a member of the female sex proceeds according to biological, empirically observable, and apparently universal facts about one's anatomical body.

If the opposition between sex and gender has proved crucial to feminist theory, a second organizing motif that has produced, as well as fractured, political alliances within feminist circles is the debate over essentialism and anti-essentialism. Some feminist theorists who see gender as the crucial category of analysis are critical of other feminists whom, insofar as they are deemed to appeal to the category of sex, they suspect of essentialism. Here I am less interested in providing more fuel to continue the now flagging essentialism/anti-essentialism debate, or in providing a point by point refutation of any one of the variety of essentialist critiques of French feminism, than I am in raising a question about the assumptions that are typically made by those who position themselves in the debate over essentialism. I am interested in asking how feminism has tended to construe itself in recent years, why it has pursued some avenues as fruitful and rejected others as unhelpful; what impasses have been produced by the measures it has adopted; and why it has blocked off certain areas of inquiry as irrelevant to its ends and aims.

The ways in which feminism characterizes itself, and the particular axes along which it has been allowed to develop over the years, have a determining influence on how women see themselves, how men see women, and what opportunities are considered viable for women by society in general and by particular women. I am not questioning the usefulness of the motifs and slogans that have been employed in the service of feminism. They have directed energy toward specific campaigns; as such they have been instrumental in achieving certain goals. Perhaps even more significant, they have helped to create a sense of unity and solidarity among women, giving them a sense of striving for common goals. They have thereby played a significant part in shaping the feminist movement as a whole. It is nonetheless worth asking what assumptions are being harnessed in order to promote certain feminist goals, and whether some of these assumptions need to be revised, questioned, or rethought. In particular, I am suggesting that we need to be wary of appealing to the sex/gender motif to such an extent and according to such rigid and narrow definitions of what counts as "sex" and "gender" that it is transformed from a useful strategy into a reified dogma.

In suggesting that the discourse of feminism has developed in a way that has prejudiced a number of activists against the work of Irigaray, I want to explore the contested site of the body within feminist discourse. One way of describing its contested site is in terms of the intersection between two conceptual grids. The body has become a ground of contention for feminists as the controversial meeting point of two feminist paradigms. I suggest that the essentialism debate has been superimposed on the sex/gender map such that women's bodies have been effectively excluded from feminist theories. I do not mean to say that bodies have been excluded from every aspect of feminism. On the contrary, it is obvious that feminists invoke women's fundamental rights to their bodies in debating many issues at the center of the feminist arena, such as abortion, pornography, and violence against women. There are numerous forums in which women's bodies have been the focus of attention—ranging from the formation of women's health groups to explicitly feminist art (Judy Chicago's work is a classic example)—that attempt to reclaim and celebrate women's bodies. My point is that while at the practical level discourses on the body from multiple points of view have proliferated, at the theoretical level feminist models have left little room for bodies.

What remains problematic for feminist discourse is articulating the relationship between two conflicting feminist demands. On the one hand, there is the desire to be treated as men's equal, and the accompanying unstated presupposition that in all significant respects women are either already, or potentially, similar to men. In other words, the message is, sexual differences are unimportant. On the other hand, there is the demand to have women's special needs recognized, and the implicit acknowledgment of the uniquely female character of these needs. Those aspects of women's embodiment that differentiate them from men, and to which feminists appeal in arguing for pro-choice or for the right to be in control of their bodies—namely, their reproductive capacities and their female sexuality—are not easily accommodated by the traditional priority feminist theory accords to gender rather than sex.[1]

Joan Scott, in her discussion of the case that the Equal Employment Opportunities Commission (EEOC) brought against Sears, demonstrates the need to complicate the tendency to neatly compartmentalize "demands for equality and affirmations of difference" as if the two were independent of one another or mutually exclusive (Scott, 1988a: 48). As she points out, "The questions always ought to be, What qualities or aspects are being compared? What is the nature of the comparison? How is the meaning of difference being constructed?" (Scott, 1988a: 44).[2]

The value and usefulness of emphasizing the potential similarities of the sexes and underplaying their differences is at the very least arguable in several areas. Indeed, the viability of the sex/gender distinction itself is undermined by rapidly changing medical technology. The increasing ease with which sex change operations can be obtained, for example, renders untenable any assumptions we may have made about the stability of the category of sex, and at the same time disrupts the gender boundaries that are usually set up along the clearly demarcated lines of male and female. The proliferation of gender identity clinics, by making gender susceptible to change, puts into question the necessity of keeping the sexual identity with which one is born.

My attempt in this chapter is both to dispel some of the confusion surrounding the debate over essentialism, and to go some way toward accounting for the persistent dismissal of Irigaray as essentialist. This part of my argument is less an attempt to exonerate Irigaray on the basis of textual evidence (although, as I hope I shall show, such evidence can be readily found), than it is an exercise in cultural history, which has the intention of shedding light on the proliferation of essentialist critiques. I argue that the distinction between sex and gender has become untenable as a grounding concept for feminism, a fact that is now being recognized by some feminist theorists. By this I mean not that the distinction itself is redundant, but that it does not tell the whole story of feminism; we need other concepts to complete the picture. To the extent that the distinction has been used to banish other concepts, we need to revise our use of it and examine the scope of its applicability.

THE SEX/GENDER MAP

The sex/gender distinction is a familiar one that has been successfully exploited by feminists in diverse ways. It is a distinction that has served to articulate both the need for, and the possibility of, social, political, and economic change. By driving a wedge between sex and gender, feminists have carved up the world roughly according to the nature/culture divide as it relates to the formation of men and women. The nature/culture divide is often specified by feminists in terms of another closely related distinction, the opposition between biology and history. Sex, nature, and biology line up on one side of the divide, while gender—socially constructed, culturally informed, and historically produced—lines up on the other side. I suggest that the ramifications that follow from the sex/gender division often remain implicit and unacknowledged, but orchestrate the academic discourse of feminist theory to a surprising extent. Perhaps we need to focus more attention on the implications of this relentless and persistent emphasis of gender over sex.

The division between the categories of sex and gender carries with it metaphysical, ontological, political, and ethical implications. Defined according to their biological sex, women and men are considered to have stable, fixed identities, empirically established by reference to the body, which thus serves as a kind of unchanging ground. On the other hand, gender formation is a result of processes of learning, social expectations, peer pressure, local and family values—all of which are culturally specific, and as such are considered to be flexible over time and malleable within limits. Ann Oakley says, for example, in *Sex, Gender and Society,* "The constancy of sex must be admitted, but so also must the variability of gender" (Oakley, 1972:16). Thus gender identity has different contents in different cultures and in different times.

If certain bodily parts are considered prerequisites to qualify as a woman, while other physical attributes define one sexually as a man, there is a range of different options when it comes to identifying oneself as gendered—both within cultures and between cultures; whether one is identified as a biological male or female, one can be more or less feminine or masculine. Thus the function of the sex/gender divide in feminist discourse comes very close to positing sex as a universal, given for all eternity, innate and unavoidable, while gender is construed as variable from one culture to another, changing over time, admitting of differences between those who are—insofar as they share one sex—designated as the same as one another. Feminist perspectives superimpose upon the sex/gender divide a variety of metaphysical and moral distinctions, including sameness/difference, good/bad, fixed/changing. Since it is desirable to change gender differentiation insofar as it is hierarchical, and to the extent that this hierarchy is used to discriminate against women, the construction of women and men in terms of gender is viewed as good. To see gender as the crucial factor in accounting for the hierarchy between men and women is to admit both the possibility of change and the possibility of acknowledging differences among individuals. Accordingly, there is an implicit moral injunction to emphasize the importance of gender as constructing one's identity, and to play down the role of sex as a determining factor. Consequently, those who persist—whether explicitly or not, whether feminist or not—in seeing sex as a relevant factor are perceived as bad, reactionary, and anti-feminist.

READING/WRITING AS/LIKE A WOMAN/FEMINIST

Considerable literature has been produced on the question of what it means to write as a woman.[3] I want to point to an underlying motif that has organized this literature in ways not always transparent to the discussants. I am concerned with a feminist allegiance to a distinction that, while it has not always been an obvious focal point, has nonetheless formed the background to the controversy over women and their writing. The distinction that has played this foundational role is the sex/gender distinction, and the planes that are defined in relation to it include sexual difference versus sexual equality. The sex/gender distinction has been so influential that it is almost taken for granted, with the result that it sometimes acts as a silent center. This pivotal distinction, which undergirds and sustains a number of precepts, has given rise to an architectural structure that stabilizes feminist perspectives in particular configurations and juxtaposes certain beliefs that have become inflexible in their relations to one another. It has become difficult, for example, to invoke the female body, sexual difference, or women's experience without alerting suspicions that one harbors essentialist tendencies. It is almost as if women's sexual specificity is an unfortunate fact that feminism has done its best to forget since the discovery of gender. But sex does not simply drop out of the picture just because it is convenient for feminism to emphasize the salience of gender construction. It is still there and it needs to be dealt with.

Mary Jacobus observes that "Women's writing occupies an unchallenged place in the politics of feminist criticism and in the classroom; yet the category itself remains problematic (defined by authorship? by style or by language? by a refusal of the very categories 'masculine' or 'feminine'?)" (Jacobus, 1986: 5).[4] An exchange that took place in the early 1980s between Peggy Kamuf and Nancy K. Miller illustrates two divergent responses to this situation. In order to demonstrate my suggestion that the sex/gender distinction generates and informs the conceptual apparatus of feminist criticism to a considerable extent, let me rehearse the pertinent details of this exchange. Kamuf's argument proceeds by adhering to the ideological assumption that women should not be defined according to their sex, but rather according to their gender. Consonant with this assumption is the suspicion that any assertion of difference between women's writing and men's writing, while it may take itself to be concerned with gender, in fact merely reinscribes biological determinism, insofar as it differentiates writers from one another on the basis of their sex. Kamuf says, referring to Patricia Meyer Spacks' *The Female Imagination*,

> Spacks's study puts together readings of a list of literary works by women in order to determine how, in her phrase, one "writes as a woman." However, by limiting the field to works whose authors are women, the critic finally gets caught in the kind of biological determinism, which, in other contexts, is recognized as a primary instance of antifeminist sexism (Kamuf, 1980: 285).

Kamuf goes on to quote Spacks, citing a passage in which Spacks makes the point that even women who consciously strive to adopt a male point of view in their writing (such as Beauvoir) cannot elude their female condition altogether. Kamuf comments further,

> Although the author sets out with a statement of faith in a psychological or cultural differentiation which can be characterized sexually ("Surely the mind has a sex . . . "), she abandons this intuition without a second thought when she must account for a woman who, by her own reckoning, has a "male" mind. By adopting the biological distinction of male/female to define a cultural phenomenon, the critic demonstrates the impossibility of limiting that definition to what "is" for, as it turns out, it "is" also what it "is not" (Kamuf, 1980: 285).[5]

Spacks' phrase "Surely the mind has a sex" echoes, whether consciously or not, Woolf's rhetorical question as to "whether there are two sexes in the mind corresponding to the two sexes in the body" (AROO: 98). Before following up this reference, I want to consider Miller's response to Kamuf. Commenting on Kamuf's article "Writing like a Woman," Miller says,

> Like Kristeva, whose interest in a female practice is related primarily to a more general concern with an avant-garde, dissident and marginal work in language, Kamuf would prefer to see "feminist" criticism address itself not to the productions signed by biological women alone,

but to all productions that put the "feminine" into play—the feminine then being a modality or process accessible to both men and women (Miller, 1982: 50).[6]

Miller's own position is that "it matters who writes and *signs* woman" (Miller, 1982: 49). She warns, "If feminists decide that the signature is a matter of indifference, if women's studies becomes gender studies, the *real* end of women in the institution will not be far off" (Miller, 1982: 53).[7]

The exchange between Miller and Kamuf has become emblematic of a tension that pervades feminist theory. On the one hand, there is the need to resist any reification, universalization, or stabilization of what it might mean to be a woman. On the other hand, there is the need to endorse the fact that being a woman informs whatever position one takes as a writer—even though every woman's position will be different and may even be comprised of a denial that the position one occupies is significantly shaped by one's sex (as Spacks suggests it is in the case of Beauvoir).

To insist on the relevance of the author's sexual identity, according to Kamuf, is to risk repeating the errors with which she faults those against whom she defines herself. It is, in the tradition of humanistic values, to set too much store by authorial intentions and meaning, and to risk falsely universalizing the category "women." Kamuf says, "to the extent that feminist thought assumes the limits of humanism, it may be reproducing itself as but an extension of those limits and reinventing the institutional structures that it set out to dismantle" (Kamuf, 1982: 46).[8] Kamuf is prepared to abandon the significance of the signature in order to avoid the naïveté that Miller embraces as a necessary evil. In insisting on the importance of the signature, Miller shows herself more willing to risk adhering to humanistic values when she affirms her belief in "books and courses based on the signature . . . even though such lists and such courses may betray a naive faith in origins, humanism, and centrality, because they also make visible the marginality, eccentricity and vulnerability of women, they concretely challenge the confidence of humanistic discourse as *universality*" (Miller, 1982: 52).

Attempting to elucidate what is at stake in women's writing, feminists seem to be caught in a series of double binds. We can, for example, insist upon the importance of women's experience of marginalization as formative of their concerns as writers—in which case we risk endorsing a number of problematic assumptions, not all of which are compatible with one another. There is, for example, the risk of identifying victimization as the defining characteristic of women's writing. There is also the risk of assuming that women's writing flows unproblematically from a subject who is not only able to directly tap into the significance of "experience," but also to communicate it successfully to others, thereby providing an accurate representation of the experience of victimization. Thus there is an appeal to common experience, despite the fact that the very experience of marginalization may well have deprived women of the ability to see themselves as subjects who are in control of their lives, and despite the fact that it is not at all clear how far any of us can be masters of our discourse, or can maintain control over the meaning our words have for others. By assuming that the exclusionary practices of patriarchy are largely responsible for informing women's standpoint, feminists tend also to assume a homogeneity of opinion among women writers (and readers), which downplays the differences among women's responses to their exclusion and the different resources individuals have to respond to it.[9] They are unable to break out of the unhelpful tautology that women's writing is written by women, or that texts that are signed by women are women's texts. Such answers not only fail to illuminate the question they are intended to answer, they also appear to affirm some kind of biological determinism. Thus Peggy Kamuf can accuse Patricia Meyer Spacks on both counts: "By 'female writing,' we discover, Spacks quite banally understands works signed by biologically determined females of the species" (Kamuf, 1980: 285).

On the other hand, feminists who do not think "feminine writing" is the exclusive preserve of women, and who thus admit the possibility that men can write like women too, risk inviting charges of desertion. Fearful of having feminism appropriated or co-opted by men, feminists view Cixous' assertion that Genet's writing can be judged feminine with extreme suspicion.[10] The suggestion that men can write like women is taken as an indicator of a post-feminist sensibility that portends—as if the death of the subject and of the author were not enough—the death of feminism. It is only by wrongly assuming that feminism has achieved its goals, that now we are all equal and we are therefore at liberty to move on to more interesting projects, that feminists imagine we can afford to recognize the femininity of men's writing too—so the argument goes.

I think that Miller is right to be cautious about ignoring the question of whether a text is written by a woman or a man, and I am sympathetic with her observation about the power of the signature: "Only those who have it can play with not having it" (Miller 1982: 53). On the other hand, Kamuf is right to point to the sense in which women must adopt a language that is not their own when she says,

To concede at the outset that it is the father who speaks and says "I" is to close the debate even before it is opened. Nevertheless, this is where we must begin to talk about women and language, women in language, if we are to end up at any distance from where we started (Kamuf 1980: 285).

The reason feminism cannot afford to shelve the question of sexual difference is indicated by Deborah Rhode, who succinctly expresses the contradiction that sexual difference represents for feminists when she says,

In an important sense, the women's movement rests on the differences it seeks to challenge. From its beginning, the feminist campaign has sought to prevent sex-related differences from limiting individuals' aspirations and achievements. Yet by definition the movement also presupposed some recognition of women's interests and concerns. In that respect, feminism assumes a shared experience it seeks in large measure to challenge.

What complicates the issue still further is the diversity of those experiences, a diversity that is gaining greater recognition within the women's movement (Rhode, 1990: 1–2).[11]

The fact that what unites women is also at the same time what women seek to overcome—namely their marginalization—produces a contradiction that feminism must confront. Women's solidarity is structured, in part, by the very mechanisms of patriarchal power that feminism seeks to eliminate, and in part by discriminatory practices that feminism is learning to address. Perhaps the problem that I initially specified by asking what it means to write as a woman needs to be focused more carefully: what does it mean for women to begin to write in a language from which they have suffered exclusion? How will that language be transformed by women's writing, and how will women be transformed as readers and writers of a language that they inherit from their fathers, a traditional language, a language heavy with the weight of a history of exclusionary practices—not only in relation to women, but in relation to its multifarious others? In order to begin to answer these questions I want to step back from current debates, returning for a moment to the echo that reverberates in Kamuf's quotation from Spacks, "Surely the mind has a sex."

Woolf's *A Room of One's Own* (written in 1929) pre-dates the ideology of the sex/gender distinction by some forty or fifty years. The term "gender" had not yet taken on the strategic significance it was to acquire for feminists in the 1970s. Holtby, a contemporary of Woolf, sees the need to introduce a distinction between sex and gender when, in her discussion of Woolf's androgynous image of "Two in a Taxi," she observes,

> One is handicapped by the confusing effect of social influence upon the English language. We ought, when talking about the difference between men and women, to be allowed to use some such neutral word as "gender" instead of "sex." For "sex" has been associated so closely with the amorous and procreative instinct, that its convenience has been destroyed, and its meaning lent an emotional significance which may be quite alien to our purpose. Especially is this true when dealing with a mind like Mrs. Woolf's, so sensitive to fine distinctions and so precise in its conceptions (Holtby, 1978: 178).

Woolf gropes toward the distinction between sex and gender, but does not express it in the terms with which we have become so familiar. She wonders whether "there are two sexes in the mind corresponding to the two sexes in the body" (AROO: 98). Perhaps we can learn just as much by directing our attention to questions that did not concern Woolf, or rather, questions which she had only just begun to formulate, as we can by considering the questions that occupied her. Noting the absence of our own answers in her text, we may be able to illuminate the ways in which now standard answers to the question of the difference between sex and gender have inflected more recent feminist discourse in particular ways. We may be able to prevent our standard answers from ascending to the level of dogma, as they are sometimes wont to do, by suggesting directions in which feminist inquiry can open up, rather than close off, new areas of investigation.

THE RISE AND FALL OF ESSENTIALISM

Woolf's exploration of the theme of androgyny should be understood as a rejection of the idea that men and women are basically the same, an idea that in practice played itself out as a privileging of traditionally masculine traits over traditionally feminine traits. Feminist demands for equality between men and women, around which feminism mobilized its forces at the beginning of the twentieth century—and which formed the context of Woolf's writing—issued in a strong tendency to envisage the sexes as essentially similar to one another. In order to achieve equal treatment in the workplace, equal reward for equal work, and equal respect in the home women resorted to strategies that emphasized the basic sameness of the sexes and directed attention away from anything that detracted from the commonalities sought between men and women. As a by-product of such strategies, women dissociated themselves from the physical differences that distinguished them from men. Julia Kristeva identifies this first phase of twentieth-century feminism as a period during which women tried to conform to some kind of masculine ideal—without questioning that ideal.[12] If Woolf kept her distance from this ideal, Beauvoir's denigration of motherhood, her aspirations to be accepted into the predominantly male world of intellectuals, and her determination to be self-supporting, became emblematic of it. Beauvoir's personal example was influential for a whole generation of feminists, and her theoretical legacy is still felt. Her call to women was to refuse the constraints of traditional femininity, unloose the bonds of their servitude, reclaim their full humanity, recognize their true freedom, and transcend the immanence by which history had defined them. These exhortations followed from the realization that "One is not born, but rather becomes, a woman" (SS: 301; DS 2: 13). Grafted on to this basic message is the familiar terminology of sex and gender. Women worked for equality in the belief that sex did not determine their destinies, gender did—and since gender was a social construct, it was also capable of change.

The second phase of feminism that Kristeva identifies might be called a reactive phase, since it is one in which there was, to some degree, a rejection of the ideals instantiated by Beauvoir's arguments—ideals which, for all the subtlety and sophistication with which she seasoned them, ended up sounding very much like an exhortation to become more like men. Insofar as Beauvoir cast herself as an exceptional woman, who managed to overcome the societal restrictions of femininity that held back most women, she identified success in male terms, and encouraged others to follow her example. Women had put up with the dictates of society for too long already. They were suspicious of Beauvoir's advice to avoid motherhood at all costs, and to direct their energies into earning their own living. Not ready to replace one set of moral injunctions with another, some feminists of the 1960s and 1970s glorified the feminine, reinvoking the joys of motherhood and rejoicing in their female sexuality. Women's consciousness-raising groups sprang up in profusion, accompanied by a renewed insistence, Beauvoir notwithstanding, that it was not the similarities of the sexes that mattered, but their differences. Intent upon self-exploration, the theme of women's commonality, solidarity, and sisterhood emerged as dominant among grassroots feminist activists. Women shared and analyzed their experiences with one another, gaining strength from the mutual corroboration of their experiences that came from the similarity of their accounts. The mutual confirmation that women offered one another no doubt consolidated the women's movement, but at the same time it exacerbated whatever classist, racist, and heterosexist assumptions structured feminist attitudes. Thus the scene was set for the ideological battle that organized itself in the 1980s around the essentialist and anti-essentialist camps.[13]

A reaction set in against the return to mother-nature and the celebration of femininity, in what might be called a third phase of feminism—characterized by, among other things, the essentialism/anti-essentialism debate. Was it safe to identify ourselves with the seemingly innocuous but in fact highly dangerous label "women"?[14] Weren't we pressing our predominantly white, middle-class heterosexism on feminists from different ethnic and cultural backgrounds and classes, of different sexual preferences, of various ages and abilities? Weren't we mistakenly assuming that women were united by some ineffable essence of femininity? How could we use the term "women" as if it named a common group, when that group was in fact as diverse as the individuals that comprised it?

"Strategic" essentialism was advocated as a way out of this dilemma.[15] Perhaps it was safe, after all, to identify ourselves as women, so long as we did so in full recognition of the fact that the term "women" falsely universalizes our experiences. Despite the genuine and crucial differences between women, there were still some political gains to be had from utilizing a label that was nevertheless inadequate to those differences.

If we witnessed, in the early 1980s, a call to beware of the potentially dangerous and reactionary elements of French feminist theories, the end of the decade saw the demise of the essentialism/anti-essentialism debate as such. It is an open question as to whether, beneath the overt rejection of the "overworked" oppositional pairing "essence/anti-essence," there lurked the vestigial remains of an issue that could not yet be put to rest.[16] In 1989 prominent feminist critics, perhaps most notably Spivak, pointed out to us that we should not allow the debate over essentialism to distract us from the real problems that should concern feminists—namely, the task of changing social relations;[17] that the difficulty of defining essentialism without essentializing it should not be overlooked;[18] that we should focus our energies not on academic, intellectual debates over "essentialism" but on transforming women's situations. Political critiques of the essentialism debate began to emerge. The point is to change the world, we were reminded, not to allow ourselves to get caught up in fine distinctions, or obsessed with articulating at the theoretical level what needed to be changed at the practical level.

While such reminders are never superfluous, they tend to reduce the relation between feminist practice and theory to one of good intentions. To say we need to transform women's situation is no doubt true; it remains, of course, notoriously problematic to know how to change social relations—from feminist perspectives, or from any other political perspective. Even if we can all agree, theoretically, that the world would be a nicer place if we were all treated as equals by everyone, vast problems remain untackled (what practical measures would achieve such ends, how to put into practice the reforms we might deem necessary, whom to entrust with the responsibility of orchestrating such changes, and so on). If, as feminists, we are to avoid naive assumptions about our ability to transform other women's lives for the better, we should be prepared to take the time to critically examine and explicate our theoretical positions. Whether we do so or not, we assume certain ideas as part of our political framework and as a result of our collective historical and cultural heritage. We may as well become conscious of the theories and ideas that lie behind our everyday rationales. Since they exist in any case, we would do well to educate ourselves about them and be reflective about the ideologies that support and sustain the models we adopt in our feminist interventions and actions. Our language is a formative element of those actions. Feminist language both is siphoned off from political actions, and it filters through to grassroots feminism—it both is transformed by political action and it transforms that action. It is elaborated from and it elaborates political positions within feminism. Slogans (one is not born, one becomes a woman; the personal is political; take back the night!) come to encapsulate feelings and motivations, and in turn these slogans themselves motivate and redirect political energies.

My own position toward the essentialism/anti-essentialism debate is one that has changed over the past few years from incredulity (how could anyone possibly mistake Kristeva or Irigaray as essentialist when their positions are not only diametrically opposed to essentialism, but they explicitly and repeatedly repudiate it?) to an attempt to understand the underlying issues that fostered such interpretations. Gradually replacing my initial disbelief of what I, somewhat arrogantly, simply dismissed as "misreadings," my interest developed not only in the "misreadings" themselves, but also in the question of how essentialist readings of the

"French feminists" could gain such prevalence so rapidly despite what seemed to me their obvious falsity. What motivated the wildly divergent readings of the same texts as essentialist or anti-essentialist? My sense was that the divergence could be in large part accounted for by the difference between the philosophical tradition out of which Kristeva and Irigaray were writing and the political pragmatic agendas that formed the background to Anglo-American feminist discourse. "French feminists," whatever else their considerable differences, were steeped in a history that took seriously the "continental tradition," which included thinkers as diverse as Hegel, Nietzsche, Freud, Marx, Heidegger, Derrida, and Lacan. By contrast, the dominant frame of reference for Anglo-American thinkers was a no-nonsense program of reform that centered on arguments for equal rights between the sexes, and that tended to look askance upon the continental tradition. The likes of Hegel, Heidegger, and Derrida were regarded, at best, with mild suspicion, at worst, as charlatans who had little to say about the real world—little more than a series of self-indulgent esoteric musings. The result was that Kristeva and Irigaray were judged in terms of the liberal discourse of equal rights and the ideal of sameness that, however inexplicit, tended to accompany it. Not surprisingly, French feminists were found wanting by these standards.[19]

My point is not that Anglo-American feminists are atheoretical, but that their theories are perhaps more immediately associated with political positions than those of the French. Consider, for example, Jaggar's classification of feminist theories into "liberal feminism, traditional Marxism, radical feminism and socialist feminism" (Jaggar, 1983: 8). Nor am I suggesting, of course, that the struggle for equal rights plays no part in French feminism. Nevertheless, the theoretical heritage of those who thematize the question of sexual difference—a blend of phenomenology, psychoanalysis, and post-structuralism—has the effect of distinguishing French feminist thought from its Anglo-American counterpart.

However much the terms "French feminism" and "Anglo-American feminism" gloss over important differences between the individual theorists each term designates—and there is no question that they do— they also signify specific cultural traditions. Critics have pointed out, for good reasons, that the term "French feminism" is a misnomer, but its inappropriateness has not prevented its wide circulation. If it is so inaccurate, why does it remain in place? Because it names a certain unease we experience in our inability to embrace these "foreign" theorists without changing some of our ideas? The fact that Irigaray's work does not fit neatly into our preconceived categories as to what feminism should look like does not mean that it cannot be read as feminism. Rather, it is indicative of the challenge that Irigaray presents to her readers in asking whether feminism has adequately formulated questions that are fundamental to it, and, correspondingly, whether feminists have a sufficiently radical view of what constitutes feminism.

Far from consolidating the split between those who are sympathetic to French feminism and those who see it as hopelessly embroiled in essentialist assumptions, as if this divide were constituted by an untraversable chasm, I try to account for the entrenched historical positions of both sides. I want to identify some of the reasons why the two sides often talk past one another, rather than to one another, and why it is just as misplaced to peremptorily dismiss essentialist critiques as irrelevant to French feminism as it is to simply take it for granted that such critiques are vindicated.

Despite attempts to negotiate or mediate the cultural legacies that differentiate the post-phenomenological and psychoanalytic tendencies of French feminism from the political activism of American feminism, these differences repeatedly reassert themselves. Citing Naomi Schor's, Jane Gallop's, and Alice Jardine's trans-Atlantic crossings (metaphorical and otherwise), Rachel Bowlby comments that "however strong the assertion to the contrary, there is a tendency for the differences between American and French critical modes to be fixed into simple, homologous oppositions between stasis and process, theme and text, pragmatism and theory, realism and (post-)modernism" (Bowlby, 1988: 66).[20] Notwithstanding its apparent radicality, and contrary to its best intentions, French feminism is still held up on suspicion that it suffers a relapse into essentialism. Fashioned by critics who have produced readings and counter-readings, the interpretative edifice of the essentialism/anti-essentialism debate continues to hold sway. If charges of essentialism as such have lost some of their effectiveness through overuse, their impact has been absorbed by feminist discourse in a variety of arenas, and their residues linger on.

While I share Rosi Braidotti's impatience with gestures that continue to distinguish between French and Anglo-American feminism on the basis that the latter is more pragmatic than the former, I do not think it is possible to simply brush aside such oversimplifications and hope to start afresh. To do so is to ignore the enormous influence that such classifications have had in creating political and intellectual alliances and disjunctions. Braidotti says that she does not want to pursue her discussion of French feminism in the direction of a comparison, or a confrontation, between the more Lacanian and therefore French-oriented school of the embodiment of the subject with the allegedly more pragmatic "Anglo-American" school. I think too much feminist theoretical energy over the last ten years has been wasted in this sort of senseless comparison. Much more important in my eyes is the way in which, through different cultural and theoretical traditions, a general direction of thought is emerging in feminist theory, that situates the embodied nature of the subject, and consequently the question of alternatively sexual difference or gender, at the heart of the matter (Braidotti, 1991: 263).

I agree that the comparison is "senseless" in many ways, but I also think that, in order to clarify the "general direction of thought" that is emerging according to Braidotti, certain misconceptions need to be addressed, among them the over-simplistic characterizations of French and American feminism that still hold sway in interpreting French feminisms. I want to take seriously the cultural phenomenon of persistent misreadings of French feminist texts and the politics of their reception, by continuing to delineate not only individual differences between thinkers, but also cultural discrepancies. If we merely ignore the multiple problems that characterize the translation of French feminism into Anglo-American terms, or pretend that they don't exist, the chances are that the distortions we permit when we inadequately substitute one language for another will return to haunt us. It hardly needs to be added that, if these problems are evident at the level of translation in the most literal sense, they extend far beyond this immediate difficulty. A number of backdrops set the scene for the stage on which the dramas of translation have been acted out in the name of the essentialism debate. These include: questions about the viability of appealing to women's experience in this post-metaphysical era that have rendered problematic conventional ideas of "authorship," "subjectivity," and "experience"; arguments over whether one can appeal to feminine specificity without invoking precisely the reified notions that feminism tried so hard for so many years to remove; and interrogations of what it means to write as a woman.

To be sensitive to the problems of translation at stake here is not merely a matter of registering the significant differences between the cultural and political contexts that situate the texts we translate and the specific contexts we, as translators, assume as our own. While the specific historical circumstances that differentiate French feminists from their Anglo-American interpreters are far from irrelevant, I would insist that their theoretical heritage is equally important.[21] If Irigaray's reluctance to embrace the language of equality (JTN: 11–13; JT: 11–14), and her hesitation to adopt the term "feminism" must be read against the background of elitist attempts by exclusive groups to usurp the feminist platform in France, her insistence upon making central the question of sexual difference cannot be reduced to a political agenda.[22] Dorothy Kaufmann-McCall documents how the group *Psychanalyse et politique,* led by Antoinette Fouque, attempted to appropriate the term that identified a diversity of groups comprising the women's movement by gaining a legal right to and a commercial monopoly on it. They officially co-opted the name MLF (Mouvement de Libération des Femmes,) a term that previously had been used as a generic label for identifying various factions of the French feminist movement.[23] This is a good example of the kind of totalizing domination that can be used in the name of feminism, and against which Irigaray warns. In an interview Irigaray remarks upon the "tyranny" that *Psych et Po* exerts over the publishing house, *Librairie des femmes.*[24]

In retaining the terms "French" and "Anglo-American" to characterize different feminist positions, there is a sense in which I am necessarily oversimplifying and overgeneralizing. I do so only in order to move beyond these labels, not in order to reify them. Far from presenting either French or Anglo-American feminists as if they were monolothic groups whose members are indistinguishable from one another, my aim is to break down some of the barriers that stand in the way of communication between these two trends in feminist thought. It does not seem possible to ignore the ways in which French and Anglo-American feminisms have been represented as antithetical to one another. Rather, we need to inquire into the reasons that lie behind these antagonistic relations, and to clarify the assumptions that support apparently divergent and entrenched positions, before we can establish any grounds for a more productive exchange between them. I am using the terms "French" and Anglo-American feminisms as short-hand designations for "theorists of sexual difference who write in the context of a continental philosophical tradition," and "their English-language readers who work in a tradition largely informed by analytic philosophy (whether implicitly or explicitly), some of whom therefore read French feminism as essentialist." I ask readers to bear in mind that I am aware that plenty of Anglo-American readers of French feminism do not see them as essentialist. I hope to provide a genealogy of the debate over essentialism and to establish a parallel between Irigaray's work and recent developments within Anglo-American feminist theory: my overall intentions are not polemical. The reinterrogation of the sex/gender distinction by so-called Anglo-American feminists is a prime example of the parallelism that I explore. This is a central thesis of my book, and it bears repeating. Let me anticipate the consequences I think it has. Once it becomes clear that the domain that we used to designate as "sex" is no longer so clearly distinguishable from that domain we named "gender," Irigaray's interrogation of sexual difference no longer threatens to disrupt the fundamental basis of Anglo-American feminism, but rather to confirm its own questioning of its foundational categories. I should note that, just as I do not intend the label "Anglo-American" to reduce all Anglo-American feminists to one position, but rather to identify a major response to French feminism, and just as I do not intend the label "French" to homogenize all French feminists, but rather to name a distinct cultural, political, and intellectual tradition, so I have no interest in arguing that these two positions—insofar as they can be regarded as such—will ever become indistinguishable. While Irigaray's interrogation of sexual difference is steeped in a psychoanalytic and post-phenomenological tradition that differs from the language of her Anglo-American counterparts, there are significant similarities between her approach and the implications of the recent loosening up of rigid distinctions between sex and gender.

SEX AND GENDER REVISITED

As Gatens acknowledges, "The problem of the relationship between sex and gender is, of course, not a new one. Freud grappled with the problem of finding a suitable definition of masculinity and femininity and their relation to men and women in the "Three Essays" published in 1905. However, the authoritative source for the recent prominence of writings centering on gender is not Freud but Robert J. Stoller, a contemporary psychoanalyst" (Gatens, 1991a: 141).[25] In a list that could be extended, Gatens cites several influential feminist authors (Germaine Greer, Kate Millett, Ann Oakley, Nancy Chodorow, and Dorothy Dinnerstein) that relied upon Stoller's *Sex and Gender*.[26] In his preface Stoller himself is scrupulously careful to emphasize the extreme difficulty, if not impossibility, of enshrining any absolute standards for the demarcation of gender from sex. Discussing the term "gender identity" he says,

> It is a working term. We know that though it deals with another realm
> of feelings, thoughts, and behavior than that encompassed by, say,

sexual activity, the two terms are contiguous and at times inextricably intermingled. With *gender* difficult to define and *identity* still a challenge to theoreticians, we need hardly insist on the holiness of the term "gender identity" (Stoller, 1968: vol. 1, vi).

Without too much exaggeration, we could say that within the discourse of feminism there has been a tendency to do just what Stoller wanted to avoid: to deify gender, to attribute to it a hallowed status that renders it impervious to questioning. It is arguable that Stoller himself ignores his own advice as he proceeds to develop the idea that there is a "*core* gender identity."[27] Paying only scant attention to the contiguity or inextricable intermingling of sex with gender that Stoller underlined, at least in his initial formulations, some feminists eagerly took up his intention to "confirm the fact that the two realms (sex and gender) are not at all inevitably bound in anything like a one-to-one relationship, but each may go in its quite independent way" (Stoller, 1968: vol 1, vii). Having stated this purpose, Stoller goes straight on to acknowledge his debt to none other than Freud, saying,

> This first became clearly evident in those monumental works *The Interpretation of Dreams* and *Three Essays on Sexuality,* wherein Sigmund Freud forced the world to recognize that much of what was called sexuality was determined by one's life experiences from infancy on and was not simply a matter of inheritance, biochemistry, and other organic factors. . . . No such profound or simple statement has supplemented or supplanted Freud's original work (Stoller, 1968: vol. 1, vii).

A strange set of alliances begins to emerge. Consulting the "authoritative" work of Stoller, to whom so many feminists turn in order to license their ideas about the flexibility of femininity, we are confronted with nothing less than a return to Freud. Not only does Stoller congratulate Freud for his profundity, but he does so in an acknowledgment that specifies Freud as the one who first began to explore the distinction that Stoller labels with the terms "sex" and "gender"—the very distinction that has become emblematic for feminism. This invocation, this history, this lineage tends to be passed over by those who suspect the French feminists of relying too heavily on the fathers of psychoanalysis, Freud and Lacan. The potential for construing gender independently of sex was seized upon by feminists, who tended to divorce the distinction from its psychoanalytic context. The abstraction of the distinction from psychoanalysis has generated a discourse in which attempts to retain a sense of its complexity have been outlawed as too dangerous. Thus Irigaray is chastised as a "French feminist" or as a "post-structuralist feminist" for veering toward essentialism, although she develops an analysis of women's position within the context from which the sex/gender distinction was originally advanced —namely, psychoanalysis.[28] Meanwhile, despite Stoller's caution, which echoes Freud's, the sex/gender distinction has become susceptible to the fixity and rigidity that both try so hard to avoid.[29] The rigidity of the distinction is then used by some feminists to dogmatically reject French feminism, and the hesitations and qualifications surrounding Stoller's formulation of Freud's original insight are forgotten. The sex/gender distinction seems to acquire a self-evidence which is no longer open to question.

Let me clarify exactly what I am suggesting. I am not seeking culprits to blame for poor scholarship or faulty reasoning. I am investigating the phenomenon of a proliferation of accusations that French feminists are essentialist, and I am offering as one possible explanation for the fervor of these accusations the extent to which feminism has become identified with a symbolic freeing of gender from sex. Notwithstanding the useful-ness of the sex/gender distinction, indeed perhaps precisely because of the dramatic improvement that this very distinction has helped accomplish, I am suggesting that there is an urgent need for feminism to move forward, to address some of the more salient oversimplifications committed in the name of changing things for the better. The very appeal and success of the sex/gender distinction has not only diverted interest away from other areas of feminist inquiry, the dominance that the distinction claims for itself also militates against serious investigation of anything that does not immediately sit well with the most superficial renderings of it—sexual difference, for example. Given feminist enthusiasm to keep sex and gender separate, the inquiry into sexual difference has acquired a bad name. It is my contention that, when properly contextualized and when properly thought through, the relevance of the sex/gender distinction to feminism not only leaves room for sexual difference, but actually requires that its significance be heeded.

Until recently, the very idea of challenging the validity of the sex/gender distinction amounted to feminist heresy. The distinction had acquired almost canonical significance, enshrined in such classic texts as Gayle Rubin's "The Traffic in Women," to which an impressive procession of scholarly citations continue to pay homage (Rubin, 1975). As I add mine to the list, let me make it clear that my aim here is neither to detract from the undoubted merit of Rubin's analysis, nor to castigate those who remain committed to the importance of employing the distinction between sex and gender in the service of securing the socio-economic and political equality of the sexes. In her own use of the distinction Rubin is careful not to posit the realms of sex and gender as separate or easily distinguishable entities. She analyzes the conjunction of sex and gender as a "system" that articulates an important "domain of social life" (Rubin, 1975: 166). While Rubin takes care to understand the sex/gender system as naming particular traits of social life, the relationship between sex and gender is often construed more simplistically in feminist discourse. The distinction tends to degenerate into a more or less straightforward division between "biology," "nature," or the "body," on the one hand, and "society," "culture," or "history," on the other hand—as if sex and gender indicate two conceptually distinct categories, which are not only readily identifiable but also defined in clear opposition to one another. The continuing strategic importance of such gestures for the purposes of achieving and maintaining equal job opportunities and salary equity, and in combatting sex discrimination in all its various manifestations, remains incontestable. My purpose is not to bring into question the undeniable usefulness of the sex/gender distinction. Rather, I propose that, despite the indisputable fact that it has effectively focused feminist energies, the distinction is in danger of being oversimplified and overworked.[30]

SCIENCE AND FEMINISM

It has become a commonplace to suggest that knowledge reflects the interests of its knowers, and that ostensible truths are informed by power relations. Yet the unsettling impact of this suggestion on the notion that "biological" sex is clearly demarcated from "socially" constructed gender has not been widely acknowledged. If science carries with it certain political agendas, if supposedly empirical truths are located within power structures and directed toward the particular ends of certain interest groups, and if the results yielded by science no longer appear to be universally applicable, a number of categories familiar to feminism begin to line themselves up differently. The grid provided by the distinction between sex and gender has structured feminist discourse in ways that feminists concerned with science throw into question. Both the reliability of the sex/gender distinction and the accuracy with which it has been employed in feminist arguments are subjected to scrutiny. As we have seen, some feminists have devoted considerable energy to distinguishing sex from gender in the interests of effecting changes. In doing so, they tend to play off gender against sex. If sex is a given, gender is not. Gender, as a social, cultural, historically specific concept is flexible and malleable, whereas sex is, by contrast, a relatively stable and fixed category. The questions that are currently being raised by feminists working in the area of science suggest a rather different scenario. It begins to look as if not only gender but sex too is a socially defined category of analysis. As Butler observes, the two realms begin to merge into one another and become indistinguishable.[31]

If, previously, biology was taken to yield indisputable truths about "nature," and scientific claims were considered verifiable according to the empirical referent of the body, now that the objectivity of scientific knowledge is being doubted, allegedly objective claims about the supposedly empirical world begin to look gender specific. Concepts such as sex and biology are just as historically mediated as gender and culture. What emerges is—to use Sandra Harding's term—the "instability" not only of gender but also of sex (Harding, 1989). Rather than being exempted from feminist analyses, sex comes back into play. It no longer seems either viable or desirable to ban the body from the feminist arena. The scientificity of the concept "sex" is open to question. The body can no longer be ignored, displaced, or disregarded by feminists. It becomes a site of contention which refuses our attempts to bracket it, to block it out, or to resist its demands for attention.

The success of the strategy of playing off gender against sex notwithstanding, once feminism acknowledges that the categories of sex and nature are historically specific, and that neither concept can be treated as if it were a stable or universal concept, a reexamination of the relation between sex and gender is called for. It is not enough to ignore sex differences and concentrate all our energy on analyzing cultural roles, as if sex could be left completely out of the picture. To do so would be to assume not only that we know what sex means, but also that its meaning has not changed and cannot change. In fact traits that once may have been considered sexual come to be identified with gender over time. Such shifts can result from feminist arguments that point to the contingency of allegedly innate characteristics. For example, if previously women's inferior intellect was attributed to the natural limitations of our sex, now discrepancies between the intellectual ability of men and women are more likely to be explained by lack of training or educational opportunity. Equally, transformations within the discipline of biology may alter the contents of that realm we traditionally designated as sex—but it would be a mistake to view such developments as purely scientific discoveries without acknowledging that the ways in which scientific disciplines define the scope of their inquiries are influenced by political forces. The extent to which feminism has informed the development of reproductive technology may be impossible to determine, but there is little doubt that it has had some impact. Not only is the sex/gender distinction unstable, so too are the boundaries separating the categories on which we typically draw to interpret it, such as the lines demarcating biology from history, and nature from culture. That these distinctions are unstable does not mean that they are meaningless.[32] They still have purchase; sex does not become entirely indistinguishable from gender. Even if the act of designating a particular realm "sex" in distinction from "gender" is itself a cultural designation, even if sex is, in this sense, always already gendered, the two realms do not entirely collapse into one another. If sex is always already gendered, it is equally true that gender is always already sexed. In other words, it is not by accident that we habitually distinguish two genders from one another; the duality of gender, as feminine and masculine, is integrally bound up with our similarly habitual distinction of the female sex (as if it were one undifferentiated whole instead of a group of separate individuals) from the male sex. Why are there only two genders? Or, as Derrida has asked, in an interview to which we shall return, what about a dream of multiple sexualities? (C: 76).

ESSENTIALISM REVISITED

I have claimed that insofar as the accusation of biological essentialism operates within a framework that unquestioningly accepts the self-evident validity of the sex/gender distinction, the charge of essentialism appeals to oversimplified dichotomies that need reworking. My suggestion is that Irigaray contests the simplicity with which the nature/culture split and the biology/history distinction have been used to interpret the sex/gender distinction.

Irigaray's interest, as I understand it, is not in universally legislating that we should all be cosmically celebrating the multiple rhythms of birth and nature. Rather, she asks whether certain features of our current way of thinking, characteristic of our particular cultural epoch, have made it difficult for us to think about what it means to be a woman. To construe feminism in terms that denigrate biology and sexual difference, deify culture, and appeal to the similarity of the sexes is—whatever the usefulness of this strategy—in some ways another inflection of patriarchal dogma masquerading under the guise of liberalism. Irigaray says,

"Equality signifies becoming totally like men" (Baruch and Serrano, 1988: 153), but elsewhere she makes it clear that, while her "thinking about women's liberation has a dimension other than the search for equality between the sexes," this does not prevent her from "joining and promoting public demonstrations for women to gain this or that right: the right to contraception, abortion, legal aid in cases of public or domestic violence, the right to freedom of expression—etc" (JTN: 11; JT: 11).[33] Irigaray's point, then, is clearly not that we no longer need concern ourselves with socio-political and economic struggles for freedom and equality, but that we need to be wary of allowing ourselves to be placated by whatever concessions are granted. Purporting to offer equal access, equal opportunity, and equal protection to all, the discourse of equality neutralizes both gender and sex, while covering over the gravitational pull that patriarchy exercises over the term "all." This "all" appears to be plural, but in fact approximates to one— one who, we hardly need specify, tends to be white, male, middle class, and heterosexual.

It is worth noting that among the (perhaps unintended) results of feminists emphasizing gender over sex there has been a fostering not only of sex-blindness, but also of color-blindness, which may have allowed discrimination more free play than it might otherwise have had. If the sex of bodies has been rendered relatively unimportant in dominant feminist discourse, in which gender was the privileged category, so the color of women (and men) has been considered more or less irrelevant. Despite the ostensibly neutral discourse of gender, the standards of patriarchy have remained more or less in place, just as the privileges enjoyed by whites over blacks have gone largely unchallenged.[34]

The differences between men and women, or between white and black, have reemerged as important considerations in a range of legal debates[35]— for example, that over affirmative action, in which the supporters of preferential hiring may require not only "formal" but "substantive" equality.[36] To insist on the significance of racial differences is not, of course, to naively endorse some theory of biological or genetic differences between races, but rather to acknowledge that if a disproportionate number of whites, compared to blacks, gain college degrees, this discrepancy can probably be traced back to earlier social discrimination. Despite legal or formal equality of opportunity, racial discrimination is socially sanctioned and institutionalized such that college entrants are pre-selected according to a variety of factors—such as which schools they attend, which in turn is determined by which catchment area they live in, and is therefore related to factors such as race, class, and income. As Onora Nell observes, "different social groups differ and so will have different success rates on various selection tests, and . . . a succession of such tests, where success in earlier ones earns privileges in preparation for later ones, will produce quite sharply divergent success rates" (Nell, 1980: 342).

I have attempted here to review recent feminist history in a way that suggests how the rebuke of essentialism was able to gather such force, and why it misrepresents Irigaray's position. I have emphasized the need for feminism to rethink the distinction between sex and gender, a distinction that has served the ends of feminism for a long time, but one which, I argue, we are in danger of taking for granted. Rather than accept the terms of debate established in the exchange between Kamuf and Miller, I have tried to recast the question of sexual difference by asking: can one appeal to an author's sex without falling into a set of naively metaphysical or humanist assumptions about authorial intention, identity, language, and domination? Irigaray's interrogation of sexual difference is, in my view, a testimony to the importance and value of balancing the need to specify that it makes a difference whether it is a man or a woman who writes, speaks, or acts, and the need for feminism to refuse to simply embrace the illusions of metaphysics.

In her initial definition of essentialism, Schor says that an essentialist is one who fails to hold apart the poles of sex and gender, one for whom the female body remains "in however complex a way the rock of feminism" (Schor, 1989: 40). I have suggested that, in her attention to the question of sexual differences and their psychoanalytic construction, Irigaray sees the need to reexamine the function and significance of the sex/gender distinction within feminist discourse. She does so in a way that brings the body back into play, not as "the rock of feminism" but as a mobile site of differences. Irigaray's attention to the body, far from amounting to a refusal of culture and history, allows her to scrutinize critically the assumptions that feminists make when they suspend questions of sexual difference to achieve political change. To accuse her of essentialism not only rejects her interrogation of certain assumptions about sameness that habitually underlie feminist struggles for equality in the political arena, it also refuses to acknowledge the challenge Irigaray issues to conventional conceptions of the enigmatic divide between nature and culture.

two THE LEGACY OF SIMONE DE BEAUVOIR

Certain passages in the argument employed by Hegel in defining the relation of master to slave apply much better to the relation of man to woman.

—BEAUVOIR

In the relationship between man and woman, for example, Desire is human only if one desires, not the body, but the Desire of the Other; if he wants "to possess" or to "assimilate" the Desire. . . . To speak of the "origin" of Self-Consciousness is necessarily to speak of the risk of life. . . . To speak of the "origin" of Self-Consciousness is necessarily to speak of a fight to the death for recognition.

—KOJÈVE

CULTURE AND THE OTHER

IN 1972 SIMONE DE BEAUVOIR WROTE, IN A RETROSPECTIVE glance at *The Second Sex,* "No feminist questions the statement that women are manufactured by civilization, not biologically determined" (ASD: 490; TCF: 504).[1] Yet we have witnessed in recent years, as I have documented, a stream of feminist criticism denouncing contemporary French feminists for falling into the trap of essentialism. This assessment of French feminism continues to gain ground, despite the efforts of some feminists to dislodge it.[2] Could her successors really have learned so little from Beauvoir?[3] I am reluctant to suppose so. For this reason I intend to return to *The Second Sex* in order to establish the relation between Beauvoir's contribution to feminist theory and the recent controversy—and confusion—over essentialism.

Perhaps the best known and most quoted sentence of *The Second Sex* is to be found at the beginning of book two: "One is not born woman, but rather becomes a woman" (SS: 301; DS 2: 13).[4] Beauvoir herself identifies this statement as "one of the leading ideas in *The Second Sex*" (ASD: 484; TCF: 497). Another leading idea that has attracted less attention, but on which I wish to focus here, is the question of what it means for women to "assume the status of the Other" (SS: xxxiii; DS: 31).[5] Feminists have tended to see Beauvoir's insistence on women's historical construction as other as a weak point in her argument.[6] Even critics who recognize the significance of Beauvoir's thematization of woman as other have not examined the difficulties it presents in relation to the Sartrian-inspired dictum to which she constantly refers, that since we are all fundamentally free, women are free to change their situations.[7] As an existentialist who endorses the ability of the individual to embrace freedom and to transcend adversity, Beauvoir is both an optimist and an individualist. She emphasizes that women can change and overcome their feminine social conditioning through the realization that they are not determined by it. In the idealism implied by her existentialist framework Beauvoir ultimately betrays her own insights into the importance of characterizing women's situation as other.[8]

In this chapter I argue not only that the significance Beauvoir attributes to women's traditional role as men's other is just as important as her idea that women are formed through cultural influences, but also that, unless feminism confronts the impact of women's status as other upon women's cultural conditioning, neither of these issues will be adequately addressed. The two strands of Beauvoir's thought that I am identifying as the role of culture and the meaning of women's construction as other are integral to one another, and must be thought in relation to each other, if Beauvoir's contribution to feminist theory is to be appreciated.[9] Only then will we be in a position to see both the usefulness and the limitations of Beauvoir's work, and to assess the advances made by more recent thematizations of women's otherness, such as Irigaray's.

One of the reasons that French feminists such as Irigaray have been dismissed as essentialist is that some feminists have been unwilling—or unable—to rethink the sex/gender distinction.[10] What I aim to show in this chapter is that, to the extent that Beauvoir saw the importance of challenging received notions of femininity, she appropriately focused the attention of feminists upon culture as the dominant force in shaping femininity. However, she did not adequately conceive of the interrelation between the role of culture and the question of women's status as other. I will suggest that, to a significant extent, the difficulty she had in relating these two aspects of her project lay in her attempt to fuse two incompatible theories. On the one hand, she drew heavily on Sartre's concept of absolute freedom, and on the other hand, she adopted a quasi-Hegelian concept of the other. Her failure to elaborate a theoretical perspective in which both elements were interwoven left her unable to see the implications of her reflections on the status of woman as other for her argument for overcoming the cultural conditioning of women as feminine. In an extension of my argument in the previous chapter, I will show that taking the thematization of women as other seriously requires—as I think Irigaray has understood—a radical rethinking of the way in which the sex/gender distinction functions in contemporary feminist discourse.

Beauvoir's existentialist starting point assumes that, through adopting a reflective distance upon the particular conditions defining one's life, an individual can rise above or transcend any situation. This analysis privileges the individual's ability to become aware of, or objectify, the situation in which one finds oneself. In the case of women, this idea translates into the suggestion that once we realize how culture limits our opportunities for action, we can act on that knowledge, challenge the constraints imposed upon us, and change our situations. I suggest that, if Beauvoir had pursued the question of women's otherness more rigorously, the significance of her argument that one is not born but rather becomes a woman would have been changed. In other words, the fact that women have always been seen as other would have impinged more directly on the way in which the nature/culture divide was construed by Beauvoir. What it means for women to have been systematically cast as other would have brought into question the adequacy of Beauvoir's well-known formulation of the idea that it is gender, not sex, that makes women what they are. Insofar as she presupposes the opposition between nature and culture, and insofar as she construes sexual difference as that which is to be overcome, Beauvoir emphasizes the difference between women as biologically sexed, and women as acculturated social beings. To the extent that this account of women's situation privileges the need to overcome any differentiation between the sexes, it is an account that ascribes a purely negative connotation to the ways in which women differ from men. Not only is the difficulty of overcoming women's historical construction as other underplayed in this scenario, there is also a tendency to take for granted the oppositional relations between culture and nature.

By emphasizing that women's situation is not given but is rather culturally produced, Beauvoir focuses on the possibility of changing women's situation so that women are no longer subordinate to men. In order to be recognized as equal, must women strive to be seen as more or less the same as men? Insofar as Beauvoir disparages traditionally feminine values, scorns motherhood, stresses the importance of women earning independent incomes, and strives to be accepted into a male world on male terms, her answer seems to be a qualified yes.[11] How well thought out is this position, and how does Beauvoir come to the conclusion that woman's otherness should be overcome?

The tension between Beauvoir's individualist existentialism and her analysis of the social causes at the root of women's oppression has often been observed.[12] Less obvious is the extent to which this tension is caused by Beauvoir's attempt to fuse two different theoretical models in her analysis of women's situation: a Sartrian model of freedom—which implies the ability of the individual to transcend any situation—and a Hegelian model of the other—which implies an irresolvable conflict between individuals. I want to approach this problem by examining the use that Beauvoir makes of Hegel's master-slave dialectic. Recalling Beauvoir's dependence on Hegel's master-slave dialectic, we discover that Beauvoir attributes no importance to the very obvious fact that Hegel's concept of the other, as elaborated in the master-slave dialectic, is an exclusively male model.[13] To the extent that she fails to see this as a difficulty, Beauvoir's analysis of woman as other is circumscribed by a totalizing way of thinking, a paradigm from which Irigaray and others who have explored what it might mean to envisage experience from a specifically feminine point of view step back. While recognizing the impossibility of finding any other place to go, as if we could ever entirely shake ourselves free of our histories, Irigaray puts into question the complacency with which feminism locates itself within the very power structures it rejects. At the same time, she brings into question the philosophical model that Beauvoir, in her synthesis of Hegel and Sartre, took for granted. By demonstrating in detail the ultimately confining implications that this model has for Beauvoir's investigation of women's situation, I hope to show the urgent need for Irigaray's rewriting of the philosophical tradition that Beauvoir assumes.

Insofar as women are disadvantaged by their role as other, Beauvoir wants women to overcome or transcend their otherness. As Kaufmann says, *The Second Sex* "views sexual difference as necessarily a source of oppression" (YFS: 121). But the task of overcoming oppression cannot merely be a matter of insisting that women are subjects just as men are, or that women should be treated as equals and construed as the same as men at least with respect to their individuality, worth, and dignity. Beyond these necessary demands, overcoming oppression also involves an effort to understand women's point of view as other. This effort is considerable because patriarchal ideologies tend to preclude the construction of women as subjects. Not only do men construct women as objectified, but women have also become accustomed to seeing themselves through men's eyes.

One task Beauvoir sets herself is "to describe the world in which women must live from a woman's point of view" (SS: xxxiv; DS: 32). This attempt is intended to uncover the particular ways in which women view the world, and to make explicit the specificity of women's experiences as distinct from men's. Insofar as Beauvoir tries to present women's point of view, her project of showing how women have typically been seen as other than (which usually means worse than) men is also an attempt to think the otherness of women—an attempt which, I suggest, never quite succeeds. Not only does Beauvoir ultimately abandon her ostensible goal of uncovering the specific point of view of women as other, adopting instead, for the most part, a masculine point of view—as I shall show in detail—she also pays scant attention to the differences among women. For the most part Beauvoir presents women as a homogeneous group—a tendency that is encouraged by the blend of theoretical frameworks she constructs as her reference point.[14] I will demonstrate how such problematic aspects of her theory of woman as other are determined to a great extent by her assimilation of Hegel's master-slave model and a Sartrian conception of freedom.[15]

THE PRIVILEGED ROLE OF THE WRITER

I intend to situate Beauvoir's attempt to think woman as other in terms of the intellectual debt she owes to Sartre, on the one hand, and to Hegel, on the other hand. But before doing so, I want to make a detour by way of some autobiographical reflections Beauvoir offers that have a bearing on the question of the other and the way in which she positions herself in relation to the other.[16] Without simply "reducing" the text to the woman, I want nevertheless to insist upon the legitimacy of such an excursion for philosophical reasons which will, I hope, become clear in a moment.[17] Let me do no more at this point than name the problem by saying that Beauvoir holds up her own life to women as an exemplary life.[18]

A case can readily be made for having recourse to Beauvoir's self-representation in her autobiographical works irrespective of her philosophical position. Whether intended to or not, her life and relationship to Sartre took on an exemplary status for a whole generation of feminists.[19] Her personal life, as represented both by herself and by others, therefore had enormous influence on feminism. Beauvoir's theoretical position is not unrelated to her personal choices, morality, and ambitions. The decision, for example, to be a writer and not to be a mother is consistent with her privileging of those activities she construes as specifically human over those capacities humans share with animals. This privileging of the creative, inventive activities of humans over the biological reproductive capacity of women is one to which I will return. For the moment I want to focus on the question of privilege in terms of the position in which Beauvoir considered herself as a writer and an intellectual. She writes:

> Far from suffering from my femininity,[20] I have, on the contrary, from the age of twenty on, accumulated the advantages of both sexes; after *L'Invitée,* those around me treated me both as a writer, their peer in the masculine world, and as a woman; this was particularly noticeable in America: at the parties I went to, the wives all got together and talked to each other while I talked to the men, who nevertheless behaved towards me with greater courtesy than they did towards their own sex. I was encouraged to write *The Second Sex* precisely because of this privileged position. It allowed me to express myself in all serenity.[21]

Reading this passage from the third volume of Beauvoir's autobiography, contemporary feminists may pause for more than a moment to wonder about this self-portrait by the author of the book which initiated so many into feminism. What do we make of Beauvoir's equation between the writer and the male when she says that she was treated "both as a writer [read man] . . . and as a woman?"[22] What did the "wives" left to talk among themselves at parties make of the woman who was to become such a celebrated feminist? What assumptions did Beauvoir make in preferring to talk to the men rather than their wives? What did Beauvoir make of the greater courtesy accorded her as a member of "the second sex"? The point at which my own hesitation arises is not incidental to such questions. It is the point at which Beauvoir acknowledges her privileged position.

I hesitate over the extent to which this acknowledgment replicates the very complicity she so carefully observes in women's acquiescence to their situation. I suggest that Beauvoir sets up the problem of finding the appropriate standpoint of women in a way that builds her privileged position into her theoretical approach.[23]

In the introduction to *The Second Sex* Beauvoir confronts the problem of who is best suited to pose "the woman question" (SS: xxxi; DS: 28). Having briefly entertained but dismissed the possibility that the neutral position of either angelic beings or hermaphrodites might be best suited to pose the question, "what is woman?" she says: "It looks to me as if there are, after all, certain women who are best qualified to elucidate the situation" (SS: xxxi; DS: 29). She explains. She has in mind those who "can afford the luxury of impartiality," those who "by and large . . . have won the game" (SS: xxxii; DS: 29). This last comment is withdrawn by 1972. Reversing her position—in the retrospective glance at *The Second Sex* with which I began—she says, "No we have not won the game: in fact we have won almost nothing since 1950 [*The Second Sex* was published in 1949]. The social revolution will not suffice to solve our problems" (ASD: 491; TCF: 504–5).[24] One of the implications Beauvoir draws from her early judgment in *The Second Sex* that "by and large" women in her position had "won the game" is that she—and others similarly privileged—"never had to sense" in her "femininity an inconvenience or an obstacle" (SS: xxxii; DS: 29). While she does not explicitly revise her judgment on this point, it seems fair to assume that such a reversal is implied. In other words, looking back, she seems to see herself as less privileged (or more exceptional) than she had at the time.

The point I want to emphasize is that Beauvoir appears to fall short of clearly articulating how she conceives of the relationship between her privilege as an educated member of the middle class and her situation as a woman. The accolade she bestows on Juliet Mitchell's work on Marxism and feminism is telling.[25] It is as if Beauvoir sees the necessity and value of such an analysis, but declines to undertake it herself. Reflections on her attitude to "politics" in her autobiographical works lead one to suspect that this is a subject on which Beauvoir's thinking remained undeveloped at the time she wrote *The Second Sex*.[26]

Returning to *The Second Sex* and to the line of thought Beauvoir follows through there, we find an acknowledgment that, despite the apparent impartiality of those who have by and large won the game, it is nonetheless "impossible to approach any human problem with a mind free from bias . . . it is better to state . . . openly [the] principles more or less definitely implied" (SS: xxxii; DS: 30). Since Beauvoir, at least at the time of writing *The Second Sex*, considered herself largely exempt from the problems normally associated with being a woman, the need to explicate the principles informing her view is in fact translated into the need to alert her readers to her theoretical framework. She thus explains the ground rules of existentialist ethics. So an attempt which began as an effort to uncover the specifics of women's situation is transformed into an explication of existentialist ethics.[27]

At times, Beauvoir approaches the situation of women as if it does not concern her personally. It is almost as if Beauvoir is a disinterested observer of other women, set apart from them.[28] Writing about the impetus behind *The Second Sex*, in *The Prime of Life*, she recalls that before the war,

> it had not yet dawned on me that such a thing as a specifically feminine "condition" existed. Now suddenly, I met a large number of women over forty who, in differing circumstances and with various degrees of success, had all undergone one identical experience: they had lived as "dependent persons." . . . Because I was a writer, and in a situation very different from theirs—also, I think, because I was a good listener—they told me a great deal; I began to take stock of the obstacles that most women encounter on their path. . . . The problem did not concern me directly . . . (PL: 572; 586–87).

It is her dual status as woman and writer that distinguishes Beauvoir's lot in life not only from the other women around her but also from other (mostly male) writers. She is both a writer and able to enjoy the courtesies extended to her because of her sex as a woman. As a writer she is accepted into male society, but only to a limited extent. She is also recognized by male society as a woman. She is seen as a man insofar as she is a writer, but she is accorded courtesy insofar as she is a woman.

There is a certain irony in the fact that the author of the text which perhaps most deserves to be considered a feminist classic did not regard herself, at least at the time of writing it, as a feminist. In 1972, in the first of a series of interviews published in translation under the title, *After the Second Sex*, Alice Schwarzer asks Beauvoir to define feminism.[29] In her answer Beauvoir makes clear that her position has shifted since writing *The Second Sex*. She says that at that time she "believed that the problems of women would resolve themselves automatically in the context of socialist development" (Schwarzer, 1984: 32). When she had refused the label of feminist then, her refusal, she claims, was based upon the belief that one did not need to take on "specifically feminine issues independently of the class struggle." In 1972, however, she is willing to call herself a feminist because she "realized that we must fight for the situation of women, here and now, before our dreams of socialism come true." She adds two other considerations to this. First, that "even in socialist countries, equality between men and women has not been achieved"; and "that a profound inequality exists between men and women even in the left-wing and revolutionary groups and organizations" (Schwarzer, 1984: 32–33).[30]

HEGEL'S CONCEPT OF THE OTHER AND SARTRE'S IDEA OF FREEDOM

Although in later years she reconsiders her position, in *The Second Sex* Beauvoir unequivocally distances herself from "the feminists" (SS: xxxi; DS: 28), preferring the perspective of what she calls "existentialist ethics." Accordingly, she sees as the task of every subject a self-transcendence, in which the subject realizes freedom through a "continual reaching out" toward new possibilities (SS: xxxiii; DS: 31).[31] The subject may, however, refuse to achieve freedom and give in to the "temptation to become a thing," that is, to submit passively to another's will (SS: xxiv; DS: 21). Transcendence thus gives way to immanence, and consciousness takes the form of the in-itself, rather than being for-itself. To treat oneself as if one is merely a thing is to act in bad faith, a possibility which is constantly open to every subject.

It is news to no one that Sartrian categories underlie Beauvoir's analysis of women's situation. But at several crucial points in the text, it is Hegel, not Sartre, to whom Beauvoir appeals, particularly in her discussion of the concept of the "Other." She says in the introduction to *The Second Sex*, for example, that human society is not "simply a *Mitsein* or fellowship based on solidarity and friendliness. Things become clear, on the contrary if, following Hegel, we find in consciousness itself a fundamental hostility toward every other consciousness; the subject can be posed only in being opposed—he sets himself up as the essential, as opposed to the other, the inessential, the object" (SS: xx; DS: 17).[32] Clearly Dorothy Kaufmann-McCall has this observation in mind when she says, "Following Hegel, Sartre sees the original meaning of other people in the world as conflict rather than *Mitsein*," but then goes straight on to conflate Sartre and Hegel, saying, "Starting from the Sartrean idea of original conflict, Beauvoir argues as a basic postulate of *The Second Sex* that man has always conceived of himself as the essential" (Kaufmann-McCall, 1979: 210).[33]

Even when feminist commentators on Beauvoir have avoided directly conflating the Hegelian influence with the Sartrian influence—as Kaufmann-McCall does in her otherwise extremely erudite and helpful article—there is an implicit tendency to produce the same effect, either by attributing little importance to the Hegelian paradigm so central to Beauvoir's work, or else by dealing with it only at a general level.[34] This is the case despite the fact that it quickly becomes clear that the Hegelian influence on Beauvoir's conceptual framework is often expressed in terms of a very specific relation: Hegel's description of the master-slave relation serves as a constant reference point for Beauvoir's discussion of the male-female relation. As we shall see, however, it is difficult to determine precisely what importance Beauvoir attributes to Hegel's master-slave dialectic, and whether its role is paradigmatic, or whether it serves more often as a foil to Beauvoir's account of the male-female relation.

Although she invokes the name of Hegel, the very fact that she chooses to focus on the master-slave relation should alert us to the influence of Kojève's interpretation of Hegel, which filtered through to Beauvoir, however indirectly. It is equally clear that in general, while she reads Hegel with great interest, she aligns herself with the philosophers of existence—among whom she includes not only Sartre, but also Heidegger and Kierkegaard—rather than the philosopher of absolute knowledge. Beauvoir analyzes her life in terms that are most reminiscent of Sartre's conception of freedom, emphasizing individual responsibility. Her reflections on her response to the German occupation of France—the period during which she read Hegel—are no exception to this. While noting her admiration for Hegel, along with the feelings of insignificance his world-historical scheme of things inspired in her, Beauvoir makes it clear that she throws in her lot with her contemporaries.[35]

It is very doubtful that either Beauvoir or Sartre attended Kojève's lectures. There is, however, ample evidence that both Raymond Aron and Raymond Queneau, whom Mark Poster includes among those who "regularly attended Kojève's lectures on Hegel" (1975: 8), were in close contact with Beauvoir and Sartre. Since Queneau edited Kojève's lectures on Hegel, it is hardly surprising that it was a topic of conversation between these friends. Beauvoir recalls one such afternoon in June 1945, saying,

> Towards the end of the afternoon, sitting on the grass next to Queneau,
> I had a discussion with him about the "end of history." It was a frequent
> subject of conversation at the time. We had discovered the reality and
> weight of history, now we were wondering about its meaning. Queneau,
> who had been initiated into Hegelianism by Kojève, thought that one
> day all individuals would be reconciled in the triumphant unity of Spirit.
> "But what if I have a pain in my foot?" I said. "*We* shall have a pain in
> your foot," Queneau replied (FOC: 43; FDC: 47).

Although in 1940 Beauvoir is daunted by the universal claims Hegel's
philosophy makes for itself, a few years later we find her taking much
more seriously the weight that Hegel attaches to history, as we see in her
recollection of the conversation she had with Queneau.[36]

If it remains unclear whether or not Kojève influenced Sartre, or vice
versa, it is common knowledge that Kojève's reading of Hegel is influenced
by his Marxism, and it might therefore seem superfluous to raise the
question of how Beauvoir's discussion of the master-slave dialectic relates
to Hegel's text as such.[37] Kojève's interpretation of Hegel is not so much
intended to produce an accurate picture of Hegelian philosophy, as it is to
engage with Hegel's thought to the extent that it sheds light on problems
that occupied Kojève. Insofar as Kojève reads Hegel through the lens of
Marxism, there is little point in attempting to establish the discrepancy
between Beauvoir's understanding of the master-slave dialectic, and Hegel's
account—at least if this attempt is merely for the sake of arguing that
Beauvoir's reading of Hegel is inaccurate.

The point of my returning to Hegel then is not to gauge the measure
of accuracy Beauvoir achieves in representing Hegel nor to establish the
inadequacy of Beauvoir's interpretation of his philosophy. Rather, I am
interested in establishing both the strengths and the limitations of
Beauvoir's feminism and how these limitations have been inherited by
contemporary feminism. By accounting for the lack of detail in the
analogy Beauvoir draws between Hegel's master-slave dialectic and the
relations between the sexes, which she is content to leave as a rough
sketch, my hope is to clarify why Irigaray and other feminists find it
necessary to reject the master-slave relation, and to bring into question
the philosophical framework that it legitimates.[38] At the same time,
however, even if it is incidental to my main concern, I will be able
to determine to a limited extent the problems Beauvoir encounters in
her attempt to reconcile her use of Hegel with her dependence upon
Sartre's existentialism.

Of course, Sartre devotes several pages of the chapter on "The Existence of Others" in *Being and Nothingness* to Hegel's master-slave dialectic, an account which is ultimately critical of Hegel (BN: 319–39; EN: 280–98).[39] It is not my intention here to provide a detailed account of his critique.[40] Neither do I intend to address the problem of whether or not Beauvoir does justice to Hegel in taking his master-slave relation out of context, except insofar as this question has a bearing on the adequacy of Beauvoir's own conceptual framework.

I shall not spend time showing Beauvoir's dependence on Sartrian categories, which has been amply demonstrated. In an interview first published in 1982 Beauvoir is quite candid about what she regards as Sartre's "superiority" as a "creative" philosopher. "Where Sartre's philosophy is concerned, it is fair to say that I took my cue from him, because I also embraced existentialism for myself. There were, however, many things we discussed and even worked on together. For example, while he was working on *Being and Nothingness,* I opposed some of his ideas, and sometimes changed things a bit" (Schwarzer, 1984: 109).[41] Beauvoir unambiguously affirms her philosophical dependence on Sartre and is modest about her contribution to existentialism.[42] Of course, however privileged she thought she was, we cannot assume that her own assessment of her contribution to existentialist philosophy is exempt from self-depreciation. Nor is there license to assume that she simply appropriated certain arguments from Sartre's *Being and Nothingness*. It would be naive to think that such an unwieldy text as *Being and Nothingness* could yield unproblematic formulae and conclusions which could readily be applied to the position of women.[43] Not only are there familiar interpretative problems associated with Sartre's philosophy of freedom, but there is also evidence to suggest that his conceptual framework is anti-feminist.[44] As the case for the incipient sexism of Sartre's categories has already been made, I do not intend to repeat it here.[45]

How much Beauvoir's discussions with Sartre affected his philosophy and which things she "changed a bit" must remain open questions. However, in her autobiography Beauvoir recalls discussions she had with Sartre about *Being and Nothingness* which are revealing for the question of how she adapted Sartre's philosophical framework for her account of women's situation.

> We discussed certain specific problems, in particular the relationship between "situation" and freedom. I maintained that from the angle of freedom as Sartre defined it—that is, an active transcendence of some

given context rather than mere stoic resignation—not every situation was equally valid: what sort of transcendence could a woman shut up in a harem achieve?[46] Sartre replied that even such a cloistered existence could be lived in several quite different ways. I stuck to my point for a long time, and in the end made only a token submission. Basically I was right. But to defend my attitude I should have had to abandon the plane of the individual, and therefore idealistic, morality on which we had set ourselves (PL: 434; FA: 448).

Beauvoir herself will later criticize the "theoretical foundation for the opposition between Same and Other," which structures *The Second Sex*, as too idealistic. She says, "If I were to write *The Second Sex* today . . . I should base the rejection and oppression of the Other not on antagonistic awareness but upon the economic explanation of scarcity" (ASD: 484; TCF: 497). She does not follow through this remark, and it remains unclear how one might substitute the idealist framework of *The Second Sex* for a materialist one, and how this fits in with her contemporaneous retraction of her earlier view that "the state of women and society would evolve together" (ASD: 491; TCF: 504). What is clear, however, is that, with hindsight, Beauvoir was not wholly satisfied with the role that the structuring opposition between the same and the other played in her text.

Beauvoir's claim is that underlying women's oppression is a basic antagonism between human beings. She says, "When two human categories are together, each aspires to impose its sovereignty upon the other" (SS: 69; DS: 107). Given her view that fundamentally all humans want to impose their will upon others, Beauvoir's question is not—why is there oppression at all?[47] The fact that man should "wish to dominate woman" is not at issue, since it is assumed that all humans wish to dominate one another. Rather, Beauvoir asks why it is that men succeeded in their quest for domination where women failed. She asks, "Whence comes" the "submission" of women? (SS: xxi; DS: 17). "Why should man have won from the start?" (SS: xxv; DS: 21). "What advantage enabled him to carry out his will?" (SS: 69; DS: 107).

The answer to this variously formulated question is summarized in the chapter on nomadic history: Beauvoir says that

the biological and economic condition of the primitive horde must have led to male supremacy. The female, to a greater extent than the male, is the prey of the species; and the human race has always sought to escape its specific destiny. The support of life became for man an activity and a project through the invention of the tool: but in maternity woman remained closely bound to her body, like an animal (SS: 73; DS: 113).[48]

Although Beauvoir says that it is an "existentialist perspective" which enabled her to see how these conditions "must have led to male supremacy," her assumption that the activities and project of human life are to be valued more highly than animal existence is inspired by Hegel. The creative, inventive capacity men exercise sets them apart from the merely biological unthinking processes that characterize women's lives, dominated, as they are, by the processes of reproduction. Both men and women ensure the continuation of life. Both serve the species, but men at the same time as they serve the species "create values": "The human male also remodels the face of the earth, he creates new instruments, he invents, he shapes the future" (SS: 72; DS: 112). Men transcend life, women merely reproduce it. Women's "misfortune is to have been biologically destined for the repetition of Life" (SS: 72; DS: 112). The opposition Beauvoir sets up between the ability to create, invent, or produce and the merely repetitive capacity to reproduce derives from Hegel's differentiation between consciousness as self-consciousness, and consciousness which is mere consciousness (animal life). Man's creative invention of values is seen as properly human, whereas the essentially repetitive existence of women, burdened by reproductive functions, makes them akin to animals. For Beauvoir, as for Hegel, man (and the term "man" is sex-specific) transcends his animal nature (SS: 71; DS: 110) by proving that "life is not the supreme value" (SS: 72; DS: 111). In a passage to which Michèle le Doeuff refers as the "Hegelian key" of The Second Sex, Beauvoir distinguishes sharply between men and women.[49] She states, "it is not in giving life but in risking life that man is raised above the animal; that is why superiority has been accorded in humanity not to the sex that brings forth but to that which kills" (SS: 72; DS: 111).[50]

THE CONCEPT OF RISK
IN HEGEL'S MASTER-SLAVE DIALECTIC

Leaving aside the highly questionable assumption that childbirth was risk-free in primitive times, what I notice about Beauvoir's explanation of what gave "early man's activity" its "supreme dignity" is the extent to which this Hegelian key is in fact anti-Hegelian. This Hegelian key, on being turned, opens on to a distinctly un-Hegelian space.

While there is little doubt that the importance the notion of risk acquires for Beauvoir derives from Hegel's description of the master-slave relation, her use of the concept of risk is Hegelian only in the loosest sense. It is essential for Hegel's account that the risk of life issues from a relation between two independent consciousnesses, two individuals each of whom is able to grant the independence of the other. By contrast, Beauvoir focuses upon the risk involved in an individual man hunting a wild animal, thereby shifting the significance of the relation away from self-consciousness. For Hegel, the significance of the master-slave relation lies in the realization of self-consciousness by consciousness, a realization which can only take place in and through another conscious—and potentially self-conscious—human being. The fact that consciousness discovers itself as self-consciousness is precisely what distinguishes it from life as it is experienced in sense-certainty, that is, as animal life at the level of mere sensation. By construing the risk of life as a confrontation between a man and a wild animal, rather than between two human beings, Beauvoir subverts the whole point of Hegel's master-slave relation.[51] She sees man as gaining his "supreme dignity" not through the recognition of another human being, but through his ability to hunt down a wild animal. Of course, the success or failure of the hunt is a matter of pride and in that sense primitive man, according to her account, seeks recognition from his peers. A good hunter is respected by other hunters. An individual contributes to the "prestige of the horde" by being seen to "put his life in jeopardy" (SS: 72; DS: 111).[52]

My point is that for Beauvoir the hunter proves himself by conquering an object which is not the same as the subjects he seeks to impress. This is not the Hegelian realization of self-consciousness by consciousness through another identical consciousness, but rather the confirmation of an individual's worth in a horde into which he has already been accepted.[53] In other words, it becomes clear that Beauvoir is assuming that there can be a subject which is self-conscious before its self-consciousness is put to the test by another. In this assumption she is following the Sartrian understanding of the self as a being which consists of nothing but freedom. Her dependence at this point of her argument on Sartre, not Hegel, is highlighted when she says, "At the moment when man asserts himself as subject and free being, the idea of the other arises" (SS: 89; DS: 131). Since Hegel says, "It is only through staking one's life that freedom is won" (PhS: 114; PhG: 144), one could almost say that for him the reverse is true. For Hegel it is rather when the idea of the other arises that man can, for the first time, assert himself as subject and free being. Or, to be more precise, it is only through others that humans become self-conscious.[54] Freedom is a concept that becomes meaningful for Hegel through the life and death struggle. Beauvoir assumes freedom as given prior to any encounter with another, while Hegel assumes the other as given, and as necessary for the realization of self-consciousness.[55]

Despite this major divergence, which goes unremarked by Beauvoir, she pursues her parallel between sexual difference and the Hegelian master-slave relation. She makes explicit the debt she owes to this account, but she does so in a passage that raises as many difficulties as it solves.

> Certain passages in the argument employed by Hegel in defining the relation of master to slave apply much better to the relation of man to woman. The advantage of the master, he says, comes from his affirmation of Spirit as against Life through the fact that he risks his own life; but in fact the conquered slave has known this same risk. Whereas woman is basically an existent who gives Life and does not risk her life; between her and the male there has been no combat. Hegel's definition would seem to apply especially well to her. He says: "The other consciousness is the dependent consciousness for whom the essential reality is the animal type of life; that is to say, a mode of living bestowed by another entity."[56] But this relation is to be distinguished from the relation of subjugation because woman also aspires to and recognizes the values that are concretely attained by the male. He it is who opens up the future to which she also reaches out (SS: 73; DS: 112).

Beauvoir thus both establishes a parallel between Hegel's description of the master-slave relation and the relation of subjugation between male and female and cautions that there are limitations to this parallel. The next few pages might be read as no more than an extended commentary on this enigmatic passage which plays such a key role in Beauvoir's argument. How far Beauvoir can be said to be Hegelian remains to be seen. The purpose of this commentary is to enable us to trace the implications of the dual function Hegel's master-slave dialectic has for Beauvoir as both the paradigm for and the antithesis of the male-female relation. By focusing on the question of exactly how Beauvoir interprets the Hegelian master-slave dialectic, I hope to clarify the character of her project as a whole, pointing to, on the one hand, those elements of her work that have proved fruitful and have been followed through by others, and on the other hand, those assumptions upon which her own work foundered. Before addressing the details of Beauvoir's engagement with the master-slave relation, I shall briefly review the account Hegel provides of the master-slave relation, the central issue of which is a contest for recognition.[57]

The possibility of recognition is held out not by any presupposed inferiority of the one who is to become the slave. For Hegel, the possibility of genuine recognition by another human being is premised on precisely the fact that one potentially free human being is confronted by another potentially free human being. The possibility of freedom for both protagonists is indispensable to an understanding of the outcome of the dialectical relation. Whoever becomes master is cast into that role through the subjugation of another—but we need to be careful about exactly what causes the submission of the slave to the master. I said that the master is "cast into" his role because it is not simply a matter of the stronger individual subjecting the weaker, or the survival of the fittest, or the master's will overcoming the slave's due to some inherent superiority. Something more interesting is at stake. It is a matter of the slave choosing, of his own free will, servitude over death. To understand why the slave chooses slavery one must see the significance of two things. The first is the role of death in the struggle that ensues between the two individuals who do battle, and the second is that, for Hegel, the possibility of recognition is bound up with self-understanding and self-consciousness. To be recognized by another is to be seen for what you are. To be self-conscious one needs the other; the possibility of self-understanding, for Hegel, depends on one's access to the perspective of another. To have one's freedom confirmed is to have someone else give you the idea of yourself as free, by making it significant, by materializing it, by living it out, by embodying it. The master has his freedom concretely confirmed by the service of the slave. In short, the enslavement of another is what makes the master free.

In order to engage in the struggle for freedom one must put one's life at risk. To gain freedom one must be willing to lose life. The slave chooses life over death, not because the slave is a coward or is weak. In choosing slavery over death the slave confronts the question of what it would mean to die for the idea of freedom, rather than to live. In his confrontation with death the slave learns that life is essential to him. It is not the master that is, in Hegel's account, the supreme lord. It is death. The slave faces death, and refuses to die because to do so is to act on a principle that becomes meaningless—at least for him, if not for others. If the slave dies, he may die free, but he will not have lived free. Freedom may have been won, but at the cost of life.

From this familiar scene depicting the struggle for freedom between master and slave, I want to retain the following points. Despite the fact that, unless the struggle results in death, the outcome is the supremacy of a master over a slave, the result of the struggle is satisfactory for neither of the participants. Whether the slave lives or dies, the master does not achieve the recognition he seeks. If the slave dies, there is no one left to confirm the master's freedom and supremacy, and if he lives, he lives as a slave, whose will has been subjugated. As a slave, the individual is deprived of the potential he had for freedom, and he thereby loses the potential value he formerly had as someone who could confirm the freedom of another. The other is now his master. What good is the slave's submission to the master when what both wanted was to have their freedom recognized by someone worthy of them? By definition, to become a slave is no longer to be worthy.

The master is not only disappointed in his quest for recognition, but he remains, according to Hegel, essentially unchanged. The slave, on the other hand, in his confrontation with death, has learned that, without life, the idea of freedom is a lifeless abstraction. Without the material conditions of life, without life at the biological level, what good is it to affirm the principle of freedom, in preferring death to life? The slave learns that life is essential to what it means to be human, or that animality or economic desire (desire as a need that can be satiated) is an inalienable element of the individual. Without life, freedom is just an abstract idea. Moreover, although in one way the slave who chooses life over death is fettered, having recoiled from death only to be bound by the chains of his master, in another way the slave, through the work that he does, is independent and creative. In work, the slave encounters the resistance of objects and becomes conscious of his ability to shape objects according to his will. Thus the slave, as creator, establishes a relationship of permanence to desire, through the objects he produces. He learns to see himself as independent—at least insofar as he is creative (PhS: 118; PhG: 149).[58] The master, on the other hand, gains only fleeting satisfaction from the fruits of the labor undertaken by the slave. In other words, the master's desires are satisfied, but desire here is understood as animal desire, and satisfaction is merely temporary. Hunger is a simple desire which is satiated when one eats, but one soon gets hungry again. Moreover, one is dependent on a slave for the satisfaction of one's hunger. If the master remains, in this respect, both static and dependent, by contrast, the slave changes his situation through his labor. Producing goods and transforming materials from their raw state, the activity of the slave is such that raw materials take on new forms. The slave makes history by transforming the natural world into products for human consumption according to the demands of his master. Laboring upon the land, he produces something other than the raw materials on which he works. The product takes on another dimension by entering into a system of circulation in which it acquires a value, according to the patterns of production and consumption with which we are all familiar.

Beauvoir asked about the situation of women as other and chose Hegel's master-slave dialectic as a major reference point. It is a complex reference point, involving, as we have seen, a confrontation between individuals, a fight in which not the master but death is absolute lord—producing an outcome which (at least according to Hegel) resolves nothing for the master, issuing in, as it does, his subjugation of one who is thereby no longer worthy of offering him the recognition he sought. Following Marx's analysis, we should note that to the extent that the master retains the surplus value that accrues from the slave's labor, the master may not have his freedom confirmed in the way he hoped for, but at the expense of the slave he does attain another sort of freedom, namely that bestowed by the accumulation of capital.

What is strange about Beauvoir's use of the master-slave relation is that she constantly draws on it as a way of illustrating how she understands the relation between men and women without ever really clarifying exactly how she understands it, what she finds of importance in it, or in what sense it is an inadequate comparison.[59] Having differentiated her understanding of the male-female relation from Hegel's account of the master-slave relation, she often reverts to a straightforward comparison, leaving the status she accords to the Hegelian account unclear.[60] The master-slave relation is both like and unlike that between men and women. In fact, Beauvoir says that in some respects Hegel's definition is more appropriate for the male-female relation than it is for the master-slave relation. It is, in one sense, more like the master-slave relation than the master-slave relation itself. "Certain passages . . . apply much better to the relation of man to woman," she says, and by way of explanation as to the lack of fit between the master-slave relation and Hegel's argument she goes on: "the advantage of the master . . . comes from his affirmation of Spirit as against life, through the fact that he risks his own life. But in fact the conquered slave has known this same risk." Anyone who is familiar with Hegel's account of the master-slave relation may be surprised by this comment. Why does Beauvoir find it necessary to remind us that the slave too has known what it is to risk life? Why does she point to the slave's confrontation with death as if this disqualifies him from being an appropriate player in the drama of the struggle for freedom? Doesn't the significance of the master-slave relation lie precisely in the fact that both master and slave risk their lives? How then could Beauvoir think that woman, precisely because she does not risk her life, is more slavish than the slave?

It is tempting to suggest that the answer to the puzzle lies in the few pages of *Being and Nothingness* that Sartre devotes to a critique of Hegel's master-slave dialectic. If Beauvoir had these passages in mind, she may well have misconstrued the significance that Hegel attaches to the idea of risk, since Sartre also plays down the fact that the slave experiences a confrontation with death. Sartre acknowledges that Hegel's account does indeed require that the slave as well as the master risk his life, but he dismisses the significance of this fact on the grounds that there is in Hegel's account a "confusion" (BN: 324; EN: 285).[61]

Whether or not Beauvoir is influenced by Sartre on this particular point, I suggest that her existentialist standpoint prevents her from taking account of several other significant features of Hegel's master-slave dialectic. It intervenes, for example, at precisely the point at which the slave, in Hegel's account, transforms his situation, and in doing so, differentiates his existence from the master's. The existentialist bias of Beauvoir's analysis, I argue, results in a failure to take the dynamic aspect of Hegel's dialectical thinking seriously. The historical development of the relation and the resulting new form of consciousness that issues from the master-slave dialectic are crucial to Hegel's analysis. Beauvoir's existentialist conviction that freedom is the defining characteristic of humans brings her into conflict with Hegel's emphasis on the historical conditions that shape consciousness.[62] It is as if freedom is always already given. This tension between freedom and history is played out in Beauvoir's belief both in a woman's ability to transcend the situation in which she finds herself and in the weight of women's historical oppression. Let me specify in detail my claim that Beauvoir allows the existentialist concept of absolute freedom to structure her thinking in such a way that she is unable to appreciate elements of Hegel's discussion that might otherwise have contributed to her analysis of women's situation.

In several places Hegel makes a point of stressing the "mutuality" of the master-slave relation. He says of the master and slave, "they *recognize* themselves as mutually recognizing one another" (PhS: 112; PhG: 143). Again, the two must "reciprocally give and receive one another back from each other consciously" (PhS: 114; PhG: 145).[63] Surely then it is essential to the struggle for recognition that both stake their lives in a reciprocal and mutual relation? Contrary to first appearances, the point is not lost on Beauvoir. For the slave may have known what it is to risk life, but, as Hegel also points out, the slave who survives has withdrawn from that risk, preferring life to death, choosing slavery over freedom. In other words, the outcome of the life and death struggle, for those who survive, is not reciprocal or mutual but "one-sided and unequal" (PhS: 116; PhG: 191).

In precisely what respect then does the master-slave relation Hegel describes apply better to the relation between man and woman than it does to Hegel's own use of it? The definition that Beauvoir takes to "apply especially well" to woman is that "the other consciousness is the dependent consciousness for whom the essential reality is the animal type of life; that is to say, a mode of living bestowed by another entity" (SS: 73; DS: 112; Cf. PhS: 115; PhG: 146). The stage of the life and death struggle Beauvoir refers to here is that at which, in Hegel's account of it, the slave has learned that "life is as essential to it as pure self-consciousness" (PhS: 115; PhG: 145). It is the point at which the slave has granted the other the independence that both sought at the outset of the life and death struggle, by recognizing him as master. The slave has failed to achieve independence himself, but has confirmed the master in his independence. In doing so, the slave has at the same time put himself at one remove from death. He has chosen to live rather than die. He has chosen to live and not to be free or independent.

Both the slave and the woman then are dependent consciousnesses. The difference between them is that woman has not encountered the fear of death, at least not through a life and death struggle. "Between her and the male," says Beauvoir, "there has been no combat" (SS: 73; DS: 112). For Hegel, it is through the encounter with the other that the slave is confronted with death. Death is the "absolute" lord for the slave. But for Beauvoir, anxiety about death is given, along with freedom, independent of any specific battle with the other. As in Sartre's philosophy, bad faith, like the possibility of self-transcendence, is a permanent possibility for the human being.[64] One is constantly tempted to "forgo liberty and become a thing" (SS: xxiv; DS: 21). The existence of others plays some part in the objectification that takes place when one reflects on oneself and one's actions. One looks at a situation from another point of view, as we say, and sees oneself from the point of view of another (even if there is no empirically present other). Unlike Hegel, for the existentialist, the role of the other is structurally constant and is not tied to any specific moment of battle. To understand myself at all, for Sartre, is always already to see myself from another's point of view.[65]

Beauvoir does not suppose that all situations are equally constraining of one's freedom, or that everyone is equally condemned to bad faith.[66] Women, however, fall prey to complicity with men in their oppression, according to Beauvoir. Beauvoir finds it difficult to account for her view that men find in women "more complicity than the oppressor usually finds in the oppressed" (SS: 802; DS 2: 565). She observes that, historically, women have been more closely tied to their bodies than men through the demands of reproduction. One might think then that woman is closer to the in-itself by definition, simply by virtue of biological accident. This explanation does not hold up, however.[67] Beauvoir goes on to say not that women are in bad faith, but that men "in bad faith . . . take authorization from this to declare that she has *desired* the destiny they have imposed on her" (ibid.). Other claims Beauvoir makes show the complexity of the problem. She says, for example, that a woman "chooses to desire her enslavement so ardently that it will seem to her the expression of her liberty" (SS: 713; DS 2: 478). To choose to desire enslavement, far from being evidence of simply being close to nature, stuck or mired in the in-itself, represents a complicated and calculated process of deceit by which a woman can gain what she really wants while appearing to submit to the will of another.[68] She can "follow the easy slope" (SS: 802; DS 2: 565), which she is in fact only too happy to do since, as we have seen, "she is often very well pleased with her role" (SS: xxv; DS: 21). To be complicitous then, is not a temporary lapse into bad faith. It is more a matter of enjoying the consolations of the powerless. In Sartrian terms, one might say that women, on the whole, fail to take responsibility for their freedom, they refuse to develop the capacity to shape their lives in terms of their own fundamental projects.[69]

Women's complicity is a subject about which Beauvoir is strangely unclear. Left as a vague assumption by Beauvoir, it nevertheless seems to carry a lot of weight in her account.[70] It is through woman's "complicity" with her role as other that "she can evade at once both economic risk and the metaphysical risk of a liberty in which ends and aims must be contrived without assistance" (SS: xxiv; DS: 21). By complying with her role as other, woman gains the advantages of economic and metaphysical security. She allows man to take care of her and to be the decisionmaker. She even enjoys her position (see SS: 88; DS: 129). At the same time, men's expectations are not incidental to women's complicity, judging by Beauvoir's observation:

When man makes of woman the *Other,* he may, then, expect her to manifest deep-seated tendencies toward complicity. Thus, woman may fail to lay claim to the status of subject because . . . she lacks definite resources, because she feels the necessary bond that ties her to man regardless of reciprocity, and because she is often very well pleased with her role as the *Other"* (SS: xxiv–xxv; DS: 21).

We have seen how women are complicitous—that they accept and even collude with the role as other—but what does Beauvoir mean by the "lack of definite resources" and the "necessary bond" that unites men and women? By a lack of definite resources, Beauvoir refers to the dispersion and isolation of women who are "attached through residence, housework, economic condition and social standing to certain men" (SS: xxii; DS: 19)—in contrast to the solidarity of the working class who come together in the workplace. Echoing Engels, she says, "The bond that unites her to her oppressors is not comparable to any other. The division of the sexes is a biological fact, not an event in human history" (SS: xxiii; DS: 19). The difficulty is that women have always been different from men and they have always been oppressed (according to Beauvoir at least).[71] The "necessary bond" that ties woman to man refers to the need for men and women to procreate for the continuation of the species. Beauvoir says of woman that "she is Other in a totality of which the two components are necessary to one another" (SS: xxiii; DS: 19).

What then are we to make of this lack of resources at woman's disposal, the necessary bond she feels to man, and the fact that her role as other often pleases her? While in one sense woman depends on man, in another sense man depends on woman. This is because she is both debased and at the same time elevated.[72] Never equal, she is either deified—and as such she is the threatening, powerful, mysterious other—or she is not-yet subject, merely potentially human, at the mercy of (reproductive) natural forces. God-like, or animal-like, she is not human-like.[73] The mythic elevation of woman is crucial for understanding the relation between man and woman. Beauvoir says that "by complete possession and control woman would be abased to the rank of a thing; but man aspires to clothe in his own dignity whatever he conquers and possesses; the other retains, it seems to him, a little of her primitive magic" (SS: 91; DS: 133). Woman would not be worthy of man's control if in some way she did not escape his control. Compare this with the truth which emerges in Hegel's account of the master-slave relation. "The object in which the lord has achieved his lordship has in reality turned out to be something quite different from an independent consciousness. What now confronts him is not an independent consciousness, but a dependent one" (PhS: 116–17; PhG: 147). The slave, in Hegel's account, does not remain determined by his dependence on a master. Through the resistance he encounters in work, his situation changes. Women, in Beauvoir's account, remain in dependent relations with men, who invest them with mythic qualities. Men mystify their relations with women, seeing them as mysterious others and thereby avoiding the impasse reached by the master who realizes that the slave, once subjected, is no longer able to grant him recognition as an equal. If, in an elaborate pattern of self-deception, men can construe women both as dependent on them and subject to them, and at the same time as elevated and mysterious creatures, they can avoid the paradox I outlined earlier.[74] Women remain immured in the position of dependents, and men construct women as ambiguous and incomprehensible others, subjugated yet defying categorization.

As we saw, there is a paradox contained within the struggle resulting in the master–slave relationship, in that the desire of self–consciousness to be recognized by another contains within it the seeds of its own destruction. The recognition required of another involves a necessary failure. Self-consciousness demands the recognition of its own worth by another who is an equal, by someone who is both worthy of him and who desires similar recognition from him. The problem is that as soon as recognition is granted, or rather, in the very act of recognition, the equality of the other disappears. In recognizing the supremacy of another, the other makes himself inferior, makes himself into a slave. In submitting to the will of another, the slave recognizes the other as his master. Characteristic of the movement of consciousness, as Hegel depicts it in the *Phenomenology of Spirit*, and as evident in the master-slave relation as at any other stage, is its dynamism. Consciousness must constantly move forward. The struggle for freedom in which self-consciousness engages is marked by the emergence of the mastery of one self-consciousness over another, only to give rise to a new configuration. Consciousness is impelled onward—it cannot sustain itself in a master-slave relationship.[75] Self-consciousness, for Hegel, "does not see the other as an essential being" (PhS: 111; PhG: 141).[76]

To the extent that woman appears to hold man in a relation of dependence to her, she seems to be less dependent, not more dependent, than the slave. On the one hand, the advantages she finds in her situation function merely at the level of compensation for her real dependence. On the other hand, it is precisely to the extent that the slave is not under any illusion about the advantages of his situation—that is, precisely insofar as he is a slave and nothing more than a slave—that he is able to transform his situation.

In attempting to comment on the passage in which Beauvoir asserts both the homology and the dissonance between Hegel's master-slave relation and her own conception of the male-female relation, so far I have only asked why, according to Beauvoir, the man-woman relation is more like the master-slave relation than the master-slave relation itself. Yet Beauvoir also asserts that woman is not like the slave. The relation between man and woman "is to be distinguished from the relation of subjugation because woman also aspires to and recognizes the values that are concretely attained by the male" (SS: 73; DS: 112). In other words, woman wants to be creative and inventive, and to engage in projects to justify herself through self-transcendence. She wants to open new possibilities, thereby taking control of her destiny, just as much as man does. But how is this unlike the slave? For Hegel, the slave, just like the master, seeks recognition. It is only because the slave wants to be recognized that he is worthy of granting the master recognition. The slave fails to gain recognition through his fear of death. By averting the threat of death, choosing servitude over death, the slave also abandons the quest for recognition that drew him into the struggle toward death in the first place. Why does woman fail to achieve her aspiration for those values achieved by man? The answer to this question is unclear for Beauvoir, whose account deviates significantly from Hegel's at this point: "woman," says Beauvoir, "does not risk her life; between her and the male there has been no combat" (SS: 73; DS: 112). As I have argued, while Beauvoir thinks that this makes Hegel's description of the animal existence of the slave even more apt for women than it is for the slave, her view misrepresents Hegel's position. For Hegel the threat of death that the slave experiences is precisely what makes him choose servitude. Confronted with death, the slave realizes that even the existence of a slave is better than no existence. In the Hegelian account, the slave manages to transform his servile existence, not through the recognition he previously sought, but through manual labor.

The question remains then, if not through any risk of death, how do women, on Beauvoir's account, acquiesce to their dependence upon men? Does Beauvoir think that women consent to a degraded existence, or is degradation inflicted on them? There is, as we have seen, a vague assumption that women are closer to the in-itself than men. At certain points, however, Beauvoir appears to offer more concrete causes. One might say that her account suffers from inconsistency, for she attributes the blame to different parties. She says, "men compel her [woman] to assume the status of the Other" (SS: xxxiii; DS: 31), having located the blame elsewhere only a few pages earlier: "If woman seems to be the inessential which never becomes the essential, it is because she herself fails to bring about this change" (SS: xxii; DS: 18). But Beauvoir also acknowledges, as Moi observes (1990a: 71), that finding the culprit is not the point. The reason women fail to achieve their aim of transcending the present and realizing values in the same way as men cannot simply be that they do not try hard enough or that men prevent them from doing so. As we have already seen, Beauvoir recognizes that women's oppression cannot be explained by finding a victim and a perpetrator, but rather is due to a complex network of factors.

Beauvoir's interrogation of women as other was inhibited, in part, by the privileged role that Beauvoir assumed for herself relative to other women, and in part by the blend of theoretical influences informing her analysis. I have shown how the combination of these two factors fed into one another in order to explain what I see as one of the abiding tensions in Beauvoir's account of women's situation. In emphasizing the malleability of culture, in line with the Sartrian belief in individual freedom, Beauvoir was unable to attribute to woman's status as other the significance that the Hegelian elements of her own analysis called for. By uncovering in Sartre and Hegel the theoretical roots of the structural incompatibility underlying Beauvoir's framework, I have demonstrated that her belief in absolute freedom allowed Beauvoir to underestimate the role history has in determining women as other. I do not want to deny that Beauvoir had the merit of seeing, perhaps earlier than Sartre, the problems to which the idea of absolute freedom led. My point is that the force of her own analysis is undermined by an internal contradiction that I think can be characterized in terms of an opposition between Sartre's optimism in the individual's ability to transcend the contingency of one's historical conditions, and Hegel's insistence on history as a formative influence on the individual.

Woman both is and is not a slave. She is even more dependent, more animal-like, more determined by another than the slave. Yet she is simultaneously unlike the slave, less confined than the slave inasmuch as her horizons are broader. She identifies not with her own restricted life, but with the aims and goals of man. She remains immersed in her dependent condition, yet does not give up the possibility of transcending it. According to Beauvoir, she chooses not to realize her full potentiality as a human being, but rather to take advantage of her femininity. In a word, she lives vicariously.

Because the life and death struggle between two independent consciousnesses plays no part in Beauvoir's comparison of the master-slave and male-female relations, she does not differentiate between the slave before, during, or after the struggle. She is therefore able to develop both the similarities and the differences between the master-slave dialectic and the male-female relationship without apparent contradiction. Because her comparison remains undeveloped, Beauvoir fails to mention the reversal that the slave undergoes in Hegel's account, or to explore any connections this might have with woman's role as other. For Hegel, the slave ultimately finds the resources to advance the dialectical progression of spirit through the transformative power of work. Beauvoir neglects the parallel that she might have pursued between the slave's markedly different position from the master, and women's significantly different position from men.

For Hegel, the slave transforms his consciousness not through aspiring to the same values as the master (although before the fear of death took hold of him he certainly wanted to be recognized, just as the master did). It is precisely as a slave—by being a slave and remaining a slave—that the transformation takes place. Through work the slave transcends all the aspects of his being that define him as a slave. He transcends his attachment to life—the very attachment which put him in slavery, in his refusal to give up life. Hegel says, "He rids himself of his attachment to natural existence in every single detail; and gets rid of it by working on it" (PhS: 117; PhG: 148). He transcends his dependence on the master and becomes an independent being. Hegel says, "The bondsman becomes conscious of what he truly is . . . consciousness, qua worker, comes to see in the independent being [of the object] its *own* independence" (PhS: 118; PhG: 148–49). The slave transcends the inessential aspect of his being, and in its place gains an awareness that, in Hegel's words, "he himself exists essentially and actually in his own right" (PhS: 118; PhG: 149).

BEYOND BEAUVOIR

Having followed through some of the problems that emerge in understanding the function of the master-slave dialectic as a model for understanding women's oppression, let me step back from the text, and ask, what would happen if Beauvoir had taken her own analysis of woman as other more seriously? In Hegel's master-slave relation the slave remains a slave, and thereby loosens his ties to natural existence, transforms his dependence into independence. What would happen if women, rather than aspiring to the same values as men, took seriously what it means to be women? What risks are at stake in affirming femininity? It is precisely by taking the approach indicated by these questions, it seems to me, that Irigaray has tried to think what it means for woman to have always been cast as other. She does so not by adhering more closely to the master-slave dialectic than Beauvoir, but rather by turning to Hegel's discussion of Antigone.

In this chapter I have begun to make clear why feminism cannot afford to limit itself to the work of changing cultural identifications which define the feminine. Questioning what it means to act *as a woman* in relation to those cultural definitions must also be confronted. In other words, it is not enough to bracket the question of sex and concentrate all our energies on gender. It continues to be crucial for feminists to stress that socially constructed differences account for discrimination against women in the socio-political sphere. To the extent that arguments for the equality of the sexes require that we emphasize their similarities, feminism has downplayed the differences between the sexes that, however much they are ignored, nonetheless remain. Renewed interest in the question of sexual difference signals, perhaps, not so much a return to biological determinism as a recognition that the separation of sex from gender that has been such a central part of feminist agendas masks an inadequate conceptualization not only of sexual difference but also of gender. Insofar as the usefulness of the sex/gender distinction, or at least the adequacy with which it is conceptualized, is now being called into question, feminism is reexamining the relation of sex to gender, after Beauvoir's once decisive and convincing separation of the two.[77] As we saw in the previous chapter, this reexamination of the distinction between sex and gender and disruption of the categories that tend to line themselves up along the sex/gender divide in an apparently unproblematic way (namely, biology versus society or history, and nature versus culture) is beginning to take place. However, there is still little recognition of the implications such a reexamination has for the question of the other. I would argue that, once the importance of revisiting the sex/gender distinction is seen in terms of Irigaray's reflections on the historical representation of women as other, any lingering doubt as to her alleged essentialism can be dispelled.

I have suggested that the significance of Beauvoir's preliminary attempt to theorize woman as other has been underestimated. Perhaps this neglect is in part due to her problematic engagement with Hegel's master-slave dialectic. Beauvoir herself, I have shown, was less than clear about the extent to which such a model could be useful for feminism. I said earlier that Beauvoir's question was not, why is there oppression at all, but rather, given that all human relationships are fundamentally conflictual, why is it that women, rather than men, have been systematically oppressed? In other words, Beauvoir takes conflict as a fundamental fact of humanity, and then asks, what is it about sexual difference that has lined up men on the side of the oppressors, and women on the side of the oppressed? Beauvoir's answer takes shape around the idea that while men risk their lives, create values, and introduce novelty into the world, women do not. While men take initiatives, women stick to repetitive biological rhythms. Having set up the problem in this way, the only solution she can find is for women to become more creative, more like the subjects that they fundamentally are—less feminine, and more masculine. To put this in terms of the sex/gender distinction, Beauvoir's answer to women's situation is to ignore the fact that the female sex is different from the male sex, and to encourage women to transcend the adversity of their situations (following Sartre's dictum to realize one's true potential as a free human being), and become to all intents and purposes like men. This means not only that sexual difference is seen as irrelevant to feminism (except as an unfortunate fact to be forgotten as much as possible), but also that freedom is construed as a disembodied and gender-neutral transcendence. Of course, if in theory gender is conceived in neutral terms, in fact women can only realize their potential freedom by overcoming their immanence—in other words, by identifying with masculine ideals and aspirations.

Insofar as Beauvoir retains the Hegelian idea that "true alterity—otherness, is that of a consciousness separate from mine and substantially identical with mine" (SS: 158; DS: 231), she does not carry out her own project of thinking woman as other, from a woman's point of view. The very language that Beauvoir uses—the language of overcoming otherness, transcending the in-itself, becoming a subject—can be used to compromise the individuality of women if it is not employed very carefully and put into question at every moment. Beauvoir sets out to uncover the specificity of the point of view of women—but she exempts herself from the problems normally associated with femininity. And as she does so, she steps out of the very situation she seeks to describe from within. She speaks about the situation of women from a privileged position, as a writer, as if it were a problem she encounters exclusively in others. She does not own the problem for herself. It is as if she has already, once and for all, overcome her otherness. She has become a writer, achieved success in a masculine world. In refusing the position of marginality, she takes up the position of one who knows the truth, standing above and beyond her situation. The fact that, at the time of writing *The Second Sex*, Beauvoir was not prepared to think fully through the implications of her privileged class position interrupted her articulation of the relation between women's situation as other and their conditioning as feminine.[78] Beauvoir's refusal to inhabit the position of woman as other, however, a refusal to stand both inside and outside, should not prevent us from seeing the radicality of her thinking in its own time.

Despite her truncated attempt to think through women's otherness, Beauvoir's final message is that sexual difference should be eradicated and women must become like men. As I have tried to show, Beauvoir did not think through the otherness of women's position far enough to allow her to see that no matter how important it remains for feminists to debunk the myths of femininity—and there is no question that it remains crucial to do so—feminism should not restrict itself to that task. For Irigaray, however, simply to eliminate women's otherness is not to overcome oppression. It is, in some senses, to remain captive to it. Irigaray sees in that form of feminism which confines itself to the classic quest for equal rights the tyranny of the same. In its abstract idealizing of individuality and equality, she finds not the emancipation of women, but the repetition of the dogma that enchains them. In directing her attention toward multiplicity, difference, and otherness, Irigaray does not refuse to acknowledge the continuing need to struggle for equality. Rather, she asks whether a feminism that confines itself to the discourse of equality assumes the logic of the male gaze, a logic which in its most successful moment could see no further than the symmetrical leveling of differences. Such a logic reflects a way of thinking that neutralizes the specificity of women's situations as distinct from men's. Women's access to subjectivity has been systematically limited, and to that extent it is necessary for women to define "a new subjective identity" (Jardine and Menke, 1991: 101). In specifying the feminine as other, Irigaray insists that "women's exploitation is based upon sexual difference; its solution will come only through sexual difference" (JTN: 12; JT: 12). Thus a "double gesture" is required: "We need both to interpret and deny that sexual difference should return to exploitation, to subordination, but at the same time to affirm the positive character of difference" (Baruch and Serrano, 1988: 154). It is "necessary to act in two ways . . . because we are at the same time inside and outside" (Baruch and Serrano, 1988: 159). Irigaray neither advises women to remain unquestioningly on the outside nor to be content to complacently inhabit marginal locations within the socio-economic and political structures that construct the power of subjects, nor does she think all our problems will be solved if we become "like men."[79] She is aware that the success some women have in becoming equal to men in socio-economic terms is often at the cost of other women remaining "trapped" as women. In both cases, women are "trapped by their refusals of difference, because difference has always served to exploit" (Baruch and Serrano, 1988: 154), which is precisely why sexual difference needs to to excavated from male history and read positively, not merely negatively. Irigaray asks whether, in some ways, the wish to be more like men does not accept a very traditional devaluation of that which has always been identified as feminine. She asks, in a gesture very different from one which simply reinvokes the myth of the eternal feminine, for a more radical rethinking than one which would merely deny the value of the feminine. The point is not that feminine practices are bad in themselves, but that the constant identification of them as feminine has been used to the detriment of women. Readers who accuse Irigaray of returning to nature tend to lose sight of this difference—perhaps because Irigaray, at times, takes it so much for granted. The multiple identities Irigaray points to require of women a delicate balancing act. Women need not be exclusively one, nor rigidly other; rather they can be both one and other. Irigaray resists conceptualizing women's occupation of their different roles dialectically, whereby one position would cancel out the other, albeit through a process of sublation (in which one position is negated by another such that it is preserved within it rather than being entirely eradicated). Being in more than one place at once is perhaps one of the things women have learned to be good at.

Beauvoir's inquiries into women's condition helped to decisively shape feminism. Irigaray records her admiration for Beauvoir, but adds that Beauvoir was "much more interested in vindication of equality than I am" (Baruch and Serrano, 1988: 164). The strategy of playing down cultural stereotypes, like the corresponding tactic of emphasizing the potential similarities between the sexes, continues to be crucial to feminist struggles for equality—but feminism must look beyond equality while continuing to work to secure it. If Beauvoir's argument that women are not born but constructed by culture is a lesson from which feminism has reaped many benefits, perhaps the time has come for feminists to concentrate their energies on thinking through another less influential aspect of her legacy. Perhaps it is time to think about the question of what it means to be other, by confronting the issue of sexual difference. This does not mean we can forget about the importance of cultural molding. It means we need to rethink culture by attending to the problem of the other more rigorously than Beauvoir was able to do in her eagerness to identify herself as having overcome her status as other. If her privileged social position—as a white, middle-class intellectual—made it easy for her to vacate her role as other, it also allowed her to minimize the problem of otherness. In returning feminism to the question of the other, feminists such as Irigaray have begun to show, as I argue, the necessity of reexamining the way in which the distinction between sex and gender operates in feminist discourse.

In order to think about women's otherness, feminism also needs to take history seriously. Not only do we need to think through the history of women's otherness, but also the history of feminism itself.[80] To do so is not to acquiesce to that history, but to appreciate both the limitations and the radicality of feminist theories by situating them in their theoretical, historical, and political context. I hope the above discussion of the strengths and weaknesses of Beauvoir's feminism will provide a starting point for rethinking one aspect of recent feminist history, namely the debate surrounding essentialism. In returning to the historical and intellectual legacy out of which Irigaray's feminism arose, I have restricted myself to the limited suggestion that one way of situating her project is to think through the relationship between two aspects of Beauvoir's feminism. While the idea that one is not born but becomes a woman has become a popular motif in feminism—indeed it has almost achieved the status of a slogan—Beauvoir's characterization of women as other has been less well elaborated. Irigaray is an exception to the rule in that she takes up the less celebrated strand of what I have identified as Beauvoir's dual legacy—namely, the task of thinking woman as other, a project that Beauvoir began but did not complete. I have argued that the relationship between the two strands of this dual legacy needs to be addressed. Feminism needs to confront the complex relations between negotiating the historical construction of gender roles (which Beauvoir expressed in terms of how one becomes a woman), and differentiating women from their traditional representation as other. In order to do justice to the interaction between gender stereotypes and processes of othering that women encounter, we need to take account of the historical and cultural construction not only of femininity as other, but also of the scientific discourses according to which we define sex, biology, and nature.

By focusing on Hegel's master-slave dialectic, I emphasize not so much that Beauvoir could have used it better than she did, but what prevented her from doing so. It would be too simple to say that her adherence to a Sartrian belief in freedom made it impossible for her to fully develop her

Hegelian insight into historical otherness, and too historical to blame Beauvoir for the shortsightedness of her individualist idealism. It might be more appropriate to say that her privileged position as a writer enabled her to make the most of her history—which, in her time, and for her, amounted to an attempt to escape her feminine condition and create, as much as is possible when one remains a woman, the life of a man.

Without detracting from Beauvoir's contribution to feminism, I want to emphasize the need for feminists to continually draw new boundaries, to take account of the shifting significance of feminist agendas, and to recognize the limitations of discourses which may once have been feminist in a revolutionary way, but which might have become reactionary, and even complicitous.

But I want to end this chapter on a more positive note. Let me do so by quoting another fine French woman writer and theoretician, Catherine Clément. In an article that draws a comparison between Beauvoir's reflections on *Old Age* and *The Second Sex*, she writes,

> *The Second Sex* whose historical importance continues to grow as the history of women's liberation develops . . . is made of multiple stories. . . . If I had to define the philosophy of Simone de Beauvoir, I would say that it is the philosophy of a peeler. She peels, quietly, the onion skins of the world, one after the other; with this kitchen knife that we call in our kitchens the "(s)paring" knife because it peels very thin skins. . . . Simone de Beauvoir has, to the highest degree, the sense of the multiple skins that constitute us; but when she detaches them, for herself and for others, it is with tenderness and precision. It is with the immemorial talent of all the peelers who, working until now in the shadows, have accomplished material kitchen work. She does the same thing in culture, but, in place of the servant or the mother of the family, let us see in her the woman writer, the woman philosopher, the woman storyteller who cooks culture for women and for men and who will not draw back before the sight of any skin, whether it be that of a dying mother or an old man (Clément, 1987: 168–171).[81]

three LOOKING AT HEGEL'S ANTIGONE
THROUGH IRIGARAY'S SPECULUM

Antigone is thrust out of the city, "extradited" from the city-state, refused a home and the most elementary domestic rituals (serving the dead, the gods, preparing food), forbidden to speak, to marry, to bear children. She is walled up in a cave on the border of the world of citizens; she may neither leave nor enter her home. Every act is forbidden her. All that she can do is carry out the deed that king and state dare not do openly but which they collude in, to the point of performing the burial: she can kill herself. She has barely been allowed a little air, a crack in the rock to permit breath. . . . It is crucial that she be given her share of life, blood, air, water, fire, not just that she be present to offer worship to something already dead: whether individuals or laws.

—IRIGARAY

"IT IS VERY IMPORTANT," IRIGARAY TELLS US, "TO QUESTION again the foundations of our symbolic order in mythology and in tragedy, because they deal with a landscape which installs itself in the imagination and then, all of a sudden, becomes law" (Baruch and Serrano, 1988: 159).[1] Among the figures Irigaray invokes are Athena, Ariadne, Kore-Persephone, and Clytemnestra.[2] Sophocles' Antigone receives even more extensive treatment.[3] As Charles Segal observes, Sophocles' Antigone retraces Kore's "lonely journey to the cave and Hades," but, unlike Kore, Antigone "does not rise again to new life" (Segal, 1983: 167).[4] Irigaray's most notable discussion of Antigone is her "The Eternal Irony of the Community" (SO: 214–26; SA: 9–162).[5] The essay is a meditation on Hegel's reflections on the tragic figure of Antigone. We saw in the previous chapter Beauvoir's problematic use of Hegel's master-slave dialectic as a paradigm for the male-female relationship. Not only does her use of this model assume that, like the master-slave relationship, the relationship between men and women is necessarily conflictual, but it also holds out little hope of any fundamental change. The only possible alteration seems to be a reversal of the terms in the male-female relationship, whereby women gain power at the expense of their erstwhile masters. In this chapter I explore Irigaray's instance of a woman who is neither master nor slave: Antigone (ES: 119; E: 115). Irigaray retrieves Antigone from the role in which she is cast by Hegel in his reading of Sophocles' play, as the other of reason, ethics, and knowledge. Unlike Beauvoir, Irigaray is not ready to negate the alterity imposed upon women by the Western philosophical tradition without first acknowledging its unplumbed resources. Rather than immediately reversing the terms of the male-female power relationship or seeking to equalize them, Irigaray exploits the marginality of Antigone's position in a way that puts into question the system that designates Antigone its inferior. Antigone is not idolized or romanticized by Irigaray. Antigone remains a product of a culture that is written by men. Irigaray calls her the "anti-woman" (ES: 118; E: 115). As Josette Féral says, "Antigone is not a woman, or at least she does not conform to society's image of a woman. She is actually representative of the woman who refuses her condition as woman and pays for her transgression of the laws with her death" (Féral, 1978: 2).

Antigone subverts the rationale of the state, putting herself outside its jurisdiction by rigidly adhering to her role within it. She refuses to submit to the demands of the community which Hegel presumes defines her, and she does so by specifying the uniqueness of her task. That task, as far as Antigone is concerned, should not be subordinated to the "greater" end of the *polis* as a whole. By rejecting the expectation that her role should be circumscribed by the needs of the state, Antigone makes herself an outsider, overturning the rationale of the system. She turns her subordinate role into a challenge to the status quo, not by abandoning her feminine duty, but by sticking to it at all costs—and she pays for her decision with her life.

Antigone's action cannot be separated from the tragic circumstances of her birth as the daughter of Oedipus. Antigone's tragedy is one that begins to be played out in her father's life, and inevitably leads her into the cave that becomes her crypt. In banishing her to an underground cavern Creon means to cut her off from the world, depriving her of sunlight, food, love—stifling her life. Irigaray brings into question a key assumption that Freud reads into the Oedipal complex in her reinterpretation of Antigone's tragedy.[6] She sees Antigone's act as challenging Freud's assumption of the essential passivity of femininity, an assumption that Irigaray puts in the context of a series of supporting assumptions—not the least of which Hegel articulates—upheld by the edifice of Western metaphysics.[7]

According to Hegel, Antigone does not, cannot, will not, attain self-consciousness. Why? Because she is a woman and not a man. She can act ethically. *But she cannot know what she is doing.* She cannot understand the rational and universal implications of her divinely inspired, sisterly act on behalf of her brother. She acts on the basis of blood kinship, on the basis of an intuitive sense of her duty. She knows *what* is right. What she does not know is *why* it is right. Since she does not know the reason for her act, that act, by itself, becomes worthless—except as an impetus to propel the dialectic forward. It has no value. It cannot even be said to be properly ethical. For an act to be ethical, the subject has to be in full possession of his faculties, and he must be able to account for his action. He must be able to explain himself verbally, conceptually, ethically. According to Hegel this requires, in short, that he must be male. He must have grasped the essence of his act and have understood its rationale.

Now, since Antigone is not well-versed in the language of reason—*logos*—she speaks not of the relation of her act to the city-state as a whole, not of how it fits in with her role in the *polis* (for if she did she might see that she takes a subordinate role to the brother she seeks to bury), but of her blood kinship with her brother. Since Polynices has turned against the *polis*, his transgression would forbid his burial in advance.[8] Antigone pays no heed to this logic, but heeds rather her passion; she speaks not as a warring soul, but of her nature as a loving creature (A: 523); not of the state, but of familial feelings and sisterly devotion.

SITE AND FORESIGHT IN IRIGARAY'S APPROACH TO HEGEL

Irigaray quotes the following passage from Hegel as an epigraph to "The Eternal Irony of the Community":

On the one hand, the uterus in the male is reduced to a mere gland, while on the other, the male testicle in the female remains enclosed within the ovary, fails to emerge into opposition, and does not become an active cerebrality. The clitoris moreover, is inactive feeling in general; in the male on the other hand, it has its counterpart in active sensibility, the swelling vital, the effusion of blood into the corpora cavernosa and the meshes of spongy tissue of the urethra. The female counterpart of this effusion of blood in the male consists of the menstrual discharges. Thus, the simple retention of the conception in the uterus, is differentiated in the male into productive cerebrality and the external vital. On account of this difference therefore, the male is the active principle; as the female remains in her undeveloped unity, she constitutes the principle of conception (SO: 214; SA: 266).[9]

Enclosed rather than external, inactive and dependent rather than active and independent, simple and undeveloped rather than differentiated and productive, the sexual anatomy of the female is presented as the inversion of the male sex organs, as their imperfect—because internal and undifferentiated—mirror image. It is no accident that Hegel's investigations on nature provide the backdrop to "The Eternal Irony of the Community," although it is his treatment of Sophocles' drama in *Phenomenology of Spirit* that provides the textual focus for Irigaray's essay.

Philosophy of Nature is the text that furnishes Irigaray with the epigraphs with which she sees fit to open her essay, rather than the more obvious sources that might have provided her with a point of entry into the tragedy of Antigone. Leaving aside his consideration of the tragic figure of Antigone in the *Aesthetics*, as well as the comments that appear on tragedy in the context of Hegel's consideration of history, or in his discussion of religion, Irigaray turns instead to what is, from our point of view, a somewhat archaic account of male and female body parts. If the sexed body is the site of the oppositions with which Irigaray begins, the ensuing reflections on Hegel's Antigone will constantly revisit this site of tension.[10]

The oppositions that Irigaray singles out as representative of Hegel's depiction of sex in the *Philosophy of Nature*—inner and outer, vital and bloodless, seeing and unseeing—guide her reading of Hegel's Antigone. With them, Irigaray sets the scene for the discordance that besets the body politic, putting it into permanent conflict with itself.[11] Dwelling first on the function of blood as that which informs the vitality of male activity, Irigaray introduces the theme that inaugurates her own commentary on Hegel's recapitulation of Antigone. In a second epigraph to "The Eternal Irony of the Community," Irigaray posits the eye, reminding us of the role of the Hegelian spectator, the overseer of dramatic action, the privileged observer of the ultimate unity issuing from tragic conflict. Quoting from Hegel's *Philosophy of Nature* again, she writes: "'In the case of the eye,' says *Sömmering*, 'it seems that the arteries are continued in finer branches, which no longer contain red blood. These branches pass initially into a similar vein, but finally into veinlets carrying red blood'" (SO: 214; SA: 266).[12] Just one eye. Just one spectator. The reconciling voice of the univocal chorus perhaps, or Hegel's philosophical reader?[13] Irigaray follows up her reference to Hegel's *Philosophy of Nature* in the final sentence of her essay when she says, "But the eye—at least in the absolute—would have no need of blood to see with, anymore perhaps than the Mind to think with" (SO: 226; SA: 281). Irigaray's ironical observation brings to mind the sense in which, as a reader, one is not in a position to understand the *Phenomenology* until one has reached its end, or, in other words until one has attained the standpoint of absolute knowledge.

How then will these deposits—body, blood, sight, sex—cohere, coagulate, regulate, and organize the themes Irigaray pursues? By opposing the king, Antigone threatens not only to break the mold of feminine simplicity and undifferentiated matter assigned to her by her sex, but also to overturn—even if she cannot do away with once and for all—the principle of inactivity to which her sex, according to Hegel, is supposed to conform. She upsets the assumption that females are necessarily essentially passive, reactive beings, even in the strict observance of their roles as guardians of the family, as mothers whose sexual organs serve as receptacles from the moment of conception to the moment of birth, incubating first the effusion of blood that swells the vital organ of the male, and then the child that develops from his seed. Women, for Hegel, assume the role of retainers, becoming one with their bodies, mere containers, providing a safe place both in the gestation period prior to giving birth and in the mourning period during which they ensure safe passage out of this life through the burial procedures of entombing and embalming. Irigaray, as we shall see in the next chapter, is interested in asking about the condition that allows women to serve the function of containers.

If we accept Thomas Laqueur's hypothesis that it was not until the late eighteenth century that studies in human anatomy began to progress from what he calls the one-sex model toward a two-sex model, then we should not be surprised that Hegel still adheres to the view that women's sexual organs can be adequately presented as if they were imprecise copies of men's.[14] Based on lectures delivered between 1805 and 1806, Hegel's taxonomy of natural sex differences retains the language of the one-sex model, while acknowledging that variations and deviations from the male ideal mark the differences between empirical men and women. No part in either sex is without its counterpart in the other sex, albeit an attenuated counterpart like the uterus (which "in the male is reduced to a mere gland"), ovary ("the male testicle in the female," which "fails to emerge into opposition and does not become an independent and active cerebrality"), or the clitoris (which is "inactive feeling in general") (SO: 214; SA: 266). If the female body parts Hegel names are inactive as opposed to active, undeveloped as opposed to self-differentiated, and internal as opposed to external, they nonetheless approximate their male counterparts. They take their place in a harmonious whole, their purpose assured with reference to an ideality that is presupposed, their function guaranteed in terms of the higher unity under which they will be subsumed. The principle of conception embodied by the female sexual parts only makes sense in terms of a life-giving potentiality that is directed toward a further goal, one that goes beyond the protective privacy of the familial sphere. Female conception is significant only insofar as it inaugurates life at another level, giving rise to a different order that is not circumscribed by familial concerns, one that is nonetheless made possible by the limited boundaries defining family ties. The private domain of the family serves as the substratum of the public domain, the *polis*. Underpinning—and sometimes undermining—the politics of the state, the family remains its necessary counterpart, its antithesis.

Drawing attention to the series of oppositions that Hegel establishes in distinguishing male body parts from female body parts, Irigaray anticipates the themes she will investigate with regard to Antigone in more ways than one. Reading the sexual body, we are already embedded in a response to Hegel's examination of the tensions that prevail within the city-state, and, before we know it, Irigaray has taken a definitive stance toward the "true spirit of the ethical order" for which Hegel looks to his Antigone. The position Irigaray has adopted, without—like Antigone—explicitly mentioning it, without demonstrating any conscious awareness of her knowledge of it, is registered initially not at the level of philosophical self-reflection, but precisely in terms of corporeality. It is registered in the material of the sexual body—the Hegelian body, at that. No doubt she takes a woman's pleasure in making what must seem to be, at first glance, such an oblique entry into the center of this text. In fact, however, we are already at its heart. Having traveled incognito, through its subterranean arteries, against the flow of the system, to arrive at this place, we find ourselves, once again, under the sway of the blood relationship. Having gained entry to the point in the text at which the decisive issue is one's ethical duty not to the living but to the dead, where the ties that bind are those that articulate the relationship of the sister to the brother, we find ourselves wondering how we could come to be in such a place. By what arcane route might we have discovered this inexplicably pivotal familial relationship? Is the privilege Hegel accords to Antigone's relation to Polynices as arbitrary as it initially appears? Or is there some principle, the origin of which remains as yet obscure, that would govern Hegel's appraisal of this particular blood relationship from the very beginning?

If Hegel's allusions to Antigone appear, to the untrained, unphilosophical eye, to be sketchy, once we begin to discern the pattern they collectively produce, they take on a permanence that comes to pervade the entire section on the ethical order of the true spirit.[15] At the same time—and according to the very same structure that Hegel's reading of the *Antigone* dictates—we begin to see that if in one way Irigaray's approach to her topic remains tangential, in another way it issues directly from Hegel's own premises. If, at first glance, an adumbration of sexual bodily parts seems an incongruous preparation for Irigaray's reflections on Hegel's Antigone, it turns out to be a hidden code that will prove invaluable as a means of interpreting Hegel's designs.

In mapping out the politics of the state, Hegel depends upon bodies—male and female both—to perform very specific and necessary roles. The two brothers, Polynices and Eteocles, offer up their bodies in warfare, while Antigone offers up herself, on the occasion of their death, to the family. Creon may wish to deny any personal sentiments of love, he may be guilty of the unbending, "unyielding" attitude of which Haemon, his son, accuses him (A: 716), but no matter how much Creon identifies with the universal law that outlaws the pleasures of the body, these bodily desires will return to haunt the sense of unity that the state had managed to construct for itself.[16] Creon tries to ignore his son's desire for Antigone, which seems to him to be frivolously contingent compared to the necessity that drives his reasonable concerns for the protection of the state: Haemon's desires must be sacrificed to the greater ends of the whole. In the end however, it is in his refusal to yield that Creon learns—too late to avoid either his own downfall or his family's destruction—that the voice of reason cannot stand alone (A: 1095–96). Just as Creon finally meets his destruction, so the ethical spirit of the community is overthrown by the forces of nature. Brute strength, sheer physical force, pure chance—these are the factors that ultimately disrupt the ethical spirit of the community in Hegel's reading.

Consider the way in which Hegel maps the relation between the "distinct ethical substances" into which Spirit divides itself—namely, the human law and the divine law (PhS: 266; PhG: 317). The part of Spirit that is human law is essentially "conscious of itself" (PhS: 267; PhG: 319), and it is because of this self-consciousness that it is called human. The universal form of the human law, says Hegel, "is the *known* law, and the prevailing custom; in the form of individuality it is the actual certainty of itself in the individual as such, and the certainty of itself as a simple individuality is the Spirit as government" (PhS: 267–68; PhG: 319). This is the law that is manifested when Creon, as the ruler of the state, authorizes an edict that forbids anyone to extend the rights of burial to Polynices. "Confronting this clearly manifest ethical power there is, however," says Hegel, "another power, the Divine Law" (PhS: 268; PhG: 319). Unlike ethical substance, which appears in the community as the human law that is "conscious of what it actually does" (PhS: 268; PhG: 319), the Divine law "has the form of immediate substance or substance that simply is" (PhS: 268; PhG: 319). Ethical Spirit is expressed in its immediacy in the family, which is a "*natural* ethical community" (PhS: 268; PhG: 320). Now, this immediacy has two sides to it. It is "on the one hand the inner Notion or general possibility of the ethical sphere in general, but on the other hand equally contains within it the moment of self-consciousness" (PhS: 268; PhG: 319). Antigone embodies the immediacy of ethical substance in burying Polynices, acting in accordance with the divine law, and on behalf of the family. She thereby gives meaning to the "general possibility of the ethical sphere in general" (PhS: 268; PhG: 319), but she "does not attain *consciousness* of it" (PhS: 274; PhG: 325). Why not? Why does Antigone not attain consciousness of "what is ethical" despite having "the highest *intuitive* awareness of what is ethical" (PhS: 274; PhG: 325)?

This question, I suggest, has a bearing on all that one might say about Hegel's philosophical universality. Should this claim seem too bold, too grand, too sweeping, I could perhaps begin to justify it by appealing to the integral role of the tragic, which in the words of Peter Szondi, is the "dialectic governing morality," in Hegel's philosophy as a whole (Szondi, 1986: 54).[17] I want to build a case for what at first glance may seem an insupportable suggestion—that Antigone's consciousness (or unconsciousness) of the ethical pertains to Hegel's philosophical universality—by recalling the ethical role that Hegel legislates for women as individuals whose interests are representative of the family. I recall the function of the family in Hegel's phenomenology and I review the extent to which nature enters into Hegel's designation of women as guardians of the family.[18] For in tragedy—of which *Antigone*, in Hegel's mind, is the supreme example, at least with respect to the honorable guilt that its characters display—it is nature that comes into collision with spirit through the universal forces of action.[19] The clash between nature and culture is central both to the present investigation, and to Hegel's project.

Hegel acknowledges the extent to which women are the driving force of the unity of the *polis*, while nevertheless excluding them from participating in its politics. The irony of women's position, in this account, is that they make possible the integrity of the *polis*, yet remain defined in opposition to it, as outsiders who threaten its equilibrium. Hegel thus both transcends women's definition as natural beings, and confines women to their naturalness.

Even if it remains to be seen just how far Antigone's ostensible ethical unconsciousness bears upon Hegel's philosophical project as a whole, at least the question has a direct bearing on a more limited domain that can be immediately specified. The question of Antigone's ethical consciousness takes shape not only in terms of Irigaray's positioning of women in her reading of Hegel, it also incorporates a reference to Hegel's incessant need to totalize, to unify, to universalize, to synthesize, to subordinate every opposition to the mutuality of a sublating third—in short, his tendency to subject each detail to what might be called the imperialism of the same.[20] This would, of course, include the negation of whatever challenge Antigone's defiant act might constitute to the "superior law" of the community (PhS: 272; PhG: 323). I am not denying that, in the course of his analysis, Hegel is able to uncover precise historical details of specific phenomena. I am merely indicating that, in the final analysis, the necessity of synthesis subordinates all such details to the logic of the same—a phrase that echoes not only Irigaray but also Levinas and Derrida.

Despite its undoubted importance for our subject, the question of why Antigone is not conscious of the ethical nature of her deed is one that probably cannot be answered in any satisfactory way. If this question is unanswerable, if it lacks any ultimate or decisive response, that does not necessarily mean that we should not risk asking it. Neither does the absence of any satisfactory solution mean that there have never been any answers, nor that there will not be others. Hegel provided some of these himself. Irigaray provides others.

Hegel says, for example, that the reason Antigone "does not attain to *consciousness* of [what is ethical], or to the objective existence of it, [is] because the law of the Family is an implicit, inner essence which is not exposed to the daylight of consciousness, but remains an inner feeling and the divine element that is exempt from an existence in the real world" (PhS: 274; PhG: 325–26).[21] Even the most sympathetic reader of Hegel must surely admit that this answer does not explain everything.

For the moment then, merely as a provisional gesture, let us see how far we can go, or rather what will happen, if we try to remain at the level of explication. In order to ask our question we had better make it clearer before we proceed.

WHY DOES ANTIGONE REMAIN UNCONSCIOUS OF THE ETHICAL?

Prior to treating the question of what prevents Antigone attaining consciousness to what is ethical, we need to make sure of some preliminaries. Let us turn back, if not to the beginning, at least to the preamble that ushers in Hegel's thoughts on *Antigone* in the *Phenomenology*. These prefatory remarks are already thoroughly steeped in the conflict that will be thrown into relief by Antigone's act of defiance against Creon only later in Hegel's text. Hegel's primary concern, in the section of the *Phenomenology of Spirit* that discusses Antigone, is the determination of Spirit as consciousness.[22] More specifically, he addresses the motivating force that divides consciousness against itself in the sphere of action. It is ethical action—action of the sort that Antigone's burial of Polynices embodies (and I choose the word "embody" rather than "exemplify" self-consciously)—that divides Spirit into substance and consciousness of substance (PhS: 266; PhG: 317).[23] Consciousness of substance is divided into two, the "law of individuality" and the "law of universality" (PhS: 267; PhG: 318). This expression of the antithesis remains only "superficial"; Hegel finds a more concrete expression of the antithesis of "ethical perception," as we have already seen, in the divine law and the human law. Just as the consciousness of substance is split in two, so substance itself is divided. There is, on the one hand, the "universal essence and End," and, on the other hand, the "individualized reality" (PhS: 266; PhG: 317). Again, Hegel will provide more particular determinations for these distinctions: the community embodies universality, while the family, as the natural community, is the vehicle of expression for the individual. As Irigaray says, "One more step (into negation)" (SO: 214; SA: 266), and we find Creon, as the exemplary male figure, representing the human law that is known by and enacted in the community, while Antigone, the exemplary female figure, represents the law of divinity embodied by the individual. To complete the scene, the two sides of substance are brought into harmony with one another through ethical action, such that individual action is performed in and for the family, but it reflects at the same time the universal ends of the community. As Irigaray says, "The chapter of *The Phenomenology of Mind* in which Hegel speaks of the family comes at the beginning of his analysis of man's relationship with spirit and culture. This chapter deals first of all with the question of the ethical order and its relationship to morality."[24] Having been assigned either to the human law or to the divine law according to another law—namely, the law dividing the male sex from the female sex—Spirit, as self-consciousness, "learns through its own act the contradiction" between the human and divine laws, "as well as the contradiction between *its* knowledge of the ethical character of its action, and what is in its own proper nature ethical" (PhS: 444; PhG: 317–18). At the most abstract level, we already have all the parts in place, but if we are to follow the line of reasoning that brings Hegel to the conclusion that Antigone does not attain consciousness of her ethical act, we need to rehearse the sequence of links in the chain by which Hegel situates Antigone within the family in whose name she commits the deed, and that will lead to her inevitable death. In other words, we will need to apprise ourselves of the associations that follow an inexorable path toward the sanctity—in Hegel's eyes—of the sister's relation to the brother.

THE FAMILY AND THE STATE—PART/WHOLE

Let me begin by quoting the definition of the family that Hegel provides in the section of *The Phenomenology of Spirit* called "The True Spirit: The Ethical Order," after which I want to follow closely the movement of the ensuing paragraphs.

> The Family, as the *unconscious*, still inner Notion [of the ethical order], stands opposed to its actual, self-conscious existence; as the *element* of the nation's actual existence, it stands opposed to the nation itself;

as the *immediate* being of the ethical order, it stands over against that order which shapes and maintains itself by working for the universal; the Penates stand opposed to the universal Spirit.

However, although the Family is *immediately* determined as an ethical being, it is within itself an *ethical* entity only so far as it is not the *natural* relationship of its members, or so far as their connection is an *immediate* connection of separate, actual individuals; for the ethical principle is intrinsically universal, and this natural relationship is just as much a spiritual one, and it is only as a spiritual entity that it is ethical. We have to see what constitutes its peculiar ethical character. In the first place, because the ethical principle is intrinsically universal, the ethical connection between the members of the Family is not that of feeling, or the relationship of love. It seems, then, that the ethical principle must be placed in the relation of the *individual* member of the Family to the *whole* Family as the Substance, so that the End and content of what he does and actually is, is solely the Family. But the conscious End motivating the action of this whole, so far as it is directed towards that whole, is itself the individual (PhS: 268–69; PhG: 320).

The issue I want to highlight here is what makes an ethical act ethical, or in Hegel's words "what constitutes its peculiar ethical character" (PhS: 268; PhG: 320). In the above passage it is only one side of ethical substance that is under consideration, that which falls under the divine law and which Antigone enacts. However, since "each of the opposites in which the ethical substance exists contains the entire substance, and all the moments of its content" (PhS: 268; PhG: 319), implicit in the expression of the family as an ethical moment is the ethical content of the community. Hegel distinguishes between the family as a "*natural ethical community*" and as a spiritual ethical unit. As a natural and unconscious unit, the family has an antagonistic relation to the state. Considered in its natural existence, its ends and aims, which consist in preserving its individual members, are set against those of the state. In this aspect, the family finds its immediate existence. However, it is only as a spiritual relationship that the family can instantiate the ethical principle in its universality.

The conditions that must be met in order for an act to be properly ethical, in the sense of spiritual, within the sphere of the family are as follows: the act must be universal, and it must have as its end the family as a whole. As such it must be directed toward an individual member of the family insofar as that individual belongs to the family. While the family relationship remains a natural one, and is immediately ethical, the conscious end of the ethical principle lies in the individual considered as one member of the family. As Hegel says, the "*positive* End peculiar to the Family is the individual as such" (PhS: 269; PhG: 320); but because the family itself is ultimately answerable to the community as a whole, whatever power and wealth is acquired on the part of the family in support of the individual has its highest determination not in the family as such but only in the family considered as subordinate to the community. Insofar as Antigone's burial of Polynices is directed toward him as an individual, it remains unconscious of its higher determination for the good of the whole.

It is crucial to bear in mind the difference between Antigone's point of view and that of spirit as self-consciousness. As far as Antigone is concerned, her action in burying Polynices is performed within the scope of the family and for a particular individual. Implicit in this motivation, however, which is partial precisely because it only takes account of the divine law, there is another meaning, one that contradicts Antigone's own justification of her action. There is a world of difference between the implicit meaning of Antigone's action, and her own account of it. In this difference lies the answer to our question about why Antigone, according to Hegel, cannot be conscious of the ethicality of her act. In differentiating between Antigone's knowledge of her own action and the point of view of spirit as self-consciousness, Hegel locates sexual difference. Or perhaps it is the other way around? Perhaps it is in differentiating between the sexes that Hegel knows Antigone cannot be consciously aware of the ethical content in her ethical act as ethical. Hegel confirms this when he says, "Nature, not the accident of circumstances or choice, assigns one sex to one law, the other to the other law" (PhS: 280; PhG 332). Just as the "ethical consciousness," according to Hegel, "knows what it has to do, and has already decided whether to belong to the divine or the human law" (PhS: 280; PhG; 332), so Hegel has already decided to equate women with nature and men with culture. His decision is informed, however, by a description of women's nature that is already embedded in an assumption that is cultural. Women's sexual anatomy, compared to men's, is inactive, undifferentiated, and inferior according to Hegel's account. This supposedly natural state of affairs is used as a basis on which to ground women's inability to develop ethical consciousness, despite the fact that the anatomical descriptions themselves are already loaded in favor of women's exclusion from the public realm.

Given Hegel's view that women are destined not to be ethical, the necessity of Antigone's action in terms of its relation to the state as a whole derives from the implications her action has for the individual in its universality. Polynices, as an individual, may have violated the law of the community, that is, the human law that binds him to his state. But Antigone, by ignoring this aspect of his individuality which is not essential, and by recognizing his individuality only as a member of her family, reinvokes (what is for her) the proper order—the order of the family, the order of sexual division within the family, and, at the same time, the ethical order. She brings him back into the fold and recognizes his membership in the family, the natural community. In her recognition of Polynices as bound to her by family ties, the family becomes not merely natural but also ethical. Although, in one sense, Polynices' attack on Thebes and his consequent death "falls," Hegel says, "within the ethical community" (PhS: 270; PhG: 322), and as such "death is the fulfillment and the supreme 'work' which the individual as such undertakes on its behalf" (PhS: 270; PhG: 322), in another sense, the crime he committed against his state has an entirely incidental relationship to his death. In Hegel's words, "In so far as he is essentially a *particular* individual, it is an accident that his death was directly connected with his 'work' for the universal and was the result of it" (PhS: 270; PhG: 322).[25]

Antigone is oblivious to the misdeeds of Polynices' life. Insofar as she buries one brother despite the fact that he not only died in an act of treachery against her state, but that in doing so he also killed her second brother, Eteocles, Antigone takes no heed of Polynices' murderous act.[26] She only acknowledges the blood ties that bind her to him in death, and in doing so, she fulfills what Hegel considers to be her proper function.[27] If she cannot right the wrongs he has done, at least she can preserve the law that she represents. If she cannot make amends for the deeds her dead brother committed in life, at least she can stand by him in death by observing her own very different duty—her duty to his body, her protection of his corpse.[28] It is as if the meaning of Polynices' actions in life are simply of no concern to her.[29] Antigone is nothing if not steadfast in her conviction from beginning to end, unwavering in her commitment to the sacred duty she feels toward her brother, a duty that entails the tragic outcome that she anticipates from the beginning of the play, namely her death (see A: 71–72). Uncompromising in the stand she takes, she identifies herself so completely with the divine law that she all but compels Creon to oppose her.[30] And Creon, for his part, although he may not know it, needs Antigone to be entirely what she is. His downfall results from his failure to admit that the law that he observes requires another to support it. Haemon tries, unsuccessfully, to persuade his father that he cannot act alone.[31] In his arrogant self-sufficiency, Creon maintains the supremacy of the state, and resolutely ignores the rights of the family.[32]

As the male ruler, upholder of the communal state, Creon's predicament is that he needs Antigone to identify fully with the family, for that is her duty and function as a woman. Without her law, his law will also be lacking.[33] The human supplements the divine, and vice versa. Hegel says, "Neither of the two is by itself valid; human law proceeds in its living process from the divine, the law valid on earth from that of the nether world, the conscious from the unconscious, mediation from immediacy—and equally returns whence it came. The power of the nether world, on the other hand, has its actual existence on earth; through consciousness, it becomes existence and activity" (PhS: 276; PhG: 328). The law that Creon represents requires the law that Antigone represents. Again, as Hegel says, "the publicly manifest Spirit has the root of its power in the nether world" (PhS: 287; PhG: 337).[34] Nevertheless, Creon claims that it is his word alone that counts.[35] And Hegel, precisely to the extent that he has always already decided in favor of universality over individuality, supports him in this. Whatever reciprocity might seem to pertain between the family and the state, between the divine law and the human law, there is a sense in which, in Hegel's account, it is always already decided in advance which law has the higher authority. The law that is conscious, by definition, is the human law, the man's law—the law that contradicts Antigone's law (PhS: 267; PhG: 319). In Irigaray's words, "Hegel admits this when he affirms that the brother is for the sister that possibility of recognition of which she is deprived as mother and wife, but does not state that the situation is reciprocal. This means that the brother has already been invested with a value for the sister that she cannot offer in return, except by devoting herself to his cult after death" (SO: 217; SA: 270). Let me add that in the same way, and following the same laws, the state has been invested with a value that the family cannot offer in return, except by devoting itself to the higher ends of the community.

THE FAMILY AND THE STATE— POTENTIALITY/ACTUALITY

Paradoxically, the real purpose of the family consists in "expelling the individual from the Family, subduing the natural aspect and separateness of his existence, and training him to be virtuous, to a life in and for the universal" (PhS: 269; PhG: 320). Just as the real purpose of the female lies in conception, the successful completion of which consists in bringing pregnancy to term—through birth or, we might say, expulsion —so the real purpose of the family is contained not in the family itself, but in the higher entity that endows it with its meaning: the law that it opposes, the human law that has its actuality in the community. Both the functioning of the family and that of the female are devoted to an end outside themselves, and insofar as that end is the same—namely, to facilitate the development of virtuous (male) citizens—there is no difference between the role of the family and that of the female, which in this respect come to be equated with one another in Hegel's scheme of things.

We see then that for Hegel any individual act which could be performed within the family considered in itself, that is, as a natural relationship without a higher end or further purpose beyond its own maintenance, will lack true ethical content. Such an act, insofar as it concerns merely the particularity of the individual, will remain at the level of a natural act based on the immediate ties of the family, and not on the spiritual aspect of its ethical content. Thus Hegel discounts the possibility of finding an ethical content in any relationship that is "accidental"—"as happens perhaps in rendering some assistance or service in a particular case" (PhS: 269; PhG: 320)—which would produce "only a particular effect" on the individual and would not "be related to the *whole* individual or to the individual *qua* universal" (PhS: 269; PhG: 321). For the same reason, we should not imagine "that service in the form of education, i.e., in a *series* of efforts, really has him in his entirety for object, and produces him as a 'work,'" nor should "we understand the service as a help in time of need by which in truth the individual in his entirety is rescued; for such help is itself a completely contingent act, the occasion of which is an ordinary reality which can either be or not be" (PhS: 269; PhG: 321). The only act that can be performed by one individual family member for another that properly belongs to the family in its ethical spirituality is one that "has as its object and content this particular individual who belongs to the Family, but is taken as a *universal* being freed from his sensuous, i.e., individual, reality" (PhS: 270; PhG: 321). Since "the ethical principle is intrinsically universal" (PhS: 268; PhG: 320), as we have already seen, any act that is done for the individual as such—that is, for the individual as the end, goal, or purpose of the family—is in reality an act done not for the family as such, but for the family considered in the light of its relation to the universal. In other words, an act may be grounded in the relations of the family, but it is in the universal aspect of the family that the act attains its true ethical spirituality. The family has its true significance in the political community of the state as a whole.

In contrast to the abstract immediacy of any discrete act that pertains only to the individual as a member of the natural family, an ethical act that is at the same time spiritual and universal has as its object an individual who "concentrates himself into a single completed shape, and has raised himself out of the unrest of the accidents of life into the calm of simple universality" (PhS: 270; PhG: 321). Such an individual can only be one who has completed his life as a citizen, the life in which "he is actual and substantial," and has become "an unreal and impotent shadow" of his former self, or a mere corpse. Were it not for the ministrations of the family—principally of the women of the family—the dead would be subjected to the unconscious powers of the natural world. It is in death that the natural ties of the family come into their own. Derrida's gloss on Hegel here is useful. He says,

> The family, the natural moment of the ethical, has as its object only the singular, the essentially singular, that is, which, without reaching the universal legality of the city, strips itself of every empiric characteristic. This pure singularity, stripped but incapable of passing to universality, is the dead—is the corpse, the impotent shadow, the negation of the living being-there inasmuch as that singularity has not yet given rise to the life of the citizen. Already dead (as empiric existence), not yet living (as ideal universality). If the family's thing is pure singularity, one belongs to a family only in busying oneself around the dead: toilette of the dead, institution of death, wake, monumentalization, archive, heritage, genealogy, classification of proper names, engraving of tombs, burying, shrouding, burial place, funeral song, and so on (G: 143; GI: 162).

By observing the duty entailed by her blood relation to Polynices, Antigone transforms the natural bond between herself and her brother into a spiritual one. By acting in such a way that unconscious desires of other creatures of the natural world are kept at bay, she exerts the power of divine law over the force of nature. She makes of death "the result of an action *consciously* done" (PhS: 270; PhG: 321).[36]

For Hegel, Antigone's burial of her brother has a significance that is unparalleled. Hegel attributes such importance to the deed neither because it is the final opportunity for her to show devotion to a loved one nor because it is the culmination of a series of kindnesses that she has been able to extend to him throughout his lifetime. On the contrary, it is the only act that Antigone can perform for Polynices that does not pertain to his public role as citizen or to his potentiality for citizenship. The sense in which her observation of burial rights surpasses any other act she may have directed toward him is not simply a matter of degree. Its uniqueness consists in the fact that it is the sole act that she can do, in her capacity as a sister for him in his capacity as a brother, the meaning of which does not immediately dissolve into a higher (in Hegelian terms, more general) determination. Any other act she may have performed for him while he was still alive would have been canceled out, as it passed from the woman to the man, from the family to the state, from the individual to the community, from the personal to the political.[37]

Even this extraordinary act of burial, which justifies Antigone's entire existence, is of course, for Hegel, ultimately a subordinate one. It becomes clear that for Hegel's Antigone the possibility of ethical action is severely limited from the start. Even this singular act, the burial deed, is destined to be taken up in the service of the human law, dedicated to the good of the whole—but not without first assuming an identity that is properly its own, in the name of the family.[38] That is why Antigone's obstinate adherence to this singular act attains such importance. In standing by her duty to Polynices in death, whatever the consequences may be—and they prove to be fatal—Antigone's intransigence gives the familial bond a determinateness that it would otherwise lack. In her intransigence lies Antigone's intuitive knowledge of the ethical nature of her act. Antigone says, in a speech that has proved to be a sticking point for Sophocles' readers since Aristotle,

> Last, Polynices knows the price I pay
>
> for doing final service to his corpse.
>
> And yet the wise will know my choice was right.
>
> Had I had children or their father dead,
>
> I'd let them moulder. I should not have chosen
>
> in such a case to cross the state's decree.

What is the law that lies behind these words?

One husband gone, I might have found another,

or a child from a new man in first child's place,

but with my parents hid away in death,

no brother, ever, could spring up for me.

Such was the law by which I honoured you.

(A: 902–13)

Only for a brother—whom she thereby infers is uniquely irreplaceable— would Antigone, she claims, disobey an edict of the state. It is this inference that has provoked so much scholarly dissent—to the point that some have judged the speech spurious.[39] Michelle Gellrich says,

> To his credit, Hegel does not figure among the cut-and-paste group of scholars. In fact he seems unbothered, at least overtly, by Antigone's argument in lines 905–12. This is because he regards the speech as a seamless part of the ethical whole that constitutes Antigone's dramatic character. For him, there is no disjunction between the general precept about burial with which she first defends herself before Creon and her later appeal to the unique irreplaceability of a brother (Gellrich, 1988: 57).

I want to make explicit why Hegel remains unperturbed by what other critics have viewed as a discrepancy in the reasons with which Antigone supports her burial of Polynices. At line 519 of the play, where Antigone says, "Death yearns for equal law for all the dead," the issue she is addressing is the difference between a brother who is marked by the state as a "criminal" in life, and another brother who was a loyal ruler of the state. In dispute here is how Antigone can ignore the fact that one of her brothers not only identifies himself as a traitor to the city in his attack, but in the process kills her other brother. How, Creon wants to know, can Antigone justify extending to the traitorous, murderous brother the same rights of burial with which the city honors its victorious leader and defender? Antigone's response is that, in death, the deeds of life are insignificant. Death levels all differences in life. She is not disturbed by her brother's treachery in the sense that her concern is not to judge the rights or wrongs of his actions in life. As she says, "It is my nature (ephyn) to join in loving, not in hating" (A: 523). The political significance of the deeds enacted by her brothers is not at stake for her. Politics is not her province; the family is. In her obedience to the tradition of honoring the dead through burial rights she observes her familial duty, a loyalty that is underscored by the ignominious fate of the particular family line that is hers, and by the fact that there is no one left but her to perform the deed. Since Ismene declined Antigone's entreaty that she help bury Polynices, Antigone has spoken as if Ismene does not exist—she is all alone in the world and friendless.[40] In the figure of Antigone the family finds its proper function in burying the dead. Antigone epitomizes obedience to her familial descent and the duties it implies. Hegel thinks, as we have seen, that the family has its proper sphere of action in observing the rights of the dead.

At lines 905–12 the issue is a different one. Here in question is not whether the deeds that Antigone's two brothers accomplished in life should affect the honor their surviving family members ought to bestow upon them in death. In question rather is whether, had Creon forbidden the burial of a child or a husband, Antigone would have taken such an extreme stand, one that puts her in conflict with Creon's edict and sends her to a certain death. She denies that she would have chosen to "cross the state's decree" in such a case (A: 907) and offers as her reason that, since both her parents are dead, "no brother, ever, could spring up for me" (A: 912), whereas it is not beyond the realm of possibility that she might find another husband or beget another child in the alternative scenario she is considering. It is noteworthy that neither a husband nor a child—insofar as the child is a product of marriage (and Antigone limits the possibility of conceiving a child to the context of marriage)— would be related to her purely through blood. Her relations both to a husband and to any children, were she to be granted the possibility of having them, would be bound up with the social conventions of the political sphere. Insofar as her ties to them would not be purely natural, but rather would be determined, to some extent, through the human institution of marriage, the bonds uniting her to them would be less than strictly blood ties. Of course, it is also the case that Antigone shares the same blood as Polynices only as a result of the physical union of her parents. In other words, her relationship to Polynices occurs in the context of a sexual union that is legitimated by the marriage contract between her parents. This particular marriage contract is tainted by the incestuous relations that obtain between Oedipus and Jocasta. Despite the fact that Antigone's parents' sexual union is sanctioned by marriage in one sense, it is radically undercut by the incest taboo in another.

Considered on its own terms then, Antigone's relationship to Polynices is purely a blood relationship.

Antigone consistently speaks for her allegiance to the blood relation, to the gods of the underworld, and she establishes her ties with nature through such allegiances. Hegel understands this as her obedience to family ties. In this respect, her isolation of her relationship to her brother from other family relations she might have had does not seem out of place with her earlier refusal to acknowledge the significance of the deeds committed by her two brothers while they lived. On the contrary, it appears to be perfectly consistent with her declaration that her nature is to love, and not to hate, and with her obligations to the dead, rather than to the living.

For Hegel, the overwhelming and exclusive significance Antigone attaches to her relationship to Polynices only serves to lend further weight to his view that women are akin to nature. That Antigone pays less heed to a marriage contract than she does to a relationship that is exclusively based on the ties of blood is entirely in keeping with Hegel's premises. Moreover, it is unsurprising that a daughter born of such a marriage as that binding Oedipus to Jocasta should not place too high a premium upon the contract of marriage. That Hegel should take such care to distinguish the relations between brother and sister, wife and husband, and parents and child acquires a heightened importance in this particular context. For these roles have not been very effectively differentiated in the family which defines Antigone's relation to Polynices.

For Hegel, women, as individuals, reach their full potential in realizing the ends and aims of the family. They are not destined for public life. Their place is in the natural community of the family, overseeing the passage of their next of kin into the next life. What, then, could be more fitting than that Antigone should defend her role with such passionate vehemence?

When Hegel concludes that "the loss of the brother is therefore irreparable to the sister and her duty towards him is the highest" (PhS: 275; PhG: 327), he cites the line from the *Antigone* in which Sophocles has Antigone state that if it had been her child who was dead, she could have conceived another. As we have seen, Antigone also says that had her husband died, she could have replaced him. That Hegel limits his reference to Antigone's remark about the possibility of losing a child, without also referring directly to the possible loss of a husband that Antigone mentions, may be due to the fact that he considers the parent-child relation to be the objective fulfillment of the husband-wife relation.[41] To the extent that the husband-wife relation "has its actual existence not in itself but in the child" (PhS: 273; PhG: 325) it is a relationship that is superseded by any children that issue from it. Marriage, according to Hegel, thus finds its true purpose in reproduction. For Hegel, "the dutiful reverence of husband and wife towards each other," mixed as it is with "a natural relation and with feeling" (PhS: 273; PhG: 325), provides no match for the relation that obtains between brother and sister.

If the relations between husband and wife are not purely ethical, but tainted with the impurities of emotional and contingent love—and we know from the *Aesthetics* that romantic love is not the subject of tragedy—the relations between parents and children fare little better.[42] They too are "emotionally affected" (PhS: 273; PhG: 325). The emotional affect of the parents' relation to their children consists in the fact that in their children they witness a development "of an independent existence which they are unable to take back again" (PhS: 273; PhG: 325). The children, for their part, "derive their existence from, or have their essential being in, what is other than themselves, and passes away" (PhS: 272; PhG: 325). They attain "independence and a self-consciousness of their own only by being separated from their source" (PhS: 272; PhG: 325), that is, only by growing apart from their parents.

Not so for the brother-sister relationship, upon which Hegel bestows the highest status of the three familial relations he considers.[43] Such is Antigone's relation to Polynices. It is a relation in which there is no desire, and which consists neither in breaking away from the other, as the child must from the parent, nor in allowing the other to become independent from oneself, as the parent must allow the child to do. The brother and sister "do not desire one another, nor have they given to, or received from, one another this independent being-for-self" (PhS: 274; PhG: 325). Irigaray's comment on this is that the reciprocity of the brother-sister relationship is undercut when Polynices enters adulthood. Any illusion of equality is dispelled with the onset of Polynices' manhood, which finds its corollary not in Antigone's womanhood, but in the denial of it. Irigaray says,

> The harmonious relationship of brother and sister involved a (so-called) equal recognition and nonviolent co-penetration of two essences, in which femininity and masculinity achieve universality in human and divine law. But this mutual agreement was possible only for as long as *adolescence* lasted and neither was impelled to act. A prolongation of childhood, a kind of Eden shielded from war and blessed by the household gods. But these idyllic and/because *immaculate* loves of childhood could not last. And each will soon realize that his or her equal is also his or her worst enemy, negation, and death. For the rule of law

is impossible in a situation of mutual sharing in which one has as much value as the other, is equitably the same. In such circumstances consciousness could not recognize its simplicity or that wholeness which is the pathos of its duty. It must therefore make up its mind to act in accordance with that part of the ethical essence which has become apparent to it—that is, to the part which would correspond to its natural allegiance to one sex (SO: 222; SA: 276).

Hegel's arguments as to why the brother is irreplaceable have proven controversial, but few of those who have discussed the problem have taken into account the full implications of Hegel's rationale for categorizing the sister-brother relationship in a class of its own. To ask as Gellrich does, why Antigone's relation with Ismene is not equally irreplaceable is, on its own terms, an entirely appropriate question (Gellrich, 1988: 59). For Hegel, however, Ismene could never be as valuable to Antigone as Polynices because (1) she is alive, and as such not an appropriate vehicle for Antigone's ethical action—any action Antigone could perform for her would remain contingent and would not address the individual as a whole; (2) she is a woman, and as such she does not act in the political sphere; (3) she has denied her obligation to the family, in the figure of Polynices—but the family is the only sphere of action that, in Hegelian terms, is properly her own. At an early stage of his discussion of Antigone in the *Phenomenology of Spirit*, Hegel provides, as we saw, two different grounds for privileging the sister-brother relationship above the other two blood relationships to which he limits his consideration—those of parent to child, and husband to wife. First, unlike the other two relationships, the sister-brother relation is "unmixed with any natural desire" (PhS: 275; PhG: 326), and second, the recognition that the brother and sister can bestow on one another does not involve either giving or receiving from one another their "independent being-for-self" (PhS: 274; PhG: 325). In addition to these two reasons, however, there is another fundamental law that governs everything Hegel says about the relation between Antigone and Polynices, the law that assigns the female sex to the Penates, the gods of the underworld, and the male sex to Zeus, the god on whom Creon calls to justify his alleged attempt to preserve political order within the state.[44] The privilege Hegel accords to the brother-sister relation cannot be explained unless we bear in mind the law that differentiates male and female, and the political consequences—or lack of direct consequences, in the case of the female—this law has for whatever action each may take.[45]

Every deed other than burial that Antigone may have carried out on Polynices' behalf finds its significance not in her duty toward her brother as a member of the family, but in her duty toward him either as a potential or as an actual member of the community that he serves. As such Antigone's act attains significance from her indirect relation to the communal law via her brother.[46] By contrast, any act of service she might have performed toward her sister would first of all be contingent insofar as her sister is still alive. Secondly, since her sister is not and never was destined for the public duties of citizenship, every act on her behalf could only ever constitute a merely familial duty. Like Antigone, the only way in which Ismene, as a woman, could ever realize the meaning of her life is in the life of the family, and not in the life of the *polis* as such. To fail to see why Polynices is irreplaceable for Antigone in a way that Ismene could never be is to ignore the obvious salience of her (Ismene's) sex. In the Hegelian scheme of things, any familial devotion Antigone could have shown to Ismene could never obtain significance equal to that which lies in Antigone's burial of Polynices. Ismene's life could only be significant in and through serving male family members, in a way that releases them to the *polis*. Such services will remain contingent rather than necessary inasmuch as they are not related to the individual in its universality. If Hegel fails to consider Ismene it is because, in his eyes, she shirks the only possibility she has for assuming her familial duty in a properly ethical deed.[47] By refusing, at least initially, Antigone's plea to join her in her act of defiance against Creon, Ismene denies the role that is prescribed for her by her sex.[48] She violates the law that identifies her as a guardian of the family as such. She prematurely transgresses the law of the sexes. No drama issues from her refusal, for she preempts conflict rather than dramatizing it.

Taking up the same issues that other commentators have organized around the theme of Polynices' irreplaceability for Antigone, Irigaray concentrates on the figure of the mother. She asks of the characters that make up the relationship that steals center stage in Hegel's analysis of Sophocles—the brother-sister relationship—

What meaning does each have for the other that draws them into this exchange? Is it recognition of *blood*? Of their common allegiance to the power of the *same blood*? Could it be their complicity in the permanence, the continuance of blood that a matriarchal type of lineage ensures in its purest and most universal being? In this sense the family of Oedipus would be quite exemplary because the mother of the husband is also his wife, thus re-marking the blood tie between the children of that union— including Polynices and Antigone (SO: 216; SA: 268–69).[49]

As Derrida observes, in ironic understatement, this is not just any family: "Antigone's parents are not some parents among others."[50] Antigone is born of the incestuous embraces of Oedipus with his mother, Jocasta. The law that binds Antigone to her brother, Polynices, is thereby doubly marked by the ties of kinship binding her to a mother who is also her father's mother. Antigone's duty to her brother is indelibly imprinted on her mind by the terrible circumstances of their birth—or, as Irigaray calls it the "dreadful paradigm of a mother who is both wife and mother to her husband" (SO: 219; SA: 272).[51] The incestuous relations between their parents no doubt resonate throughout the lives of her brothers and sister too, but the circumstances are not the same for all of them. Irigaray says, "whereas Ismene is termed a sister because she shares *the same blood* as Antigone, and whereas Polynices is termed a brother because he was born of *the same mother*, Eteocles is brother because he is the son of *the same father and the same mother*" (SO: 217; SA: 270).[52] The only sibling to be born of the same mother as Antigone, but not of the same father is Polynices. What does Irigaray make of this?

> Whatever her current arguments with the laws of the city may have been, another law is still drawing her along her path: Identification with her mother. *But how are mother and wife to be distinguished?* This is the dreadful paradigm of a mother who is both wife and mother to her husband. Thus the sister will strangle herself in order to save at least the mother's son. She will cut off her breath—her voice, her air, blood, life—with the veil of her belt, returning into the shadow (of a) tomb, the night (of) death, so that her brother, *her mother's desire*, may have eternal life. She never becomes a woman. But she is not as masculine as she might seem if seen from an exclusively phallic viewpoint—for it is tenderness and pity that have motivated her. Rather, she is a captive of a desire whose path has reached a dead end, has never been blazed. And did she seek the relationship with the mother in *Polynices* because he was the more feminine of the brothers? The younger? Or at any rate the weaker, the one who is rejected. The more irritable and impulsive one, who in his anger will seek to open the veins of his blood again. He who is armed for/by love of a woman, married, unlike his siblings, and through that foreign match condemning his sister to die buried alive. At least in his passion for blood he has annulled the right of his brother—*Eteocles*—to command, has destroyed his brother's—his elder's?—relation to power, reason, property, the paternal succession.[53] And has, with the same blow, killed himself (SO: 219; SA: 272).[54]

By highlighting Antigone's identification with her mother,[55] Irigaray brings us back not only to the female body—which we never really left behind—but also to the destiny that was set in motion long before Antigone came on the scene: the dreadful paradigm, the family curse that will continue to work itself through the sons and daughters who share the same blood as Antigone, unless something is done to prevent its progress. Could this be why Antigone is not permitted—does not permit herself—to become a wife or a mother?[56] Antigone is implicated by virtue of the circumstances of her birth, which is the result of Oedipus' incestuous marriage to his mother. The issue, for Hegel, is not whether Antigone has done anything to deserve the fate that she assumes. She is, by definition, guilty.[57] Her guilt is also her knowledge.

We need to separate three different levels at which Antigone is situated in relation to the question of whether or not she knows what she is doing or is conscious of the ethicality of her act. These are the intuitive, the political, and the familial. First, insofar as Hegel regards the purity of Antigone's ethical awareness of her act as residing merely in her intuitive knowledge of it, Antigone can be said not to know the true ethical nature of her act. She may feel passionately that the right thing to do is to bury her brother, but she does not attain to ethical consciousness of her act. Second, Antigone knows that her action is in flagrant contradiction of Creon's edict. In this sense, she knows that she transgresses the political law. But since she considers the divine law to be the only law to which she is answerable, and does not recognize the validity of any other law, there is a sense in which she cannot know what her action constitutes from an ethical point of view. Precisely to the extent that she does not—cannot, according to Hegel—recognize the political, neither can she comprehend her action as ethical. It is at this level that Hegel oversimplifies—if he can ever be charged with such a sin—the question of whether or not Antigone can be conscious of the ethical nature of her act. For Hegel, the reason that Antigone observes the divine law and sets this law over and against the human law is that it is in her nature, as a woman, to do so. Given the hierarchical relation that Hegel assumes between the female/divine/individual law, and the male/human/communal law, Antigone is barred from realizing the full significance of her act. In Hegelian terms, in observing her allegiance to the family, she dedicates her life to a particular individual, and although her act has universal implications, these are not available to her as a woman in their universality. Ultimately, what this turns out to mean is that, however steadfastly Antigone might adhere to the law that is proper to her, and however heroic her action is as a tragic

105

figure, she herself can never attain the true ethical spirit. For the ethical spirit, in its highest determination, is universal, communal, and political, rather than singular, individual, or familial.

There is a third level at which Antigone is excluded from the possibility of being conscious of the ethical content of her act. That is the sense in which Antigone is under the family curse (*atē*) of the house of Labdacus. It is her destiny to meet an untimely death, born as she is of such a monstrous marriage—the daughter of Oedipus and Jocasta. It runs in her blood, as it were. Thus we have a series of assumptions about the significance of Antigone's actions that both begin and end in the destiny that is mapped out for her in her family identity. As a woman, she represents the gods of the household, and she incarnates the principle of individuality. As such she is the guardian of the family. The sister of Polynices, it falls to Antigone to honor her brother in death. As the daughter of Oedipus, in the shadow of his incestuous alliance with his mother—her mother—Antigone is destined to live out her life, and go to her death, under the curse of the house of Labdacus. It is the necessity and the circularity of this logic that Irigaray notices, picks up, and comments upon:

> *What an amazing vicious circle in a single syllogistic system.* Whereby the unconscious, while remaining unconscious, is yet supposed to know the laws of a consciousness—which is permitted to remain ignorant of it—and will become even more repressed as a result of failing to respect those laws. But the stratification, on top/underneath, of the two ethical laws, of the two beings-there of sexual difference—which in fact have to disappear as such after the death of the brother and sister—comes from Self, of itself. The movement by which the mind ceaselessly sublates necessity, clinging to the top of its pyramid more easily if the other is thrust deeper down into the well.[58] Thus the male one copulates the other so as to draw new strength from her, a new form, whereas the other sinks further and further into a ground that harbors a substance which expends itself without the mark of any individualism. And it is by no means sure that the rape to which she continues to be subjected is visible in broad daylight, for the rape may equally well result in her retreating down into a crypt where she is sealed off (SO: 223; SA: 277–78).

If Antigone qualifies as a heroic figure by committing her crime knowingly, rather than—like Oedipus—unwittingly, her deed thereby expressing "the unity of actuality and substance" (PhS: 284; PhG: 336), the purity of her ethical consciousness is underwritten by another still more fundamental qualification: her femininity in the form of the sister (PhS: 274; PhG: 325). It is more fundamental because it determines the basis on which she stakes her life, and at the same time restricts the awareness she has of her act as ethical. She may conform most completely to ethical consciousness, but whatever knowing is involved is not self-conscious. She has "the highest *intuitive* awareness of what is ethical" but "she does not attain to *consciousness* of it, or to the objective existence of it, because the law of the Family is an implicit, inner essence which is not exposed to the daylight of consciousness, but remains an inner feeling and the divine element that is exempt from an existence in the real world" (PhS: 274; PhG: 325–26). For Hegel, Antigone's knowing is feminine knowing. It is intuitive, nocturnal, an inner feeling, divinely inspired, exempt from reality. Should Antigone's act of public defiance seem for a moment to disrupt the principle of inactivity that must govern the organic meaning of her life, that moment will pass. The act is not conscious.

Deprived of the pleasures of motherhood by a destiny over which she exerts no control, Antigone's only compensation is that she can still confer life by honoring the dead, entombing the corpse of her brother, ensuring a proper burial in the name of her ill-fated family, the family who "weds the blood-relation to the bosom of the earth" and "thereby makes him a member of a community" (PhS: 271; PhG: 323).

In any case, whatever act she undertakes is always already defused, remaining as it does at the level of individuality and only passing into lasting significance through its relation to the universal. This particular act is already situated in relation to the totality. Even if she appears to subvert the principle dictated by her sex, trespassing on the realm of activity that is reserved for the men, in fact her act has never been self-initiated. The blood tie is what governs her public defiance of the king's law.[59] And the blood that runs through her veins is tainted by the unconscious incest that Oedipus committed when he married his mother—Antigone's mother. Irigaray says, in *Sexes and Genealogies*, "Hegel explains that the daughter who remains faithful to the law relating to her mother has to be cast out of the city, out of society" (SG: 1–2; SP: 14). Following the same line of thought in *Speculum* Irigaray says,

> Even if woman must die in the attempt, she will carry out her mission. Virgin? Her deed will be all the more exemplary. Condemned by the

king? She will have shown all the more clearly the contradictions in the system. As the ruler's unworthy anger shows. For if woman does not religiously, blindly, support the attributes of power of the king, judge, or warrior, that power may well decline, or prove useless, since the real issue is always men's competition for power. That said, the patriarchal regime could scarcely be expected to tolerate Antigone's loud assertions about the mother's "phallic" empire, the rights of blood, her defiance of the king's scepter and the penis of his heir! In patriarchy, the revival of relations between mother and daughter always creates conflict (SO: 118; SA: 147–48).

To the extent that her action breaks out of the principle that governs her sex, Antigone's individuality must be quelled, her action must be neutralized, her sex must be contained. Just as the "male testicle in the female remains enclosed within the ovary" so the audacity of Antigone's public transgression of Creon's edict calls for her enclosure within a cave. The body remains the site of this enclosure—the female body, the maternal body, the mother of both Oedipus and Antigone, the stigma from which Antigone could never have divorced herself no matter how heroic her acts, no matter how noble her character.

THE ETERNAL IRONY OF THE COMMUNITY

For Hegel the relation between family and state is both necessary and hierarchically arranged in terms of the relation between parts and whole. Similarly, the relation between the sexes is ordered according to the same schema, the female representing the family, and the male representing the state. According to the same structured series of oppositions that repeatedly emerge—female/male, night/day, inner/outer, natural/political—the family is the site of potentiality for the individual to develop into a fully fledged communal being. Male, of course, since the female is tied up with the family from the beginning. In a negative movement, the individual departs from his familial grounding in the organic life, supported by the mother, and moves on out into the public sphere, the realm in which his individuality acquires a higher, universal, communal significance. The family thus does its part for the whole community, by letting the individual go, by remaining eternally a site of possibility, by allowing the individual to realize the true potentiality that exists for him in the shape of the external world in its universal form.

It is tempting to read the relationship between, on the one hand, the part and the whole, and, on the other hand, potentiality and actuality, as relationships that fit snugly together, go neatly hand in hand with one another. It may appear that the human or communal is identified with the male ethic, and the divine or familial is identified with the female ethic, as if the balance of power were indisputable and straightforward. But Hegel warns against this. "Now, although human right has for its content and power the actual ethical substance that is conscious of itself, i.e., the entire nation, while the *divine* right and law has for its content and power the individual who is beyond the real world, yet he is not without power" (PhS: 271; PhG: 323). Hegel expands this judgment in paragraph 455, where he emphasizes the need to see the relation between the state and the family as a relation between the whole and its parts, and where he reflects upon the purpose of war. The "superior law" of the community, which is individuated in the form of government, allows "the Family to expand into its constituent members, and to give to each part an enduring being and a being-for-self on its own" (PhS: 272; PhG: 323–24). While allowing such developments, the powers of government cannot afford to let its individual members and local organizations forget the higher purpose of their existence, or the protection afforded them by the state as a whole. "Spirit is at the same time the power of the whole, which brings these parts together again into a negative unity, giving them the feeling of their lack of independence, and keeping them aware that they have their life only in the whole" (PhS: 272; PhG: 324). In a passage that is crucial for the present discussion Hegel comments upon the role of war, which is of course the occasion of Polynices' death:

> The Spirit of universal assembly and association is the simple and negative essence of those systems which tend to isolate themselves. In order not to let them become rooted and set in this isolation, thereby breaking up the whole and letting the [communal] spirit evaporate, government has from time to time to shake them to their core by war.[60] By this means the government upsets their established order, and violates their right to independence, while the individuals who, absorbed in their own way of life, break loose from the whole and strive after the inviolable independence and security of the person, are made to feel in the task laid on them their lord and master, death. Spirit, by thus throwing into the melting-pot the stable existence of these systems, checks their tendency to fall away from the ethical order, and to be submerged in a [merely] natural existence; and it preserves and raises conscious self into freedom and its own power. The negative essence

shows itself to be the real power of the community and the force of its self-preservation. The community therefore possesses the truth and the confirmation of its power in the essence of the Divine Law and in the realm of the nether world (PhS: 272–73; PhG: 324).

Hegel's reference to death as the real master in the master-slave relation is of particular interest to us given the way in which that relation serves as a paradigm for Beauvoir's attempt to configure the relation between male and female. By his reasoning in this passage Hegel establishes that war is conducted not solely for purposes of defense, nor merely for concerns extrinsic to the state's internal structure, such as its contingent relations with other states. It is also a necessary means of imposing internal civic order. War is the means by which the community safeguards the unity of its members, and protects its members from dissolving their communal bonds into individual and partial motives, which disregard the unity of the whole. When Hegel states that "the negative essence shows itself to be the real power of the community and the force of its self-preservation," he acknowledges that it is the individual that poses the most serious threat to the preservation of equilibrium in the state. In doing so, he echoes the sentiment of Creon's words when he declares that it would be better to be beaten by a man than a woman—for, as we saw, women are cast as guardians of the family, roles in which their action consists in representing the family in the form of the individual. Men, on the other hand, direct their activity toward the communal spirit of the whole, acting on behalf of the interests of the state. Sophocles writes:

> If men live decently it is because
> discipline saves their very lives for them.
> So I must guard the men who yield to order,
> not let myself be beaten by a woman.
> Better, if it must happen, that a man
> should overset me.
> I won't be called weaker than womankind
> (A: 674–80).[61]

In his fear of being beaten by a woman, Creon admits to the danger inherent in the individual's capacity to wreak havoc within the community.[62]

Hegel finds in the fear to which Creon gives expression "the everlasting irony [in the life] of the community" (PhS: 288; PhG: 340).[63] While there is no question that the law of the community, human order, and male rule remains "superior" in Hegel's eyes, the threat posed by the divine law is manifest in the individual's action on behalf of the family, and it is embodied in the female figure of Antigone. In response to this threat, government, says Hegel, deems it necessary to go to war. Confronted by the power of its women, and fearing for its safety, government goes so far as to put the (male) members of its community at risk before the (male) members of another. A strange turn of events indeed. How could such a reversal have taken place?

In acknowledging the threat of womankind as the impetus behind war, Hegel reverses the logic that one might have expected. Instead of simply castigating women in their role of helpless and powerless victims, the weaker sex in need of protection from the stronger sex—their male counterparts, who go off and fight wars on behalf of the community—Hegel suggests exactly the opposite. The exigency of war results from the government's need to prevent the members of its community from collapsing into divisive and self-interested conflicts that ignore their own wider interests as members who belong to a state. Hegel thereby acknowledges in a backhanded way the extent of the power of women, while nonetheless insisting that their motives do not transcend the unconscious, natural, familial bonds that circumscribe them from the start.

We are confronted with a scenario in which men go to war ostensibly for the protection of the whole state, but in fact in order to preempt the internal dissension that would break out were it not for the threat of war—which, if it is not entirely artificial and imaginary, is still a fabrication. This synthetic threat may pass itself off as having to do with outside invaders, but in fact has just as much to do with tensions internal to the city-state. To the extent that individuals believe in the external threat of war, they do indeed stand in need of protection from it. At the same time, however, it is their own individuality from which they are being protected. This is the myth that wards off the ridicule and laughter of the women, in the face of which the state could not hold up, were the threat not contained. Women, it seems, must be protected from themselves, otherwise they would forget to act in unison, as a whole. It is in their own best interests that they be confined to their proper spheres, and even if that means confining them to an underground cave, burying them alive, then so be it. What would happen, after all, should they be inadvertently let loose, given free rein, allowed to deliver their laughter in full-bodied

hilarity? What would happen if their ridicule of the state were openly con-
doned, acknowledged, conceded, recognized?

WOMAN'S PLACE IN THE DIALECTIC
OF NATURE AND HISTORY

In reading Sophocles' dramatization of tragic conflict within the body
politic, in what ways, if any, will Hegel have transcended, surpassed, or
redefined the relations between men and women as represented by the
oppositional mutuality he establishes between male and female body
parts? How far will Hegel's understanding of Sophocles' *Antigone* be governed by the views he espouses about sexual difference in the *Philosophy
of Nature*? To what extent will his interpretation of the drama he judges to
be "the most magnificent and satisfying work of art" (AFA, vol. 2: 1218)—
at least from the point of view of its resolution of the tragic "'pathos' of a
specific individual" (AFA, vol. 2: 1217)—rearticulate his preconception
that the female sex is essentially inactive, undeveloped, and undifferentiated, a mere imitation of its male counterpart, and an inadequate one at
that? This question can be recast in a way that addresses more directly the
question of sexual difference. Is Hegel guilty of that familiar fault that
seems to characterize so much of the tradition of Western philosophy,
whereby woman is equated with, confined to, conflated with nature?
Implicit in this question about woman's equation with nature is, of course,
another question, or rather another aspect of the same question, the question of whether, in her very equivalence to what we call natural, woman
is excluded from culture, which accordingly remains the privileged
domain of man.

By extending this train of thought to Irigaray, I want to ask a second
question, one that is still more pertinent to a debate that has dominated
feminist theory for some time now. Before passing on to Irigaray
however, let me note the following: To move straight to this second
question is to act as if there were no difference between, on the one
hand, posing a question about the role of nature in Irigaray's commentary
on Hegel's discussion of Antigone, and, on the other hand, questioning
the relation Hegel establishes between women and nature. By including
Irigaray within the compass of the first question, as if her inclusion in its
orbit were unproblematic, I am only delaying a confrontation that will
not tolerate being put off for very long, one whose return can be pre-
dicted with certainty: the question of sexual difference. This strategic
delay gives me the opportunity to note a further, and perhaps still more

intransigent—although not unrelated—difficulty in the procedure I have begun to employ.

A moment ago, in raising the question of women's relation to nature in Hegel, I spoke of an implied contrast between nature and culture. This contrasting pair of opposites is never very far from the surface of Hegel's meditation on Antigone, a meditation orchestrated by a series of now-familiar oppositions to which the distinction between nature and culture is no foreigner—singular and universal, family and state, human and divine, female and male, passive and active, night and day.[64] In fact, it is in opposing the forces of nature that the conflict between Antigone and Creon finds its ultimate resolution in justice according to Hegel. The wrong that Creon inflicts on Polynices by disallowing his burial consists in leaving him at the mercy of the power of nature, which makes him into a "mere thing" (PhS: 278; PhG: 329). Hegel says, "the wrong which can be inflicted on the individual in the ethical realm is simply this, that something merely *happens* to him" (PhS: 277–78; PhG: 329). Antigone's achievement is to make concrete the "enduring reality" of Polynices' blood, and thereby prove that he "still lives on in the household" (PhG: 277; PhS: 329). By burying Polynices against Creon's wishes, Antigone transforms "what has simply *happened*" into a "*work deliberately done*, in order that the mere being of the wrong, its ultimate form, may also be something *willed* and thus something agreeable" (PhS: 278; PhG: 330).

If, unlike Creon, Antigone remains circumscribed by the family, in another way her destiny is not so distant from Creon's. Even if they are in no position to realize it themselves, Antigone and Creon are united in their opposition against the power of nature. Both seek, and both fail, to overcome natural forces, albeit in different ways. Yet, at the same time, Hegel sees Antigone herself as no more than an instrument of nature, as the vessel through which Polynices' death is transformed from something merely natural into something willed, deliberate, human. Antigone, in Hegel's account, as a mere woman, is relegated to the realm of the merely natural. She does not transcend nature but merely submits to it, by playing out the role allotted to her by her sex, as guardian of the family. If, early in Hegel's reading, in the section on "The Ethical World: Human and Divine Law: Man and Woman," Antigone submits to nature, by the time we reach the end of the next section, "Ethical Action: Human and Divine Knowledge: Guilt and Destiny," we find Creon too submitting to nature. The overriding force of nature—the magnificence of which the chorus has sung (A: 332–75) and which Heidegger, among others, makes so central to his understanding of the play—is nowhere more apparent than in the closing pages of this section.[65] The full consequences of the destruction and vengeance that have been unleashed during the action of the play take their toll. Not only does Antigone's sex prove to be subject to natural powers, so too does Creon's. The whole community, to the extent that it is not free of nature's power, experiences an ethical crisis.[66] A community that sought to preserve itself by dishonoring a traitor finds itself the victim of hostile powers that "rise up" and destroy it (PhS: 287; PhG: 339). True to the movement of Hegelian philosophy, insofar as it privileges the whole, human law must engulf the "separatism" of the "independent families presided over by womankind" (PhS: 287–88; PhG: 340). The body politic tries to maintain itself by "consuming and absorbing"—the language of ingestion is not lost on Irigaray (SO: 220; SA: 274)—the wayward nature of woman. In its very attempt to digest, to assimilate, and in this process of incorporation, to outlaw, the "purely private pleasures and enjoyments" (PhS: 288; PhG: 340) that are embodied by women, the political community nonetheless finds itself subject to the body it wants to banish. It is brought down, laid to waste, demolished by that which it most wants to deny, but on which it discovers itself wholly dependent. The irony lies in the fact that it is precisely the same power through which woman makes a mockery of the state to which in the end the state must appeal. For all the "earnest wisdom" (PhS: 288; PhG: 340) that sets it apart from contingent individuality, from the personal and private life of the family, government nonetheless must find a way of appeasing the natural forces that rule women, the blood ties that have such an ancient heritage and such intransigent defenders as Antigone. For in the resources of the family, says Hegel, the state "finds its weapons" (PhG: 288; PhS: 341). To the extent that Antigone's position is consistently associated with the "power of youth," the state, in the figure of Creon, learns that it must foster the very individuality that it attempted to crush.[67] The livelihood of the state depends on that which threatens it, namely "raw and irresponsible youth" (PhS: 288; PhG: 341). Hegel expresses this contradiction in a sentence that could almost have been written by Foucault, when he says, "The community . . . can only maintain itself by suppressing this spirit of individualism, and, because it is an essential moment, all the same creates it and, moreover, creates it by its repressive attitude towards it as a hostile principle" (PhS: 288; PhG: 341).[68] The state confronts its failure in its attempt to suppress what it must revive—namely, the spirit of individualism. This is because it was nothing more than the physical prowess of Eteocles, with a measure of good luck thrown in, that determined the success of the state and the survival of the community. If the only thing standing between the survival of the state and its defeat is the strength of its soldiers and mere chance, then the state owes its existence to causes that are not purely human but rather inhuman, natural, and uncontrollable. Hegel says, "Because the existence of ethical life rests on strength and luck, the *decision is already made* that its downfall has come" (PhS: 289; PhG: 341). The fact that nature has played a part in the preservation of the state and in its ability to withstand a traitorous attack reveals its instability. In Hegel's words, "The germ of destruction inherent in the beautiful harmony and tranquil equilibrium of the ethical spirit itself" is revealed (PhS: 289; PhG: 342). For all its civilized government and culture, the *polis* is still subject to the hazardous and indiscriminate laws of nature, still answerable to the gods of the old order. The very performance of tragedies enacts the struggle between nature and culture, but however eloquently Sophocles can portray this conflict, neither he nor his audiences can eliminate the threat of nature. The natural laws of physical strength destroy any hope of the permanent peaceful coexistence of the two opposing moments of ethical consciousness. If the state insists on the sacrifice of bodily enjoyment to the good of the whole, the desires of the body prove finally to be irrepressible.

How, then, does Irigaray situate Hegel's celebration of Antigone, "that noblest of figures that ever appeared on earth?" (Hegel, 1955: 441). It is not by a direct challenge to Hegel, nor by attempting to overthrow his authority as an interpreter of Greek tragedy. She does not merely posit an alternative reading of the Antigone, nor mount a defense of the drama on the grounds that Hegel fails to appreciate the complexity of the play. Had she wanted simply to challenge his authority, she might have pointed to a wealth of detail that Hegel overlooked in his urgency to compress the various aspects of Sophocles' tragedy into a framework that may be fluid in some respects but is rigid in its overall movement, allowing him to underplay some features of the text at the expense of others—producing, for example, a unity in the figure of Antigone that is belied by the diverse motives she reveals in Sophocles' text.[69] But Irigaray resists a head-on confrontation with Hegel, accepting, in general terms, the reading of Sophocles' *Antigone* that Hegel advances. She works within his terms of reference, reproducing the structured oppositions that lead Antigone along the narrow and constricting passage that begins with her decision to perform the burial of her brother, and ends in her death. While she follows the same path as Hegel, Irigaray also makes ambiguous the borders that define this passage of confinement, casting it in an ironic light, bringing into question the hierarchy of the oppositions supporting it, reproducing them but adding a new dimension to them, giving them a new angle, reading the text with a new twist. She replicates the moves that Hegel produces, but at the same time she steps back from the scheme he endorses—acting the part of Hegel's Antigone, perhaps.

What are we to make of Irigaray's unearthing, uprooting, and transplanting the "eternal irony of the community" into another discourse? Upgrading a phrase that Hegel uses almost in passing, taking it up as the title of her commentary on Hegel in *Speculum*, Irigaray might be upbraided for celebrating, with Hegel, the status of women as marginal—which is indisputably how they appear in Hegel's text, despite the nobility he extols in the figure of Antigone. However much she disengages from his project or reverses his intentions, does she not also signal his authority?

Does Irigaray not incriminate herself as a party to Hegel's identification of women with nature, the unconscious, the indeterminate—dragging us down, with Antigone, into the nether world, entombing us with her, so that we too are destined to be walled up in her underground cave? In doing so does she not refuse to acknowledge women's proper existence beyond the nether regions, equating us with the body rather than the mind, with feeling rather than reason, with intuition rather than knowledge? Does she not risk holding us captive with Antigone, who only partakes in the public domain through her association with her brother? In short, does not Irigaray do women a disservice by reinscribing sexual difference, by embracing the time-honored distinctions between body and mind, passivity and activity, the natural and the political, the private and the public? Does she not thereby inscribe or mark, re-inscribe or re-mark, the female ethic as somehow less than, and answerable to, the politics of men? Perhaps I can best respond to these questions by returning to Irigaray's Hegelian Antigone and, along the way, recording the divergence between Irigaray's approach and a number of other contemporary attempts to grapple with the difficulties Hegel presents for feminism.

ANTIGONE'S EVASION

By burying her brother, Antigone not only acts in accordance with her familial duty, she knowingly defies the king's authority by ignoring Creon's injunction that no one is to bury Polynices because of his attack on Thebes. Antigone fulfills her responsibility to the law she represents, and she does so in full knowledge of the law she thereby violates—Creon's law, the man's law, the law of the state, the law according to the human conventions established by the ruler of the *polis*. She knows what she is doing. The fact that she is aware of Creon's law but does not recognize it makes her all the more ethical—and all the more guilty—in Hegel's eyes. According to Hegel, ethical consciousness and guilt go hand in hand. "The ethical consciousness is more complete, its guilt more inexcusable, if it knows *beforehand* the law and the power which it opposes, if it takes them to be violence and wrong, to be ethical merely by accident, and, like Antigone, knowingly commits the crime" (PhS: 284; PhG: 336).[70] Unlike Oedipus, who was unaware of transgressing the law of incest until after the fact, Antigone knows the law that she opposes from the start. "Oedipus," says Hegel in the *Aesthetics*, "has killed his father; he has married his mother and begotten children in this incestuous alliance; and yet he has been involved in these most evil crimes without either knowing or willing them" (AFA, vol. 2: 1214). Because Oedipus is unconscious of what he has done, "without having willed it" (ibid.), the tragedy of the collision in *Oedipus Rex* and *Oedipus Colonus* is of a more formal type than what Sophocles demonstrates in *Antigone*, or what Aeschylus develops in *The Seven Against Thebes*. In Hegel's view,

> The chief conflict treated most beautifully by Sophocles, with Aeschylus as his predecessor, is that between the state, i.e., ethical life in its *spiritual* universality, and the family, i.e., *natural* ethical life. These are the clearest powers that are presented in tragedy, because the full reality of ethical existence consists in harmony between these two spheres and in absence of discord between what an agent has actually to do in one and what he has to do in the other (AFA, vol. 2: 1213).

Antigone thus enacts, in the most determined way, the familial ethic dictated by her sex, and at the same time, by the very same token, by the very same act, she disrupts the meaning of the sacred law that she nevertheless follows to the letter. As Mills says, "Hegel misses what is most significant: Antigone must enter the political realm, the realm of second nature, in order to defy it on behalf of the family, the realm of first nature. In so doing Antigone transcends Hegel's analysis of the 'law of woman' as 'natural ethical life' and becomes a particular self" (Mills 1987: 27). For Knox too, "Antigone's defiance of the *polis* is a political as well as a religious action" (1983: 75).[71]

What prevents Hegel from seeing Antigone's act as a political intervention? In terms of the structure that pervades his thinking, the answer is simple: women and politics do not go together. Women, by nature, are not political beings. The political sphere—the human sphere—is by definition the realm of self-conscious action, but self-conscious ethics is not for Antigone. As a woman, she is confined to the realm of the family, governed by divine providence. If it is easy to discern the structure by which Antigone is excluded from the human, self-conscious life of the state, but representative of the divine, unconscious bonds of the family, it is much less simple to see how and why this structure came into play in the first place. What is clear is that Antigone epitomizes the tragic figure for Hegel, in that she knows full well that her action will be judged criminal by the human law. She does not consider that the authority of the human law is higher than that of the law that she recognizes—namely, the divine law—but she is prepared to accept the punishment of her denial. While refusing to acknowledge that, for her, the human law is superior to the divine law, at the same time she acknowledges that, for the rulers of the *polis*, the human law is superior. As a consequence of her refusal to compromise, she accepts the punishment meted out to her by the leader of a community which she does not recognize as the highest court of law. She is willing to die and yet she herself does not recognize Creon's word as final. For Hegel this means that she fails to attain the ethicality of her act.

Rather than launch prematurely into a feminist reclamation of the heroic nobility of Antigone's act by turning it into what Gellrich calls "an encomium of female rebellion and kinship bonds"; or, in the words of the same critic, by interpreting the play as a "defense of political authority and governmental controls of individualistic extremism" (Gellrich, 1988: 46), let me try to avoid both alternatives and remain for the moment within the question that has served as a guide thus far. If, in burying Polynices, Antigone acts in full awareness of the consequences of her action, in what sense does she remain unconscious of the ethical content of her act? How can she both know what she is doing and remain unconscious of its ethicality?

One critic responds to the problem of "Hegel's complex and contradictory discussion of the role of women" by declaring that the "ad hoc nature of his logic becomes nonsensical" (Barber, 1988: 5–28). Benjamin Barber reaches this conclusion because Hegel's logic "draws inferences from nature that nature cannot support," because "its technical portrait of anatomical nature is badly flawed," and "above all because it contradicts everything Hegel otherwise tells us about dialectic and the relations dialectic conceives between nature and spirit" (Barber, 1988: 17). While Barber's article has the merit of admitting the problematic status of women in Hegel's philosophy, his discussion is too vague to advance the debate much beyond an evasion of the problem, by means of blanket dismissals of Hegel's logic. His view is that Hegelian dialectics is supposed to supersede nature, and that its failure to transmute women's naturalness into spirit provides evidence of the inadequacy of Hegel's method in general.[72] Barber does not do justice to Hegel's concept of nature, which is no simple, fixed, or stable entity. As Seyla Benhabib observes, Hegel's political philosophy can be seen in terms of the constant transformation that nature undergoes:

> *Geist* which emerges from nature, transforms nature into a second world; this "second nature" comprises the human, historical world of tradition, institutions, laws, and practices (*objektiver Geist*), as well as the self-reflection of knowing and acting subjects upon objective spirit, which is embodied in works of art, religion, and philosophy (*absoluter Geist*) (Benhabib, 1991: 132).[73]

Benhabib goes on to ask if Hegel's concept of *Geist* permits him to "transcend the 'naturalistic' basis of gender conceptions in the modern period, such as to place the relation between the sexes in the social, symbolic, historical, and cultural world?" (Benhabib, 1991: 132). Benhabib challenges Hegel's portrayal of women without losing sight of the extent to which, in Hegel, nature is always available for reworking. No doubt the success of Benhabib's challenge to Hegel resides in part in her refusal to underestimate Hegel's sophistication. While I hope that the present discussion also manages to avoid underestimating Hegel, my interest in Hegel's relation to feminism has a different orientation, one that it gains from the recent development in feminist theory that casts doubt upon the sex/gender distinction that Benhabib's question to Hegel appears to take for granted.

We have already seen that while the distinction between sex and gender cannot simply be abandoned, the adequacy with which some feminists conceptualize it is currently being questioned by a growing body of feminist criticism—of which Laqueur's work, to which I referred near the beginning of this chapter, is in many ways a product, as he himself recognizes. By focusing our attention on Hegel's understanding of female anatomy as an inferior version of the male sex, Irigaray suggests that Hegel does not simply reduce women to biology. Rather, he reads the feminine ethic back into his account of the sexual body, reading the organism according to the circumscribed ethical action that has been allotted to women in advance of any inquiry into their bodily existence. According to Hegel, Antigone is not conscious of the ethicality of her act because she is answerable to the implicit, inner, divine realm of family kinship, the dark subcontinent of emotions, feelings, passions, pleasures, the undercurrents that the state seeks to subdue, its underbelly. These inner depths in the hidden recesses of the body will rise up and destroy those in power precisely because the latter assume absolute rights over the incomprehensible forces of the underworld. Inasmuch as humans presume themselves to be able to overcome any other force, they will experience their downfall. Antigone's death proves to be the occasion for such a catastrophe, unleashing the subterranean powers of a primeval world, governed by timeless laws that devour the ethical spirit from within.[74] Through her love for her brother, Antigone destroys Creon. Taking Haemon and Eurydice with her in death, she accomplishes the destruction of Creon's family. Her action not only leaves Creon's spirit broken, but brings the ethical spirit of his community down with him. Creon stands in sharp contrast to both Antigone and Haemon, neither of whom deviates from their intentions. Whereas Creon regards Haemon's vow to kill himself, if Antigone is punished by death, a mere threat, it is Creon's own declarations that prove to be empty, not his son's.

The youthful dedication of Antigone to her brother, and that of Haemon to Antigone make a mockery of Creon's firm belief in the iron rule of discipline. Creon underestimates the strength of family bonds and is made to pay for his error through the loss of his own family. Death and destruction prove to be his undoing. The death of his only son, and the subsequent death of his wife, show Creon that the powers invested in a political leader are not so great and all encompassing that they can overcome the ties that bind Antigone to Polynices, Haemon to Antigone, and Eurydice to Haemon. The clash between *physis* and *nomos*, the personal and the political, individual and universal, family and state, divine and human, between the old gods and the new, youth and age, inner and outer, implicit and explicit, unconscious and conscious, night and day, pleasure and discipline, and, finally, between female and male is brought to a head in a confrontation between nature and culture. How far is man's struggle against nature also his struggle against woman? How much is Hegel's treatment of Antigone a meditation on the need to tame her wild spirit, to calm her unruly disposition, or to balance the spontaneity of her actions by the neutralizing influence of the community?

Tragedy, for Hegel, results in the collapse of the ethical ideal into a world of warring forces in which nature triumphs over the tranquillity of the city, and in which conscious human action gives way to unconscious, unknowable, incalculable forces. In this respect, it is not Creon's action (which overreaches itself in its attempt at complete mastery) but Antigone's that allows the Hegelian dialectic to proceed. In raising the possibility that Hegel might be guilty of aligning women with nature, it is as if we—those of us who have witnessed repeatedly that alignment—knew in advance what it might mean to perform it. It is as if the very terms themselves, women as much as nature, were not, at least in some ways, up for question. If the terms "women" and "nature" are to a limited extent and in some moments in question for Hegel, they are all the more so for Irigaray. By naming the immensely problematic split between nature and culture as if I hoped to explain by it something in Hegel's treatment of women in his discussion of the figure Antigone, I undertake a difficult task. I am in danger of taking for granted the explanatory force of this fundamental pair of opposites—nature/culture—in referring women and men to either side of the divide, as if that simple referral could illuminate once and for all the content and meaning of the difference between the sexes—as if the first pair of opposites could serve as some kind of stable ground for the second, as if the concepts of nature and culture were easily defined, separated, segregated from one another, as if they were not interminably, irrevocably bound up with one another, as if their meaning were self-evident and their independence incontestable.

To say that Hegel simply decided to equate women with nature not only misconstrues the inextricability of nature and culture, it also misstates the problem by implicating him in women's history of subordination, as if it were his personal responsibility. Neither Hegel nor any other single individual can have simply decided, by fiat or with one blow, to circumscribe women in nature once and for all. How far Hegel can be held responsible for taking his place in a long tradition that has institutionalized women's inferiority over and over again, and in what ways this might be said to be true, are not questions that tolerate quick answers. Nevertheless it remains the case that Hegel's alignment of women with nature—however unstable both these categories are rendered at times in his thinking—is so far entrenched in a tradition that inscribes and reinscribes women as inferior that it is difficult to read his texts against the grain of that tradition. But that is precisely what Irigaray helps us to do. The questions Irigaray brings to Hegel and to the philosophical tradition for which he stands (and what better choice than Hegel—a thinker who attempted to think the history of philosophy and to incorporate it into his own system) fall outside the tradition that Hegel assumes. Precisely because Hegel's confrontation with the tradition of philosophy was so dazzlingly comprehensive, because he took the history of philosophy so seriously, we can learn from rereading Hegel—if we allow ourselves to do so without being blind to the prejudices of his time, nor to his conviction that he stood at the pinnacle of philosophical thought. Irigaray shows not only that Hegel assumes in advance that Antigone is prohibited from properly ethical action, but that he does so by reading her failure to act as if it were inscribed in her body. Being a woman is enough to disqualify her from doing anything that is not already circumscribed by her body—which Hegel reads as passive. Hegel sets up the female body as the ground of Antigone's inactivity, assuming that her apolitical nature stems from her anatomy. But his very description of female anatomy is already permeated by the principle that Antigone, as a woman whose sphere of ethical action is circumscribed by the family, cannot act. This assumption is brought under critical scrutiny by Irigaray, who sees Hegel's construction of the female body as a continuation of a long-established belief that is not so much a function of biology as it is the result of the conviction that femininity is by definition passive, inactive, and ineffectual. Irigaray shows how Hegel's comprehension of female anatomy is infused with the cultural assumptions and ethical imperatives that he prescribes for and imputes to women. By demonstrating the extent to which Hegel's account of women's "nature" is bound up—in what she calls (as we just saw) "an amazing vicious circle" (SO: 233; SA: 277)—with Hegel's cultural prescriptions for women, Irigaray destabilizes what Hegel takes to be the rock and foundation of his cultural prescription of women's roles, namely, the "natural" function of women's bodies.

Nancy Tuana demonstrates the implausibility of conceiving of the sex/gender divide in terms of such a rigid dichotomy, preferring to see the distinction as "interactionist" (Tuana, 1990: 86). She explains traditional accounts of sex and gender, and the need to overcome the metaphysical tendency to posit absolute binary oppositions, by referring to what she calls the "fabric metaphor" (Tuana, 1990: 83). The relation between sex and gender, as it is often understood, can be compared to the way in which the vertical threads of the warp cross and interweave with the horizontal threads of the woof in a piece of fabric. The vertical threads represent the genetic factors, while the horizontal strands represent the environmental factors that determine any given characteristic or trait. This model, according to Tuana, does not adequately conceptualize the interactive relation between genes and environment, or between sex and gender, insofar as it continues to conceive of the two contributing factors as inherently separable from one another. Tuana says that the fabric model

> does serve to emphasize the mutual intertwining of genes and environment, but models it in such a way that each remains a separate mechanism unaffected by the process of their intertwining. The threads of the warp are separate and discrete from those of the woof, a model which precludes the possibility of a dynamic interaction. . . . This relationship cannot be treated as additive. One cannot parse out the contributions of genes, of the developmental environment, of culture, etc., and sum the results. To do so restricts the range of relationships possible and leads one to adopt a simplistic nature/nurture dichotomous thinking (Tuana, 1990: 83–84).

Tuana makes clear the complexity of the relation between nature and nurture, and, by extension of her argument, the complexity of the relation between sex and gender. She emphasizes the importance of going beyond a merely "additive" understanding of the relationship between nature and nurture. While this model marks an advance over the traditional separation of nature from culture, it falls short of understanding the sense in which there is a *dynamic interaction* between nature and nurture to the extent that this image still retains the idea that nature is "a distinct and separate . . . *mechanism* from the *mechanism* of nurture" (Tuana, 1990: 81). What is needed, on Tuana's view are models of "dynamic interaction" (1990: 81), or "frameworks which enable us to see biological and cultural adaptation as interdependent" (1990: 84–85).

If one concedes that biology and culture have a mutually interactive relationship, then their impact on one another would extend to our ideas of what counts as biology and what counts as culture. What constitutes biology as a discipline is influenced by cultural developments, including technological advances, and what counts as culture is similarly affected by biological determinants—which in turn are comprised, in part, by cultural influences. If one understands the relation of gender to sex as genuinely inextricable, as Tuana suggests, it becomes more difficult than it might seem initially (perhaps even impossible) to separate those aspects of traits that are due to gender from those due to sex. The categories themselves impinge on one another, overlapping in ways that will always be shifting, contingent, and not entirely transparent to us. Another way of stating the same point in more general terms is that we always define the relationship between sex and gender from a cultural standpoint. The fact that we cannot help but identify culture and nature from within a given culture does not mean that culture is always the more influential of the pair, but rather that culture and nature are bound up with and implicated in one another in ways that are not reducible to quantitative analysis. The result is that feminine and masculine traits cannot be simply attributed either to sex or to gender. The very concepts of sex and gender not only resist easy or stable definitions, their instability also puts into question the applicability of the causal model of reasoning to which attributions of particular traits to sex or gender tend to appeal. To return to the fabric metaphor, neither set of threads is static and unchanging. Each is affected by the presence of the other in ways that make it impossible to ever completely isolate one from the other. It is not just that nature and culture interact at each node at which they intersect with one another, but that after each such interaction, what counts as culture and what counts as nature will themselves be changed by that interaction. Of course, even this way of conceptualizing the relation between culture and nature remains inadequate insofar as no node of interaction could be properly isolated from its context (Tuana, 1990: 81). What we call nature can never be definitively separated from what we call culture.

In his "Remarks on Antigone," Friedrich Hölderlin says: "It is a great resource of the secretly working soul that at the highest state of consciousness, it evades consciousness."[75] In this chapter I have been concerned with the meaning of that evasion, with its consequences for Hegel's Antigone as a woman, and with Irigaray's appropriation of and rethinking of these consequences in *Speculum*. Antigone's fate, her tragedy, is contained in the aspect of her existence that assigns her to her sex. The entire tragic consequences of her action are entailed by the simplicity with which she adheres to her female nature, by which she denies herself the only opportunity available to her to realize her full potential as a woman, namely motherhood. In this lies the nobility and greatness for which Hegel congratulates her, insisting nonetheless that she lacks the ethical spirit that would confirm her understanding of community. Having followed the rationale of Hegel's reading of the figure of Antigone we are in a better position to judge the wisdom of Irigaray's refiguring of Sophocles' Antigone as a call to create a new ethics of sexual difference.

It is necessary, according to Irigaray, to "renew the line of feminine genealogy" in order to render possible a new ethics of sexual difference (TD: 120–21). Such an ethics would no longer cast Antigone as an outlaw—an "anarchist" (TD: 103–104) whose actions amount merely to insubordination, or to a violation of the state's decree.[76] Rather, it would acknowledge the validity of her actions, which issue from a set of laws other than those represented by Creon: respect for the order of the cosmos, the terrestrial order, maternal genealogy, the engendering of life, respect for the gods and for the rights of burial (TD: 82–83, 84). Antigone's burial of Polynices is only seen as a disruption of the state by those who possess full citizenship, that is, by men who are able to exercise their civil and political rights.

In the same way that Creon paid no heed to the laws that governed Antigone's action, Irigaray thinks that contemporary civil codes continue to ignore the specific rights and duties of women. To the extent that this is true Irigaray characterizes the laws that organize society—which is still largely managed by men (TD: 85)—as uncivil.[77] These laws are regulated, according to Irigaray, by the fascination with the "infinite subtleties" involved in the "manufacture, commerce and possession of goods" (TD: 85). Among the incivilities permitted by a society governed by the commerce of goods, Irigaray includes the disregard of the natural environment—"of nature, the sun and the earth, water and air" (TD: 87); a lack of respect for the "genealogy of women," which consists in an idealization of virginity on the one hand, and the violence of incest and rape on the other hand (TD: 87–88); and the abuse of images of women in pornography and advertising (TD: 88).[78]

Because the civil and political rights that men enjoy are permeated with a lack of respect for women, Irigaray does not think that it is possible to effectively extend these civil rights to women, without revising our conception of what constitutes such rights. What is needed is a reconceptualization of the civic sphere, so that the supposedly neutral (but in fact masculine-biased) social and political rights and duties that have traditionally defined this sphere, are specified further, in terms of rights and duties pertaining to sexual difference. Practically, in addition to endorsing the civil rights of women (TD: 96), this entails making visible the unwritten, unacknowledged, secret laws that have characterized relations among women. (TD: 94). In other words, it is necessary to create a symbolic order for women that will not only subtend their civil rights, but will also call for a new conception of the civic realm, one that takes account of sexual identity. Unless some attempt is made to formulate the rights and duties specific to women, any success feminism has in securing equality for women will tend to confer privileges upon women as if they were token men. Moreover, it will tend to operate in line with the prejudices that structure the various hierarchies that patriarchy embraces. To the extent that feminist efforts to secure equality with men fail to systematically subject the patriarchal system to critique, they will perpetuate the exclusionary practices in which patriarchy engages—confirming, for example, its norms of racial discrimination and compulsory heterosexuality. The possibility of articulating an ethic of sexual difference is bound up with the need to insist on recognizing the validity of the specific rights and duties of specific groups distinct from their identity as defined by the social whole. Insofar as this project appeals to the importance of specifying multiple ways of existing in a society, it opens the way for an ethics that extends beyond sexual difference.

four IRIGARAY, HEIDEGGER, AND THE GREEKS

> If the couple of lovers cannot
> care for the place of love like
> a third term between them,
> then they will not remain lovers
> and they cannot give birth to
> lovers. Something gets solidi-
> fied in space-time with the loss
> of a vital intermediary milieu
> and of an accessible, loving,
> transcendental.
>
> —IRIGARAY

THE QUESTION OF BEING,
THE QUESTION OF SEXUAL DIFFERENCE

READERS OF *BEING AND TIME* WILL HAVE RECOGNIZED
more than a fleeting resemblance between the way in which Irigaray
articulates the question of sexual difference and the procedure that
Heidegger employs in posing the question of the meaning of Being. If the
task that preoccupied Heidegger in his time was the attempt to think the
ontological difference or the relation between Being and beings, for

Irigaray it is sexual difference, or the relation between men and women, that demands our most urgent attention.[1] She says, in the opening lines of *An Ethics of Sexual Difference,* "Sexual difference is one of the important questions of our age, if not in fact the burning issue. According to Heidegger, each age is preoccupied with one thing, and one alone. Sexual difference is probably that issue in our own age" (IR: 165; E: 13).[2] Just as Heidegger took the question of Being to be a question that was covered over or forgotten by the philosophical tradition, so Irigaray suggests that a question which still remains hidden, one which underlies our most basic ways of thinking and theorizing, is that of sexual difference.

For Heidegger, metaphysics, in the wake of Plato and Aristotle, concealed not only the meaning of the question of Being, but the question itself. Irigaray credits metaphysics with the impossibility of raising another question, sexual difference. According to Heidegger the forgetting of the question of Being means, among other things, that access to that question has to be regained. Making it possible to ask the question of the meaning of Being is the purpose of *Being and Time*, in which Heidegger undertakes a preparatory analysis in order to allow the significance of the question of Being to emerge from the various distortions to which metaphysical philosophers have systematically subjected it. Irigaray's *Speculum* can be seen as offering a similar preparatory analysis for the theme she will interrogate more directly in *An Ethics of Sexual Difference.* Irigaray sees *Speculum* as the beginning of her phenomenological analysis of female morphology, or of the imaginary body.[3] In the series of commentaries that constitute *Speculum,* which includes "The Eternal Irony of the Community," considered in detail in the previous chapter, Irigaray lays bare the exclusion of women and their concerns from the history of Western philosophy. Even when philosophers have attended to the themes of femaleness and femininity, as Hegel does, they have defined women as subordinate to and dependent on men, who remain the principal actors in the philosophical drama. In *Ethics*, written a decade after *Speculum*, Irigaray continues to demonstrate the systematic exclusion of femaleness from male texts, but she also concentrates her analysis in a more thematic way on the question of the meaning of sexual difference. In this chapter I want to draw some parallels between Irigaray's depiction of the failure of the philosophical tradition to address the place of woman, and Heidegger's project in *Being and Time* and in the Marburg lectures dating from the same period.[4] While this will necessitate the rehearsal of some of the developments in recent feminist history that I spelled out in detail in the first chapter, I think it is important to show precisely how

Irigaray's readings of the history of philosophy and her relations to contemporary feminism are filtered through her understanding of Heidegger. Not only will this establish the extent to which Heidegger's way of thinking provides a model for Irigaray, it will also serve to make the point that Irigaray's theoretical approach to sexual difference, far from being grounded in any version of essentialism, is thoroughly entrenched in the phenomenological insight that the body is always already a "lived body." That is, bodily experiences in the material world cannot be understood in abstraction from the contexts and meanings that inscribe experiences in all their particularity. If Heidegger's analyses of "being-in-the-world" (which I shall expand upon) laid the groundwork for an account of bodily experience that overcame Cartesian dualism, the phenomenological and post-phenomenological thinkers that followed in his footsteps—most notably Levinas, Maurice Merleau-Ponty, and Sartre—provided more detailed analyses. Irigaray expands these analyses to include sexual difference.

Heidegger embarks on what an introductory section-title of *Being and Time* calls "The Task of Destroying the History of Ontology" (BT: 41; SZ: 19). Like Derrida's "deconstruction," a term inspired by Heidegger's destruction of ontology, this task is intended to liberate thinking from the restrictions metaphysics imposes on it.[5] Heidegger says that he has no interest in "a vicious relativizing of ontological standpoints," and that "this destruction is just as far from having the *negative* sense of shaking off the ontological tradition" (BT: 44; SZ: 22). Far from negating or abandoning the history of philosophy, Heidegger wants to rethink that history with a view to the boundaries and structures that propelled its course, "to stake out the positive possibilities of that tradition, and this always means keeping it within its *limits*" (BT: 44; SZ: 23). Concretely, what constitutes these limits according to Heidegger is the failure to think the question of Being. He reads metaphysics as a series of gestures in which the question of Being is deflected along different avenues so that eventually the question itself becomes meaningless to philosophers, and irrelevant to philosophy. Irigaray's rereading of the history of philosophy is no more a total repudiation of male philosophers than Heidegger's destruction of ontology is an assault on Kant or Hegel. Rather, Irigaray seeks to expose the limits of philosophical systems that conceal or ignore the question of sexual difference, and at the same time to suggest how the inclusion of this question significantly reshapes philosophical discourse. Neither Heidegger nor Irigaray think it is possible to overcome Western meta-physical thinking in the sense of leaving it behind completely in order to move on to something new. We cannot simply shed the history of metaphysics without first understanding how it has shaped and informed our thinking. Insofar as metaphysics remains determinative of even the thinkers who try to break away from or rethink its most fundamental categories and assumptions, it is less a matter of divorcing oneself entirely from metaphysics, and more a matter of finding a new relation to it.

Heidegger exposes the absence of the question of Being in the history of metaphysics. For Heidegger, the question of the meaning of Being needed to be excavated from the trappings of metaphysical subjectivity. Having once been present, at the dawn of Western philosophy, under the pens of the likes of Heraclitus and Parmenides, and—in certain instances, Plato and Aristotle—the question of the meaning of Being lay in ruins, concealed by a metaphysical language that could only think in terms of beings. For Irigaray, the question of sexual difference appears at certain places in the texts of the Greeks, only to be submerged in the systems and treatises of the philosophers who "developed" the earliest philosophical insights that have come down to us in the Western tradition. The moments of extravagance Plato allowed himself, by allowing a woman to speak of love in the *Symposium*, for example (albeit, as we shall see, in reported speech and at two removes from reality), have been buried under a history of heterosexual texts by men. The excesses of the Pre-Socratics are largely forgotten, neutralized and tamed by the logical expertise of their descendants. Even the Greeks themselves, notably Aristotle, had a hand in systematizing the more extreme cosmological flights of fancy of the Pre-Socratics—as the poetic insights of Heraclitus and Parmenides, Thales, and Anaximander have come to be seen.

The juxtaposition of Heidegger's quest to ask anew the question of Being and Irigaray's attempt to highlight the question of sexual difference is of central importance for understanding Irigaray's work. I want to show how Irigaray both learns from Heidegger's questioning of Being, and also turns the question that she inherits from Heidegger in another direction. In Heidegger's case, the issue was how to think the relationship between beings in their Being, without reducing Being to beings. For Irigaray, the tendency of the Western tradition to reduce everything to the level of beings or things extends even to its representation of women. She attributes the tradition's departure from the Greek way of thinking to a preoccupation not merely with beings, but with a very specific type of human being: men. She says, "If, traditionally, in the role of mother, woman represents a sense of *place* for man, such a limit means that she becomes a *thing*, undergoing [occasional] changes from one historical period to another. She finds herself defined as a thing" (IR: 169; E: 17).

Heidegger's way of framing the question of Being not only serves as a constant source of reference for Irigaray in *An Ethics of Sexual Difference*; its impact can be discerned throughout Irigaray's work. Indeed, Irigaray could only have raised the question of sexual difference—at least in the terms that she formulates it—in a post-Heideggerian climate, just as Levinas claims that it would have been impossible to rethink alterity without presupposing Heidegger's radical questioning of the onto-theological tradition.[6] As we shall see in detail in the next chapter, this does not prevent Levinas from insisting upon the need to go beyond Heidegger. In the same way, while Irigaray inherits from Heidegger a way of thinking that allows her to rescue the question of sexual difference from the oblivion into which the philosophical tradition had cast it, she also takes her distance from Heidegger, arguing that he remains trapped within the very metaphysical system he seeks to put in question.[7] It would be a mistake to allow the polemical assertions about Heidegger in *L'oubli de l'air* to completely overshadow the profound influence his philosophy had on Irigaray's thinking as a whole.[8] Irigaray certainly takes a critical distance from Heidegger, but even the strategy she uses demonstrates the impact of Heidegger's approach, for she achieves her distance by incorporating Heidegger into the very tradition he sought to overcome—in much the same way that Heidegger incorporates (after learning from them) Hegel or Nietzsche into the history of Western metaphysics.

Heidegger had to search for a way of asking the question of Being such that it became intelligible—a task of immense difficulty, because the tradition had not only been unable to answer the question of Being, but had at the same time covered over any access to the thinking of Being that the Greeks may once have had. Heidegger thus challenges the tradition with a question that it finds unintelligible, since he brings into question the traditional relationship between a being (*seiend*) and Being (*Sein*), in which the latter, the substantive, is understood as the ground and principle of beings. Similarly, Irigaray finds herself confronted with the enormous barrier of resistance that feminist theory, which is as much a product of the history of philosophy as any other body of thought,[9] offers the discourse of sexual difference, in the name of defending equality. If metaphysics is incapable of comprehending the question of Being without bringing into question its fundamental concepts, contemporary feminism can no more accept Irigaray's questioning of sexual difference without reexamining some of its most basic principles. Just as, in Heidegger's time, the meaning of Being had to be adequately formulated, so the question of sexual difference remains obscure in our own era. In a world that would like to dismiss feminism as a weary set of tarnished slogans, and to return to the complacency of its time-honored patriarchal ways, the question of sexual difference has all but been occluded—and not merely for traditional reasons.

The question of sexual difference labors under a double burden of history. In the first place, the absence of women from the intellectual canon, from Plato through Hegel, prevented any serious questioning of sexual difference largely because it did not occur to the philosophers to raise the issue. In the second place, in the shorter history of the feminist movement, there is a deeply felt conviction that the project of raising the question of sexual difference must be suppressed. This recent development has more immediate effects on the project of raising the question of sexual difference than the long years of neglect by the male tradition of philosophy. It is not a case of feminism simply having omitted to ask the question of sexual difference. It is rather a matter of some feminists harboring beliefs about what feminism should be that amount to a vested interest in making sure the question does not get asked. Convinced that there is only one way of articulating feminist demands, that it consists of declaring equality as the major goal, and that it involves fostering the similarities between women and men to the exclusion of practically any other consideration, some feminists are far from open to posing sexual difference as an issue.

Reasons proffered for actively ignoring the question of sexual difference include its obviousness, its irrelevance, and its capability of distracting from the "real" issues of feminism. It is obvious, we are told, that sexual difference exists in some ways, and its very self-evidence means that it does not have to be thought about. The differences are either dismissed as trivial, or considered intractable: in either case, it is assumed, there is no need to think any further about them.[10] In fact the best thing for feminists to do is to make a concerted effort not to think about them, since they usually work in favor of men and against women. To think about them is not only to run the risk of exacerbating their significance, it is also to dwell on the misfortunes of history instead of getting on with the job of changing history. What we should be doing is minimizing the significance of these differences, not constantly reasserting them. Sexual difference is therefore seen as beside the point of feminism—the point being to gain equality through consideration of gender differences, apparently more pliable and capable of change. Like Heidegger's challenge to philosophy, Irigaray's insistence on the issue of sexual difference challenges the terms in which the feminist debate is played out, rendering obsolete the exclusive claims of equality over sexual difference, gender over sex, and anti-essentialism versus essentialism by breaking down these very oppositions.

In suggesting how the possibility of raising the question of sexual difference has been rendered unattainable, I am loosely following Heidegger's threefold enumeration of the presuppositions that foster "the belief that an inquiry into Being is unnecessary" (BT: 22; SZ: 2). Heidegger points out that Being is said to be "the most universal concept" (BT: 23; SZ: 4), but adds that its universality, or the fact that it is understood whenever we conceive of anything that is, does not mean we are clear about its meaning. On the contrary, its very inclusiveness or generality indicates the need for further elucidation. Second, Being is regarded as "indefinable," a characteristic that Heidegger thinks is "deduced from its supreme universality" (BT: 23; SZ: 4). Again, far from settling the question of the meaning of Being, Heidegger thinks that this "indefineability of Being . . . demands that we look that question in the face" (BT: 23; SZ: 4). Similarly, the fact that the concept of Being is held to be "self-evident" signals for Heidegger not that the question should be put to rest, but rather the need to "work out an adequate way of *formulating* it" (BT: 24; SZ: 4). In drawing upon Heidegger's elaboration of the difficulties involved not merely in answering the question of Being, but in articulating the question itself, I hope to illuminate Irigaray's questioning of sexual difference. My purpose is not to establish an exact symmetry between these questions, which would be misleading, but rather to show more generally how Heidegger's way of questioning is a source of inspiration for Irigaray.

What does it mean to raise anew the question of sexual difference? Or, perhaps, to raise the question as such for the first time?

In *Being and Time* Heidegger's ontological analysis takes the concrete form of posing the question of the meaning of Being through the vehicle of *Dasein*. Heidegger introduces the term *Da-sein* as a way of overcoming the assumptions of more traditional ontologies, exemplified in their "most extreme form" by Descartes (BT: 122; SZ: 89).[11] Cartesian dualism construes the subject as a "thing which thinks," and other objects in terms of their "corporeal nature" (M: 153 and 146). Subject and object are therefore conceived as two different types of substance, which Descartes characterized respectively as thought and extension. Given that he assumed the separation of an (initially at least) disembodied thinking subject from the material or physical world, Descartes posed the problem of providing a firm foundation for knowledge. Searching for a ground of certainty, he framed the relationship between an I that thinks and corporeal reality in terms of the epistemological problem: how do I know that these objects I seem to perceive really exist? Since sensory perceptions and dreams sometimes mislead (as when a straight stick submerged in water appears to bend, or when I believe I am somewhere other than in bed asleep), Descartes deemed them unreliable, and suspended all his beliefs until he found one that could not be doubted. Proceeding according to a method of doubt whereby he doubted even well-established beliefs, which on the surface seemed to him indisputable and self-evident, such as belief in the existence of God, Descartes sought indubitable truth.

> I have long had fixed in my mind the belief that an all-powerful God existed by whom I have been created such as I am. But how do I know that He has not brought it to pass that there is no earth, no heaven, no extended body, no magnitude, no place, and that nevertheless [I possess the perceptions of all these things and that] they seem to me to exist just exactly as I now see them? And, besides, as I sometimes imagine that others deceive themselves in the things which they think they know best, how do I know that I am not deceived every time that I add two and three, or count the sides of a square, or judge of things yet simpler, if anything simpler can be imagined? (M: 147).

Even when he recognizes that "I think therefore I am" (*cogito ergo sum*), Descartes can only verify the existence of other objects and other people after having established a legitimate basis for this thought. For Descartes, this consists in the ontological proof of God's existence.[12]

Heidegger's objection to this mode of inquiry is that it takes for granted that the primary orbit of philosophical questioning is epistemological, that is, it assumes that the most basic relation between the "I" and the world is one of knowledge. For Heidegger, on the contrary, the foundational mode of experience is not one of knowing, but one of existing in a context defined in terms of always already meaningful and significant relations. Heidegger says, "The phenomenon of Being-in [residing in, dwelling alongside] has for the most part been represented exclusively by a single exemplar—knowing the world. . . . Knowing is a mode of Dasein founded upon Being-in-the-world" (BT: 86–90; SZ: 59–62).

Rather than take as their point of departure the familiar activities that characterize day-to-day existence, philosophers have overlooked the mundane experiences of everyday life, in favor of ontological inquiries that abstract from the affairs of daily life.[13] By removing themselves from the plane of practical concerns that generally occupy us, philosophers have tended to assume the priority of theory over practice. In Heidegger's view, theory does not provide the most obvious point of entry into a philosophical inquiry precisely because, by adopting a theoretical point of view, philosophers have already put in abeyance the activities that dominate our normal existence. Because philosophy has not come to terms with the phenomenon that Heidegger calls "Being-in-the-world," it has exhibited a persistent bias toward the theoretical possibilities of *Dasein*, although these constitute only one approach among many. In Sartre's terms, philosophy adopts the exceptional mode of reflection as if it were the norm of behavior, instead of acknowledging that to reflect upon the world is to render thematic that which is usually taken for granted. Not only does the reflective level of thought take unquestioned precedence over the pre-reflective, but philosophy, in treating its subject of inquiry as pre-eminently theoretical, also neglects the fact that one can only adopt a reflective attitude on the basis of the pre-existent context that precedes the act of reflection.[14]

Rather than assume that the connection between a Cartesian subject and the physical world is problematic and tenuous, and that it needs to be established through proofs that have the certitude of mathematical deductions, Heidegger takes on the task of describing the relations *Dasein* has to the things that are "closest to us," taking as his clue "our everyday Being-in-the-world, which we also call our '*dealings*.' . . . The kind of dealing which is closest to us is . . . not a bare perceptual cognition, but rather that kind of concern which manipulates things and puts them to use; and this has its own kind of 'knowledge'" (BT: 95; SZ: 67). The kind of knowledge that Heidegger has in mind is nothing extraordinary, but rather the relations we have with things in the most commonplace occurrences and everyday activities, such as "writing, sewing, working, transportation, measurement" (BT: 97; SZ: 68).[15] The entities we encounter in such concern Heidegger calls "equipment," pointing out that in our involvement with equipment, we discover that "there 'is' no such thing as *an* equipment," but rather a "totality of equipment." It "always is *in terms of* [*aus*] its belonging to other equipment: ink-stand, pen, ink, paper, blotting pad, table, lamp, furniture, windows, doors, room" (BT: 97; SZ: 68). Heidegger emphasizes the extent to which we usually take for granted the relations that we have with the objects around us, the things that are just lying around, and which, far from being objects of philosophical reflection, precisely recede into the background in normal circumstances. It is in reference to his famous example of the hammer that Heidegger articulates the way in which tools perform their function most effectively, not by obtruding, but rather through their serviceability—in other words, just by being "ready-to-hand" and serving their proper function, without becoming a theme for investigation on their own terms.[16] Heidegger says,

> In dealings such as this, where something is put to our use, our concern subordinates itself to the "in-order-to" which is constitutive for the equipment we are employing at the time; the less we just stare at the hammer-Thing, and the more we seize hold of it and use it, the more primordial does our relationship to it become, and the more unveiledly is it encountered as that which it is—as equipment. The hammering itself uncovers the specific "manipulability" [*Handlichkeit*] of the hammer. The kind of Being which equipment possesses—in which it manifests itself in its own right—we call *readiness-to-hand* [*Zuhandenheit*] (BT: 98; SZ: 69).[17]

Central to Heidegger's analysis of Dasein's existence is his account of the "equipmental" relations that define individuals in the context of their day-to-day interaction with objects and others in contexts such as that of the workplace. It is in terms of the usefulness of things, their instrumentality, that Heidegger defines *Dasein*'s experiences. *Dasein* can therefore be understood as Being-there, as human being thrown into the world—defined by a network of significations that connect and situate individuals in terms of a variety of projects.

In our dealings with the world we tend to take for granted the reliability of the equipment that we use, and it is perhaps because of this tendency *not* to thematize our dependence upon equipment but rather just to use it that philosophers have overlooked its significance: it is too obvious to have become a theme for philosophical investigation. It is only when the referential context (see BT: 107–22; SZ: 77–88) in which the tasks assigned to various instruments or tools breaks down—when a pen runs out of ink, when we cannot find the tool we need, or when we try to open the door with the wrong key—that we become aware of the specific character of the equipmental world. As Heidegger puts it,

> to miss something in this way amounts to coming across something un-ready-to-hand. . . . It reveals itself as something just present-at-hand and no more. . . . The helpless way in which we stand before it is a deficient mode of concern, and as such it uncovers the Being-just-present-at-hand-and-no-more of something ready to hand (BT: 103; SZ: 73).

The phenomenon of Being-in-the-world allows Heidegger to approach *Dasein's* existence in terms of the general character of the experiences that constitute its life. The total structures of such familiar experiences are explored by Heidegger by means of what he calls "Existentiales" (BT: 70; SZ: 44), one of which is "Being-alongside" (BT: 80; SZ: 54).[18] Being-alongside the world is being absorbed in the world, caught up in or distracted by whatever activities demand our attention. It is through "concernful absorption" (BT: 101; SZ: 71) in the world that we encounter the things or objects that constitute a meaningful matrix of tasks and projects, and which Heidegger analyzes in terms of the instrumental relations we have with a "totality of equipment" characteristic of our particular "world" or immediate environment. In its turn, "Being-alongside" is founded, according to Heidegger, upon "Being-in" (BT: 81; SZ: 54). By this expression Heidegger means to distinguish between the way in which *Dasein* exists in the world, and the way in which water is "in" the glass (BT: 79; SZ: 54). The relationship between *Dasein* and its "world" is not analogous to the sense in which water is contained by a glass because *Dasein* "encounters" objects as signifying in a network of concerns that motivate and define its projects and tasks. This mode of existence is elaborated in terms of what Heidegger calls the equipmental world. The care Heidegger takes to distinguish the container-type relationship, which pertains to objects, from *Dasein's* mode of existence in its "concernful absorption" foreshadows, albeit faintly, the thematic attention Irigaray gives to the "place" that woman provides. In both cases, insufficient attention has been given to the spatial model assumed by philosophers in their attempt to represent the subject's relation to its surroundings (in Heidegger's case), or the male subject's relation to women as mother/provider/sustainer (in Irigaray's case).

Dasein is the only being that always already has Being as an issue for it (BT: 32; SZ: 12), or who lives within an understanding of Being, without having formulated explicitly the question of Being as such—or, as Heidegger puts it in his lectures on Nietzsche, the "question of the truth of Being" (1981: 10). As human beings we understand Being in the simplest events, whenever we see a particular object, or feel a certain way. For example, when we assert, "The sky *is* blue," or "I *am* merry" (BT: 23; SZ: 4), we understand Being in an average, vague sort of way, without, however, having posed Being as a question, that is, without turning our attention specifically to what we mean when we say Being in the form of "it is" or "I am." We thus already have access to Being—albeit in an imprecise and therefore incomplete way. "*But this vague and average understanding of Being is still a fact*" (BT: 25; SZ: 5), as Heidegger says, and as such it serves as his point of departure. Heidegger's task in *Being and Time* is to increase the precision of that average understanding by examining the concrete structures of our day-to-day existence. This he accomplishes through what he calls an existential analysis of *Dasein's* ways of Being-in-the-world, an analysis that will lead him to the meaning of Being: time.

Just as Heidegger takes as his point of departure the average understanding that *Dasein* has in its very way of Being, or in the manifold ways in which it comports itself in the world, so Irigaray uses an equally obvious, and equally unthematized, fact that underlies the very existence of feminism, that of sexual difference. The very existence of feminism is premised on sex differences but, although its initial impetus involved the recognition that women were treated differently from men in significant respects, these differences were seldom a matter of thought for feminism. They were assumed as given, rather than elaborated or made thematic. Not only were the differences rendered obvious by their sheer extensiveness, but also the solution—their eradication, or, at least, their obfuscation—was deemed obvious. Thus the meaning of sexual difference remained unthought by feminism, much like the meaning of Being was neglected by philosophy: to dwell on the question of difference seemed to be a distraction to the aims of feminism, just as Heidegger's questioning of Being seemed beside the point to a metaphysical tradition for the reasons already enumerated—its apparent universality, indefineability, and self-evidence (see BT: 22–23; SZ 2–4). Sexual difference, according to Irigaray, suffers the same fate at the hands of feminism (insofar as feminism uncritically embraces the ideal of equality) as the question of Being suffers, according to Heidegger, in the history of Western philosophy. Sexual difference is what gets passed over but remains an unstated ground of feminism; Being is what is forgotten yet allows beings to appear as they are.

Let me pause to clarify the status of my claim about sexual difference, and to situate it in terms of my overall argument. In referring to feminism's tendency to play down sexual differences, and in suggesting that this tendency is built into the very conception of feminism, at least in its earliest formulations, I do not mean to ignore the increasing body of work that has begun to acknowledge the importance of difference. In fact, the very emergence of these legitimate claims, alongside Irigaray's, that we need to "take the idea of sexual difference seriously" (Braidotti, 1991: 273), attest to the point I am making.[19] The necessity of the fairly recent call to thematize sexual difference comes from the consistent failure of feminism to have done so in its earlier manifestations.

From the first, feminism formulated its requests, desires, and demands in terms of propositions that followed the structure "we want to be like you. We want to enjoy the same privileges, have the same rights, the same opportunities, the same authority, and to be treated in every way as equal to you." Or, in MacKinnon's words "we're as good as you. Anything you can do, we can do."[20] So, written into the acknowledgment of the very inequity of women's situations in comparison to men's—socio-economically, in terms of careers, skills, and achievements—was a denial of women's differences from men. Whatever differences there were, it seemed clear, were deemed irrelevant, superfluous, and expendable, at least for the purposes of feminism. Sexual differences may have been put on the agenda for the first time, but only as a sign of what had to be changed, disposed of, suppressed. The aim of feminism was surely to eliminate the significance of these differences. Little thought was given to the fact that one cannot, however much good will there is, eliminate in one stroke what took over two thousand years to accomplish: a history in which women were essentially deprived of their full subjectivity. Like Levinas, Irigaray is wary of dispensing with subjectivity. Like Levinas too, her affirmation of subjectivity is neither a gesture that is innocent of the challenges that the discourse of post-modernity has posed to the subject, nor is it a simple reiteration of the traditional claims made in the name of subjectivity. The question of the subject is no simple one for Irigaray, particularly since some critics would identify her as belonging to that allegedly irresponsible clan of post-modernists accused of declaring the death of (among other things) the subject. When Irigaray warns against the "heedless destruction of subjectivity" (Jardine and Menke, 1991: 103) she does so because women seem to be in danger of losing what they have never been properly granted. More specifically (and this formulation of the problem not only returns us to Heidegger, but also recalls Marx), Irigaray's warning comes out of her awareness that women have been consistently and systematically objectified as mere things through systems of exchange. She asks, "Will the future emphasize the subject or the object? (c)ommunication and exchange of meaning or the ownership of possessions?" (Jardine and Menke, 1991: 103).[21] It is the preponderance of beings or objects that prompted Heidegger's questioning of the meaning of Being in an era dominated by technology, an era that carries with it irreversible environmental and social changes.[22] What lies behind Irigaray's question is the threatened occlusion of sexual difference and the irreversible neutralization and homogenization that accompany it. Why does the occlusion of sexual difference threaten?

Irigaray reads the history of Western philosophy as a history in which the question of sexual difference has been obliterated. What this means is not only that philosophers—from Plato to the present day—have failed to pose the question of sexual difference, but that the question itself has been buried, suppressed, or banished from the arena of legitimate philosophical consideration.[23] Irigaray's insistent emphasis on the question of sexual difference is not simply a matter of drawing attention to an area that happens as a matter of empirical fact to have been neglected. The question of sexual difference has been excluded from the philosophical orbit as a matter of principle. Irigaray's concern is to investigate the dynamics of this systematic relegation of sexual difference to the sidelines of philosophical discourse, and to ask why and how sexual difference has been written out of the history of philosophy.

Irigaray thinks that, far from being incidental to the history of philosophy, the failure of philosophers to raise the question of sexual difference is symptomatic of their sex. It did not occur to philosophers to ask about sexual difference until women, who had been excluded not only from philosophical learning but from all forms of public debate and theoretical discourse, began to draw attention to the fact that all the philosophers happened to be men. Only when their sex became an issue—if not for the (male) philosophers themselves, then for women, who were excluded from philosophy on the basis of their sex—could the possibility of raising the question of sexual difference at all emerge. Until then, philosophy did not even recognize the issue of sexual difference as a philosophical problem. Philosophy was so male-identified that its maleness was invisible to it.[24] Philosophy took itself to be neither male nor female. It assumed the neutrality of its discourse precisely because there was never any reason to suspect that its discourse could be other than what it was.

How are we to gain access to the question of sexual difference without the case already having been decided against it? First of all by reinterrogating the basis on which the question has been put out of play, and second, by demonstrating that insofar as feminism refuses to pose the question of sexual difference, it remains blind to its own male-dominated, phallocratic assumption that difference is inadmissible. To accomplish the first of these goals, Irigaray reinterprets the history of philosophy with a view to situating the question of sexual difference on the philosophical map, a task that Irigaray sees as both urgent and necessary. Such a task requires a redrawing of the whole philosophical map, bringing into question the entire edifice of Western philosophy. The question of sexual difference can only be properly posed by reconceptualizing philosophy from the ground up, from the Greeks on, from the point at which women first began to suffer exclusion—in other words, from the inception of philosophy. Thus Irigaray rereads the philosophers in the light of sexual difference. She points to the lacunae, the gaps, or, as she says, to "those *blanks* in discourse which recall the places of [woman's] exclusion" (SO: 142; SA: 176); to what gets passed over, evaded, missed—not necessarily intentionally or deliberately, but sometimes unwittingly or unconsciously.

Irigaray's excavation of the philosophical canon is accomplished through laying bare the persistent sexual bias that informs even the very possibility of the philosophical project as such. She shows that the very language of philosophy, the very terms in which it formulates its questions, militates against the meaningfulness of sexual difference. To write philosophy is to speak the voice of universality, to seek for ultimate causes behind appearances, to account for why "reality" is the way it is, to unify, synthesize, and systematize.[25] And yet it did not occur to these writers of philosophy to ask about sexual difference. It was not a question for them. After all, why should sexual difference have occurred to Aristotle?[26] His maleness was not an issue for him.

When, finally, in the eighteenth and nineteenth centuries, women began to demand the vote, access to education for all women, and entry into the professions, when women slowly began to speak for themselves, things began to change. For the first time, the difference between the sexes began to be a political issue—but only in a very limited way—in male terms, and under circumstances that were dictated according to very specific agendas. The issue was argued largely in terms that endorsed men's privileges as the only privileges worth attaining, thereby almost incidentally deflecting attention—both men's and women's—away from the expertise specific to women. The issue of sexual difference was on the table in one sense then—to the extent that women were finally calling attention to themselves collectively as having been unfairly treated. We were finally asking why we had been excluded, as women, from the privileges that men took for granted. But in formulating the problem in this way—notwithstanding the fact that this formulation was not merely expedient, but perhaps even necessary as the only way in which the problem could first be broached—certain prejudices were confirmed. For example, it was assumed that men's lives were better—that is, more worthy, valuable, and interesting than women's lives. And, no doubt, in some respects they were, but not in all. When women looked at their position vis-à-vis men's, they evaded, rather than confronting, the question of sexual difference. At the very moment that it depended on the recognition that there were significant differences between men and women that needed to be addressed, feminism assumed that, to change things for the better, women had to become more like men. Women would be granted the privileges that men already enjoyed, thereby confirming the superiority of men's lives over women's.

As feminism developed, it hit upon one particular formulation that proved to be extremely helpful in providing leverage for the granting of its demands, and at the same time extremely effective in burying still deeper the question of sexual difference (as if it could be put to rest once and for all, when in fact it had barely begun to be an issue). As we saw in chapter one, gender was construed as malleable, and sex as static and unchanging, a distinction according to which certain characteristics were repeatedly attributed to sex, while others were consistently said to be caused by gender identification. A series of transformative gestures, ranging from consciousness raising to political, legal, and economic reforms, acknowledged that even if femaleness remains incontestable, gender roles can, at least to some extent, be altered. Inasmuch as feminist gestures and processes appealed to the similarities of the sexes, not only was the question of sexual difference forgotten—it was deliberately obscured.

While every feminist is all too familiar with the strategic importance of emphasizing gender construction over sex determination, less obvious perhaps is the cost of allowing this mind set to settle the issue of sexual difference without ever having really investigated it. One of the by-products of putting all our considerable energies into transforming gender roles so that they are less confining—not only for women, but also for men—is the occlusion of sexual difference. Indeed, mainstream feminism could almost be characterized as an object-lesson in covering over sexual difference. Irigaray sees this as a sign of surrendering to the assumptions of the dominant discourse.

> When Freud maintains that the little girl discovers that compared with the little boy she has "no sex," and that this "castration" will completely arrest her in her auto-eroticism, that statement makes no sense, other than culturally. . . . But one must above all think that there is an older complicity between the values recognized in discourse, and those admitted for sexuality. . . . Thus, to place genitality in a privileged position amounts in fact to according a privileged status to the values which unify, but also the values of production, the values of "making," and with the aim of bringing to light "making"—in this case with the child. But all these determinations of a "good" sexuality are not an invention of Freud.

Here again, he describes and normalizes, in the name of psycho-analytic science, the effect of social and cultural norms in sexuality.

That the criteria for a valid sexuality should be the same as those of valid discourse, and that the criteria should be acceptable for a masculine sexuality should not be surprising. It is men who determined those criteria for evaluation. By contrast, women, left outside any active participation in the elaboration of socio-cultural norms, have been submitted to "laws" which owed nothing to them (WE: 65–66).[27]

As women, we are in a relation of exclusion from culture.[28] To understand that is not to capitulate to it. It is to take the first step toward genuinely transforming our relationship to culture. Once we take that step, and acknowledge our marginality, we have the possibility of rectifying our exclusion from culture. But as we do so, we need to ask ourselves at every turn what we are hoping to accomplish, and what models underlie our hopes. Are we hoping to make men marginal in the way that we have been, according to a model that would reverse the master-slave relation?[29] Or do we want to occupy more or less the same space as men, joining them in their technological mastery over nature? Or, again, do we want to bring into question both the idea of simply reversing the power-relationship, so that women can get revenge on men or become powerful at men's expense, and the idea that we all have to occupy more or less the same space, adopting the roles of mastery and dominance? Can we envisage a situation that neither involves the subjection of some group of individuals, nor the relentless exploitation of the world's resources for technological ends? Could there be a situation in which differences exist that do not imply hierarchy? Irigaray says that what interests her "is precisely sexual difference without hierarchy" (Baruch and Serrano, 1991: 154).

Irigaray's attempt to think difference in a nonhierarchical way is not limited to sexual relations. It extends to a rethinking of all our relations, not only with other people, but also with nature. The possibility of rethinking sexual difference cannot be separated from the need to rethink the model of domination that is implicit in the processes of production and exchange that are characteristic of our age. Technological mastery has become the norm, so much so that it is difficult to envisage any other basis for our relationships. In challenging the idea that sexual difference can only be thought hierarchically, Irigaray is at the same time questioning the model of technology that she sees as informing all our relationships.[30] Heidegger's influence is easily discernible in Irigaray's insistence that the very possibilities of thinking are circumscribed by the assumptions of a technological age.

Heidegger's appeal to the end of philosophy, which Derrideans echo when they declare the closure of metaphysics, has received wide press.[31] Less attention has been paid to the relation between the overcoming of metaphysics and Heidegger's emphasis on the predominantly technological character of the modern era. Technology both enables Heidegger to envisage a new relationship to the metaphysical tradition, and makes the rethinking of metaphysics urgent and necessary. Technology is not merely the culmination of metaphysics. As Schürmann says, for Heidegger, "Technology does not only complete metaphysics, it is itself a metaphysics, the metaphysics of our age" (1987: 184).

Heidegger wanted to indicate something that he knew was impossible to think as such, namely the Being of beings. Impossible, because Being can only be thought in relation to particular beings or objects, and never simply as pure Being. To think "pure and simple Being," in abstraction from concrete objects would amount to no more than positing quasi-Platonic idealities, free-floating forms. Heidegger's attempt to think Being was not, as it was for the tradition, a matter of searching for essences, grounds, principles, or reasons. It was a matter of trying to ask what it is that allows beings to be what they are and nothing else.

What allowed Heidegger to begin to articulate the conceptual distinction between a particular object or being and Being as such (even if Being could not in fact be divorced from beings, objects, or things) was the proliferation of a particular type of being, and a change in the relation between those beings and human beings. The beings in question were those beings that take center stage in the post-industrialist, capitalist epoch of the twentieth century, that is, the objects and things that govern our daily existence in a network of technological and, increasingly, technocratic systems. Whereas the equipmental and technological world that Heidegger characterized as a "machine economy" and which includes airplanes and radios (QCT: 135; H: 87), tanks and telecommunications equipment (1982b: 116), factories and mines (QCT: 15; VA: 19), was initially conceived of as a means of increasing the efficiency of tasks otherwise performed more laboriously and painstakingly by human beings, certain shifts have taken place so that it is no longer clear whether some of these instruments are there to help us, or whether we are there to help them. According to Heidegger, while it may once have seemed clear that human beings invent objects as tools to perform certain tasks, it is no longer so clear.[32] Instead, it now seems to be more a matter of our being controlled by objects, of our tasks being set for us by networks of communication that define us, and of our lives being coordinated according to schedules set by computers, cars, and systems of communication. There are both good and bad aspects to these technological innovations that have transformed our lives in such significant ways. But one aspect of this transformation that Heidegger does not neglect to point out is the need to rethink the fundamental relations between human beings and the objects that surround them in this increasingly sophisticated (at least in terms of technology) world in which we live. Questions that arise during his attempt to understand the relation between human beings as creators/producers and human beings as individuals who are answerable to the demands of technology include: what function does technology serve?[33] What purposes do the communication networks that organize our day-to-day activities have? What is the scope of science and technology, and what should be its scope?[34] These questions gain importance precisely because objects that formerly served circumscribed purposes now threaten to dictate those purposes themselves. "Technology," Heidegger says, "conceived in the broadest sense and in its manifold manifestations, is taken for the plan which man projects, the plan which finally compels man to decide whether he will become the servant of his plan or will remain its master" (PI: 34; ID: 98). What needs to be rethought then, is whether we properly understand the relation between ourselves and the objects we once thought of ourselves as creating, but which now seem to be producing and regulating us in certain ways. But it is not enough to remain caught up in a conception of technology that "reduces everything down to man," confirming "our own opinion that technology is of man's making alone." If we do so, "We fail to hear the claim of Being which speaks in the essence of technology" (PI: 34; ID: 98). Heidegger thinks that so long as we remain at the level of objects themselves in our questioning of them, we cannot hope to gain any new insights into our relations with them. He says, "Let us at long last stop conceiving technology as something purely technical, that is, in terms of man and machines. Let us listen to the claim placed in our age not only upon man, but also upon all beings, nature and history, with regard to their Being" (PI: 34; ID: 98). Heidegger continues this thought by referring to this claim of Being in terms of "the framework" (*Das Gestell*) (PI: 35; ID: 100), and *Ereignis*, the event of appropriation (PI: 36–41; ID: 100–106)—terms that resonate with Irigaray because of their spatial connotations. One way of articulating the direction in which Heidegger's thinking of technology points is in terms of his reflections on truth as *aletheia*. Technology may appear to be simply an issue of the human domination of nature, but this appearance conceals a more original truth about technology. As John Sallis describes it, Heidegger's analysis of the essence of technology is the

> opening in the wake of which nature comes to appear as a store of energy subject to human domination. It is that opening in which natural things show themselves as to be provoked to supply energy that can be accumulated, transformed, distributed, and in which human things show themselves as subject to planning and regulation. What is at issue in Heidegger's analysis of technology is that original issue to which his thought is already addressed from the beginning. It is that issue in which converge his efforts to radicalize Husserlian phenomenology and to renew Greek ontology, the issue of disclosedness, of original truth (1978: 54).

Heidegger's attempt to think the essence of technology arises out of a concern that Irigaray shares, one that is reflected in her call for a new ethics. Perhaps where this can be seen most clearly is at the end of her preface to *Sexes and Genealogies*, where she stipulates the need for "an ethics of the couple as an intermediary place between individuals, peoples, States. Wars break out when peoples move too far away from their natural possibilities, and when abstract energy builds up so much that it can no longer be controlled by subjects or reduced to one or more concrete responsibilities" (SG: 5; SP: 17–18). Irigaray's warning against the danger of unleashing forces over which we abdicate our control is not only reminiscent of Heidegger's reflections on technology. In advocating renewed attention to our responsibility for one another, and in alerting us to the dynamics of war, Irigaray rearticulates themes that Levinas develops at length.

SPACE/TIME

According to Irigaray we need to rethink the most fundamental assumptions of the Western tradition of philosophy if we are to gain access to the enigma of sexual difference. Foremost among these are space and time. "In order to live and think through [sexual] difference, we must reconsider the whole question of *space* and *time*" (IR: 166; E: 15). Here too Irigaray takes her lead from Heidegger, who, in his formulation of the question of Being, found it necessary to rearticulate the most basic philosophical categories, those that structure and inform the subject's experience of the world—namely, space and time.[35] Although most readers will more readily associate Heidegger's name with a rethinking of time, Heidegger makes it clear, especially in his later work, that such a reworking of temporality requires us to reconceptualize space as well. In 1962, in a retrospective glance at his earlier work, he explicitly states that he was mistaken to have construed space as derivative of time in *Being and Time*.[36] While space does not occupy the organizing role Heidegger gives to time in *Being and Time* and *Basic Problems of Phenomenology*, notions such as location and spatiality become increasingly significant in Heidegger's later work. In order to continue his questioning of the meaning of Being, Heidegger's terminology progressively develops, from the 1930s onward, to reflect his concern with site and place. Terms such as framing (*das Gestell*), occurring in Heidegger's work as early as 1936 in the essay "The Origin of the Work of Art," carry this resonance.[37] Reflecting upon the truth of the work of art, Heidegger describes the work of art as an event that can be understood in terms of a conflict between what he calls "world" and "earth." One example he uses is that of a Greek temple.

> Earth is that whence the arising brings back and shelters everything that arises without violation. In the things that arise, earth is present as the sheltering agent.
> The temple-work, standing there, opens up a world and at the same time sets this world back again on earth, which itself only thus emerges as native ground . . . (OWA: 42; H: 31–32).

The path of thought that Heidegger develops here in relation to the work of art is rich and complex, and cannot be followed in detail here without taking us too far afield.[38] I merely want to establish that Heidegger's vocabulary already shows his interest in place/space/location. In elaborating his use of the word "world" Heidegger appeals to the concept of space:

> By the opening up of a world, all things gain their lingering and hastening, their remoteness and nearness, their scope and limits. In a world's worlding is gathered that spaciousness out of which the protective grace of the gods is granted or withheld. Even this doom of the god remaining absent is a way in which world worlds.
> A work, by being a work, makes space for that spaciousness (OWA: 45; H: 34).

Heidegger develops the idea of the strife that occurs between world and earth with reference to the concepts of rift (*Riss*) and the idea of framework (*Ge-stell*). He says of the rift to which earth and world belong that it

> carries the opponents into the source of their unity by virtue of their common ground. It is a basic design, an outline sketch, that draws the basic features of the rise of the lighting of beings. This rift does not let the opponents break apart; it brings the opposition of measure and boundary into their common outline. . . . This composed rift is the fitting or joining of the shining of truth. What is here called figure, *Gestalt*, is always to be thought in terms of the particular placing (*Stellen*) and the framing or framework (*Ge-stell*) as which the work occurs when it sets itself up and sets itself forth (OWA: 63–64: H: 51–52).

This series of terms that Heidegger introduces in connection with the work of art is not an isolated foray into the question of place, but rather represents an ongoing concern. The terms *Ereignis* and *Ge-stell* come to play key roles in some of Heidegger's essays, while an abiding, if not central, concern with place is reflected in many other works, including "Building Dwelling Thinking."[39] In this lecture, which Heidegger first presented in 1951, he writes, "To say that mortals *are* is to say that *in dwelling* they persist through spaces by virtue of their stay among things and locations."[40]

Heidegger comes to see that the project of rethinking the commonly held assumptions about time involves a similar revision in our understanding of spatiality because the notions of space and time are integrally bound up with one another. He thus has recourse to the terminology "time-space," in order to indicate that one cannot be thought without the other.[41] In thinking space, we tend to build in unexamined temporal assumptions (space is usually thought in terms of the present), and in thinking time, we tend to use spatial metaphors (the linear representation of historical time works by analogy with spatial extension).[42] When Irigaray uses the locution "*l'espace-temps*," a term that is central to *Ethics*, she is no doubt assuming this genealogy.[43]

Derrida's essay "*Ousia* and *Grammē*," which investigates Heidegger's critique of the metaphysical tradition's understanding of temporality from Aristotle on, provides an analysis of the complex interrelation between space and time.[44] Indeed, Derrida's commentary on Aristotle's essay on time in *Physics* Book 4, chaps. 10–14 perhaps provides the model for Irigaray's interpretation of Aristotle's consideration of place. Given the unparalleled influence that Heidegger's philosophy has on Derrida, it is hardly surprising that there are echoes of Derrida in her work.[45] If the textual strategies Irigaray employs resemble Derrida's in many respects, however, Heidegger's way of interrogating Being also remains paradigmatic for her principal question, the question of sexual difference.

In his later texts, Heidegger can confront the question of Being in different ways, having established that, as beings who are involved in projects and engaged in the world, we already have preliminary access to the question in our everyday comportment toward things in our dealings with them. One of the most significant essays in which he reworks the question he had explored in a preparatory way in *Being and Time* is "The End of Philosophy and the Task of Thinking" (Heidegger, 1978). It is this essay that Irigaray takes as the starting point for her meditation on Heidegger, *L'oubli de l'air*. Heidegger reformulates the fundamental themes that he had elaborated under the heading *Being and Time*, suggesting that the title can be rewritten as "Opening and Presence (*Lichtung und Anwesenheit*)" (BW: 392; SD: 80).[46] The passage from "being and time" to "opening and presence" has a peculiar pertinence for Irigaray's claim that the project of raising the question of sexual difference involves a rethinking of space and time. What Heidegger indicates by the word "opening" or "clearing" (*Lichtung*) is a free space or region that allows things to appear as present and even as absent (see BW: 384; SD: 72).[47] He poses the question of "whether the opening, the free open, may not be that within which alone pure space and ecstatic time and everything present and absent in them have the place which gathers and protects everything" (BW: 385; SD: 73). Heidegger compares the sense in which the opening allows that which is present and absent to appear to the way in which a forest clearing allows a play between lightness and darkness, resonance and echo. When a forest is cleared of trees in one place, an opening is created that allows light in. Heidegger says, "Light can stream into the clearing, into its openness, and let brightness play with darkness in it. But light never first creates openness. Rather, light presupposes openness" (BW: 384; SD: 72). Heidegger's emphasis on the way in which light presupposes the opening is a restatement of the appearance of beings presupposing Being. Beings appear in time, and as such their existence is not limited to the present, but they also have a past and a future. However, it is the present alone in terms of which we habitually interpret beings. By exploring the question of Being through the multi-dimensional temporality of beings that present themselves as existing, Heidegger's thought not only prepares the way for his own reflections on opening and presence, but also for the questions Irigaray raises both in *L'oubli de l'air*, published in 1983, and in *Éthique de la différence sexuelle*, published a year later (but based upon a course she gave in 1982 at Erasmus University in Rotterdam).

If Irigaray's interrogation of the conditions under which objects appear follows Heidegger in significant respects, it subverts his intentions in other ways. Most obviously, her reflections take a direction that Heidegger's inquiries did not, a direction that is guided by the central question of her age, that of sexual difference. In particular, Irigaray's consideration of the philosophical tradition inverts one of Heidegger's most profound insights— namely, his interpretation of Being as time. Irigaray asks, what if being was first of all spatial? Her question is not so much a refusal of time as it is a way of making clear how Heidegger's questioning of temporality was also an exclusion of the place of woman. Even when, in his later work, Heidegger rehabilitates, to a certain extent, the existential importance of spatiality, even when he is no longer content (as one could argue he was in *Being and Time*) to see spatiality as derivative of a more primordial temporality—there is still no space or place for the question of woman. By bringing to bear the question of sexual difference on the very texts that Heidegger reads as fundamental for posing the question of being as time, Irigaray shows not only how time and space must be thought together, but also how philosophy and feminism must be thought together. It is no accident that while Heidegger claims a foundational role for Aristotle's essay on time, Irigaray makes what could be read as a strategic counter-claim in her assessment of Aristotle's treatment of place. Strategic because Irigaray is not making place foundational for space or space foundational for time—she is not doing transcendental philosophy, or even fundamental ontology—she is asking what it has meant, philosophically, to ground certain phenomena on others, who has been responsible for the heirarchies that are promulgated in such a process, and who has been excluded by such systematic thinking.

Both Aristotle's account of place and that of time are to be found in *Physics* Book 4, and both are introduced in the context of a discussion of motion or movement. Irigaray observes in the first section of *An Ethics of Sexual Difference*, which served as the introductory lecture to her course, that woman in the role of mother is "used as a kind of envelope by man in order to help him set limits to things. The *relationship between the envelope and things* represents one of the aporias, if not the aporia, of Aristotelianism and the philosophical systems which are derived from it" (IR: 169; E: 17). For Heidegger, on the other hand, Aristotle's treatise on time "essentially determined" "every subsequent account of time" (BT: 49; SZ: 26). In place of "a detailed Temporal Interpretation of the foundations of ancient ontology," Heidegger offers "an interpretation of Aristotle's essay on time, which may be chosen as providing a way of *discriminating* the basis and limitations of the ancient science of Being" (BT: 48; SZ: 26). He promises this interpretation in *Being and Time*, but it is not provided until the following year, in the lectures now published as *The Basic Problems of Phenomenology* (Heidegger, 1982a).

Heidegger reads Aristotle's essay on time as one of the principal sources in which the temporal nature of Being—and the way in which Being determines time—were obscured. Irigaray reads Aristotle's essay on place as one of the inaugural texts of the Western tradition to obscure the place of woman. In doing so, Irigaray's interpretation cuts two ways. With regard to Aristotle, she sees in his text the obliteration of sexual difference. Aristotle asks about the nature of place, about the ways in which bodies are contained in their places, about what can be said of places that contain growing things—but he neglects to ask about those bodies that serve as receptacles for human bodies (see ES: 36–40; E: 43–46). He forgets to ask, in this context, about the containers that women in their role as mothers have provided, about their limits as containers, or about their boundaries as mothers. With regard to Heidegger, Irigaray's reading of Aristotle's consideration of place as a writing out of the question of sexual difference is also a deliberate reordering of Heidegger's passage of thought from "being and time" to "opening and presence." Heidegger moves from the formulations of *Being and Time* to formulations that evoke place, a shift of emphasis that Irigaray takes up and applies to Heidegger's starting point. By reading Aristotle as one of the first in a philosophical tradition that covers over sexual difference, and Heidegger as one of the most recent in that tradition, Irigaray both incorporates Heidegger within the tradition from which she would escape, and acknowledges Heidegger's part in overcoming that tradition.

ARISTOTLE ON PLACE

For Irigaray the illusion that metaphysics has not managed to dispel since Aristotle is that woman has the status of a container, an external covering, a kind of envelope for man. This myth is retained, but still not thought through, in the image of the maternal mother as "*castrator*," for example (IR: 169; E: 17). Irigaray asks,

> Does the father replace the womb with the matrix of his language? But the exclusivity of his law refuses all representation to that first body,

that first home, that first love. These are sacrificed and provide matter
for an empire of language that so privileges the male sex as to confuse
it with the human race (SG: 14; SP: 26).

Because "her status as envelope and as thing(s) has not been
interpreted," the function she provides—enabling man to be what he is,
giving him a place, first in the form of a maternal body, and then in the
form of a domicile—remains both indispensable and unthought. Irigaray
says, "She remains inseparable from the work or act of man, notably
insofar as he defines her, and creates his own identity through her or,
correlatively through this determination of her being" (IR: 169; E: 17).
There is, however, a possibility of evading this determination by creating
an "interval" (IR: 169; E; 17) between the place that she has traditionally
been—"the place of the other" (IR: 169; E: 18)—and the place that she
would become if she had "a 'proper' place" (IR: 169; E: 18). Irigaray
develops the idea of the interval, that gap between what women have
always been and what they could become, in the third lecture of *Ethics*,
which she calls "The Place, the Interval," and where she provides a
commentary on Aristotle's treatment of place in *Physics* Book 4 chaps.
2–5. Before turning to this discussion, let's remind ourselves of the aporia
that Heidegger uncovers in Aristotle in order to establish more precisely
the relation between Heidegger's reading of Aristotle and the subsequent
metaphysical tradition, and Irigaray's rereading of the Aristotelian tradition
and her partial inclusion of Heidegger within it.

A good deal hangs on the Heideggerian claim that there is one
dominant way of interpreting time, that this interpretation gives priority
to the present, and that Aristotle is at least exemplary of this tendency, if
not somewhat responsible for it. Heidegger suggests that metaphysics
operates on the basis of an unwarranted presupposition in its attempts to
conceptualize the nature of time. The mistake that unites metaphysical
thinkers, notwithstanding the differences that mark their discussions of
time, is to believe that they could, in Derrida's words, "think time on the
basis of a being already silently predetermined in its relation to time" (OG:
47; OGe: 53). That silent pre-determination of Being is the understanding
of Being as presence. Heidegger argues that in asking about time,
metaphysics draws upon a conception of Being that is already permeated
by an unacknowledged privileging of the present.

At the heart of the Western philosophical tradition lies a confusion that
Heidegger claims to discover in the way in which metaphysics, from

Aristotle on, confronted the Being of time. The error consists of taking for granted a certain conception of Being that already interprets temporality in a very specific way and then asks about the nature of time in a way that assumes this unexamined notion of Being. According to Heidegger the tradition unquestioningly understands Being in the sense of present-at-hand (*Vorhanden*), so that in interrogating the nature of time, it takes for granted that the kind of being that time has is the kind of Being things have. It asks about the Being of time, having precluded any other answer than one that repeats the (inadequate) notion of Being that it assumed in the first place. The answer to the question "what is time?" is thereby built into the question. Heidegger says the Greeks "take time itself as one entity among other entities" (BT: 48; SZ: 26), and since the Greek interpretation of time remains determinative for the metaphysical tradition in Heidegger's view, time is still construed as one being among others. Insofar as the traditional understanding of Being already implicitly understands itself in a temporal way, the "truth" about time is decided in advance by metaphysics.

When metaphysics asks about the Being of time it is caught within a circle of its own making. The very formulation of the problem assumes the answer—namely, that time, like Being, must be understood in terms of the dominant temporal ecstasis, the present. Heidegger subscribes neither to the assumption that Being means essentially Being-present, nor to the idea that our understanding of time emanates primarily from our experience of the present. Both assumptions are regarded by him as characteristic of metaphysical thinking. There is a sense in which metaphysics neither has access to the nature of time outside of Being (which tends to be under-stood as Being-present) nor to the temporality of Being (which tends to be understood as present-Being). What is most real about time seems to be its being present, but this amounts to no more than asserting that the present is in being. In questioning the nature of time, metaphysics turns up the response that time is what is most real about time, or that what is most in being is the present. This not only leaves unexamined the temporal presuppositions that inform the metaphysical notion of Being, but also assumes a host of additional notions that accompany this metaphysical interpretation of Being. Existence, reality, truth, meaning, values—all the standards and concepts that metaphysics celebrates are implicated in an illusion that metaphysics sustains without unraveling, that it knows the truth about time and Being.

Heidegger claims that the traditional conception of time is contradictory. On the one hand, time has been conceptualized as essentially transitory, while, on the other hand, the tradition has assumed, without explicitly stating it, that time stands still. The contradiction has not been brought to light, according to Heidegger, because philosophers have consistently failed to see that the question of Being is integral to time—a failure that should not surprise us if we agree with Heidegger that "thinking the most difficult thought of philosophy, means thinking Being as Time" (1981: 20). The confusion has been allowed to persist because the tradition has implicitly appealed to the present as that which is most real about time.

Ordinarily, time is envisaged as ever-changing, in continuous flux, like the river into which, as Heraclitus said, no one can step twice. Nevertheless, in their attempt to articulate the truth about time, philosophers call upon the idea of time as modeled on an eternally present now. Insofar as they take for granted that the actual "now" is the only real time, philosophers tacitly presuppose that time stands still. By considering the past as a present which has passed away, and the future as a present which is yet to come, true time, they assume, must be present. If the past and the future only qualify as time by virtue of their respective status as quasi-presents (as presents which are "no longer" and "not yet"), what is it about the present that makes it real? The answer is that the present is understood as constant, identical with itself, a unity, unchanging. But this is precisely the opposite of the overt characterization of time as ever-changing. With this last thought we return to Aristotle's famous aporia, the classic paradox of time: time is what it is not. Time exists only in passing. As soon as you try to specify a given moment, it has already changed into another moment. As Hegel sees in his account of the negation of the "now," "this," and "here" in his discussion of sense-certainty, "now" is at the same time the most specific and the emptiest or most universal designation (PhS: 58–66; PhG: 79–89). Although everything about the passing of time suggests motion, philosophers, in order to think this essential transitoriness, have in fact depended upon the static idea of the eternal: time is still understood, as in Plato, to be a moving image of eternity. That is, its reality is understood as a present that stands still.

Aristotle raises the question of whether or not time can be said to exist. It is a question to which he never provides an explicit answer, but one which, insofar as Aristotle goes on to discuss time, is answered at least implicitly—for it must have some kind of existence to be under discussion at all. Heidegger claims that the kind of existence that Aristotle, and the tradition that follows him, assumes for time is Being as present-at-hand. In other words, time is assumed to be *a* being—a thing or object. This assumption is one that not only covers over the question of how time exists—its specific type of existence—but also the question of the meaning of Being. The temporality of Being is concealed along with the evasion of what kind of existence time has.

The existence or non-existence of place presents a similar problem for Aristotle. In his account of place, Aristotle begins his discussion by acknowledging that

> it is generally assumed that whatever exists, exists "somewhere," (that is to say, "in some place") in contrast to things which "are nowhere" because they are non-existent—so that the obvious answer to the question "where is the goat-stag or the sphinx?" is "nowhere" (P: Book 4, chap. 1. 208a).

Having noted the common opinion that whatever exists is assumed to be in some place, Aristotle goes on to enumerate several considerations that put into question this common assumption, and which lead him "to reopen the question that appeared to be closed and ask whether there is such a thing as 'place' at all" (P: Book 4, chap. 1. 209a).[48] The final two considerations consist of Zeno's dilemma and of the problem of how to assign a place to things that grow. Irigaray opens her discussion of Aristotle by commenting on these two considerations, amplifying Aristotle's list of examples to include women, who, because they do not have a place of their own, also appear to be non-existent. She quotes Aristotle, who recalls Zeno's dilemma: "If everything that exists, exists in some 'place,' then if the place itself exists it too must have a place to exist in, and so on *ad infinitum*" (ES: 34; E: 41).[49] "As for woman," says Irigaray, "she is place. Does she have to locate herself in bigger and bigger places?" (ES: 35; E: 41). But the place that woman is, Irigaray comments, has no origin, no place. All places have their place— except woman, who is the place of others, but who has no place for herself, who is deprived of a place of her own. "If she is to be able to contain, to envelop, she must her own envelope," says Irigaray (ES: 35; E: 42).

Aristotle understands by place that which we assign to what immediately surrounds a body, its "immediate envelope" (P: Book 4, chap. 2. 209a). In understanding place in this way, Aristotle means the "special and exclusive place" of an object, rather than a space that is "'common' to it and other things." (P: Book 4, chap. 2. 209a). The example he gives makes it clear that to assign a proper place to a particular body does not necessarily mean that the place can contain no other bodies. Rather, what we call the place of an object is its most immediate environment, rather than its environment in a more general sense. He explains that, properly speaking, the place that humans live is the earth, although in another sense their place could be said to be the universe, or the air. But since humans are in the universe because they are in the air "which air is in the universe," and they "are in the air because on the earth," Aristotle thinks of the earth as the proper place for humans, and not the universe or the air. The earth is more properly the place of humans because it is a more local and specific designation of where they live than the universe or the air.

Two observations are in order. First, Aristotle addresses the concept of place in the context of a discussion of local movement. At the beginning of his account of place, he says that the "primary and most general case of 'passage' or transitional change from 'this' to 'that' is the case of local change from this to that 'place'" (P: Book 4, chap. 4. 208a). Aristotle reiterates this consideration later on in his discussion when he says, "no speculations as to place would ever have arisen had there been no such thing as movement, or *change* of place" (P: Book 4, chap. 4. 211a). Second, Aristotle specifies "that the immediate or 'proper' place of a thing is neither smaller nor greater than the thing itself" (P: Book 4, chap. 4. 211a) and that it is that which "embraces" the thing. We have to assume, then, that when Aristotle specifies the "earth" as the proper place of humans, he means the particular part of the earth on which humans stand at a given time, and not the earth in general. He also stipulates that "the place where the thing is can be quitted by it, and is therefore separable from it" (P: Book 4, chap. 4. 211a), indicating that as humans move about the earth, so their places change or become different.

Aristotle provides a list of examples of things that can be "said to be 'in' another" (P: Book 4, chap. 3. 210a). A part is said to be in a whole, as a finger is included in a hand; the affairs of Greece lie in the king's hands, in the sense that in the king lies the efficient cause of the affairs of Greece. Aristotle concludes his list of examples with the statement: "But the primary sense, from which all these are derived, is that in which we say that thing is 'in' a vessel, or more generally 'in a place'" (210a). Conspicuously absent from his list of examples is any mention of woman as a vessel or container for the child. Aristotle goes on, "And here the question may arise whether a thing can be in itself or whether it must always be in something other than itself, if it be anywhere at all" (210a). So Irigaray's question is, if woman has no place other than herself, can she be anywhere at all?

Woman has no other. She herself has always been the other for others. She has been other than the one (the masculine subject in terms of which woman is always defined), she has given shape to the objects that constitute the master's life by providing an order to the things he consumes—creating boundaries, articulating limits, offering the elements for him to form a coherent whole.

Aristotle considers, and rejects, three possible ways of further identifying place before he settles on a fourth possibility. Place is neither "form (*morphe*)" nor "matter (*hyle*)" (two of the four Aristotelian causes), nor is it "internal dimensionality," nor yet "some kind of dimensional extension lying between the points of the containing surface" (P: Book 4, chap. 4. 211b). Aristotle concludes that place must be "the fourth of the alternatives, namely, the limiting surface of the body continent—the content being a material substance susceptible of movement by transference" (P: Book 4, chap. 4. 212a). However, what is of most interest to Irigaray is not so much his ultimate conclusions, nor even the evidence he amasses in order to arrive at them, but rather his rationale for rejecting the third option, which Irigaray quotes,

> But because the encircled content may be taken out and changed again and again, while the encircling continent remains unchanged—as when water passes out of a vessel—the imagination pictures a kind of dimensional entity left there, distinct from the body that has shifted away. But this is not so; for what really happens is that (instead of anything being *left*) some other body—it matters not what, so long as it is mobile and tangible—*succeeds* the vacating body without break and continuously (see ES: 48–49; E: 53).[50]

What about mucous, blood, milk, skin—how tangible are these? Are these imaginary "intervenients," or "dimensional entities"? Or are they too fluid, too amorphous, too much associated with the female body, the provider of places for others to count? What about the boundaries or limits of the human body—skin (see ES: 44–53; E: 49–57)—or the passage that the maternal body provides as the container for the child as it enters into the world, or the enveloping that the female body performs sexually, as the container "for the man" (ES: 41; E: 47)? What about the bodily fluids and mucous that surround both the act of birth and the sexual act (the act that is "the most divine act" [ES: 51; E: 55] according to Irigaray)? Why is mucous or the enveloping fluids that are secreted in the sexual act left out of Aristotle's account (ES: 44; E: 50)? Why does the protective membrane so vital to the process of birth, or the blood and milk that are essential to the fetus and the infant, have no place in a consideration of bodily places and transitions? Throughout her discussion of Aristotle's treatment of place,

Irigaray is concerned with the separation or suppression, within the Aristotelian tradition, of the relation between the first and the last place, the place provided by the mother, and the quest for the infinity of God (ES: 34–36, E: 41–43; ES: 49, E: 54; and ES: 50–54, E: 55–58). Or, to put the same question in another way, with how one passes from the physical to the metaphysical (see ES: 55, E: 59; and ES: 36, E: 42–43).

Woman has been treated as a provider of places for men, according to Irigaray, intra-uterine places, sexual places, but the *place* of these places that woman provides—and is—has itself remained unthought (see ES: 35–36; E: 42–43).[51] "The womb is never thought of as the primal place in which we become body" (SG: 16; SP: 28). The continuity between Heidegger's questioning of the meaning of Being, and Irigaray's meditation on woman as place should be apparent by now. Just as Being remains unthought but necessary to everything that is, or that without which beings would not be what they are, so women remain the condition for men to be what they are—namely, the philosophers, the inventors, the technicians, the scientists. Women provide the potential, the material requirements, the physical comforts, while men actualize these into the life of the mind, the spirit of adventure, the ability to abstract from the concrete.

Woman remains the unthought in relation to man, that which is taken for granted, that to which thought never attends as such, but on which it depends. Thought cannot take place without bodies to think. In this sense, the abstract is based upon the concrete. Irigaray says,

> It is crucial that we keep our bodies even as we bring them out of silence and servitude. Historically we are the guardians of the flesh. We should not give up that role, but identify it as our own, by inviting men not to make us into body for their benefit, not to make us into guarantees that their body exists. . . . Let us not forget, moreover, that we already have a history, that certain women, despite all the cultural obstacles, have made their mark upon history and all too often have been forgotten by us. . . . What this amounts to is that we need above all (though there's no one thing that has to be done before another) to discover our sexual identity, the specialness of our desires, of our autoeroticism, our narcissism, our heterosexuality, our homosexuality (SG: 19; SP 31–32).

Thinking can only occur if bodies are taken care of—if they are nourished, cleansed, renewed. This renewal, this rebirth—tasks which have typically been relegated to women—is a theme that Irigaray takes up both in her discussion of *eros* in Plato's *Symposium* to which we now turn, and in the essay on Levinas that concludes the collection *An Ethics of Sexual Difference*, "The Fecundity of the Caress," and which will be discussed in the next chapter. The figure of Diotima is also a religious, mythic, symbolic representative of those women who, "despite all the cultural obstacles," have "made their mark upon history."

DIOTIMA'S DISCOURSE ON EROS IN PLATO'S *SYMPOSIUM*

Irigaray finds in Greek philosophy two opposing but integrally related tendencies. The first moment is one that transcends the philosophical tradition inaugurated by the Greeks, and the second moment is one that founds the essential characteristics of that tradition. What this means is that there are certain insights present in the Pre-Socratic fragments, and in the philosophies of Plato and Aristotle, that are obscured, not only in the subsequent philosophical systems that owe so much to the Greeks, but also in the very same texts that contain these insights. Thus, in her reading of Socrates' speech in Plato's *Symposium*, a speech on the subject of love, in which Socrates describes his alleged encounter with Diotima and reports what she said to him, Irigaray portrays Plato, with Diotima as his mouthpiece, both as having caught sight of love as some kind of "*intermediary*" (SL: 32; E: 27) and as having lost sight of this intermediate character of love.[52]

The intermediary position that love occupies between a series of oppositions is the defining characteristic of love—according to Irigaray's reading of the words Plato puts in Diotima's mouth.[53] These are words that Diotima herself barely understands (SL: 37; E: 37). Her lack of understanding is entirely in keeping with the role that Irigaray carves out for her—for is she not one of those mythical figures of the spirit, an "angel" who mediates between immortality and mortality? Or if not Diotima herself, then certainly the subject of which Diotima speaks, Love. Irigaray says that angels

> circulate between God, who is the perfectly immobile act, man, who is enclosed within the horizons of his world of work, and woman, whose job it is to look after nature and procreation. . . . They cannot be reduced to philosophy, theology or morality and appear as the messengers of ethics evoked by art—sculpture, painting or music—though they can

only be discussed in terms of the gesture that represents them (E: 22–23; IR: 173–74).[54]

Love mediates between mortals and divinities. We learn this when Irigaray quotes Plato at length at the point in the *Symposium* at which he has Diotima, through the figure of Socrates, describe Love's parentage. The passage not only informs Irigaray's 1982 reading of Plato's *Symposium*; it is one to which Levinas also drew attention, first in 1947, with the publication of *Existence and Existents*, and again in 1961, in *Totality and Infinity*. Love then "is not immortal, nor yet mortal," says Plato (Plato, 1975: 203).[55] Love is a child of Plenty and of Poverty who has both his mother's and his father's characteristics. He is homeless (like his mother) yet "eager in invention and resourceful" (SL: 34; E: 29), the true son of Plenty, who was himself, Plato tells us, the son of Invention. He is neither resourceless nor wealthy, neither ignorant nor wise, but midway between the two.

Diotima's description of love as part human and part divine, as halfway between Poverty and Plenty, ignorance and wisdom, is also a source for Levinas' understanding of eros (see EE: 85, DE: 145; and TI: 114–15, TeI: 87). As we shall see in more detail in the following chapter, Levinas characterizes eros as essentially ambiguous, following Diotima's account of love both as a child of need and as the offspring of abundance. On the one hand, eros is situated on the plane of economic need—the lover lacks what it loves, and, according to a simple structure, in order to be satisfied, the object of love must be obtained. "Need," says Levinas, "a happy dependence, is capable of satisfaction, like a void, which gets filled" (TI: 115; TeI: 87). On the other hand, eros is situated on the plane of a desire that cannot in principle be satiated, a desire that transcends the structure of needs that can be met. Levinas expresses the difference between eros as need and eros as desire in these terms: "in need I can sink my teeth into the real and satisfy myself in assimilating the other; in Desire there is no sinking one's teeth into being, no satiety, but an uncharted future before me" (TI: 117; TeI: 89). Eros is both a bodily demand akin to enjoyment, and at the same time an excessive desire that goes beyond the measures of materiality or the economies of pleasure.[56]

Quoting Diotima's statement of the immortality of fecundity, Irigaray says that "Diotima's method miscarries here (*échoue la*)" (SL: 38; E: 33). She is referring to Diotima's statement that "The union of a man and woman is, in fact, a generation; this is a thing divine; in a living creature that is mortal, it is an element of immortality, this fecundity and generation" (SL: 37; E: 32).[57]

There are two noteworthy aspects of Irigaray's observation in addition to its Heideggerian resonances. The first concerns Irigaray's use of the image of midwifery for Diotima, and the second concerns the status of love as intermediary—a position that Irigaray, in contrast to Diotima, wants to preserve.

Irigaray's use of the verb "to miscarry" recalls the famous image of Socrates as a midwife, as one who delivers people of their thoughts, thoughts which sometimes turn out to be nothing but wind-eggs.[58] That Diotima is said to miscarry could be due to Diotima's inability to bring to fruition the thought that, on Irigaray's account, she had begun to bear. Or again, it could be due to the incompetence of the midwife, Socrates, the one who acts as a mediator on behalf of Diotima, carrying her words both to the other participants of Plato's dialogue, and to us, the readers of Irigaray's commentary on Plato. While we are not told explicitly that Socrates is to blame for Diotima's miscarriage, Irigaray indicates her suspicion of Socrates' competence as a midwife more than once. She reminds us that Diotima "*is not there, Socrates reports her views*. Perhaps he distorts them unwittingly and unknowingly" (SL: 38; E: 34, Irigaray's italics). Again, Irigaray registers surprise about what Diotima is alleged to have said, and introduces doubt about the adequacy of Socrates' translation of Diotima's ideas when she says, "Carnal procreation is suspended in favor of the engendering of beautiful and good things. Immortal things. That, surprisingly, is the view of Diotima. At least as translated through the words uttered by Socrates" (SL: 41; E: 37). Throughout her discussion of Socrates' rehearsal of Diotima's words, Irigaray refers neither to Plato, the author of the text, nor to Socrates, the speaker at this point of the dialogue, but rather to Diotima, whose presence in the text is assured only by Socrates' rendering of a previous conversation he claims to have had with her. Irigaray thus gives back to Diotima her own words. Even the title of Irigaray's discussion recoups for Diotima any losses she may have incurred in having her words appropriated by Plato, and represented by Socrates. But Irigaray is careful. She acknowledges that we have no way of knowing what it was that Diotima said (assuming that she existed as a historical figure and was not a purely mythical or fictive figure of Plato's own invention, serving as a vehicle of expression for his own ideas). Andrea Nye, in her reading of Irigaray's essay on Diotima, remarks that Irigaray does not "recognize Diotima's authority," that she "judges Diotima as a lapsed French feminist," that she "sees Diotima as capitulating to Platonic metaphysics," and that she "sees in Diotima's philosophy another attempt to deprive women of their specific sexual pleasure."[59] But Nye's critique of Irigaray, and her own corrective attempt to reclaim for Diotima her rightful due, is based on a reading that neglects the dramatic context of Plato's dialogue. Having acknowledged that some scholars contest the actual existence of Diotima, arguing that "Diotima is a fictional priestess invented by Plato to give divine authority to Socrates" (1989: 46), Nye then goes on to assume not only that Diotima existed but that Plato's intention was to produce an accurate representation of her.[60] In a dialogue whose dramatic sense depends as much on the identity of the interlocutors as it does on what they are saying to one another, we cannot afford to forget that Plato's presentation of Diotima's thought is filtered through Socrates' (perhaps faulty) memory. How far Diotima remains Plato's dramatic invention we cannot tell: we have no way of knowing what embellishments, elaborations, or "corrections" Plato may have made in recording Diotima's words, even supposing her to have existed.

Irigaray neither makes the mistake of taking for granted that Socrates represents Diotima faithfully, nor indeed does she assume that Plato is providing an accurate historical depiction of events that really happened. Rather, by pointing to Diotima's physical exclusion (imaginary or real) from the discussion of love that follows the banquet—a dinner at which no women are present in the flesh (as it were), for even the flute-girl is dismissed—Irigaray emphasizes the uncertainty that surrounds not only Diotima's words, but her very existence.[61] Thus she sets the scene for the theme that not only provides the site of interrogation for *An Ethics of Sexual Difference*, but which she interrogates throughout her work: how can we begin to ask about sexual difference, when the inclusion of women is not yet, still not, assured in discourse? When their very existence as women is in question, still a contested site? It is the question hovering over Diotima's existence that makes her such a provocative figure for Irigaray. It is no doubt true, as Nye observes, that Irigaray "works from a text glossed by many readings that shape and distort Diotima's teaching to make it compatible with Platonic dogma" (Nye, 1989: 47), but it is also true that Irigaray is only too aware of this. She is concerned with precisely the strength with which the "Platonic" interpretation of Diotima's speech has held fast throughout the years of translating the *Symposium*. Let's take a closer look at exactly what Irigaray means when she announces that Diotima's method miscarries, moving on to the second observation about this miscarriage.

Irigaray asks whether Diotima's separation of love into mortal and immortal, a division that deprives love of its intermediary position between the two, is "the founding act of the meta-physical?" (SL: 38; E: 33). By hyphenating the word "*méta-physique*" Irigaray implies that one part of its meaning has lined itself up with immortality, while the other part of its meaning—namely, the physical and material aspect—is relegated to the other side of the divide. From Plato's time on, theoretical questions or meta-level speculations have been associated with the spiritual dimension and the divine, while matter, bodies, and sensuality are identified with humans, with the mortality of life. In the closing lines of her essay, Irigaray refers again to the "risk" that Diotima's method gives way to a "meta-physics" (SL: 44; E: 39). In her reference to metaphysics she echoes Heidegger. Heidegger suggests that the Greeks understood—without formulating it thematically—something essential to thought, something that the tradition inspired by the Greeks themselves covered up. What, then, does it mean in this context for Irigaray to raise the question of sexual difference? It means that she wants it to be a question—to remain open, not to be decided either in favor of male or in favor of female. It means that she does not envision an androgynous society, where the bisexuality of both men and women makes them all but indistinguishable. It means that she sees the obliteration of sexual difference—before it has even begun to be recognized as an issue for so many individuals, as disastrous, not only for women, but, in a different way, for men too.

Characteristic of Irigaray's reading of the philosophers is a return to the elements—water, earth, fire, and air. It is not by chance that Irigaray, in her rehabilitation of the elements, draws on the very philosophers that figure so prominently in Heidegger's analysis of the history of Being—namely, the Pre-Socratics. If we must look to Heidegger as one of Irigaray's precursors in her return to the Pre-Socratics, we should consider too the influence of Nietzsche, before Heidegger, and Levinas, after. We should forget neither Nietzsche's invocation of the Greek world, which concerns Irigaray in *Marine Lover*, nor Levinas' appeal to the elemental, which, as we shall see in the next chapter, he associates with the feminine—a gesture that Irigaray reiterates without adhering to the role that the feminine plays for Levinas.

Irigaray's reconstruction of a feminine morphology appeals to the material elements and seeks to expose the limits to which the male philosophical tradition submitted when it lost interest in the sustaining elements of the Pre-Socratic world view. But this appeal is not one that makes her an easy target for essentialist critics. In returning to the elements as they figure in Pre-Socratic thought, far from naively reasserting the priority of matter over form, Irigaray seeks to challenge the schism between the two that philosophers after the Greeks began to assume—the schism that culminated in Descartes' mind and body dualism. In *L'oubli de l'air* Irigaray reads metaphysics as a "forgetting of the elements" (OA: 10) not only of the air, but also of fire and water: "Metaphysics is written neither in/on water, nor on/in the air, nor on/in fire" (OA: 10). Metaphysics, in its incessant search for grounds on which to construct its theories, is based on the solidity and density of the earth. Insofar as Heidegger did not leave behind the proclivity of metaphysics to gravitate toward terrestrial explanations, his thinking, Irigaray claims, remains metaphysical. He too forgets the air, which does not have the density of the earth. Still searching for solid ground, Heidegger is caught within the foundational discourse of metaphysics, according to Irigaray. Despite the fact that, at times, in his attempt to think the clearing as an opening, for example, he catches sight of the air, that which holds the place of place— he remains earth-bound.

In his attachment to the earth, in his forgetting of the air, Heidegger was unable to develop his understanding of the interrelation of space and time to the point of redeploying the traditional conception of time, in which time remains interior to the subject, and space is seen as exterior to it (IR: 167; E: 15; and OA: 89–96). Irigaray suggests a reversal of the metaphysical assumption that the subject is, first of all, a master of time. She asks whether this mastery is not based on an incorporation or appropriation of space, a materiality that first constitutes subjectivity (OA: 89). Her inclusion of Heidegger within the metaphysical tradition with which he sought to break is orchestrated by Irigaray's attempt to resuscitate the question of woman's place. Breathing new air into a tradition that all but strangled the question of what constitutes women's subjectivity, Irigaray rehabilitates the most basic philosophical concepts so that they become attuned to what metaphysics leaves unthought: sexual difference. In her questions as to what governs the rationale of woman's constant provision for others, as the giver of birth, as the mediator, as the homemaker, Irigaray reworks the traditional meanings not only of space and time, but also matter and form, potency and act. Her reworking of the Aristotelian causes is a recurrent theme in Irigaray's discussion of Nietzsche, particularly in "Veiled Lips," the second part of *Marine Lover*.

NIETZSCHE'S VEILS

In *Marine Lover* (1980)[62] the impact of Derrida's reading of Nietzsche in *Spurs* (1976) can be discerned in Irigaray's repeated reference to woman as a veil,[63] as masked, as acting a part,[64] as doubling herself,[65] as "posing as . . . " (ML: 83; AM: 89), as duplicitous, (ML: 116; AM: 124) as semblance, as "undecidable" (ML: 88; AM: 94) "without ever being either one or the other" (ML: 86; AM: 93), as always giving herself out as other than she is,[66] as concealing the truth.[67] On Derrida's reading of Nietzsche too, woman both dissimulates and is dissimulated by the metaphysical tradition, is both gift and deception:

> Either, at times, woman is woman because she gives, *because she gives herself*, while the man for his part takes, possesses, indeed takes possession. Or else, at other times, she is in fact *giving herself for*, is simulating, and consequently assuring the possessive mastery for her own self. The *for* which appears in the "to-give-oneself-for," whatever its value, whether it deceives by giving only an appearance of, or whether it actually introduces some destination, finality, or twisted calculation, some return, redemption, or gain, into the loss of proper-ty (*propre*), this *for* nonetheless continues to withhold the gift of a reserve (S: 108–10, 109–11).

Irigaray supplements Derrida's reading of woman as dissembling gift with another series of images of woman's function that recall her discussion of Aristotle on place. She reads woman as the envelope, the sheath, the cover-ing of man, as that which embraces without being held herself.[68] She "remains without limit or boundary" (ML: 115; AM: 123). As she reads woman as that which embraces others, as the mirror (ML: 86, 88; AM: 93, 94) and mimic (ML: 118; AM: 126) of others, she continues her critique of metaphysical biases toward the specular and the visual, toward solidity and density, toward unity and totality. Irigaray says, "Out of the storehouse of matter all forms are born. She brings them into the world, she 'produces.' From between her lips comes every new figure: a warm glowing heat comes out of that self-embrace and becomes 'visible'" (ML: 92; AM: 98). If woman is "without any qualities of [her] own" (ML: 82; AM: 88), if "her only value is an assumed value" (ML: 84; AM: 90), if "she is unable to talk about her-self as he does, without getting lost in the process" (ML: 83; AM: 90), if she "never signs up for the game without losing herself" (ML: 84; AM: 90), and if "she is always already othered but with no possible identification of her, or of the other" (ML: 86; AM: 93), this is not because she has no qualities or value, or skills, no place or identity of her own. It is rather because meta-physics does not speak her language. It is "because she herself is unable to present herself" (ML: 87; AM: 93), because "she is 'foreign' to the unit. And to the countable, to quantification" (ML: 86; AM: 92). Because she is not one, she therefore cannot be anything. Irigaray says, "She goes and comes, in herself and outside of herself, ceaselessly. According to at least four dimensions: from left to right, from right to left, from before after, from after before, the threshold of the inside to the outside of the body" (ML: 115; AM: 123). Again,

> She is not repeated, reproduced, in traditional representation because she is already split "within herself." And the economy in being cannot account for this. For fear of putting all its properties into question: one, simple, self-identical, grounded, derivable, etc. Even if that economy goes so far as to admit the work of repetition in presence, the splitting of the unit within itself remains foreign to it (ML: 89; AM: 95).

Woman cannot be presented, cannot be said, except in a voice that is not hers. "Femininity is part and parcel of the patriarchal order. Woman is hidden in the thought of the father" (ML: 96; AM: 102). To talk about woman is always to misrepresent her. It is always to talk about her from the point of view of the other, and therefore not to talk about her at all, but rather to talk about what she is for the other. "To talk about her— even supposing a woman could do it—to try and talk about her, comes down to exposing oneself to being only the object, the aim, of a repetition of negation, of denial" (ML: 84; AM: 90).

The difficulty of talking about woman in the language of patriarchy, the only language that we have available, is that she is necessarily represented as the other of man, and never as herself. She herself can only construe herself in the language she inherits from her fathers. She can only see herself as belonging to another. So, Irigaray says, "I had been taught that a woman who belonged to no one was nothing, and I laughed, I really laughed to hear such startling news. How surprising that I had believed them for so long" (ML: 5; AM: 11). Just as the language of patriarchy tends to talk in terms of possession and exchange, so the vocabulary of philosophy tends to talk in terms of universals, subsuming parts into wholes.

> My whole body is divided up into neatly ruled sections. Each of them allotted to one private owner or another. Which belongs to whom?— shrieks such and such a part. And no one replied, for each man claimed

the whole. If his whole comes to seem merely a part, then he no longer recognizes it and prefers to give up the whole so he can keep his dream safe and sound (ML: 4–5; AM: 11).

The problem of philosophy only being able to talk in the name of universality is a problem that Irigaray addresses in several contexts, her discussion of Levinas being one of the most notable. It is the impact of Levinas' philosophy to which I will turn, after a concluding summary of the relation between Heidegger's questioning of Being and Irigaray's questioning of sexual difference as I have characterized it in this chapter.

HEIDEGGER'S RELATION TO METAPHYSICS AND IRIGARAY'S RELATION TO FEMINISM

Heidegger's attempt to think Being in distinction from beings is paralleled by Irigaray's attempt to think women in distinction from the traditional representation of them as other than men, or as not-men. Just as Heidegger conceives of Western metaphysics as having subsumed Being under certain categories of beings, from which Being henceforth became apparently inseparable, so Irigaray points to the pervasive tendency in Western philosophy to subsume women under categories that devolve from their lack of maleness. To the extent that women's differences from men are only seen as signaling their inferiority to men, feminism's only hope of addressing the problem is to encourage women to identify themselves with masculinity, shedding as many signs of their femininity as possible.

In Heidegger's reading of the history of philosophy, once Being is reduced to a specific type of beings, namely those that are present-at-hand, the assimilation of Being to beings appears to be natural; moreover existence, understood in terms of presence-at-hand, embodies values to which philosophers appeal as if they were self-evident standards of truth by which to gauge reality—standards such as presence, validity, clarity, and permanence. For Heidegger to question the priority of beings over Being, then, is tantamount to challenging the very foundations of philosophy. Similarly, in doubting the adequacy of feminist analyses based on the assumption that women need to eliminate the differences between themselves and men, Irigaray throws into question the underlying presupposition that if women's differences from men were always registered as a lack the only solution could be to make good that lack. Irigaray's solution is to reconceptualize the terms of the problem by refusing to think difference merely privatively, and insisting on the positive significance of women's differences from men. Sexual difference is no longer to be construed in terms of women's deviance from the male norm, but rather as original difference. Irigaray thinks that one of the root causes of the failure to positively conceptualize the feminine gender is a more general refusal to think otherness apart from the same, or difference apart from the totality. She says,

> If the female gender does make a demand, all too often it is based upon a claim for equal rights and this risks ending in the destruction of gender. . . . But any operation is an error if the self is equal to *one* and not to *two*, if it comes down to *sameness* and a split in sameness and ignores the other as other (SG: 115; SP: 130).

In thinking the "other as other" Irigaray is influenced above all by Levinas' conception of radical alterity. Before examining this conception of the other as other, let me pause to observe that Irigaray's emphasis on the need to establish "a new *ethics* of sexuality" (SG: 3; SP: 15), her belief that "Sexual difference represents one of the great hopes for the future" (SG: vi: SP: 8), and her conviction that "If we are to remain alive and regenerate ourselves as living beings, we need sexual difference" (SG: 107: SP: 121), do not prevent her from endorsing the struggles traditionally undertaken in the name of feminism (see JTN: 11; JT: 11). It "does not mean that women should be paid less. It does mean that salaries and social recognition have to be negotiated on the basis of identity—not equality" (SG: vi: SP: 8). Just as Freud overlooks "the fact that the female sex might possibly have its own 'specificity'" (TS: 69: CS: 68), so too a feminism that construes itself strictly in terms of equality neglects, in Irigaray's view, the fundamental need to establish sexual difference "on the level of the *subject*" (SG: 107: SP: 121).

> Claims that men, races, sexes, are equal in point of fact signal a disdain or a denial for real phenomena and give rise to an imperialism that is even more pernicious than those that retain traces of difference. Today it is all too clear that there is no equality of wealth, and claims of equal rights to culture have blown up in our faces (SG: vi: SP: 7–8).

Claims for equality do not go far enough precisely insofar as they fail to take account of the differences between the sexes, races, and classes they are called upon to equalize. Irigaray thinks that we have not understood sexual difference as long as we try to eradicate it by reducing "*all others to the economy of the Same*" (TS: 74: CS: 72), or to take it up as "*the otherness of sameness*" (TS: 152: CS: 148). She advocates that what is needed rather is "a 'radical' evolution in our way of conceptualizing and managing the political realm" (TS: 127: CS: 125), one in which, as the title of the lead essay in *Sexes and Genealogies* has it, "Each Sex Must Have Its Own Rights" (SG: 1–5; SP: 13–18).

five LEVINAS AND THE QUESTION OF THE OTHER

Only a subject that eats can be for-the-other.

—LEVINAS

The Desire that is the independence of the separated being and its transcendence, is accomplished —not in being satisfied and in acknowledging that it was a need, but in transcending itself, in engendering Desire.

—LEVINAS

The metaphysical event of transcendence—the welcome of the Other, hospitality— Desire and language—is not accomplished as love. But the transcendence of discourse is bound to love. We shall show how in love transcendence goes both further and less far than language.

—LEVINAS

They love each other like the bodies that they are.

—IRIGARAY

They give themselves to each other and abandon what has already been created.

—IRIGARAY

Like sculptors who are going to introduce themselves, entrust themselves to one another for a new delivery into the world.

—IRIGARAY

. . . she also revives herself in the warmth and does not simply receive it from the other.

—IRIGARAY

THE IMPOSSIBILITY OF BEING OTHER

IN THE LAST CHAPTER I DEVELOPED AN ANALOGY BETWEEN Heidegger's analysis of the Western tradition of philosophy as the history of the oblivion of Being and Irigaray's questioning of sexual difference. One of my aims was to demonstrate that just as Heidegger found it necessary to regain access to the question of Being in the wake of a series of metaphysical systems that had all but rendered it meaningless, so

Irigaray must establish a way of posing the question of sexual difference anew. For woman "mimes so well what is asked of her" that she "has forgotten . . . her own sex" (TS: 152; CS: 148). What is needed, then, "is a discourse in which sexuality itself is at stake so that what has been serving as a condition of possibility of philosophical discourse, of rationality in general, can make itself heard" (TS: 168; CS: 163). Irigaray's task then is to put the issue of sexual difference on a new footing, so that the case is not always already decided against it by the discourse of equal rights—that is, so that women's differences from men do not automatically signify inferiority. Sexual difference needs rethinking so that it is not a question of retaining the masculine ideal as the standard in terms of which women are measured—whether as similar to, or different from that assumed ideal. In either case, women are referred back to the same economy, an economy that Irigaray seeks to put into question:

> Her sex is heterogeneous to the whole economy of representation, but it is capable of interpreting that economy precisely because it has remained "outside." Because it does not postulate oneness, or sameness, or reproduction, or even representation. Because it remains somewhere else than in that general repetition where it is taken up only as the *otherness of sameness* (TS: 151–52; CS: 148).

While in one sense—by virtue of her exclusion from it—woman is already "outside" representation, in another sense, her exclusion does not automatically provide her with the resources to interpret it from another standpoint. Reinterpretations of the place that woman is (such as Irigaray presents in *An Ethics of Sexual Difference*) have to be worked at, produced, and crafted. As Irigaray says, "There is no simple manageable way to leap to the outside of phallogocentrism, *nor any way to situate oneself there, that would result from the simple fact of being a woman*" (TS: 162; CS: 157).

Many of the conflicting misreadings to which Irigaray's work has given rise stem from a failure to attend to the complexity of the question she raises about sexual difference. In affirming sexual difference, Irigaray speaks out of the need for women to become other than we are in more ways than one. Most obviously, women have been seen as, and we have seen ourselves as, other than men insofar as men traditionally have been privileged by the balance of power between the sexes. This masculine privilege has structured the very ways in which we make sense of our lives, informing language and structuring the social, economic, religious, and political systems that this privilege has helped to erect. Like Beauvoir (and many other feminists), Irigaray construes the fact that women have been systematically cast as the other of men as a major problem, but unlike Beauvoir, Irigaray does not think that the solution lies in eradicating the differences between women and men so far as is possible. Nor does she advocate that women should emphasize their differences from men simply for the sake of being different: to identify dominant masculine traits and then to embrace the opposites of these wherever possible would be pointless. Nothing fundamental would change: women would still be responding to masculine privileges, they would still be defining themselves in terms of previously established and unquestioned masculine ideals, but instead of striving to appropriate these for themselves, they would merely be reacting against them. The question for Irigaray is neither how women can become similar to men, nor merely how women can become different from men. Insofar as these two questions simply reverse one another, neither challenges the presumed authority of the masculine ideal. Each position simply reestablishes it as an ideal, whether by measuring women up against it to see how similar the sexes can become, or how different they can become. Irigaray writes of woman, "She therefore needs her own linguistic, religious and political values. She needs to be situated and valued, to be *she* in relation to her self" (EP: 3). This is not a call for women to specify their differences from men, but rather "to become women" (JTN: 85; JT: 106) on their own terms, and not in comparison to men. In order to do so, says Irigaray, "she must go through a complex and painful process, a real conversion to the female gender" (JTN: 21; JT: 24). Such a task is not merely a matter of disentangling and retrieving from the tradition the positive ways in which women have identified themselves as women, and discarding the negative images. A more radical approach is required:[1] it is a question of creating new models and images for women that do not succumb to the constraints of patriarchal discourse in which women can only represent themselves through "the loss of [their] sexed subjective identity" and the adoption of "what they believe to be a neutral position" (JTN: 21; JT: 24). Because women "are excluded and denied by the patriarchal linguistic order" (JTN: 20; JT: 23) they can only enter it by denying their "sex and gender" (JTN: 21; JT 24). It is notable that Irigaray begins to use the terminology of "sex and gender" in her later works, and also that the issue, for her is sex *and* gender—not just gender.[2] Irigaray's interest in sexual difference, far from signaling a lack of concern with gender, betokens her recognition of the need to examine the relation between sex and gender.

In rethinking this relation, in creating a tradition for themselves, women cannot merely extract from a male tradition positive images of themselves; they must rewrite that tradition, or "move back through the 'masculine' imaginary, that is, our cultural imaginary" (TS: 162; CS: 157) in order to "(re)discover a possible space for the feminine imaginary" (TS: 164; CS: 159) based not on the tradition that has always designated women as its other, but on the relations between women in "among themselves" (TS: 164; CS: 159). In order that the feminine imaginary does not merely revert into a replica of the masculine imaginary, what it means for woman to have always been "the other" needs to be rethought:

> Since philosophical discourse has set forth the laws of the order of discourse, it will be necessary to go back through its decisive moments looking at the status imparted to the feminine within discursive systematicity, *so that psychoanalytic interpretation will not fall back into the norms of philosophical discursivity.* In particular as regards the function that is assumed there by the "other": in the most general terms, the feminine. The question being how to detach the other—woman—from the otherness of sameness (TS: 169; CS: 163).

In asking about how to think sexual difference Irigaray does not restrict the scope of her question to women's differences from men, she also introduces the question of how to think sexual difference in terms of absolute alterity or radical otherness. She thereby joins Levinas in his attempt to break with a venerable tradition, which, since Parmenides, has judged it impossible to think otherness in abstraction from sameness, to conceive of difference except in relation to the same or multiplicity as anything other than a repetition of the one. Under the heading, "How She Became Not-He," Irigaray writes, "instead of remaining a different gender, the feminine has become, in our languages, the non-masculine, that is to say an abstract nonexistent reality" (JTN: 20; JT: 23). In asking about the possibilities for women to be radically different or to be other in a radical way, Irigaray is influenced by Levinas' critique of metaphysics as the systematic suppression of alterity. Both Irigaray and Levinas challenge the logic of metaphysics whereby one cannot conceive of otherness without referring back to the concept of the same as the guiding principle. Neither thinker denies the indisputable priority that the Parmenidean notion of the one, the same, being has achieved, but both question the status of this priority and the logic by which it is sustained. By the standards of that logic, what Levinas proposes—to think the other in a way that is not reducible to the same—is quite literally unthinkable, as he himself concedes and as Derrida confirms (WD: 126–28; ED: 185–87).[3] By the same token the dramatic reorientation Irigaray calls for is a "cultural transformation, the nature of which we can barely conceive" (JTN: 21; JT: 25), in which sexual difference is thought for the first time as radical difference, rather than as a variant of the same.

For such a radical reorientation to be achieved, says Irigaray,

> women must of course continue to struggle for equal wages and social rights, against discrimination in employment and education, and so forth. But that is not enough: women merely "equal" to men would be "like them," therefore not women. Once more, the difference between the sexes would be in that way canceled out, ignored, papered over (TS: 166; CS: 161).

Because "the exploitation of women does not constitute a *limited* question, within politics, one which would concern only a 'sector' of the population, or a 'part' of the 'body politic,'" what is required is a disruption of

> the entire order of dominant values, economic, social, moral, and sexual. [Women] call into question all existing theory, all thought, all language, inasmuch as these are monopolized by men and men alone. They challenge *the very foundation of our social and cultural order*, whose organization has been prescribed by the patriarchal system (TS: 165; CS: 160).

This includes, for Irigaray, a reassessment of religious symbols and imagery, and the development and elaboration of women-identified religions that recognize female divinities.[4] While Irigaray insists that there is a sense in which women "all undergo, even without clearly realizing it, the same oppression, the same exploitation of their body, the same denial of their desire" (TS: 164; CS: 159), this does not entail that women all experience that oppression, exploitation, and denial in the same way. The force of the "all" derives from patriarchy's exclusion of women *as women*, rather than Irigaray's own prescriptions for women. Irigaray thinks that

> the most important thing to do is to expose the exploitation common to all women and to find the struggles that are appropriate for each

woman, right where she is, depending upon her nationality, her job, her social class, her sexual experience, that is, upon the form of oppression that is for her the most immediately unbearable (TS: 166–67; CS: 161).

Since critics think that Irigaray's writing "fails to recognize that female sexuality is experienced differently, at different times, in different cultures" (Moore, 1988: 169), it is worth stressing the point that Irigaray, far from insisting on the singular importance of sexual difference, makes a point of emphasizing that each woman's struggle will be different and will depend on which form of oppression is "for her the most immediately unbearable." In my view, the above passage demonstrates that Irigaray was attuned to such differences as early as 1977 (when *Ce sexe qui n'en est pas un* was published), that is, well before it became fashionable to be so. In 1990 Butler summed up the situation admirably when she wrote that "The theories of feminist identity that elaborate predicates of color, sexuality, ethnicity, class, and ablebodiedness invariably close with an embarrassed 'etc.' at the end of the list," and added that "This illimitable *et cetera*, however, offers itself as a new departure for feminist political theorizing" (Butler, 1990: 143). Irigaray, as I read her, offers one basis for making such a departure by revisiting the question of otherness.

Irigaray's refusal to identify with any group that "purports to determine the 'truth' of the feminine, to legislate as to what it means 'to be a woman,' and to condemn women who might have immediate objectives that differ from theirs" (TS: 166; CS: 161) is a testimony to the seriousness with which she takes differences at all levels. She is just as concerned to acknowledge the differences among women as she is to assert sexual difference. This point is often overlooked, I suggest, precisely because of a failure to understand Irigaray's challenge to the tendency of Western thought to reduce everything to the same. In this chapter I want to provide the Levinasian background to Irigaray's attempt to confront the question of what it means to allow difference by entertaining the possibility of radical otherness.

The problems women face in their attempt to change the process of othering that has defined them through the eyes of men extend to fundamental assumptions about what it means to be a subject, assumptions that are embedded in the functioning of language and institutionalized in socio-political norms (see SG: 107; SP: 121–22). Irigaray is quite clear that "any theory of the subject has always been appropriated by the 'masculine'" (SO: 133; SA: 165);[5] she is opposed to any idea of constructing women's subjectivity simply in terms of their equality with men, since this would abrogate their differences (TS: 166; CS: 160). I do not think this means that she thinks it is either necessary or possible to dispense with subjectivity altogether. On the contrary, she sees the loss of the subject as a danger. Kaja Silverman has suggested that Irigaray "proves herself quite willing to relinquish subjectivity" (1988: 160) but Irigaray is aware of the "risk that the subject (as) self will crumble away" (SO: 135; SA: 167). Far from being, in Silverman's words, "willing to forgo subjectivity" (1988: 161), Irigaray is wary of the erosion of the subject. When Irigaray says that "female sexuality is not unifiable . . . cannot be subsumed under the concept of the subject" (WE: 64)[6] this is not because she has no interest in retaining—or rather creating for the first time on its own terms—the idea of female subjectivity. It is because she wants to develop a notion of women as subjects that does not succumb to the metaphysical constraints of masculine subjectivity, one that is not defined in terms of the unitary, fully present, mastering subject, one that does not refer back to the one as a repetition of the same. It is not subjectivity *per se* of which Irigaray is critical, only the dominant mode of interpreting subjectivity, which excludes multiplicity, plurality, and difference in favor of sameness, univocity, and totality.[7]

To change the historical subordination of women it is necessary to reexamine assumptions that are basic to our way of thinking. Irigaray says, "Social justice, and especially sexual justice, cannot be achieved without changing the laws of language and the conceptions of truths and values structuring the social order" (JTN: 22; JT: 25). Irigaray's consideration of the role that history has cast for women as the other of men (see JTN: 24–25; JT: 28–29) does not merely focus on women's subordination, as if this problem could be isolated from other fundamental traits of the culture that has fostered it. It is also a matter of seeing the continuity between the roles that the discourse of equal rights has defined for women, and the ways in which various groups have been cast as other, sometimes by women themselves.[8] In raising the question of otherness, Irigaray is not only thinking of sexual difference—although this is obviously central to her concerns as a woman—she is posing the difficulty of thinking otherness at all.[9] Or rather, since to speak of the other by resorting to the concept of otherness is already to embrace the very contradiction Irigaray sees in any attempt to make otherness a problem, we might say Irigaray's project is to raise the question of the possibility of speaking otherwise. How do we become other than this other that history has designated us? Can we think women as other without systematizing otherness, without construing it in terms of the totalizing discourse that defines woman as other? Irigaray raises these questions in terms of women but her question about whether it is possible to speak otherwise, and what such a possibility could mean is a question that has much wider implications. It is a question that concerns the "patriarchal foundation of our social existence," and in asking it she is seeking to be self-conscious about the relation of feminist politics to "phallocratic power" (TS: 165; CS: 160). For Irigaray it is not only necessary to become "*politicized*" (TS: 164; CS: 159), it is also necessary to recast the political so that it does not merely reinscribe patriarchal forms of domination, or, as she puts it, "from a feminine locus nothing can be articulated without a questioning of the symbolic itself" (TS: 162; CS: 157). Irigaray is skeptical of feminism if it is understood simply as a process of politicization that does not also question the models and ideals that govern politics.

By examining the impact of Levinas' philosophy on Irigaray's work, and considering her critique of Levinas, I want to focus on one of the most important, yet neglected, sources of her attempt to think woman as other.[10] What distinguishes Levinas' philosophy is the radicality with which he thinks the ethical relation to the other. If the impetus of Levinas' questioning derives from an ethical concern, his philosophy demands a rethinking not only of the ethical relation but also of the priority that philosophy has typically accorded ontology over ethics.[11]

LEVINAS AND PHENOMENOLOGY

Being and Time remains, for Emmanuel Levinas, "one of the finest books in the history of philosophy" (EI: 37; EeI: 33).[12] Fundamental as the analyses of *Being and Time* are for him, Levinas is not immune from pointing out the shortcomings of the early Heidegger.[13] The relation Levinas has to phenomenology is ambiguous. Phenomenology bears the brunt of Levinas' attack on Western philosophy, as its most recent incarnation, yet, at the same time, it provides the philosophical starting point for whatever distance Levinas gains from that tradition. The ambiguity of Levinas' relation to phenomenology is played out in his relationship to its most prestigious advocates, Husserl and Heidegger.[14] Although his early work—for example, *The Theory of Intuition in Husserl's Phenomenology* (1930) and *En découvrant l'existence avec Husserl et Heidegger* (1949)—remains exegetical in some respects, it already displays a strong tendency to criticize Husserl from a Heideggerian perspective.[15]

This does not prevent Levinas from adopting at times a polemical tone, against the later Heidegger in particular, even invoking Husserl in support of his skepticism of Heideggerian etymologies.[16] While it is tempting to explain this reversal of allegiance by claiming that Levinas' increasing disillusionment with the possibilities of Heideggerian thought has its origin in political events, Levinas himself denies this. He comments,

> I know that the homage I render to *Sein und Zeit* seems pale to the enthusiastic disciples of the great philosopher. But I think the later work of Heidegger, which does not produce in me a comparable impression [compared to *Sein und Zeit*], remains valuable through *Sein und Zeit*. Not, you well know, that it is insignificant, but it is much less convincing. I do not say this owing to Heidegger's political engagements, taken several years after *Sein und Zeit*, even though I have never forgotten those engagements, and though Heidegger has never been exculpated in my eyes from his participation in National-Socialism" (EI: 40; EeI: 37).

Heidegger's national socialism (of which Levinas was aware as early as 1933) notwithstanding, one cannot overlook the abiding influence Heidegger's thinking had on Levinas.[17] Levinas concludes his article "As if Consenting to Horror,"

> It is impossible to be stinting in our admiration for the intellectual vigor of *Sein und Zeit*, particularly in light of the immense output this extraordinary book of 1927 inspired. Its supreme steadfastness will mark it forever. Can we be assured, however, that there was never any echo of Evil in it? The diabolical is not limited to the wickedness popular wisdom ascribes to it and whose malice, based on guile, is familiar and predictable in an adult culture. The diabolical is endowed with intelligence and enters where it will. To reject it, it is first necessary to refute it. Intellectual effort is needed to recognize it. Who can boast of having done so? Say what you will, the diabolical gives food for thought (AC: 487–88).[18]

Even in repeatedly stating the difference between his own thinking and Heidegger's—indeed by the very fact that he finds it necessary to do so ever more emphatically—Levinas acknowledges the profound influence of Heidegger. If Levinas invokes Husserl's name in his attempt to articulate the difference between his own philosophy and Heidegger's, it is not in order to endorse a thinking that would be pre-Heideggerian.[19] Despite his considerable reservations about Heidegger, Levinas also thinks that someone "who undertakes to philosophize in the twentieth century cannot not have gone through Heidegger's philosophy, even to escape it" (EI: 42; EeI: 40).

In his 1990 prefatory note to "Reflections on the Philosophy of Hitlerism," Levinas aligns Heidegger with the tradition he characterizes as putting freedom first, prior to any commitment. He understands the horror of Nazism, or the possibility of "elemental evil," as a possibility that is

> inscribed within the ontology of a being concerned with being [*de l'être soucieux d'être*]—a being, to use the Heideggerian expression, "*dem es in seinem Sein um dieses Sein selbst geht.*" Such a possibility still threatens the subject correlative with being as gathering together and as dominating [*l'être-à-reassembler et à-dominer*], that famous subject of transcendental idealism that before all else wishes to be free and thinks itself free. We must ask ourselves if liberalism is all we need to achieve an authentic dignity for the human subject. Does the subject arrive at the human condition prior to assuming responsibility for the other man in the act of election that raises him up to this height? (RP: 63).

Levinas defines the subject not as that which "before all else wishes to be free and thinks itself free," but rather in terms of an always prior commitment, a fundamental responsibility. To some extent, Levinas' understanding of the subject as first of all ethical can be seen as a reaction against the idea of a subject whose freedom extends to the possibility of suspending all commitment, a freedom that entails skepticism. For it is in this situation that modern society, seeking refuge from the inauthenticity and lack of sincerity that pervades it, disillusioned by its apparent inability to settle upon any solid commitments, and retreating from skepticism, turns to "the Germanic ideal of man" according to Levinas.

Levinas is content neither with idealism's construal of the subject as pure freedom, nor with the materialist conception of the body as a "contingent fall of the spirit into the tomb or prison of a body" (TO: 56; TA: 37). Contrary both to the glorification of the body in materialism, and to its denigration by idealism, Levinas seeks to articulate a third approach. As he says in "Transcendence and Height," "We are looking for a way out of idealism, but we do not find it by having recourse to realism" (TH: 93). Levinas would neither "diminish" the "irreducible originality" of pain, suffering, and effort—as does the idealist tradition of Western thought that regards the body as degenerate, as an "obstacle" (RP: 67; 1934: 204) to be overcome—nor would he accept the materialist alternative that looks to "The mysterious urgings of the blood" or "the appeals of heredity and the past for which the body serves as an enigmatic vehicle" (RP: 69; 1934: 205). Combining the insights of idealism and materialism, while attempting to avoid the pitfalls of both, Levinas discerns in solitude a simultaneous "freedom" and "materiality" (TO: 57; TA: 38), in which the subject's "freedom is immediately limited by responsibility" (TO: 55; TA: 36). Thus we are faced with what Levinas calls a "great paradox: a free being is already no longer free, because it is responsible for itself" (TO: 55; TA: 36).[20] Here, as elsewhere in Levinas' texts, it is possible to discern a pre-figuring of what Irigaray calls the "sensible transcendental," a concept that she explains in terms that are very similar to Levinas' explication of the paradox of an other-worldly freedom and materiality, or what he will later refer to as sensibility. Irigaray understands the "sensible transcendental" as "that which confuses the opposition between immanence and transcendence" (SL: 44; E: 39).[21] With this concept Irigaray wants to avoid a "closed universe" in which the absolute "kills, saps vitality," and "destroys its first roots" (SG: 109; SP: 123). Like Levinas' idea of the free being that is no longer free because it is always already responsible for itself, Irigaray's notion of the sensible transcendental conflates categories that traditionally philosophers have kept apart. The "sensible transcendental" is nothing if not paradoxical. Irigaray draws on this conflation of abstraction and materiality in order to insist on the need to retain the otherness of the other. Refusing the Hegelian gesture, which allows the female—in the figure of Antigone, for example—to be only "representative of *the other of the same*" (SG: 111: SP: 125), kept in a subordinate place, associated with the immediate world of immanence, and dissociated with the mediated abstract world of ideas, Irigaray wants to emphasize the "path between heaven and earth" (SG: 108: SP: 123). This between, or intermediary middle ground—like the position articulated by Diotima, as we saw in the previous chapter—plays an important role for Irigaray. We shall see that even Levinas—who is clearly a source for the notion of the sensible transcendental—is guilty at times, according to Irigaray, of separating the two realms that Irigaray brings together with this phrase. In his discussion of the lover and the beloved Levinas falls prey to the most traditional trope—the inability to resist the temptation to maintain the transcendental and the sensible as separate from one another. The consequences of this will be spelled out in the final section of this chapter in terms of man's tendency to "go to the top and stay there and leave others, women for example, to occupy the low ground" (SG: 108; SP: 123).

THE FACE-TO-FACE RELATION

In order to understand the sense in which, for Levinas, the subject is always already committed, I will elaborate a central organizing theme in Levinas' philosophy, the face-to-face relation. A relation that places the subjects facing one another differently in regard to one another, the face-to-face relation cannot be adequately comprehended by any external agent, or by what Levinas calls a third party.[22] Nor can it be satisfactorily represented by one of the subjects involved in the relation, as if one could abstract from the relation itself without any loss of meaning.

The meaning of the face-to-face relation does not derive from the equality of its terms—language which already distances itself from the ethical impulse of the relation itself. Any attempt to represent it from the outside in terms of concepts will inevitably alter its significance. To represent the meaning of the relation from the point of view of an impartial observer, a neutral onlooker, already reduces the face to face to the categories of being (see TI: 293; TeI: 269). To treat the face to face in terms of being is to introduce an ethical relation as a relation between two entities, as if what matters most is their essential similarity to one another; as if ethics were only concerned with the equality of individuals who derive their identity by partaking of an ideal, or by embodying a universal principle. As equals, individuals are situated within a moral community whose prior claim is presupposed.[23] To claim the priority of the face to face is, above all, an expression of Levinas' insistence upon the fact that ethics comes before ontology.[24] The face to face is a relationship that exceeds the categories of being and nothingness.

Levinas asks philosophy to entertain the possibility that its very meaning and significance might derive from another order; a request that is not at all the same as denouncing philosophy as redundant, or pronouncing philosophy as having come to its end. Levinas distances himself from the idea of the end of philosophy, an idea about which he finds Hegel and Heidegger, despite their differences, in agreement.[25] He advises caution in thinking "the possibility of a conclusion or a closure of the philosophical discourse," and asks, "Is not its interruption its only possible end?" (OB: 20; AE: 24).[26] In other words, for Levinas, the ethical continually disrupts the equilibrium of being, repeatedly dislocates meaning, constantly disturbs the complacency with which we establish universal maxims for what we benevolently imagine to be the good of the whole.[27] This does not mean that Levinas doubts the necessity of universal laws, nor the legitimacy of observing ethical standards of behavior. It means that the moral laws by which we live bear a significance beyond their universality. The interruption they suffer in taking account of the face to face is precisely what renews their efficacy, and what justifies the moral codes we construct by which to live.

Levinas' concern with ethics is directed not toward formulating universal principles, whose applicability presupposes a group of more or less similar and fully formed rational subjects. "My task," he says, "does not consist in constructing ethics; I only try to find its meaning" (EI: 95; EeI: 90). Ethics, for Levinas, is understood as a breach of the concept of identity, which an ethical system that consists of articulating moral dictums would take for granted. This breach of the traditional concept of identity can be explained further with reference to the meaning Levinas gives to the notion of "separation" in *Totality and Infinity*.[28] With this word, Levinas names the movement by which a subject identifies itself—by which it assumes an identity, becomes identical with itself through time, begins to act as if it were a subject. To act as a subject it is necessary, according to Levinas, to have already encountered infinity. Subjectivity, he says, is "founded in the idea of infinity" (TI: 26; TeI: xi). To be a subject is to discover oneself already in relation to the other. This discovery takes place in the concreteness of living a life that is full of needs, needs which demand satisfaction. Let me spell this out by explaining in turn what Levinas means by the other, infinity, needs (as distinct from desire), and enjoyment.

THE OTHER. Levinas contends that the philosophical tradition of the Western world has paid too little attention to the other and, at the same time, that it has assumed the primacy of ontology, at the expense of ethics. In *Totality and Infinity* Levinas argues for the priority of ethics, a term which he employs in a different sense from traditional ethics insofar as the latter tends to assume the universal applicability of moral principles, and an essential similarity between individuals. The moral subject presupposes itself as a model, to which other subjects are analogous. By contrast, the ethical relation *par excellence* for Levinas is what he calls in *Totality and Infinity* the face-to-face relation, a relation that involves my recognition of the other's alterity, or irreducible otherness. In the face-to-face relation, as ethical relation, the I experiences an infinite obligation to the other. Unlike the Christian belief that I should love my neighbor as myself, or the Kantian dictum according to which I should treat others with the respect that I would like to command myself, Levinas' conception of ethics starts not from an analogy between myself and the other, but precisely from our differences. The comparison between me and the other is formulated explicitly in the Christian conception of ethics, which holds that I should love my neighbor as myself, assuming that my obligation to the other can be understood on the basis of myself.[29] Levinas sees such a comparison as possible only on the basis of a prior disjunction between self and other, derivative of the face-to-face relation. Any equality between myself and the other is dependent on the originary experience of the other as one who transcends me, approaches me from a dimension of height, or puts me in question.[30] The original inequality and asymmetry of the face-to-face relation precedes and is the condition of the universality of ethics.[31]

INFINITY, OR BEYOND BEING. By way of explicating the idea of infinity, Levinas draws on Descartes' third Meditation, in which Descartes shows that the idea of God cannot have been derived from the I, but must have come from some external source (see M: 162). God's perfection is not a concept which could have been thought up by the Cartesian I. Surpassing the imperfect I, exceeding any capacity belonging to the I itself, the idea of God, Descartes reasons, must have been put in me from the outside. The Cartesian I who has the thought of God is certain of God's existence not through knowledge, but precisely to the extent that the concept of God overflows any idea which could have derived from the I's own imperfection. I am certain of God's existence because I cannot even have imagined a being so far superior to myself. God's excellence, or perfection, is such that Descartes concludes he must exist. Similarly, for Levinas, the other cannot be contained in any idea I might have of the other, cannot be adequately thought by way of a concept. The other is exterior to me, transcendent to me, involves no return to myself. The relation with the other is in place "despite me," irrespective of what I wish.[32]

It is no accident that it is in Descartes' proof for the existence of God that Levinas discerns the idea of the infinite.[33] Not that he wants to resurrect the proof itself. In *Otherwise than Being* he very deliberately disassociates himself from "the dangerous way in which a pious thought, or one concerned with order, hastily deduces the existence of God"

(OB: 93; AE: 119).[34] For Levinas, the only access to God is through the face of the other. The face-to-face encounter has nothing to do with proving that God exists. Rather, the other who presents himself as absolutely or irreducibly other, also signals God—a God who, even if Levinas himself thinks of God from within the Judaic tradition, is not, Levinas says in an interview, "uniquely Jewish" (Levinas, 1989b: 107).[35]

Levinas maintains that his philosophy is separate from his theology.[36] Insofar as Levinas insists that philosophy derives its energy from pre-philosophical experiences, and he includes among these "founding experiences" that of "reading the Bible," one can accept the claim (EI: 24; EeI 19). There is no question however that Levinas' philosophical agenda is shaped to a significant extent by his Judaism.[37] This does not mean that Levinas reserves for Judaic religious feeling the highest moments in intellectual history. It is the philosophical idea of a Greek philosopher that stands out as having broken most radically with the Eleatic notion of being. Plato provides Levinas with evidence that one can go beyond being. Pre-eminent among those rare moments in the history of philosophy that interrupt philosophers' adherence to the priority of being is Plato's insistence, against Parmenides, that there is something other than being. In the Platonic scheme of things, being is intelligible not of itself but because of the idea of the good. For Plato it is possible to talk about something other than being, outside being, without reducing this other to being. Indeed, within the Western tradition of philosophy, Plato's idea of the good beyond being (*epekeina tes ousias*) perhaps comes closest to expressing the sense of infinity with which Levinas is concerned, and which he sees the tradition as having obscured. Plato "posits transcendence as surpassing the totality" and "catches sight of" desire as "the need of him who lacks nothing, the aspiration of him who possesses his being entirely, who goes beyond his plenitude, who has the idea of Infinity. The Place of the Good above every essence is the most profound teaching, the most definitive teaching, not of theology, but of philosophy." (TI: 103; TeI: 76).

Derrida is careful to stress the words "in our own way" when he quotes Levinas' statement: "We thus encounter *in our own way* the Platonic idea of the Good beyond being." Derrida explains: "*In our own way*, which is to say that ethical excendence is not projected toward the neutrality of the good, but toward the Other, and that which (is) *epekeina tes ousias* is not essentially light but fecundity or generosity" (WD: 86; ED 127).[38] What is beyond being for Levinas is not an abstract or ideal conception of the good, but the social relation, which first takes place not in terms of

Hegelian recognition where the I is contested by the other, but as welcome, as a giving in which I am answerable for the other.[39] The face of the other signifies my obligation to the other, not solely because the other has empirical needs—but because I am put in question by the very existence of the other.

DESIRE, NEED, AND ENJOYMENT. Fundamental to Levinas' project in *Totality and Infinity* is the claim that there is a significant distinction between need and desire.[40] It is a distinction to which the tradition of philosophy has been insufficiently attentive, in Levinas' view.[41] When the subject experiences need, the relationship between the I and what it needs can be described in terms of a lack. In order for a need, such as hunger, to be satisfied, that which confronts me as other—the food from which I live, the air I breathe—undergoes a transformation of which I am master. The things from which I live sustain me, they become part of me. As Levinas says, "Their *alterity* is thereby reabsorbed into my own identity" (TI: 33; TeI: 3).[42] To need something is to relate to something outside myself in such a way as to negate its alterity. For Levinas, to know is also to reduce something to the same. He makes the point concisely in *Otherwise than Being* when he says, "In knowing, which is of itself symbolic, is realized the passing from the image, a limitation and a particularity, to the totality" (OB: 64; AE: 80). To know is to bring something under a concept, to relate it back to me, to make it familiar, to objectify it, to incorporate it into my own identity. By understanding it, not only do I refer it back to me. I also relate it to the whole, to the system of knowledge in general. Otherness is consumed in my conceptualization of it. Knowing is a movement that reduces the object to me, leaving no room for difference. I am made whole, and the whole encompasses me.[43] Levinas is suspicious of the totalization that he believes to be inherent in philosophical discourse, or in any attempt to think, to conceptualize, to systematize, to theorize. He sees in philosophy the tendency to reduce everything to the same—to categorize, to subsume, to unify.

Before the constitution of the I as a subject proper, before the advent of the I as such, the I is able to control its environment to some extent. It is also at risk—its control is not absolute. It is subject to the vicissitudes of its environs and to the uncertainty of the future. In *Totality and Infinity*, Levinas describes how the insecurity of dwelling in the element, in the shape of "concerns for the morrow" (TI: 149; TeI: 123), is stilled in possession and labor. "The element is fixed between the four walls of the home, is calmed in possession" (TI: 158; TeI: 131).

Concretely, the relation between the I and the elemental world is accomplished through enjoyment.[44] Levinas says,

> The world offers the subject a participation in existing in the form of enjoyment, and consequently permits it to exist at a distance from itself. The subject is absorbed in the object it absorbs, and nevertheless keeps a distance with regard to that object (TO: 67; TA: 51–52).[45]

In emphasizing the enjoyable aspects of life Levinas departs from Heidegger's analysis of *Dasein's* existence as Being-in-the-world. Heideggerians tend to take for granted the idea that the materiality of things is only meaningful in the context of our actions in the world. As we saw in the previous chapter, in Heidegger's analysis of things as equipment, the hammer points toward the meaningful framework of my existence by occupying a place within a chain of signification, whereby each thing has a reference to the next in an organized series of intentions. Things signify not of themselves, but precisely in terms of other things, receiving their meaning through specific situations. I am situated within a world in which I operate tools, which function as serviceable in the purposeful activity with which I am engaged. Ensuring that everything runs smoothly and efficiently, objects thus take on meaning through my industry, singled out as a theme for attention only when they break down, bringing to a halt the system of referral in which they usually take their place.

It may be correct to see the significance of things in the uses they have for us, in the tasks we assign to them—but according to Levinas, to interpret our relations with things in the world primarily as equipment is to ignore not only the effort involved in work, but also the enjoyable aspect of living.[46] To view the world in terms of equipment ignores the concrete satisfaction that characterizes our activities even as we work for our living: it abstracts from the corporeal, it forgets embodiment and makes of life a plan or project without any substance. Levinas distances himself from Heidegger's analysis of the world in terms of tools as early as 1947:

> In turning on a bathroom switch we open up the entire ontological problem. What seems to have escaped Heidegger—if it is true that in these matters something might have escaped Heidegger—is that prior to being a system of tools, the world is an ensemble of nourishments. Human life in the world does not go beyond objects that fulfill it. It is

perhaps not correct to say that we live to eat, but it is no more correct to say that we eat to live (TO: 63; TA: 45).[47]

The Heideggerian view of the world as one in which I plan and have projects, where everything has its place ordered according to a hierarchy of ends—the world of the "for-the-sake-of-which"—may appear to overcome the Cartesian dualism against which it is directed, but Levinas asks if it ultimately reduces everything to thought. Might it not also suspend my enjoyment of the world, might it not overlook the satisfaction and happiness which constitute the concrete living of a life? Is Heidegger too quick to identify my relation with the world in terms which already abstract from the immediacy of enjoyment? Levinas maintains that there is a meaning in enjoyment that is not captured by his philosophical predecessors. According to Levinas, phenomenology, which consists in bringing to light the phenomena it seeks to describe, restricts itself to the "being of *existents*," subjecting the existent to the "light of generality" (TI: 189; TeI: 164), and "forgetting . . . the *there is*" (TI: 191; TeI: 166), or that which cannot be reduced to existents or beings, things or objects.[48]

In *Otherwise than Being*, the disturbance caused by the other invades the complacency of the I who, in enjoyment, protects its complacency by residing in a home. The "immediacy of the sensible" is said to be "an exposure to wounding in enjoyment," or "the imperfect happiness which is the murmur of sensibility" (OB: 64; AE: 81). In the "passivity or patience of vulnerability" the I is already for the other, not for itself, as "in a tearing away of bread from the mouth that tastes it, to give it to the other" (OB: 64; AE: 81). Thus enjoyment, in *Otherwise than Being*, becomes a "moment of sensibility" (OB: 72; AE: 91), as sensibility takes on a different meaning than in *Totality and Infinity*, where it bore the sense of consumption (OB: 191; AE: 94).[49] In *Otherwise than Being* Levinas explains the sense in which sensibility is to be understood:

This sensibility has meaning only as a "taking care of the other's needs," of his misfortunes and his faults, that is, as a giving. But giving has meaning only as a tearing from oneself despite oneself, and not only *without* me. And to be torn from oneself despite oneself has meaning only as a being torn from the complacency in oneself characteristic of enjoyment, snatching the bread from one's mouth. Only a subject that eats can be for-the-other, or can signify. Signification, the one-for-the-other, has meaning only among beings of flesh and blood (OB: 74; AE: 93).

Identifying terms which would have been kept apart in *Totality and Infinity*, Levinas says, "Subjectivity is sensibility . . . is signification" (OB: 77; AE: 97)—which might be read as a summary of the above description.

The I of enjoyment has needs, but needs which it can satisfy for the most part.[50] It eats and lives, thereby forming something like a world. The model appropriate to this living off the land—at least in *Totality and Infinity*—is that of consumption, a model in which the things I eat become part of me, they become what I am, they have their alterity negated.[51]

Levinas says, "Desire does not coincide with an unsatisfied need; it is situated beyond satisfaction and nonsatisfaction" (TI: 179; TeI: 154). Or again, "metaphysical desire tends toward *something else entirely*, toward the *absolutely other*" (TI: 33; TeI: 3). In retaining the word "metaphysical" to refer to an intention which is other-directed in such a way that it can never reach its term, or in other words, is infinite, Levinas has at least two (apparently) contradictory aims. On the one hand, he designates by the term "metaphysical" a relation that cannot be contained within any attempt to conceptualize it, which exceeds the boundaries of metaphysics as traditionally conceived, which precisely goes beyond a philosophy which would ground itself in being. Levinas says, in one of the concluding paragraphs of *Totality and Infinity*, "Philosophy presents itself as a realization of being. . . . In this work metaphysics has an entirely different meaning. If its movement leads to the transcendent as such, transcendence means not appropriation of *what is*, but its respect" (TI: 302; TeI: 279). If Levinas subverts the very supremacy metaphysics claims for itself, by maintaining—in a sense we have yet to make clear—that ethics as transcendence is primary, one wonders why he wishes to retain the term "metaphysics" at all.

On the other hand, Levinas does not want to—nor could he, should he wish to—leave metaphysics behind. To insist on the face to face as primordial, to insist on ethics as primary, to insist on metaphysical desire as fundamental, is not to ignore being, nor to fail to give being its proper due. Levinas does not—cannot—remove being from his discussion. In the early pages of *Otherwise than Being*, he says, "The way of thinking proposed here does not fail to recognize being or treat it, ridiculously and pretentiously, with disdain, as the fall from a higher order or disorder" (OB: 16; AE: 19). In Levinas' discourse, being is displaced from its primary and foundational status—not altogether dispensed with. To state the consequences of this displacement, or rather to find other ways of stating the displacement itself, one could observe the following. Ethics initiates ontology, and not the other way around. The I understands itself on the basis of a meeting with the other—not because it is challenged by another I who has equal claim to its property, due to some known or assumed essential similarity of human beings to one another. The I is challenged by the other only in the sense that the other arrests the rhythm of life precisely because it disrupts the familiarity of what Levinas calls "living from," that is, nourishing oneself, attending to the needs of daily life. The other introduces something new, approaches as radically other, and resists absorption into the I's habitual reduction of the alterity of things to itself, through consumption, labor, work, and knowing.

Levinas does not pretend to eschew being—he knows that such an attempt, even if desirable, is impossible. He does not avoid metaphysics. One of the many accomplishments of Derrida's essay, "Violence and Metaphysics: An Essay on the Thought of Emmanuel Levinas," is to focus our attention on the importance of metaphysics as a theme in *Totality and Infinity*.[52] Rather than naively thinking he can overcome metaphysics, Levinas points to its ethical origin. In claiming that the face to face has priority, he does not deny the claims of universality. Rather he shows its inception: he reveals how universal claims originate. "The universal law," says Levinas, "itself refers to a face to face position which refuses every exterior 'viewing.' To say that universality refers to the face to face position is (against a whole tradition of philosophy) to deny that being is produced as a panorama, a coexistence, of which the face to face would be a modality" (TI: 304–5; TeI: 281). This is how Levinas situates universality in terms of the relation between the same and the other:

> The relation with the Other does not only stimulate, provoke generalization, does not only supply it with the pretext and the occasion (this no one has ever contested), but is this generalization itself. Generalization is a universalization—but universalization is not the entry of a sensible thing into a no man's land[53] of the ideal, is not purely negative like a sterile renunciation, but is the offering of the world to the Other (TI: 173–74; TeI: 149).

For Levinas, the face to face founds language.[54] The I's confrontation with the other enables a subject to differentiate itself from all the others, and by the same token to begin to collect things under concepts. Through language the subject can gather together and represent the fruits of its labor. A transformation is thus effected. The things from which the I lives, the "elemental" in which it is submersed, become objects of exchange, subject to the designs of others. Henceforth, the products of my work take on values bestowed on them by commerce. To share a world in common with others is also to produce goods which are susceptible of meanings over which I have no control. The act of representation, a giving of my world to another, is at the same time the possibility of conceiving of a world at all.[55] The gift is offered only on the basis of oneself. In other words, it is through the other that the I both becomes an I—identifies itself as such—and is able to generate the categories of being, or to universalize. The other produces the I by putting it in question. To be put in question is to have the things I live off be contested by a subject who approaches me. Language is the movement through which these new events occur, the constitution of the subject as such, and the putting in common of a world. Expressed in language, things are at the disposal not only of the I, they are also exposed to the other.

INEQUALITY, ASYMMETRY, AND SINGULARITY

In a remarkable section of *Totality and Infinity*, "The Ethical Relation and Time," Levinas confronts several major philosophical questions. Among them are questions that attend to the difficulty which is the central theme of the present discussion, that of describing desire without reducing it to need. This difficulty can be expressed in various ways. How can one refer to the meaning of a relation which is transcendent without being limited by the language of being? One has to resort to the language of being—but how can one nevertheless go beyond its limits? How is it possible for two beings to be in relationship to one another and yet to remain independent of one another, or to resist the limitation or confinement of their definition according to a system which treats them as two types of the same, as more or less identical? How is it possible that they remain significant or meaningful outside their participation of the whole? How can they avoid absorption into categories which tend to subordinate them to a conceptual totality? Can alterity signify outside a schema which produces a synthesis, in terms which relegate others to their place, in a system of thought which classifies them as parts of a whole? These questions are provoked by the same difficulty that troubles Derrida in a series of questions he poses to Levinas in "Violence and Metaphysics." Questions such as "How could there be a 'play of the Same' if alterity itself was not already *in* the Same, with a meaning of inclusion doubtless betrayed by the word *in*?" and "How can the 'Other' be thought or said without reference—we do not say reduction—to the alterity of the *eteron* in general?" (WD: 126–27; ED: 186).

The question of how the same can be related, but not reduced to, the other not only recurs as a constant organizing theme of Levinas' *Totality and Infinity*, it also reverberates throughout his entire corpus.[56] In the particular section under discussion on time and ethics, the problem is posed first in terms of relationality and then in terms of transcendence. "We must explicate," says Levinas, toward the beginning of this section, "the power that beings placed in relation have of absolving themselves from the relation. This power entails a different sense of absolution for each of the separated terms" (TI: 220; TeI: 195). He will begin to explicate this power of absolution with reference to transcendence a few pages later: The "transcendence of the Other with regard to me . . . being infinite, does not have the same signification as my transcendence with regard to him" (TI: 225; TeI: 200). Again, the I is not "transcendent with regard to the other in the same sense that the other is transcendent with regard to me" (TI: 223; TeI: 201).

The formulation of the face-to-face relation in terms of transcendence is important for the present examination of the role of desire in Levinas' philosophy for the following reasons. First, to understand the ethical relation as a relation of transcendence is to grasp the significance of Levinas' insistence that the face to face is characterized by the inequality of its terms. Second, because the face to face is a relation of transcendence, it is possible to see how this essentially "asymmetrical relation" can also "take on the aspect of a symmetrical relation" (TI: 225; TeI: 201). Third, the idea of a relation that is genuinely transcendent is what underlies the claim that Levinas makes for the pre-original and disruptive force of the face to face in relation to the universality, objectivity, and rationality for which it both calls and from which it withdraws.[57]

First, I will consider the question of equality.[58] At first glance, one might have cause to worry over Levinas' refusal to posit a relationship of equality as the primordial ethical relation. In affirming that the face-to-face relation, the ethical relation *par excellence*, is to be understood as a relation of inequality, is Levinas thereby stating his belief in the inherent superiority of some individuals over others? Answer, no. The inequality of the relation consists in the obstinate alterity the other maintains in relation to me, in other words, in the other's absolute transcendence. The face-to-face relation, says Levinas, "commences in the *inequality* of terms, transcendent to one another, where alterity does not determine the other in a formal sense . . .

the alterity of the other does not result from its identity, but constitutes it: the other (*autre*) is the Other (*autrui*)" (TI: 251; TeI: 239).[59] In order to understand the significance Levinas gives to the term "inequality," it is crucial to differentiate it from the idea that some individuals are better than others. For Levinas, not only is the application of the term "inequality" restricted to the face-to-face relation as it is experienced from within that relation. Inequality is precisely converted into equality when considered from another point of view, external to the relationship itself.[60] The way in which I feel myself to be unequal or inferior to the other who approaches me from a height, as other, from alterity—this inequality "does not appear to the third party who would count us . . . the inequality *is* in this impossibility of the exterior point of view, which alone could abolish it" (TI: 251; TeI: 239). With this claim, that the inequality of the face-to-face relation consists precisely in its invisibility to anyone who is outside the relation itself, we begin to see how Levinas can maintain that the face to face both founds equality, while itself remaining essentially unequal. From the experience of inequality, Levinas says, "equality is founded" (TI: 214; TeI: 189). This transformation of inequality into equality is at the same time the meaning that is deduced from the face to face by the "third party" or the others, by the observer who "looks at me in the eyes of the Other" (TI: 213; TeI: 188). Thus Levinas can speak of the other presenting himself as equal in the ethical relation despite, or even because of, his emphatic statement of the essential *inequality* of the face to face. He says, "The poor one, the stranger, presents himself as an equal. His equality within this essential poverty consists in referring to the *third party*" (TI: 213; TeI: 188). This apparent contradiction is in fact what Levinas sets out to demonstrate as constituting the ethical situation. The movement that governs the shift from the responsibility I have for the other to the social demand for justice is thereby described. It is the same movement by which the asymmetry of the face-to-face relation is rendered symmetrical—as we shall shortly see.

The face to face is defined by the inequality of its terms in relation to an other, but in a different sense it is also a relationship in which the other is presented as an equal. This is an example of the state of affairs which the entire effort of *Totality and Infinity* is an attempt to describe. There is, says Levinas, an "inevitable *orientation* of being 'starting from oneself' toward 'the Other'" in the face-to-face relation. "The priority of this orientation over the terms that are placed in it summarizes the theses of the present work" (TI: 215; TeI: 190). In other words, being itself appears only in relation to the other. The identity of the I itself—the being of the I—is given through the other.

One might say that when the terms, or the individuals themselves, are treated as prior to the face to face, prior to that which puts them in relation, prior to the I's ethical responsibility for the other—then the third party comes into play, designating the two subjects facing one another as equals. Equality is deduced from an original inequality.[61] Considered from the point of view of those involved in the relation, within the terms of the face to face, the inequality remains. There is, then, a paradoxical quality of the face-to-face relation, whereby it contains a reference to others, despite the fact that this very reference undoes the uniqueness and originality of the ethical obligation that defines the relation.

Unlike his characterization of the face-to-face relation, Levinas presents the erotic relationship as lacking an explicitly social dimension. In contrast to the reference that the ethical face-to-face relation has outside itself, to all the others, the relationship of eros remains closed and impenetrable. If anyone interrupted the society established by lovers, the intimacy of the moment would disappear. Eros depends on the secrecy of lovers, which is violated by the intrusion—perhaps even by the thought— of others. The absolute exclusivity of the erotic relation marks one of the differences between the erotic relation of desire and the metaphysical desire with which Levinas characterizes ethics in the face-to-face relation. I will return to a consideration of the differences between the ethical relation of the face to face, and the erotic relation between lovers.[62]

In *Otherwise than Being*, the paradox that the face-to-face relation somehow contains a reference to the third party, or that the exclusive and personal relation the I shares with the other is at some level witnessed by the whole of humanity—the others who look at me in the eyes of the other—is compressed into one word: proximity.[63] With this term Levinas expresses the complex relations between the face to face and the need for universal justice that he traces in *Totality and Infinity*. This is why Levinas can say that "Proximity . . . might be called humanity, or subjectivity, or self" (OB: 46; AE: 58).[64] It would barely be possible to find an equivalence between these terms in the language of *Totality and Infinity*, a principal concept of which is the I as separated being. To be separated is precisely not to be counted amongst the totality of humans that would make up humanity. To be a subject who identifies itself as a self is not yet to be a sociological statistic, an anonymous member of society. It is to dwell in the elements, to enjoy life, to be happy—and to find that one is already committed in infinite obligation to the other.[65] It is to discover oneself in the midst of oblivious freedom, in the midst of spontaneous enjoyment of the good things life has to offer, already implicated by the face-to-face relation.

If in *Otherwise than Being* the word "proximity" does the work of several ideas mapped out in *Totality and Infinity*, the word "substitution" stands in for several further, related ideas. Substitution is specified there as the "very subjectivity of a subject" (OB: 13; AE: 16). Substitution denotes the impossibility of refusing responsibility for the other—the I is the only one who can take the other's place.[66] The other's address to the I involves the reversion of the ego to the self, where the I is called upon and where there is no escaping the call, or—in the language Levinas develops in *Otherwise than Being*—the I is elected as unique and irreplaceable (OB: 56–57; AE: 72–73).[67] In *Otherwise than Being*, as we began to see with reference to his conceptions of enjoyment and sensibility, Levinas develops a new terminology for the questions he posed in *Totality and Infinity*.[68]

In the same way that, through establishing laws which apply to individuals, inequality is converted into equality, the asymmetry which defines the face-to-face relation is "effaced" and replaced by symmetrical relations. To say that the ethical relation is originally asymmetrical is another way of characterizing it as initially non-reciprocal.[69] Of course there is a reciprocity, which is acknowledged in the morality established by communities, but reciprocal relations are set up on the basis of non-reciprocity. In Levinas' words, "the knot of subjectivity . . . consists in approaching in such a way that, over and beyond all the reciprocal relations that do not fail to get set up between me and the neighbor, I have always taken one more step toward him—which is possible only if this step is subjectivity" (OB: 84; AE: 106). Once responsibility is abstracted from, once the I becomes equivalent to others, the asymmetry of the relation disappears into the moral positions that individuals take with regard to others. To quote Levinas again, "I and other become interchangeable in commerce . . . the particular man, an individuation of the genus man, appearing in history, is substituted for the I and for the other" (TI: 226; TeI: 201). History deals in positions and places, not in the unique identity that is established in the personal individuation that consists in identifying myself as I, as distinct from others. History, for Levinas, talks in generalities, it reduces the I to all the others.

The third and final point I want to explicate concerns how the transcendence of the face to face opens on to universality. Universality ensures equality (TI: 242; TeI: 219). It draws out the implications of the face-to-face relation, it makes permanent the ethical meaning of my recognition of the other as other. It creates reasons for why I should consider the other, and in doing so it changes the ethical relation of the face to face into an impersonal dictate of public morality, perhaps as a principle of an institution or as an edict of the state—in any case it is to be judged according to the measures employed by history. This transformation from the demand felt by a subject who is henceforth ethical, to the objective standards erected by a prudence learned from historical lessons, carries with it new dangers—the risk of tyranny, for example (TI: 300; TeI: 276), and the neutralizing effects of "impersonal reason" or the "power and domination" that the philosophy of being imposes, despite its intentions (TI: 275–76; TeI: 252–53). These are necessary risks, which cannot be avoided, but neither should they be forgotten.[70] Irigaray makes a similar point when she says, "There is no universal valid for all men and women aside from the natural economy. All other universals are partial constructions and, as a result, authoritarian and unjust" (JTN 83; JT: 103).

To stress the primacy of the face to face as the origin of rationality (TI: 203; TeI: 177), or to "surprise the echo of the saying" in the "said" (OB: 27; AE: 34), are the resources with which Levinas seeks to remind us of the risks inherent in politics and history. These are his attempts to keep us vigilant while we read the philosophers of being.

Levinas says,

> I have tried to describe the difference between Desire and need by the fact that Desire cannot be satisfied; that Desire in some way nourishes itself on its own hungers and is augmented by its satisfaction; that Desire is like a thought which thinks more than it thinks, or more than what it thinks. It is a paradoxical structure, without doubt, but one which is no more so than this presence of the Infinite in a finite act (EI: 92; EeI: 97).

For my part, I have tried here to demonstrate this paradox with reference to the conversion of inequality into equality, of asymmetry into symmetry, and finally, of the transformation of the singular and personal relationship of the face to face into the claims of universality. I have indicated that this paradoxical structure also governs the transmutation of the saying into the said. If Descartes' idea of God is the best reference point for the modern world to grasp the significance of Levinas' insistence that we notice the interruption of totality by the infinite, it is Plato (at least in *Totality and Infinity*) to whom he turns in the ancient world.[71] Renewing Plato's attempt to overcome the notion of Eleatic being, Levinas nevertheless gives the ethical an altogether different meaning than the idea of the good as a universal. Or rather, he insists that the original ethical impulse is already violated once it is understood in the neutral impersonal light of reason. Against Socrates, Levinas finds in teaching the possibility of absolute novelty—a novelty which comes from the other and is not always already implicit in me. The interlocutor does not awaken in me knowledge which was lying dormant. The other first makes it possible to "know thyself."

EROTIC DESIRE AND THE ETHICAL RELATION

In describing the ethical transcendence of the face-to-face relation we saw the importance of the third party or what might loosely be called the public element of the face-to-face relation. The third party transforms the face to face into a relation of equals, undoing its essential inequality, exchanging the specific indebtedness experienced by the I in front of the other for a general call for justice, and rendering the asymmetry of the relation symmetrical. Substituting the specificity of the face to face for a social demand that individuals display reasonable behavior, ethics becomes an impersonal recognition of the need for the fair treatment of others. This transformation, although originating in the experience of the face to face, at the same time violates the originality of the ethical experience. I have dwelt upon the meaning of the third party not only because, in understanding it, we see the complexity of the face-to-face relation. Even more important for the present discussion, in *Totality and Infinity* it is the third party that signals the most decisive difference between the ethical relation of the face to face and the erotic relation between lovers. I will show this in detail.

If the face to face is one of the most important concepts in *Totality and Infinity*, the distinction between the "saying" and the "said" is one of the key ideas in *Otherwise than Being*. The excess of the face to face overflows all attempts to represent it in principle and not just for the moment—not merely until we know more or until we find a more appropriate means of exposition. This excess, and the difficulty language has in speaking of it, is perhaps the central problem of *Otherwise than Being*, where Levinas elaborates a new terminology for expressing the priority of ethics over ontology. With the distinction between *le dire* and *le dit*, the saying and the said, he emphasizes the excess of meaning that overflows any statement, and the impossibility of ever completely reducing the saying to the said. Levinas offers a particularly concrete commentary on the distinction between the saying and the said by referring his readers to the experience that "even the philosopher" has, that of feeling responsible for the other in trying to make oneself understood (a feeling that has impressed itself upon me repeatedly in writing this book!). In the effort of doing so, the fact that the other might feel the same way does not register. Levinas says, "The subject affected by the other cannot think that the affection is reciprocal, for he is still obsessed with the very obsession he could exercise over him that obsesses him. Not to turn into relations that reverse, irreversibility, is the universal subjectness of the subject" (OB: 84; AE: 106).

Does Levinas' treatment of eros in *Totality and Infinity* represent a significant departure from his earlier descriptions of the erotic relation as a relation of alterity? What does the near eclipse of eros in *Otherwise than Being* indicate? Such questions are far from incidental to a concern already touched upon, which proves central for Irigaray—namely, how can Levinas claim to think the alterity of the other in relation to the I, without collapsing the two terms "I" and "other" into the same? In other words, does Levinas avoid the totalization with which he faults the tradition, and even if he does, can his philosophy still make sense as philosophy? Does not the very movement of philosophy consist in reducing the same to other, in conceptualizing, in relating the parts to the whole, in producing some sort of organization out of chaos, or in synthesizing, ordering, systematizing, thinking one thing in terms of another, sorting out differences, and seeing similarities among things which make up some kind of a whole? These are questions that Levinas would no doubt consider "facile" (OB: 155; AE: 198), like the objections he raises himself only to reply that they "do not answer the proximity of the neighbor" (OB: 155; AE: 198).[72] They are questions nonetheless that will also be highlighted in Derrida's responses to Levinas.

In *Totality and Infinity*, Levinas' philosophical agenda is still governed by the concepts of the same and the other, no matter how much his thought strains against the limitations of such conceptualization. In *Otherwise than Being*, Levinas no longer frames his questions by asking how the same can remain itself in the face of the other. Typical of his procedure in *Otherwise than Being* are the following questions, which Levinas poses in the opening section of chapter four, the chapter Levinas tells us is the germ of this work:[73] "How can the passivity of obsession find a place in consciousness, which is wholly, or is in the end, freedom?" and "How in consciousness can there be an undergoing or a passion whose active source does not, in any way, occur in consciousness?" (OB: 102; AE: 129). While recalling the structure of the questions that dominate his procedure in *Totality and Infinity*, the emphasis Levinas places on consciousness here signals Levinas' intention to break down still further, if he can, the opposition between the same and the other. He is not attempting just another existentialist philosophy of consciousness. As early as 1947 we find him already dissatisfied with such a goal. He is rather trying to locate and articulate the alterity which dominates consciousness from the outset.[74]

With terms such as "substitution," "passivity," and "obsession," Levinas conjures up the idea of responsibility as the-one-for-the-other, and as "the other in me" (see, e.g., OB: 125; AE: 160). He thereby avoids the formalism that even the language of *Totality and Infinity* conceded, by construing ethics in terms of the face-to-face relation. In *Otherwise than Being,* the I and the other are understood no longer in terms of the face to face, which still represents its terms in opposition to one another, as if in a mode of confrontation or struggle, however benign. To the extent that the terms of the face to face are still reducible to entities, Levinas finds that relation insufficient. No longer retaining the face to face as his model in *Otherwise than Being,* he alters the meaning of familiar terms, investing them with a sense of responsibility, and employing them to do the work which was formerly demanded of the face to face. By giving a different nuance to words like "substitution," "proximity," and "obsession"—we could add to the list—Levinas opens the way to an understanding of responsibility as maternity. Maternity comes to stand for the vulnerability that is always already prior to any commitment I could have toward the other.

THE ECLIPSE OF EROS AND
THE EMERGENCE OF MATERNITY

The movement Levinas' thinking undergoes, such that maternity can become emblematic of responsibility, is what concerns me here (see OB: 75; AE: 95). Maternity not only coalesces with ethics in *Otherwise than Being,* it represents the ethical *par excellence.* This is indeed a strange turn of events, since the place reserved for the feminine in *Totality and Infinity* was that of the coquettish animality of eros, which lacks the seriousness of ethics and the rigor of the masculine world. The feminine was acknowledged either in the domestic realm of habitation, as a gentle discreet presence, or in the "vice of the clandestine" (TI: 265; TeI: 243), in the night of the erotic. If eros still has a place in *Totality and Infinity* (however marginal, however unworthy of ethics as such), it drops out of sight altogether in *Otherwise than Being.* The feminine is admitted only as maternity.

Plenty could be said about the stereotypical restrictions on sex roles in play in Levinas' texts. Levinas limits the appearance of the feminine figure either to the realm of the erotic (where, in one respect, it turns out to be a poor imitation of the ethical), or to the elevated heights of maternity. It is not, perhaps, too extreme to accuse Levinas of expressing the traditional denigration and deification of the feminine in the restricted possibilities he extends to the feminine. Do we not find an insistence on the domestication of women in Levinas' portrait of the feminine in habitation? Is his identification of the feminine with eros anything other than an indictment of women as sexually alluring, echoing the condemnation the tradition has bestowed on the figure of Eve? However far it might be from his intentions, it is hard not to find in Levinas' work the opposition between good wife and mother and wayward sex symbol. Is there any more to his motif of the feminine than the well-worn antithesis of whore *versus* maternal Virgin Mary? Or perhaps we had better say, taking account of Levinas' Judaism, the antithesis of Eve's transgression of the law *versus* the silent footsteps of Rebecca, which reverberate with the sounds of solicitude for the other?[75]

If, in *Totality and Infinity*, eros and ethics were kept apart, treated under separate headings (eros is "beyond the face"), Levinas no longer concerns himself with this difference in *Otherwise than Being*. Indeed, in *Otherwise than Being*, eros all but disappears. Why? The answer involves an understanding of the role of fecundity and paternity, and their relation to voluptuosity in *Totality and Infinity*. To anticipate this discussion, let me say that eros is only acknowledged in that it issues in the child. The fecundity of eros is admitted, but the voluptuosity of eros is outlawed. The feminine is written out of the text. Having been written out of *Totality and Infinity*, one might say, the eclipse of the feminine as eros makes room for the maternal in *Otherwise than Being*.

Several other questions thus emerge concerning the entry of maternity into the ethical considerations of *Otherwise than Being*. For example, why is the language of paternity and fraternity (the language of the Jewish fathers, the language of patriarchy—perhaps the common language of both) replaced with that of maternity? Why when, in *Totality and Infinity*, fecundity means the relation between father and son, does Levinas introduce maternity as the dominant metaphor for responsibility in *Otherwise than Being*? Can this be attributed to his stereotypical attitude to sexual roles, or has a change taken place in his thinking? Even if a change in his language can be discerned, is Levinas paying any more than lip service to feminism? Is his invocation of the maternal simply the traditional attitude toward women reasserting itself in a different guise?

Before embarking on the detailed examination of Levinas' treatment of eros that is called for in order to sort out the function and significance of the feminine in his work and thereby to prepare for Irigaray's critique of Levinas, I want to mention, if only in passing, a detail that would have detained only the most careful reader of *Otherwise than Being*. One might want to say that Levinas does not neglect eros altogether in *Otherwise than Being*. The use of the word "caress" might be invoked to signal this.[76] But is this caress not sanitized of the sexual reference it contained in *Totality and Infinity*? Is its meaning not circumscribed by the love a mother expresses for a child, rather than erotic passion?[77] Is not the passion it connotes passion in the sense of passivity, as the eternal patience of the maternal, rather than that excited by the voluptuosity of the other in the society of lovers, which maintains itself in the secrecy of the night, invisible to the public gaze?

The role of eros in Levinas' philosophy, and how it relates to the sense he gives to ethics, has been peculiarly absent from commentaries on Levinas' work. Even Derrida's essay, "Violence and Metaphysics," which in other respects provides perhaps the most comprehensive survey of the themes which structure *Totality and Infinity*, reserves Levinas' treatment of the feminine for another time.[78] Derrida explains, in a footnote,

> It would be useless to attempt, here, to enter into the descriptions devoted to interiority, economy, enjoyment, habitation, femininity, Eros, to everything suggested under the title *Beyond the Face*, matters that would doubtless deserve many questions. These analyses are not only an indefatiguable (sic) and interminable destruction of "formal logic" they are so acute and so free as concerns traditional conceptuality, that a commentary running several pages would betray them immeasurably. Let it suffice to state that they depend upon the conceptual matrix we have just outlined, without being deduced from it but ceaselessly regenerating it (WD: 315, note 40; ED: 161).

To the extent that my remarks constitute a commentary, I take the risk of betraying immeasurably the analysis Levinas provides under the title "Phenomenology of Eros," a risk that Levinas would say all language must take, insofar as it reduces the saying to the said. Guided by a concern with the feminine, my approach to the question of what place is occupied by eros in Levinas' philosophy will address the section devoted to a phenomenology of eros in *Totality and Infinity*, as well as the earlier texts of 1947.

In *Time and the Other*, it is eros, not ethics, that Levinas thinks "furnishes us with a prototype" of the other (TO: 76; TA: 64). Although the relation with the other is already conceived by Levinas as the face to face or "the encounter with a face that at once gives and conceals the Other" (TO: 78–79; TA: 67), it is eros, and not ethics—as in *Totality and Infinity*—that the face-to-face relation describes.[79] Might it not be possible to explain the early emphasis on the radical alterity of the feminine, and the later deference to the ethical relation, as a simple shift of emphasis? Levinas first tried to interpret the feminine as the other *par excellence*, and then shifted his attention to the ethical. One might want to claim that he shifts ground simply because he finds that his understanding of the erotic relation in terms of the feminine is less adequate to the task of breaking away from Parmenidean being than is the ethical tie between the I and the other. Such a claim, however, will not hold up to examination. Not only is it clear that from the start Levinas is concerned with ethics, it also becomes clear that in later years Levinas does not entirely revoke or repudiate the earlier attention he gave to the feminine. I will first show that Levinas is concerned with ethics even in the 1940s, and then that he still attributes importance to the feminine as late as 1979.

The different meaning Levinas finds in the face-to-face relation cannot be attributed to the fact that he has not yet, in 1947, developed any interest in ethics. There is no doubt that the question of ethics guides his analyses even at this early stage of his thinking. The "hope for a better society" (TO: 58; TA: 40) already animates his philosophy. It motivates the suspicion of Heidegger that Levinas already harbors when he questions philosophies which think they can afford the luxury of concerning themselves solely with solitary anxiety and the meaning one's death has for oneself (see TO: 61; TA: 43–44). Levinas' own concern with death is not only its meaning for the self, but also for others. In denouncing the luxury of meditating only on the meaning of death for oneself Levinas does not need to put a name to the philosopher he has in mind. It is only too evident that his disillusionment with philosophers of existence extends even to one whose capacity for thought yielded what remains, nonetheless, among the finest books in the history of philosophy.

The question is not simply, then, why Levinas' early interest in eros gives way to an interest in ethics. He does not merely transpose the question of alterity from the domain of eros to ethics. The problem is rather that while in 1947 there is little hint of any clash of interest between eros and ethics, by 1961, with the publication of *Totality and Infinity*, the erotic relation—as the supreme embodiment of alterity—has been relegated to the sidelines. While Levinas by no means entirely neglects eros in *Totality and Infinity*, it is certainly made to play the supporting role to the relation that takes center stage, namely the face-to-face ethical relation. What causes this realignment and what role does sexual difference have in it? Is there a tension between the early attention Levinas accords to eros, and the upstaging of eros by ethics that characterizes *Totality and Infinity*? I will bear these concerns in mind as I show that ethics all but eclipses Levinas' early analyses of eros.

Although several of the key elements that will come to characterize the face-to-face relation as ethical in *Totality and Infinity* are already present in Levinas' 1947 account of the other, the explicitly ethical dimension of the face to face is nowhere to be found. Thus, alterity already "appears as a nonreciprocal relationship" (TO: 83; TA: 75), and Levinas stipulates that the relation between the I and the other "is not symmetrical" (TO: 83–84; TA: 75). Clearly these statements anticipate the analyses that, as we have seen, are central to the inequality of the face-to-face relation upon which Levinas dwells at length in *Totality and Infinity*, but the closest Levinas will come to elaborating the ethical dimension of the face to face in *Time and the Other*, is in his reference to the other as "the weak, the poor, 'the widow and the orphan'" (TO: 83; TA: 75). Levinas is quoting the famous biblical phrase that recurs throughout *Totality and Infinity* to designate the other.[80] For the remainder of his discussion, Levinas develops the notion of alterity not in terms of the ethical relation, but under the heading of eros. We must, Levinas admonishes us, "recognize its exceptional place among relationships" (TO: 88; TA: 81). Most significantly for our present discussion, he specifically identifies alterity first and foremost with the feminine. He says: "I think the absolutely contrary contrary (*le contraire absolutement contraire*), whose contrariety is in no way affected by the relationship that can be established between it and its correlative, the contrariety that permits its terms to remain absolutely other, is the *feminine*" (TO: 85; TA: 77). In *Existence and Existents*, also published in 1947, Levinas says, "The plane of *eros* allows us to see that the other par excellence is the feminine" (EE: 85; DE: 145). If there is any doubt left as to the significance Levinas attaches to the feminine as alterity, Levinas dispels it when he appeals to sexual difference as that which runs up "against the unity of being proclaimed by Parmenides" (TO: 85; TA: 78). Since Levinas' entire philosophical project is expressed in his attempted break with Parmenidean being, such a claim is not without significance. Levinas is suggesting that it is feminine alterity that provides the most fruitful possibility of providing a radical break in the hegemony of Eleatic being as oneness, sameness, unity, allowing the other to remain other without being reduced to the logic of the same.

In "Violence and Metaphysics," Derrida subjects Levinas' attempt to overcome the Eleatic notion of being to careful scrutiny. It is curious, then, to discover that he pays no attention to the change that occurs in Levinas' attitude toward the feminine as eros. He acknowledges the radicality of Levinas' announcement in *Time and the Other* that he will attempt to "break with Parmenides" (TO: 42, TA: 20; in WD: 89, ED: 132), but neglects to record that in *Time and the Other* this attempt is made with explicit reference to the feminine, and not to ethics. In *Totality and Infinity*, it is the face to face as ethics which takes precedence. Eliding the alterity of the feminine as eros into the sense of the other as ethically transcendent, Derrida acts as if there were no difference between them. It is true that in *Time and the Other* the encounter with the feminine qualifies as a relation with alterity for reasons akin to those that will describe the alterity of the ethical relation in *Totality and Infinity*. Love as the feminine "consists in slipping away from the light" (TO: 87; TA: 79); the feminine transcends in "withdrawing" from the categories of being (TO: 88; TA: 81); the caress knows not "what it seeks," remaining resistant to the model of intentionality (TO: 89; TA: 82), and escaping the conceptual grasp of the philosopher.

Yet, if *Time and the Other* presents no compelling reason to attend to the differences between eros and ethics (although even there, as we shall see, Levinas himself insists upon the differences between various modes of alterity), in *Totality and Infinity* there are insurmountable differences. Eros involves a return to self; it is not unambiguously transcendent like the ethical relation. To love is not only to love the other, but also to love oneself in love.

Since the erotic or feminine relation involves a return to self, the alterity it involves is understood by Levinas as less radical than that of the other in the ethical relation of the face to face, a relation which is non-reciprocal, a relation without return. This does not prevent Levinas from affirming the importance of the feminine precisely in relation to alterity as late as 1979, that is, after the face to face has been developed as an explicitly ethical relation. In the preface to *Time and the Other*, which Levinas wrote in 1979—after the publication of both *Totality and Infinity* (1961) and *Otherwise than Being* (1974)—Levinas not only maintains the relevance of his analysis of femininity, he takes trouble to emphasize it. "I should like to stress two points," he says toward the end of his preface. He recalls that "Femininity . . . appeared to me as a difference contrasting strongly with other differences, not merely as a quality different from all others, but as the very quality of difference" (TO: 35–36; TA: 14). But he adds an important qualification: "one would have to see in what sense this can be said of masculinity or of virility; that is, of the differences between the sexes in general" (TA: 14; TO: 36). Why the qualification? Are these the words of someone who has become attuned to the sexism of his own work? Has Levinas realized, between 1947 and 1979, how enormously complex the problems posed by the feminine are? Or do we find in his remark nothing more than a mild gesture of conciliation that does not begin to address the seriousness of the problem his analysis of the feminine presents? Or perhaps the sign of a guilty conscience because he knows that his work does not answer the feminists he addresses? Would not his guilt suggest—following Levinas' own meditations on the subject—that he acknowledges the problem, however hesitantly and obliquely? I suggest that none of these responses are adequate. Rather, we must admit the seriousness of the problem, but ask what indications lie in Levinas' presentation, which he himself does not develop but others do, and which yield a new perspective for feminism. Before doing so, I want to follow in some detail the analysis of the feminine Levinas provides in *Totality and Infinity*.

We have seen that one of the organizing themes structuring *Totality and Infinity* is the distinction Levinas establishes between desire and need. The distinction provides us with access to the account of love, an account which is full of conflicting details that Levinas weaves into one another with infinite care, some strands of which I will try to unravel here. These pages are among the most beautifully written of *Totality and Infinity*, their movement more akin to poetry than philosophy, and if to treat them as if they offered just so many theses is to do violence to them—as it undoubtedly is—I can only exhort the reader to go back to the text itself.[81]

"Love remains a relation with the Other that turns into need, and this need still presupposes the total, transcendent exteriority of the other, of the beloved. But love also goes beyond the beloved" (TI: 254; TeI: 232). Levinas announces love as a desire which turns into need in his preliminary description of "The Ambiguity of Love"—and he thereby introduces a multi-layered problem that I will try to sift through. Taking one layer at a time, we can begin with Levinas' suggestion that love remains a relation with the other.

In his account of eros Levinas uses a surprising number of formulations that bear a striking resemblance to those he will use to describe the ethical relation of the face to face. Love is "predestination, a choice of what had not been chosen" (TI: 254; TeI: 232); the caress defies intentionality (TI: 260;

TeI: 238), it goes beyond the possible, and what it seeks "is not situated in a perspective and in the light of the graspable" (TI: 258; TeI: 235); erotic nudity "says the inexpressible" (TI: 260; TeI: 237). All of these descriptions are in keeping with the sense in which love—like the ethics of the face to face—is genuinely transcendent. But, unlike the face to face as such (although through the third party this is also true of ethics, albeit with very different results) love reverts into need. Not only does desire, as eros, transcend, it also falls short of genuine transcendence. The desire of love "is broken and satisfied as the most egoist and cruelest of needs" (TI: 254; TeI: 232). Love becomes the underside of transcendence, it reverses ethics. It is "without responsibility," and in it the "face fades," producing "neutrality" and degenerating into "animality" (TI: 263; TeI: 241)—all of which could not be more distant from the face to face as a relation of transcendence.

Flouting—and explicitly so—the rules of formal logic, Levinas insists that both these tropes—love as both desire and need—contradictory though they are, belong to the order of eros. For in love "transcendence goes both further and less far than language," it is "situated at the limit of immanence and transcendence . . . as though the too great audacity of the loving transcendence were paid for by a throw-back this side of need" (TI: 254; TeI: 232).[82] Like Irigaray—whose "sensible transcendental" is surely indebted to Levinas' description of love—Levinas is fully aware that he is stretching the rules of philosophy to breaking point, threatening to escape the bounds of comprehension.[83] He says,

> An enjoyment of the transcendent almost contradictory in its terms . . . the possibility of the Other appearing as an object of a need while retaining his alterity . . . this simultaneity of need and desire, of concupiscence and transcendence . . . constitutes the originality of the erotic which, in this sense, is *the equivocal* par excellence (TI: 255; TeI: 233).

This passage presents clearly the idea of eros as the equivocal *par excellence*. Still, I have yet to make concrete the suggestion that love both transcends and does not transcend, that it goes both further and less far than language, that it is both like and unlike ethics. In order to do so, let me relinquish any attempt to follow exhaustively the descriptions Levinas provides, and focus initially on the concept of signification.

In the middle of his description of eros, Levinas pauses to remind us that "the face signifies by itself" (TI: 261; TeI: 239). The face is the origin of language, it founds all meaning: "One does not have to explain it, for every explanation begins with it" (TI: 261; TeI: 239). The reason Levinas stops to recall the originary and founding role that the face has for signification, is because it puts into perspective the sense in which eros "dissimulates" (TI: 260; TeI: 238), how "erotic nudity" can be "an inverted signification" (TI: 263; TeI: 241), and what it might mean to see in the equivocation of eros a non-signification, or a "non-signifyingness" that refers to a "signifyingness" (see TI: 264, TeI: 241; and TI: 262–63, TeI: 240). In other words, eros can only refuse the discourse of light, avoid the concept of intentionality, and subvert the very order of meaning because it refers to the face, or because language is already in place. There can only be non-signification because signification already exists, or because the order of meaning is already established. In this sense, eros is always consequent upon ethics. The innuendo and deflagrating laughter (TI: 263; TeI: 241), the exorbitance and profanation (TI: 256, TeI: 234; and TI: 258, TeI: 235), the wanton immodesty of exhibitionism (TI: 257; TeI: 234), in short, the "disrespect" of eros "presupposes the face" (TI: 262; TeI: 240). Levinas' point is also expressed in terms of the secrecy upon which the relation of eros depends. He emphasizes the clandestineness of lovers, their need for privacy, the fact that eros requires intimacy, the exclusivity of lovers. But, Levinas insists, "the in appearance asocial relation of eros will have a reference—be it negative—to the social. In this inversion of the face in femininity, in this disfigurement that refers to the face, non-signifyingness abides in the signifyingness of the face" (TI: 262–63; TeI: 240).

The concept that is ultimately the most crucial, I suggest, for distinguishing between eros and ethics is the third party. Eros excludes the third party. "The relationship established between lovers in voluptuosity, fundamentally refractory to universalization, is the very contrary of the social relation. It excludes the third party, it remains intimacy, dual solitude, closed society, member of a dual society, an intimate society, a society without language" (TI: 264–65; TeI: 242–43). Recall how the third party is both implied by, yet absent from the face to face as such. Levinas says that the inequality of the face to face "does not appear to the third party who would count us. It precisely signifies the absence of a third party capable of taking in me and the other, such that the primordial multiplicity is observed within the very face to face that constitutes it" (TI: 251; TeI: 239).[84] The absence Levinas speaks of here is not the same as the absolute exclusion of the third party from the erotic relation between lovers. The third party is absent from the face to face as a relation, but the presence of others is implied in it; the demands of justice issue from the ethical relation *par excellence*.[85] In eros, any intrusion of others will not lead to anything beyond the destruction of intimacy. In ethics, on the contrary, the presence of the other in the eyes of the one that challenges me from on high is the condition of morality. The face to face founds justice.

In eros, it is not the presence of the other as the third party that can lead to anything beyond eros—lovers are only interrupted by outsiders. This does not mean, however, that eros has no signification beyond itself. There is an other involved in the relationship of eros, but it is a very specific other—namely, the child. The ultimate meaning of eros for Levinas lies in fecundity, in the production of the child. He says, "The profanation that violates a secret does not 'discover,' beyond the face, another more profound I which this face would express; it discovers the child" (TI: 267; TeI: 254).

By what trajectory does Levinas give eros a central place in 1947, but find it wanting in 1961? Why is it that the only aspect of eros responsible enough to gain admission in *Totality and Infinity* is that of fecundity? And by 1974, in *Otherwise than Being*, why does maternity occlude paternity, while eros is abandoned altogether?

In *Time and the Other* the idea of alterity is introduced through the notions of death and the future, which dominate the first part of Levinas' analyses of the other. In the final sections of *Time and the Other*, Levinas elaborates alterity in terms of the feminine and eros. In *Totality and Infinity*, ethics as the face-to-face relation takes center stage, and eros is sent off to the side wings. If, in *Totality and Infinity*, signification and non-signification are found respectively in the ethical relation of the face to face, and in the erotic nudity of voluptuosity, in *Otherwise than Being* they become part of the same movement. Signification includes or is also non-signification. The saying cannot exist without the said, and yet the said always undermines the saying, always makes it say something else, renders it other, betrays its intention. Words can signify intentions, but not without already losing sight of another meaning, not without already substituting the categories of being for the pre-original sensibility which signifies as the-one-for-the-other. Always in retreat, the saying nevertheless needs the said, from which it withdraws.

LEVINAS AND FEMINISM

So far, in tracing the movement of eros through Levinas' texts, we have tended to see in it the failure of the feminine to be ethical. There is no question that there are ample grounds for emphasizing the negative aspects of Levinas' attitude toward the feminine. One could almost call it pejorative. Does Levinas not seek to wipe clean the traces of the erotic that remain in his philosophy? All that seems to remain of the feminine in *Otherwise than Being* is the figure of the maternal, purified of any reference to erotic sensibility. Sensibility itself signifies responsibility. Maternity— responsible, ethical suffering, bearing the weight of the world—eradicates the troubling and dissembling nudity of voluptuous eros.

This summary can be reconstructed, paying attention specifically to the feminine. Eros has no place in the later texts of Levinas. And as eros disappears, so does the feminine, only to be replaced by maternity, which is apparently the only acceptable face of the feminine. This much is clear. Yet we should not allow ourselves to be blinded by the obvious case that can and should be made against Levinas to the extent of ignoring the contribution of his thinking through the problem of sexual difference. The importance of Levinas' rethinking of the other lies, for us, in the model it provides for Irigaray's rethinking of sexual difference. If Levinas' philosophical project can be characterized as an attempt to break away from the hegemony of the same that has dominated the visage of Western philosophy, Irigaray undertakes to think sexual difference according to this radical Levinasian departure from Parmenides. Neither project is without its problems. Since both Levinas and Irigaray, in their own ways, seek to put into question the very standards of intelligibility according to which the Western philosophical canon has functioned, there is a sense in which Levinas' reconceptualization of ethics and Irigaray's rethinking of sexual difference are quite literally incomprehensible.[86]

Derrida takes up the problem of what Levinas might mean by characterizing Western philosophy as governed by the imperialism of the same. Has not every possibility of radical alterity been explored and rejected by the dialecticians of thought? If not the Greeks, then surely Hegel has pre-empted any claim that otherness could be absolute or original in any way? What are we to make of Levinas' claims for the feminine as positing an unheard of relation with alterity? Even if in *Time and the Other* he prefaces this claim with a meditation on the alterity of death, and even if the priority of the feminine gives way to the ethical transcendence of the face to face in *Totality and Infinity*, and to obsession as a responsibility of the-one-for-the-other in *Otherwise than Being*, we should not lose sight of the fact that Levinas neither discards the feminine as unimportant, nor ignores it altogether.

Levinas' analysis of the feminine in *Time and the Other*, as we have already begun to see, is highly problematic for feminism. When Levinas tells us, in the final section of that book, entitled "Fecundity," that he is "going to return to the consideration that led [him] from the alterity of death to the alterity of the feminine" (TO: 90; TA: 85), the concept he has in mind is paternity. Aware, no doubt, that feminists will not like his resolution of eros into paternity—which appears to put the feminine firmly back into second place, according to an all too familiar trope—and presumably intending to alleviate the offense which he knows his remarks might cause, Levinas anticipates certain objections in advance. He assures us that his construal of the feminine does not "refer to any romantic notions of the mysterious, unknown, or misunderstood woman" (TO: 86; TA: 78). This is the explanation that follows:

> Let it be understood that if, in order to uphold the thesis of the exceptional position of the feminine in the economy of being, I willingly refer to the great themes of Goethe or Dante, to Beatrice and the *ewig Weibliches*, to the cult of the *Woman* in chivalry and in modern society (which is certainly not explained solely by the necessity of lending a strong arm to the weaker sex)—if, more precisely, I think of the admirably bold pages of Léon Bloy in his *Letters to His Fiancée*, I do not want to ignore the legitimate claims of feminism that presupposes all the acquired attainments of civilization.[87] I simply want to say that this mystery must not be understood in the ethereal sense of a certain literature; that in the most brutal materiality, in the most shameless or the most prosaic appearance of the feminine, neither her mystery nor her modesty are abolished (TO: 86; TA: 78–79).

Resisting the temptation to dismiss Levinas' protestation that he does "not want to ignore the legitimate claims of feminism" as disingenuous, I want to inquire more closely into the grounds he adduces for it. Levinas argues that there is an "exceptional position of the feminine in the economy of being." The radicality of this position should not be underestimated. I will indicate, following Derrida's analysis, how decisive Levinas' attempted break with Parmenides is. No matter how problematic Levinas' depiction of the feminine is in other respects, it challenges the logic of metaphysics with a radicality hitherto unprecedented. That is, Levinas' call to rethink philosophy starting from the face-to-face relation cannot be understood without bringing into question the conventional priority that ontology has enjoyed over ethics. Levinas claims to think otherness, difference, or alterity not by starting from the same, the one, the totality, but precisely as absolutely other.

In *Time and the Other* Levinas uses a striking image to express his attempted departure from the totalizing language of philosophy, an image to which he returns in later years.[88] He says, "To take up the existing in the existent is to enclose it within unity and to let Parmenides escape every parricide his descendants would be tempted to commit against him" (TO: 43; TA: 22). Derrida capitalizes on the image of parricide, using it to put into perspective Levinas' assessment of the impact of Greek philosophy on the tradition, and his attempt to break with it. On the one hand, there is the privilege that Levinas gives to Plato's idea of the good beyond being, and on the other hand, there is, pervasive in the tradition, Parmenides' insistence on excluding otherness from being. Derrida says of the bold gesture with which Levinas announces his intention to break with Parmenides,

> Thus, Levinas exhorts us to a second parricide. The Greek father who still holds us under his sway must be killed; and this is what a Greek— Plato—could never do, deferring the act into a hallucinatory murder. . . . Why was the repetition of the murder necessary according to Levinas? Because the Platonic gesture will be ineffectual for as long as multiplicity and alterity are not understood as the absolute solitude of the existent in its *existence*. . . . The relationship to the other arises from the depths of this solitude. Without it, without this primordial secret, parricide is philosophy's theatrical fiction (WD: 89–90; ED: 132–33).

As Derrida reminds us, following Levinas' own observation in *Time and the Other* (TO: 44; TA: 24), Levinas' word "existent" can be understood as more or less equivalent to Heidegger's "*Dasein*"; its mode of existing, therefore, approximates to Heidegger's concept of *Existenz* or that sense of existence which is specific to *Dasein*. Levinas insists that Heidegger does not recognize the drama of the instant (EE: 75; DE: 129) that constitutes the I's solitary existence. Levinas' descriptive analyses of this drama of solitude abound. To recall just a few of these telling descriptions, Levinas finds the ego "chained" to itself (EE: 84; DE: 143). He speaks of the "irremissible" burden of its existence (EE: 78; DE: 134), of the tragedy which consists in being unable to escape oneself, always encumbered with oneself (EE: 79; DE: 135), of the I as always having "one foot caught in its own existence" (EE: 84; DE: 143). It is this sense of being riveted to, mired in, stuck with myself that gives my existence its definitive character (EE: 84; DE: 144)—and it is this definitive character that the philosophical tradition from Parmenides on, according to Levinas, has failed to capture. Derrida summarizes the position Levinas held in 1947:

> In effect, if the Parmenidean tradition—we know now what this means for Levinas—disregards the irreducible solitude of the "existent," by the same token it disregards the relationship to the other. It does not think solitude, it does not appear to itself to be solitude, because it is the solitude of totality and opacity (WD: 91; ED: 136).

For alterity to be radical, not only must the other be absolutely transcendent, but the I must also exist multiply. Multiplicity is present even in the Levinasian I, which has a dual existence—in the sense of realizing, for example, the impossibility of escaping itself.[89] It is this sense of oneself as inescapable, the idea of one's being or existence as irremissible, that Levinas recognizes in his insistence on the solitude of the I. But if solitude marks, for Levinas, the failure of Parmenidean being in 1947, the situation changes with the publication of *Totality and Infinity* in 1961, according to Derrida. There, says Derrida, Levinas seems to regard whatever differences characterize interiority as illusory (WD: 93; ED: 139), as a "false heterology" (WD: 94; ED: 140), as less than fundamental (WD: 109; ED: 162). Says Derrida,

> If formerly, interiority, the secret and original separation, had permitted the break with the classical use of the Greek concepts of the Same and the Other, the amalgamation of Same and Ego (Same and Ego homogenized, and homogenized with the concept, as well as with the finite totality) now permits Levinas to include within the same condemnation both Greek and the most modern philosophies of subjectivity, the philosophies most careful to distinguish, as did Levinas previously, the Ego from the Same and the Others from the other (WD: 109–10; ED: 163).

Derrida's suggestion that a significant shift takes place in Levinas' thinking when in *Totality and Infinity* he amalgamates two concepts he had thought separately in 1947 bears scrutiny. While agreeing with him that there is a significant shift between 1947 and 1961, I have emphasized different reasons for this shift. We have seen, in following the motif of the feminine in Levinas' work, that in *Totality and Infinity*, it is acknowledged in a way that leaves eros in the shadow of ethics. In *Totality and Infinity*, although we know that erotic desire is not completely neglected, it is certainly less important than the ethical relation of the face to face.

The dissatisfaction Levinas anticipates he will find in his feminist readers led us to focus on the uneasy position Levinas endorses when, having first introduced the feminine as the motif that decisively breaks with the Parmenidean tradition, he finally turns, in his analysis of fecundity, to paternity. Describing the relation of father to son, Levinas says, "I do not *have* my child; I *am* in some way my child. But the words 'I am' here have a significance different from an Eleatic or Platonic significance. There is a multiplicity and a transcendence in this verb 'to exist,' a transcendence that is lacking in even the boldest existentialist analysis" (TO: 91; TA: 86). Does this signal a subordination of the feminine to the role of the father? Levinas' self-commentary indicates that his own answer to this question would be negative. Summing up his analysis of alterity in *Time and the Other*, he says, "I began with the notions of death and the feminine, and have ended with that of the son. . . . The unity of these situations—death, sexuality, paternity—until now appeared only in relation to the notion of power that they exclude" (TO: 92; TA: 87). And now (the reader might ask herself)? Levinas answers:

> This was my main goal. I have been bent on emphasizing that alterity is not purely and simply the existence of another freedom next to mine. . . . The coexistence of several freedoms is a multiplicity that leaves the unity of each intact, or else this multiplicity unites into a general will. Sexuality, paternity, and death introduce a duality into existence, a duality that concerns the very existing of each subject. Existing becomes double. The Eleatic notion of being is overcome (TO: 92; TA: 87–88).

For his part then, Levinas sees no contradiction in maintaining that each relation—with death, with the feminine, and with the son—is a relation of alterity which is at the same time a relation sufficient unto itself as a relation. One can be in relation to feminine alterity without compromising or changing the relation one has with one's son. The relation of alterity one has with the son affects neither one's relation with death, nor one's relation with the feminine as other—at least not in the sense that one relation could not exist without the other relation. At the risk of stating the obvious, let me add that Levinas can readily maintain that these relations "one" has are separable and possible, without colliding with one another or conflicting with one another or canceling one another out, for the very simple reason that he assumes unquestioningly the position of a heterosexual man. Derrida has in mind a similar concern when he says of Levinas' philosophy that it could not have been written by anyone other than a man.[90]

It is not only legitimate, for a woman reading his texts, to ask what difference the fact that they are written by a man might make, it is imperative—at least if one is concerned both to understand Levinas' philosophy, and to try to formulate questions and strategy which bear on feminist practices. Formally speaking, Levinas' self-commentary is encouraging. In claiming that relationships of alterity can leave each other "intact" without compromising or interfering with one another, Levinas would seem to rule out the possibility that the relationship the feminine has to paternity is one of subservience, as if the relationship with the feminine were somehow sublated in the relationship with the son. Levinas never tires of refusing the Hegelian gesture of negation, whereby the alterity of the other is surpassed and rendered identical with the I, only to succumb to yet another encounter with otherness which in its turn is sublated in the I. In claiming that his whole point is to differentiate between various alterities, to maintain their differences and not to collapse them into the same, Levinas appears to pre-empt any suspicion that feminism casts on his work—namely, that it is gender-specific in a way that merely confirms and reflects the power imbalance that persists between the sexes, as if that were unproblematic. In claiming that his point is not to resolve one relation into another, to collapse the relation with the feminine into that with the son—as if the latter had ultimate priority—Levinas might seem to get himself off the feminist hook.

However, the rules governing the production of Levinas' text are clearly not purely formal. His cultural and religious identification, his political beliefs, and his sexuality are all factors that also come into play. Levinas recognizes this when in 1979 he writes in the preface to the second edition of *Time and the Other*, "Femininity—and one would have to see in what sense this can be said of masculinity or of virility; that is, of the differences between the sexes in general—appeared to me as a difference contrasting strongly with other differences, not merely as a quality different from all others, but as the very quality of difference" (TO: 36; TA: 14). One would have to see in what sense this could be said of masculinity. (Who would have to see—who is this we? We feminists, one supposes.) Let's move on to look at Irigaray's response to Levinas.

IRIGARAY'S CRITIQUE OF LEVINAS

In 1984 *Éthique de la différence sexuelle* appeared, the final chapter of which Irigaray devoted to Levinas' conception of eros. She calls the conclusion of her book, which had previously been published as a separate article in 1982, "The Fecundity of the Caress: A Reading of Levinas, *Totality and Infinity* section IV, B, 'The Phenomenology of Eros.'"[91] That Irigaray chose to conclude her book with a reading of Levinas, indeed that she chose to write a book on the ethics of sexual difference at all, and that in concluding it, she chose to concentrate on the comparatively small section of *Totality and Infinity* in which Levinas discusses eros—none of these facts are insignificant. Irigaray's work as a whole is profoundly influenced by Levinas' conception of ethics.

Ostensibly a commentary on Levinas' phenomenology of eros—a discussion which takes up only a small portion of *Totality and Infinity*—Irigaray's first essay on Levinas may take as its starting point the subject of eros, but it also suggests a reading of Levinas' work as a whole. It thus includes a consideration of Levinas' notion of the feminine not only as eros, but also in the context of the dwelling (section II, D, *Totality and Infinity*), and it addresses the relationship between ethics and eros in Levinas' philosophy. Throughout "The Fecundity of the Caress," Irigaray recalls the formulation of love that she borrowed from Diotima, who sees eros as some kind of rebirth of the self and the other.[92] The lovers, says Irigaray "bestow on each other—life" (FC: 235; E: 177). It is for this reason that eros does not first appear as eros, and that voluptuosity is not aware of itself as such. Eros is "prior to any *eros* defined or measured as such" and voluptuousness is "Voluptuous without knowing it" (FC: 231; E: 173). Just as the subject has, as yet, no reason to parcel itself off from the world, so it has no reason to distinguish one sensation from another. In one of its senses eros stands for enjoyment in general, or that desire which Levinas equates with need, desire that, like a hunger, can be satisfied, as distinct from metaphysical desire, the responsibility for the other which is in principle insatiable.

Yet eros, for Levinas, as we have already seen, is essentially ambiguous. It is both like and unlike ethics, and hence it is both capable of being sated, and in this respect it is akin to animality or need, and at the same time insatiable, and in this respect it is similar to metaphysical desire, to ethics, to infinity. Eros is not just a simple hunger, although it has certain characteristics which put it on a par with economic pleasure. It is also transcendent, it goes beyond the simplicity of needs. It is both an "appetite of all the senses" and an "indefinable attraction to the other, which will never be satiated" (FC: 232; E: 174). It is, to quote a word which is so crucial for Irigaray's reading of Levinas, on the "threshold" (*le seuil*) of need and desire, marking the limits of the dwelling, separating the subject from the world, creating a boundary behind which the subject can withdraw from the public gaze and into the clandestine twilight of the lovers' embrace. Halfway between sense and nonsense, between clarity and obscurity, eros evinces not so much a duality as a thoroughgoing ambiguity. In eros, the truths and certainties of the world, the will to mastery and control, are suspended (see FC: 232; E: 174).

The effect of eros then, is to recast a subject who has learned to control its world, who has achieved mastery of itself, back into a state of flux where the borders of self and other, between the I and the world, are no longer so clear, where the gap between the I and the other is not so well-defined, nor so easily grasped. Thus Irigaray says of the new birth of eros, "The light that shines there is different from the one that makes distinctions and separates too neatly" (FC: 234; E: 176). Irigaray consistently characterizes the lover (*l'amant*) as transcendent, and the loved one (*l'aimée*) as "plunged into the abyss" (FC: 233; E: 175).[93] The lover attends to his "solitary call to his God" (FC: 244; E: 187) while the loved one "sinks into the abyss, founders in a night more primeval than the night, or finds herself dispersed in the shards of a broken mirror" (FC: 238; E: 181). He "relegates her to infancy, animality, or maternity," thereby "Separating her off into the subterranean, the submarine. . . . Uprooting the beloved from her fundamental habitat" (FC: 239; E: 181).[94] Consumed with his "ethical responsibilities" (FC: 241; E: 184), distracted only temporarily by the gesture of eros, the lover turns back to the serious things of life, to transcendence. Irigaray says, "The loved one would be relegated to the abyss so that the lover might be sent back to the heights. The act of love would amount to contact with the irrationality of discourse, in order to send the loved one back to the position of fallen animal or infant" (FC: 241; E: 183). Irigaray repeatedly appeals to the transcendence of the lover, which is dependent upon the submergence of the loved one in a world without ethics: the lover sends his loved one "back down to the abyss so that he may rebound into the transcendent" (FC: 249; E: 191). Using her as a refuge, only to discard her as profane, the gesture of eros returns her to the abyss, meanwhile catapulting him up to the lofty heights of divinity, to communion with his God, to the righteousness of responsibility. So Irigaray's question is, "But what of her call to the divine?" (FC: 239; E: 182)—a question that is not only dictated, as one might think at first glance, by Levinas' concern with God, but also with Irigaray's own agenda.

Is Irigaray to be faulted for imagining a new relation to the divine, one that incorporates a sense of the female sexual lover? Is she to be blamed for seeing Levinas' rethinking of alterity not only as a stumbling block for women, but also as a resource? To put the same question yet another way, is Irigaray to be castigated for still reading the male philosophical tradition, for still talking—at least in places—the language of philosophers, even as she brings into question that language at every moment? By adopting a procedure of close reading, interspersed with critically ironic gestures, Irigaray not only locates herself in a certain relation to Levinas and the philosophical tradition of which he is representative. She also situates herself in terms of several other ideologically hazardous terrains. Adopting Levinas'—or any other philosopher's for that matter—point of reference, however much she disengages with his assumptions, revises his project, or reverses his intentions, does she not thereby also signal his authority?

How are we to weigh the strategic gains to be had from positioning oneself in relation to a master discourse, even if one looks on it askance? Are the losses we incur too great, or is this a risk worth taking? Irigaray might be upbraided for celebrating, with Levinas, the status of women as marginal—which is indisputably how they appear in Levinas' texts, despite the respect he has for the biblical figures of Sarah, Rebecca, and Rachel.

How then can Irigaray avoid endorsing, however ambiguously, hesitantly, or unwittingly Levinas' stance on women? Does she not legitimate the necessary inferiority Levinas imputes to women? To be sure, Irigaray replicates the moves that Levinas produces, but at the same time she steps back from the scheme he endorses (see Berg, 1982: 14–15). Performing, in my view, an urgent and necessary role, Irigaray is neither content to simply dismiss Levinas as a thinker whose attempt to rethink the other has no relevance for feminism, nor is she satisfied with unquestioning or slavish devotion to the texts of the male tradition. She insists on rereading "the dominant discourse" (TS: 119: CS: 119), not in order to perpetuate it, but by "interrogating men's 'mastery'" (TS: 119; CS: 119), in the knowledge that we cannot afford to ignore the legacy of the Western tradition that has shaped our very ways of thinking. At the same time Irigaray, perhaps more than most, is aware that the tradition we inherit does not determine all our possibilities for thinking. Her critical deployment of the resources offered her by the tradition owes its energy not only to that tradition, but also to her difference from that tradition. She says that

> unless we limit ourselves naively—or perhaps strategically—to some kind of limited or marginal issue, it is indeed precisely philosophical discourse that we have to challenge, and *disrupt*, in as much as this discourse sets forth the law of all others, in as much as it constitutes the discourse on discourse (TS: 74; CS: 72).

While it is certainly true that, in some senses, in attending to traditional philosophical concepts, her thinking is encompassed by the tradition even in the very attempt to bring it into question, it is also true that her thinking is never entirely determined by the discourse against which she necessarily defines her own position. It is as well to acknowledge her debt to a tradition that she cannot possibly ignore, as to pretend it does not exist—for to do so would be simply to remain blind to its consequences, its power, its effect. It is because of the philosophic "reduction of the other in the Same" that Irigaray sees the "necessity of 'reopening' the figures of philosophical discourse—idea, substance, subject, transcendental subjectivity, absolute knowledge—in order to pry out of them what they have borrowed that is feminine, from the feminine, to make them 'render up' and give back what they owe the feminine" (TS: 74; CS: 72). Irigaray, then, turns Levinas' concern with God into an agenda of her own. The subtitle of her second essay on Levinas, "Questions to Emmanuel Levinas," is "On the Divinity of Love," and the subject of divinity reappears as a focus in much of her other work.[95] Irigaray acknowledges her debt to Levinas' reflections on religion, and to Derrida—who in turn is inspired by Levinas—when she says,

> We are witnessing . . . a modification in the use of language by certain philosophers who are turning back toward the origins of their culture. Thus Nietzsche and Heidegger, but also Hegel before them, interrogated their foundations in ancient Greece, and in religion Levinas and Derrida are interrogating their relation to the texts of the Old Testament. Their gesture goes with the use of a style that comes close to that of tragedy, poetry, the Platonic dialogues, the way in which myth, parable, and liturgies are expressed (Jardine and Menke, 1991: 101).

Irigaray is able to show that Levinas' characterization of ethical transcendence is achieved by confining the female to the animality of desire. The one who transcends is the man—who thus represents one side of the ambiguity Levinas ascribes to eros. The one who is relegated to the carnal embodiment of desire, akin not to ethics but to enjoyment, is the woman. By making clear the sexual demarcation between the two aspects of eros, which Levinas refers to as conflated in the "ambiguity" of the erotic, Irigaray shows that it is only at the expense of female desire and female subjectivity that male desire succeeds in transcending the body, exceeding the limited model of need and satisfaction that structures enjoyment, and breaking out of the egoism of the self. To be responsible for others, the message is, you have to be a man. For all its radicality—and Irigaray admits that Levinas' philosophy of desire has potential—Levinas' account of eros ultimately falls back on the familiar and traditional elevation of men at the expense of women. Irigaray says of Levinas' philosophy of ethics: "Although temporarily useful and worthy of respect up to a certain point, this ethics no longer knows its faults" (QE: 114).

For Levinas, as we have already seen, while there may be some aspects by which eros is construed as a relationship involving genuine alterity, ultimately it is only in its resolution in the child, through paternity, that eros is acknowledged as issuing in otherness. Irigaray focuses on the sense in which eros is fecund "prior to any procreation" (FC: 234, E: 176; FC: 235, E: 177),[96] and argues, contrary to Levinas, that "The son does not resolve the enigma of the most irreducible otherness" (FC: 234; E: 176–77). The importance of Irigaray's insistence that the alterity of eros is not only to be found in procreation—which, for Levinas, means the birth of the son—is twofold. If lovers encounter or produce an irreducible otherness in erotic relations which is not merely an aspect of procreation, the significance of eros is not only extended beyond physical fecundity, beyond the pretense that eros is legitimate only to the extent that it leads to maternity. At the same time the heterosexuality that is assumed in Levinas' model of eros is challenged by Irigaray (see QE: 113). By insisting on the otherness of eros as such, irrespective of any procreative aspect it may have, Irigaray both resists reducing the feminine to the maternal, and opens Levinas' discussion of eros to the possibility of homosexuality. She says, "before the son appears, the loved one's fulfillment tells him, shows him, the mystery of fecundity" (FC: 235; E: 177). This mystery is not restricted to the female lover—there is a mutual fecundation in the erotic experience of eros, "for those who take the time to reopen their eyes" (FC: 235; E: 177). "Prior to any procreation, the lovers bestow on each other—

life. Love fecundates each of them in turn, through the genesis of their immortality" (FC: 235; E: 177).

If Irigaray concedes that Levinas catches sight of the rebirth of both lovers in eros outside of fecundity, she criticizes him for not making more of this mutuality. Irigaray continues her analysis by emphasizing the stultifying and paralyzing effects that the lover has on the regeneration of the loved one, according to Levinas' account. "Bidding her to freeze into the shapes that separate her from herself. Deprived of the suppleness of her amorous mobility . . . annexing the other . . . [he] paralyzes the other's movement" (FC: 238–39; E: 181–82). By pointing to the idea that the lover restricts the movement of his loved one, negating her differences and imposing sameness, Irigaray reads Levinas' account of eros in terms of the structure I have already outlined; the male is transcendent and responsible to God, while the female is relegated to animal desire and subterranean needs. The Levinasian lover sees in the rhythms of gestation only the potentiality of the child, ignoring any difference in the loved one herself. Irigaray turns to the imagery of the myth of creation to make her point:

> When the lover relegates her to infancy, animality, or maternity, he leaves unsolved, in part, this mystery of a relation to the cosmos. . . . Believing that it is given once and for all, to be exploited endlessly, carelessly, irretrievably. Cultivating one's already-enclosed garden. The work of a landlord, without regard for the natural world that makes fecundity possible, without God's concern for this universe of incarnation, for the harmony of its allurements (FC: 239; E: 181).

Again, Irigaray says—highlighting the restricted subjectivity that Levinas' equating the feminine with eros allows women—

> Even if she plays, within this male territory, at disguising herself in numerous displays, various coquetries, which he will interpret as part of love, she remains without an identity or a passport with which to traverse, to transgress, the lover's language. A more or less domesticated child or animal that clothes itself or takes on a semblance of humanity? (FC: 239; E: 182).

Irigaray pursues the image of the garden of Eden that is clearly invoked above in challenging Levinas' conception of eros as profanation (see FC:

233–34; E: 186). At the same time she suggests that Levinas leaves women no real possibility of breaking out of the mold into which they are cast by men, for it is men alone that Levinas recognizes as ethical subjects, on Irigaray's reading of Levinas. Whatever disguises, displays, or coquetries women adopt, they are trapped by having been excluded from the possibility of being other than they are, suggests Irigaray. Whatever new strategies they devise to break the mold, they will find themselves reinscribed in their old position.

The exclusion of women from representation, and the impossibility of representing otherness within the gaze of the same is the focus of Irigaray's attention when she raises the question of how the touch of eros can be remembered. Suggesting that "Touch never shows itself, not even if its exactness could thus be made manifest" (FC: 236; E: 178–79), she goes on to point out that to represent the "source of all the senses—the sense of touch" (FC: 237; E: 179) by way of images or photographs is to immobilize "the perpetual unfolding and becoming of what is alive," or to render as if it were static the "unceasing palpitation" (FC: 236; E: 179) that marks the caress of eros. The only way that eros can have a future— if not in memory that must resort to images which cannot represent the "letting go and giving of self" (FC: 237; E: 179), then in life itself—is by giving new life to the lovers. As Irigaray says, "Return to a certain night whence the lovers can arise, differently illuminated and enlightened. They give themselves to each other and abandon what has already been created. By themselves and by reason" (FC: 237; E: 179).

At this point let me step back from Irigaray's critical reflections on Levinas in order to review the terrain covered in this chapter. Throughout the course of Levinas' work he constantly renews his attempt to catch sight of the possibility of maintaining a relationship with absolute otherness or radical alterity. How can one be in a relation to the other, without negating the other's alterity, without reducing it to oneself, without the use of some mediating category, based on mutuality, or commonality, or some supposed standard of truth?

I have traced the distinction that Levinas offers between desire and need, a distinction that depends on an affirmation of otherness which does not degenerate into the always already known, which does not proceed by negating difference nor by claiming the priority of preconceived categories over what may overturn old conceptions and produce something altogether new. To insist on knowing everything, to render the unknown knowable, to contextualize the foreign by placing it within the familiar comfortable world of the subject's experience, is to grasp everything exotic—all that is other than oneself—and to make it available for use according to one's own purposes and projects, to take control of it, and to put otherness at one's own disposal.

Despite the alterity that characterizes the worldly things that nourish the subject, enjoyment remains a mode of experience which reduces the food I eat or the air I breathe to the I that does the eating and breathing. To inhabit the Levinasian world is ultimately to be a subject who comports itself toward that world in a way that takes command of it. The subject engages otherness, but it does so in a relationship of mastery, ensuring its own supremacy at every turn. Through strategies of possession, it identifies as its own the things it enjoys, making whatever it has contact with into its belongings, endowing things with the permanence of objects, providing them with a definite environment, calling that environment a home, designating part of the world a dwelling place, producing a domain that one can call one's own, parceling off from the world a pocket of security, protecting oneself against others who do the same. It gains time, creating within the vast open spaces of the world a place to withdraw, a resting place, a retreat for oneself. In the enjoyment of the world, in the possession of things, the other is defined, the unknown is rendered knowable, reduced in the last analysis to my comprehension, negated, nullified—destroyed?

Eros disrupts the familiarity of enjoyment and possession, breaks the circle one establishes among the things one enjoys in relation to oneself. In the erotic relation, as Levinas describes it, the other has the capacity to remain other in the face of the same. Irigaray sees this when she says, "Voluptuousness can reopen and reverse this conception and construction of the world" (FC: 231; E: 173). She sees that for Levinas "the touch of the caress" leaves the other intact even while seeking its alterity, it "weds without consuming" and "perfects while abiding by the outlines of the other" (FC: 232; E: 174). The Levinasian caress respects the other as other. "This touch binds and unbinds two others in flesh that is still, and always, untouched by mastery," this touch "seeks out and affirms otherness, while protecting it" (FC: 232; E: 174).

The importance of Levinas for Irigaray is his refusal to submit the otherness of the other to the demands of logic. The paradox that both Levinas and Irigaray maintain in their different discourses consists in leaving room—or perhaps creating a space—to think difference without reverting to sameness. What this means in Irigaray's terms is a continual emphasis on the irreducibility of sexual difference to the terms of equality. While it is still necessary to fight for equal rights it is even more urgent, in

Irigaray's view, to be vigilant about reminding ourselves that the very necessity of the abstract idea of equality emerges from irreducible differences. Irigaray's rejection of the sex/gender ideology that serves as the dominant frame of reference for Anglo-American feminism stems from its tendency to measure success in terms of the extent to which the situations of the two sexes become similar. Her point is that, as long as the presuppositions of what constitutes success remain unquestioned, the chances are that the alienation and domination inherent in current social relations will be perpetuated in the name of equality.

If Levinas provides a model for Irigaray's rethinking of the question of sexual difference by giving an account of a relationship in which the other can retain alterity without being reduced to the neutral categories of the same—to the demands of an I—his philosophy still falls short of an ethics of sexual difference. In Irigaray's words, "Although he takes pleasure in caressing, he abandons the feminine other, leaves her to sink, in particular into the darkness of pseudo-animality, in order to return to his responsibilities in the world of men-amongst-themselves" (QE: 183). Irigaray sums up her position when she says that:

> the description of pleasure given by Levinas is unacceptable to the extent that it presents man as the sole subject exercising his desire and his appetite upon the woman who is deprived of subjectivity except to seduce him. So the woman's pleasure is alienated to that of the man, according to the most traditional of scenarios of temptation and fall. In my opinion, if there is a fall, it is located in the reduction of the feminine to the passive, to the past tense and to the object of man's pleasure, in the identification of the woman with the beloved [*aimée*] (QE: 185).

Before the Levinasian I discovers itself as ethically related to the other, as already implicated in a relationship of obligation, it cannot properly be said to "be" a subject. This is why Levinas is so insistent on the idea that ethics precedes ontology. The subject is constituted in and through its relation to the other. The I only identifies itself as an I once it takes account of the other. Its realization of its selfhood is integrally linked to its discovery of the other. There is not, for Levinas, first a subject, and then a relation to the other. By its relation to the other, the I discovers not only its responsibility as a subject, but subjectivity itself. The I's relation to absolute otherness provides the subject with an understanding of its subjectivity for the first time. To put it slightly differently, we might say that it is in the call to responsibility which comes from elsewhere, or in the challenge that the other issues to the I in the face-to-face relation, that the I first becomes an I. In being challenged the subject sees itself, for the first time, as an I capable of distinguishing itself from the world it has hitherto inhabited. Already involved in the world, having set up a dwelling, the I only comes to separate itself from the things from which it lives once it is called into question by the other. Up until that point the I does not need to recognize itself, to conceptualize itself as autonomous or as distinct from the elements in which it dwells. It is inserted into the world without having had to conceptualize its relation to that world. Irigaray sees eros as a return to this tactile world of sensation, where things do not yet need to be thought as separate from the subject.

In this chapter I have argued for the importance of Levinas' philosophy for Irigaray's project. Let me conclude by reviewing the advances that Levinas sees his philosophy as having made over fundamental ontology in order to specify with greater clarity the distance Irigaray takes not only from Levinas but also from Heidegger. The direction in which Levinas takes Heidegger's inquiry into being is an ethical one. Levinas' goal is to demonstrate the priority of ethics over ontology, that is, to show that philosophical reflection and the central tasks of the philosopher—identifying concepts, universalizing, abstracting from the concrete—gain their impetus from a source that is extra-philosophical.[97] Philosophy, for Levinas, begins with the other. Or, rather, it has always already begun, prompted by the other. Levinas suspects that however radical Heidegger's inquiry into being may be in its attempt to overcome traditional metaphysics, it does not manage to bring into question the priority of the self over the other.[98] The ethical relation remains therefore subordinate to Heidegger's hermeneutical project, in *Being and Time*, of uncovering the truth of *Dasein's* own understanding of its relation to the world.[99] By returning our attention to ethics, understood not primarily in terms of metaphysical principles that issue from general truths about a community of rational and more or less identical subjects, but rather in terms of the asymmetrical face-to-face relation, Levinas places the radical alterity of the other at the center of his analysis. If Heidegger's analysis of the question of being provides Irigaray with a model for interrogating the philosophical tradition in the light of its neglect of sexual difference, it is Levinas who provides the reorientation of phenomenology toward the ethical relation with the other.

Borrowing from Heidegger, Irigaray suggests that as long as the question of sexual difference is framed as a question about the privilege of one sex over the other, the question of difference itself is avoided rather than addressed. Borrowing from Levinas, Irigaray asks about the possibility of thinking radical alterity, where difference is not defined in opposition to some presumed and already known standard, where otherness is not circumscribed by the same. Having examined Irigaray's relation to Levinas and Heidegger, my final task will be to situate Irigaray's relationship to Derrida in terms of this philosophical inheritance.

six DERRIDA, IRIGARAY, AND FEMINISM

Of course, it has been a necessary phase, strategically speaking, to build Women's Studies. But what should be the next step? Only this first move, this first effort? Or something totally new? And is it only a question of strategy—is not strategy itself the real risk?

—DERRIDA

One can only wonder: what are the risks and the stakes of the institution of women's studies? Do the women who manage these programs, do they not become, in turn, the guardians of the Law, and do they not risk constructing an institution similar to the institution against which they are fighting?

—DERRIDA

In the subtitle of Speculum, I wanted to indicate that the other is not, in fact, neutral, neither grammatically, nor semantically, and that it is no longer possible to utilize indifferently the same word for the masculine and the feminine. Now this practice is current in philosophy, in religion, in politics. We speak of the existence of the other, of the love of the other, of the suffering of the other, etc., without asking ourselves the question of who or what represents this other.

—IRIGARAY

RETHINKING PHENOMENOLOGY

W HEN IRIGARAY ASSERTS THAT, FOR DERRIDA, "*THERE IS nothing outside the play of différance (il n'est pas de hors jeu de la différance)*" (VL: 157), what is the register of her observation? Does it signal a trivialization of Derrida's work that indicates a failure to move beyond the most banal level of ostensible interpretation? Does the tenor of Irigaray's comment put her in the company of those who have reacted with indignation to the idea that "There is nothing outside the text?" (OGr: 158; DG: 227).[1] Or does Irigaray represent a more profound challenge to the framework within which Derrida's questions are typically formulated?

The reader coming to Irigaray's first essay on Derrida in ignorance of her responses to Heidegger and Levinas could be forgiven for mistaking as naive and uninformed her rendering—for it is not merely a critique—of Derrida's strategies. By reading it in the context of the continental tradition out of which both Irigaray's and Derrida's thought emerges we may be able to find a more productive way of gauging their relation. We might do well to bear in mind, for example, the sense in which, since Hegel, continental philosophers have created a tradition of thought that takes account of its own historical development. Among Hegel's greatest contributions to philosophy was his insistence upon conceiving of philosophy as historical. Hegel did not merely record historical developments as a chronicler might produce a list of events; he paid attention to the internal logic of philosophical development in the sense that Merleau-Ponty establishes in his essay "Hegel's Existentialism." According to Merleau-Ponty, the *Phenomenology of Spirit*

> does not try to fit all history into a framework of pre-established logic but attempts to bring each doctrine and each era back to life and to let itself be guided by their internal logic with such impartiality that all concern with system seems forgotten. The introduction states that the philosopher should not put himself in the place of human experiences; his task is simply to collect and decipher these experiences as history makes them available. It is in this sense that we can begin to speak of "Hegel's Existentialism," since he does not propose to connect concepts but to reveal the immanent logic of human experience in all its sectors (Merleau-Ponty, 1964: 65).

Phenomenology thinks through its own origins in a way that brings to fruition the tradition out of which it was born, allowing it to flower and to issue in new blooms. The image is not incidental to Hegel, who in the preface to the *Phenomenology of Spirit* refers to the blossoming of a bud in his call to philosophers to attend to the historical development of philosophy:

> The bud disappears in the bursting-forth of the blossom, and one might say that the former is refuted by the latter; similarly, when the fruit

appears, the blossom is shown up in its turn as a false manifestation of the plant, and the fruit now emerges as the truth of it instead. These forms are not just distinguished from one another, they also supplant one another as mutually incompatible. Yet at the same time their fluid nature makes them moments of an organic unity in which they not only do not conflict, but in which each is as necessary as the other; and this mutual necessity alone constitutes the life of the whole. But he who rejects a philosophical system does not usually comprehend what he is doing in this way; and he who grasps the contradiction between them does not, as a general rule, know how to free it from its one-sidedness, or maintain it in its freedom by recognizing the reciprocally necessary moments that take shape as a conflict and seeming incompatibility (PhS: 2; PhG: 10).

Hegel's legacy is reflected in the phenomenological movement as a whole, for it is only by situating themselves in relation to their predecessors that Husserl saw the need to radicalize Descartes' project, and that Heidegger advanced beyond Husserl's phenomenology. Husserl took seriously Descartes' starting point by applying the Cartesian method all the more rigorously, while at the same time pressing beyond the normative ideal of science that Descartes presupposed by inquiring into the scientific method itself (Husserl, 1977: 7–8). Heidegger, in his turn, took up Husserl's phenomenological method only to move beyond it. If Hegel's comprehension of the movement of history came to an abrupt halt when he had to situate himself in that history—as Merleau-Ponty says, he "understood everything except his own historical situation" (1964: 64)— Husserl retained some of Hegel's idealism. Hans-Georg Gadamer observed, writing in 1962,

In certain ways, the concept of self-understanding is an heirloom of transcendental idealism and has been propagated in our own time as such an idealism by Husserl. It was only through Heidegger's work that this concept acquired its real historicity. . . . Even in *Being and Time* the real question is not in what way being can be understood but in what way understanding *is* being, for the understanding of being represents the existential distinction of Dasein (1977: 49).

Perhaps no one has done more than Gadamer to illuminate the sense in which Heidegger's translation of Husserl's phenomenology must itself be understood in terms of Heidegger's reinterpretation of ourselves as historical beings. Hegel encountered his own thought as a limit, but Heidegger experiences Hegel's limitations as an invitation to go beyond Hegel, not by ignoring his thought but by thinking it through to its own limit—and beyond. Heidegger can stress the sense in which the need to surpass a thinker need not be a repudiation of that thinker; on the contrary, it can be a token of the greatest respect. John Sallis shows, in his article "The Origins of Heidegger's Thought," how Heidegger's thought both assumes and builds upon the phenomenological method as conceived by Husserl, and challenges the foundations of that method. Heidegger thinks the "unthought" in Husserl's appeal "to the things themselves" (Sallis, 1978: 48) in an effort "to be more phenomenological even than Husserl himself. He seeks to radicalize phenomenology by adhering even more radically than Husserl to the phenomenological demand to attend to the things themselves" (Sallis, 1978: 47). By asking what remains unthought in Husserl's appeal to the things themselves, Heidegger uncovers the question of being. Taminiaux also shows how in *Being and Time* Heidegger "combines with [h]is recognition of debt [to Husserl] a sense of departure" from Husserl's investigations, and from phenomenology as Husserl understood it (Taminiaux 1978: 58).

Husserl made it possible for Heidegger to raise a question which may not have been Husserl's own, but which Heidegger could not have articulated without first thinking through thoroughly Husserl's own investigations. In a gesture to which I have already referred more than once, Levinas acknowledges a similar dependence on Heidegger, insisting on the need to "leave the climate of that philosophy" although not "a philosophy that would be pre-Heideggerian" (EE: 19; DE: 19). Derrida reiterates Levinas' gesture in acknowledging that perhaps "logocentrism is not totally absent from Heidegger's thought" (OGr: 12; DG: 23), while nonetheless emphasizing that

> the critical movement of the Husserlian and Heideggerian questions must be effectively followed to the very end, and their effectiveness and legibility must be conserved. Even if it were crossed out, without it the concepts of play and writing to which I shall have recourse will remain caught within regional limits and an empiricist, positivist, or metaphysical discourse (OGr: 50; DG: 73).

To think differently the most profound thoughts of a thinker is perhaps to remain true to that thinker—more so than blindly and unthinkingly adopting what one takes to be the basic tenets of a philosopher. Gadamer sees this when he says,

> Nowhere does the understanding mean the mere recovery of what the author "meant," whether he was the creator of a work of art, the doer of a deed, the writer of a law book, or anything else. The *mens auctoris* does not limit the horizon of understanding in which the interpreter has to move, indeed, in which he is necessarily moved, if, instead of merely repeating, he really wants to understand (1977: 210).

The idea that the truth of a philosopher can be borne out even in its apparent overcoming should not surprise us if we take seriously Heidegger's meditations (discussed in chapter four) on the Greek idea of truth as *a-letheia*, as un-concealment—a truth that is uncovered from its own oblivion, revealing its hidden side as having been forgotten. The need for a rethinking of philosophy from the ground up—in the sense that Heidegger elaborates in "The Way Back into the Ground of Metaphysics" (Heidegger, 1975c: 265), as a thinking back through the roots of metaphysics—is one that Irigaray takes up in her own way. That is, Irigaray sifts through the earth to find the remains of the scattered question of sexual difference: she pieces together the shards of a forgotten question, she traces the roots of her question to its earliest burial, she forms her question out of fragments, and she thereby transforms what was not yet a question into a powerful and obligatory matter for thought. Irigaray says "I ought to reconstitute myself on the basis of a disas-similation . . . of a culture, of works already produced by the other. Searching through what is there—for what is not there" (ES: 9; E: 17, translation adapted).

My reasons for undertaking this brief excursus into the self-consciously historical relationship that binds together phenomenologists and post-phenomenologists in a way that allows them to reveal the hidden truths contained in the thought of their predecessors are threefold. First, Heidegger's retrieval of the question of the meaning of being from the oblivion into which metaphysics had cast it, and the sense in which this retrieval of the forgotten question of being can be thought in terms of the structure of *aletheia* has functioned as a leitmotif throughout this work. The parallel between Heidegger's question of being and Irigaray's question of sexual difference was explicitly demonstrated in chapter four, but it was already implicit as a guiding motif in my discussion of the sex/gender distinction in chapter one.[2] There is a sense in which sexual difference forms the silent center of feminist theory, which is left unthought as such, but which nevertheless acts as a pivot around which feminist categories are constructed. In thematizing the question of sexual difference Irigaray is not merely shifting the terms of the debate, but also revealing its underlying presuppositions. She asks what lies behind the surface phenomena in a manner similar to Heidegger, who reappropriates Husserl's reflections on the "givenness" of the world in the name of the question of being. From Heidegger's point of view, Husserl does not succeed in properly answering to the call of *"Zur Sache Selbst"* (To the Things Themselves!)[3] because he remains trapped by methodological concerns which make him a closer adherent to Cartesian thought than he would like to have thought. As Taminiaux says, Husserl's call *"Zur Sache Selbst"*

> subordinates the Thing towards which it directs the phenomenologist's attention to the primacy of method, in such a manner that the *Sache* is phenomenologically admissible only to the extent to which it satisfies the methodological requirements of validity which were expressed for the first time by Descartes and which deem that the only entity the presence of which is indisputably valid is the *ego cogito* (Taminiaux, 1978: 64).

Second, one of my aims is to establish Irigaray as a major figure in the continental tradition in her own right, by demonstrating how the evolution of her thought and the formulation of her questions is indebted to a path of questioning mapped out by Beauvoir, Hegel, Nietzsche, Heidegger, Levinas, and Derrida.

Third and finally, I want to emphasize, contrary to the popular conception of Derrida's work, the extent to which his thought can no more be understood in isolation from the tradition that it nonetheless seeks to put into question than Irigaray's questions can be divorced from the tradition that provokes them. If in some ways and at some moments Derrida and Irigaray align Heidegger and Levinas with the metaphysical tradition, they also take up Heideggerian and Levinasian themes as a means of overcoming that tradition. In general terms, the Heideggerian theme of the metaphysics of presence and the Levinasian theme of the other are integral to both Irigaray and Derrida in their rethinking of the tradition. In the next section of this chapter, as a preface to elaborating Irigaray's reading of Derrida, I want to specify more exactly how the influence of Heidegger and Levinas plays itself out in Derrida's understanding of the feminine.

In "Choreographies," Derrida asks his interviewer, "Must one think 'difference' 'before' sexual difference or taking off 'from' it? Has this question, if not a meaning (we are at the origin of meaning here, and the origin cannot 'have meaning') at least something of a chance of opening up anything at all, however im-pertinent it may appear?" (C: 70). At the beginning of her article, "Questions to Emmanuel Levinas," Irigaray asks, "Is there otherness outside of sexual difference?" (QE: 111). While it is posed with a different emphasis, Irigaray's question to Levinas addresses the same difficulty that Derrida inherits from Levinas—namely, can difference be thought without sexual difference? It becomes clear as Derrida deflects his interviewer's questions in "Choreographies"—changing roles with her, asking her the questions and deferring his answers to her own—that he is not just improvising his moves as he goes along. For one thing he is drawing on a text he had written beforehand, and for another, he explicitly calls Levinas on to the stage as a third dancing partner.

The text that Derrida draws on in "Choreographies" is "At This Very Moment in This Work Here I Am."[4] One might say that in drawing on his essay on Levinas Derrida returns to Levinas a debt that was never incurred. A debt, that is, that can never be repaid because its context is not the economic structure in which one pays back loans. The history of Derrida's relationship to Levinas is one that can hardly be cashed out in terms of what Derrida owes Levinas—or vice versa—bound up, as it is, with the debt both of them owe to Heidegger, Hegel, and others. "At This Very Moment in This Work Here I Am" is a text, then, that responds to Levinas at one level, but goes beyond any expectations Levinas might have of Derrida. Giving Levinas back more than he would have hoped for, giving back an inordinate amount, Derrida's text does not just exceed all of Levinas' expectations. It does more than that. It transgresses the movement of Levinas' thinking, sets it thinking against itself, turns it around. Specifically, it overturns the priority Levinas gives to the masculine. Derrida follows the letter of Levinas' text, pays attention to the ostensible privilege of the masculine, and finds that its spirit reverts to the feminine.[5] A reversal from masculine to feminine takes place in Levinas' text despite itself. One might say Derrida accomplishes this reversal, but he does so within the terms set by Levinas' own texts. Moreover, he does so at what he understands to be Levinas' invitation. He works from the inside out. He is not approaching Levinas from outside. He is not demonstrating some hidden presupposition on which Levinas' logic must depend in order to produce its effects. He shows rather how certain statements Levinas makes work against what Levinas says, how they produce a meaning Levinas could never have intended, and yet they do this according to a rule that Levinas himself articulates—perhaps not a rule so much as a phenomenon, or rather, a necessity, an obligation. In other words, Derrida seeks the "saying" in Levinas' "said." Levinas uses the same phrase to mean opposite things, constantly interrupting the meaning of his own text (see AV: 27; EM: 38)—as Derrida shows, for example, in his analysis of Levinas' phrase "at this moment" (AV: 24–25; EM: 35–36). In the same way, according to the same logic of interruption, Derrida shows that while Levinas wants to maintain the possibility of otherness, that possibility is always already inscribed within the same. Yet this is something of which Levinas shows himself fully aware. What is the difference then between Levinas' self-commentary and Derrida's commentary on him? Merely a difference of emphasis? Perhaps, but it is a difference that produces very different results—for feminists, for example.

I am not concerned here with facile assertions about the arbitrary meaning of a given text. I am not claiming merely that the text can mean anything you want it to, that any reading is as good as another, that it doesn't matter if Derrida takes up Levinas' meaning and reverses it so that it means the contrary. I am concerned with a directive that Derrida takes over from Levinas, a lesson he learns so well that he takes it to extremes— for example, he shows that Levinas, quite literally, cannot know what he is talking about. By taking Levinas seriously, by taking him at his word, Derrida shows both the extreme rigor of Levinas' thought, and the way it goes beyond itself, pointing further than what it says. At one level, Derrida asks whether Levinas' thinking remains a commandment, for all its hesitations about authority, totality, sameness, domination. He finds a way of asking this by putting to work a thought he finds in Levinas, the thought of radical ingratitude. What would it mean, Derrida asks, for someone to exercise an ingratitude so radical that it not only returns the gift to the giver, declaring the gestures of giving and receiving null and void, but also exempts itself from any blame or responsibility, refusing to be identified as beneficiary and therefore disclaiming all responsibility for returning the gift?[6] A gift that is returned to its origin is not a gift, and one who returns it is no longer a receiver. What if Derrida "chooses" to obey the rules of Levinas' game to the extent of wondering what it means to put Levinas in the position of receiving something? (I put the word "chooses" in quotation marks because the obligation, on Levinas' understanding, is not one which the subject is free to take up or leave alone as if one had complete unfettered freedom—rather one finds oneself always already answerable to the other, always already responsible.) What if Derrida obeys the rules of Levinas' game, even while inverting it, asking Levinas to adopt the position of one to whom Derrida gives something (be it a text, a thought, or friendship)? At a certain point in his text Derrida turns to face Levinas—if not to address him directly, then at least obliquely. "In listening," says Derrida,

> I was nonetheless wondering whether I was comprehended, myself, and how to stop that word: comprehended. And how the work knew me, whatever it knew of me. So be it: to begin by reading his work, giving it to him, in order to approach the Work, which itself does not begin with "his" work nor with whoever would pretend to say "my" work. Going toward the Other, coming from the Same so as not to return to it, the work does not come from there, but from the Other (AV: 39; EM: 51).

Derrida (who no doubt recognizes some version of his "own" thinking in Levinas' work) gives back to Levinas his text in his reading of it—reshapes it, reproduces it—and Levinas' text ends up, in some respects at least, saying the opposite of what it overtly affirms. Overtly asserting the priority of the father and the son over the profanity of erotic otherness, Levinas' saying ends up giving way to the non-serious, unethical playfulness of feminine eros. "He" gives way to "she." Enacting what he has learned from Levinas, Derrida throws it back to him, making it recoil upon itself, making it reconstitute itself into something otherwise, and in a certain way, Derrida thereby brings into harmony what Levinas insists on keeping separated, dissonant, disjointed. Derrida brings together eros and ethics— he closes the gap or distance between them that (in his later works) Levinas likes to maintain, in order to claim that it is in fact the feminine that takes precedence in the strange logic that Levinas uses, despite its secondary status on which Levinas insists. The question remains, both for Derrida and for us, exactly what this secondariness amounts to.

Derrida suggests that Levinas' work, despite itself, posits woman as "wholly other" (AV: 44; EM: 56). In a series of movements, which remark the figuring of the feminine in Levinas' work, and to which I merely allude here, Derrida allows his concern with the phrase, "He will have obligated" (AV: 11; EM: 21), to be recast as the saying, "She will have obligated" (AV: 47; EM: 60). Taking up what it might mean to display a radical ingratitude (see AV: 13, EM: 24; AV: 46, EM: 58) toward an author whose work (*oeuvre*) forbids any symmetry, outlaws equality, and asks for no return, Derrida wonders how he can respond to Levinas. "If anyone (He) tells you *from the start* (*d'abord*): 'don't return to me what I give you,' you are at fault even before he finishes talking" (AV: 14; EM: 25). So when Derrida asks whether the "secondary status of the sexual, and therefore, He [Levinas] says, of feminine difference . . . comes[s] to stand for the wholly-other of this Saying of the wholly other" (AV: 43; EM: 55), he accepts that he is at fault: "what I am writing at this very moment is faulty" (AV: 44; EM: 56). Derrida thereby raises the question of what it means to be faithful to Levinas' text. Derrida's answer is as follows:

> If in order to give without restituting, I must still conform to what he says of the Work in his work, and to what he gives there as well as to a re-tracing of the giving; more precisely, if I must conform my gesture to what makes the Work in his Work, which is older than his work, and whose Saying according to his own terms is not reducible to the Said, there we are, engaged before all engagement, in an incredible logic, formal and nonformal. If I restitute, if I restitute without fault, I am at fault. And if I do not restitute, by *giving* beyond acknowledgment, I risk the fault (AV: 14; EM: 24).

I quote these sentences not because I intend to follow out all the complications to which they give rise, and in which they take root, but in order to signal one of the directions that my own reading of Levinas takes—namely, that the feminine functions at the order of the saying in Levinas' text, which remains, in its external appearance, at the order of the said, thoroughly male. To the extent that the distinction between the saying and the said is an elaborate expression of the distinction between implicit/explicit, Irigaray is right to read in Levinas a suppression of the feminine. But to the extent that Levinas' rethinking of the other (including his reflections on the feminine) as radical alterity provides the model for Irigaray's recasting of women's otherness, Levinas' legacy is more positive.

In answering (or putting back into question) McDonald's questions to him in "Choreographies," Derrida not only responds to some of the problems his own texts have presented to feminists, he also responds to some of the problems Levinas' texts present for feminists. By drawing on essays in which Levinas addresses the feminine in Judaism, he thereby mediates between Levinas and his feminist readers.[7] McDonald opens her questions by asking Derrida about woman's place. Predictably, Derrida is reluctant to give woman a place in the sense of prescribing, at least in any but the least traditional sense, the proper place for woman. It is unclear whether McDonald asks about what place Derrida would give to woman in the knowledge that Derrida is strongly influenced by Levinas, or whether she is familiar with Levinas' conclusion in "And God Created Woman" that the feminine takes "second place" (AG: 177; EC: 148).[8] In any case, Derrida is. He emphasizes the need for "re-sexualizing a philosophical or theoretical discourse, which has been too 'neutralizing'[9] . . . without regression in relation to what might justify . . . the procedures—or necessary steps—of Levinas or Heidegger" (C: 75).[10]

I want to briefly consider Derrida's reflections on Heidegger and woman. In "Restitutions," (1987b) Derrida provides a reading of Heidegger's "The Origin of the Work of Art." Here too, as in "At This Very Moment in This Work Here I Am" (and in so many other texts), Derrida is interested in the question of who has responsibility for a text, who may be responsible for it, whose property it becomes. Derrida takes issue with Meyer Schapiro's "The Still Life as a Personal Object—A Note on Heidegger and Van Gogh."[11] Heidegger adopts Van Gogh's painting, *Old Shoes*, to serve as an example of equipment. The shoes that are depicted serve as an example of objects that are well-worn through use. The old shoes serve, then, at least initially, as an invocation of the familiarity such items have to their users. Emphasizing that the main point of Heidegger's discussion of the Van Gogh painting is the status of the painting as an *example*, Derrida is concerned that Schapiro altogether ignores the exemplary function that the painting plays for Heidegger. By insisting that there is evidence for the shoes having belonged to Van Gogh himself and not to a peasant woman, as Heidegger supposes, Schapiro may feel that he has made a significant discovery—but in Derrida's view he has missed the point. Heidegger refers to the shoes in Van Gogh's painting as an illustration of the kind of objects that everybody takes for granted. By focusing on who owned the shoes, Schapiro neglects to see them as exemplary of useful objects. According to Derrida, this is because he divorces the formal elements of Heidegger's essay—in this case, the question of who owns the shoes—from the context of the peasant's world that Heidegger calls up for his readers.

Furthermore, Schapiro, on Derrida's account, fails to relate the question of the ownership of the shoes to other formal elements in Heidegger's essay. For example, the shoes appear not only as useful, but also as mere things on the one hand, and as a work of art, on the other. The relationship among these three aspects of the thing—as a mere thing, as a product, and as a work—is, Derrida says, like a shoe lace: "Each 'thing,' each mode of being of the thing, passes inside then outside the other. From right to left, from left to right. We shall articulate this *strophe* of the lace: in its rewinding passing and repassing through the eyelet of the thing, from outside to inside, from inside to outside . . . " (TP: 299; R: 341). The figure of laces weaving in and out of the shoe leather, through the eyelets, illustrates for Derrida a movement that he will also call the work of the trace. In describing the existing relationship among the three modes of the thing's being that Heidegger discusses, and by referring to the trace, Derrida places a new emphasis on the relationship between the shoes in Van Gogh's picture and the shoes outside the picture—that is, the relationship between the shoes as unused, abandoned, unlaced, bare, and the shoes as clothing for the peasant woman, the shoes as invested, inhabited, informed by the body (TP: 265; R: 302).

In his reading of "The Origin of the Work of Art," Derrida uses this difference between inside and outside to comment on sexual difference. Derrida notices Heidegger's dependence on the "sex of reattachment," as he calls it (TP: 306; R: 349), whereby the owner of the shoes is recognized only in neutral terms when the shoes appear "in" the picture—that is, as a product characterized by usefulness. However, considered "outside" the painting, the shoes become the clothing of a peasant woman. "There is something like a rule in the peasant woman's appearance on the scene," says Derrida (TP: 307; R: 350). He continues:

> Heidegger designates in this way the (female) wearer of the shoes outside the picture, if one can put it that way, when the lace of discourse passes outside the edging of the frame, into that *hors-d'oeuvre* which he claims to see presenting itself in the work itself. But each time he speaks of the exemplary product in the picture, he says, in neutral, generic fashion—that is, according to a grammar, masculine fashion: "*ein Paar Bauernschuhe*," a pair of peasant's shoes. Why are the feet of the thing, in this case some shoes, then posited as the feet of a woman, a peasant woman? (TP: 307; R: 350)

The peasant woman knows her shoes only in their reliability, and she thereby figures only as an example of a worker in the fields. Woman is prevented from knowing the shoes in their "truth"—as they appear for the philosopher who looks at Van Gogh's painting of the shoes as a work of art.

In a more recent essay, Derrida makes tangible his conjecture that sexuality is a regulating, if unacknowledged, theme in Heidegger's philosophy: "It is by the name of '*Dasein*' that I would introduce the question of sexual difference," says Derrida in "*Geschlecht*" (1983: 421).[12] The very neutrality of the term *Dasein* occludes sexual difference while at the same time always already having decided in favor of the male tradition. The naming of *Dasein* becomes for Derrida a way of thinking what Heidegger leaves unsaid, just as Derrida's reading of Heidegger's "The Origin of the Work of Art" points to the unwritten rule of the peasant woman's appearance: she can only appear as an example, as a figure who represents what we take for granted. She can only appear in the background, as it were, of the painting, as that which is assumed, as an example of common knowledge, as the figure who establishes familiar territory. If in one way woman is always already there, in another way, her place remains unthought. Derrida begins to write woman into Heidegger's text by noticing her absence—but this rewriting is necessarily equivocal. In *Spurs*, where Derrida takes up the question of woman in relation to Heidegger's reading of Nietzsche, he suggests that there is a metaphysical necessity in the disappearance of woman. This disappearance is also an opening for metaphysics, an opening on to a thinking not governed by metaphysics. Derrida writes:

> Just as there is no such thing, then, as a Being or an essence of *the* woman or the sexual difference, there is also no such thing as an essence of the *es gibt Sein*, that is, of Being's giving and gift. The "just as" finds no conjuncture. There is no such thing as a gift of Being from which there might be apprehended and opposed to it something like a determined gift (whether of the subject, the body, of the sex or other like things—so woman, then, will not have been my subject) (S: 120; 121).

Providing a self-commentary on *Spurs*, Derrida says,

> Why must there be a place for woman? And why only one, single, completely essential place?
> This is a question that you could translate ironically by saying that in my view *there is no place for woman.* That was indeed clearly set forth during the 1972 Cerisy Colloquium devoted to Nietzsche in . . . *Spurs/Eperons.* It is without a doubt risky to say that there is no place for woman, but this idea is not anti-feminist, far from it; true, it is not feminist either. But it

appears to me to be faithful in its way both to a certain assertion of women and to what is most affirmative and "dancing," as the maverick feminist [Emma Goldman] says, in the displacement of women. Can one not say, in Nietzsche's language, that there is a "reactive" feminism, and that a certain historical necessity often puts this form of feminism in power in today's organized struggles? It is this kind of "reactive" feminism that Neitzsche mocks, and not woman or women. Perhaps one should not so much combat it head on—other interests would be at stake in such a move—as prevent its occupying the entire terrain (C: 68).[13]

Derrida's relationship to feminism has proved notoriously problematic. Elizabeth Meese, citing *Spurs* (Derrida, 1979: 65), claims that

Derrida and some deconstructive critics tend to see Feminism only as monolith, exemplified in the most inflammatory terms in *Spurs*: "Feminism is nothing but the operation of a woman who aspires to be like a man. And in order to resemble the masculine dogmatic philosopher this woman lays claim—just as much claim as he—to truth, science, and objectivity in all their castrated delusions of virility. Feminism seeks to castrate. It wants a castrated woman. Gone the style (Meese, 1990: 25).

While this quotation looks damning on its own, it is worth remembering that Derrida is commenting specifically on the feminism of those "women feminists so derided by Nietzsche" (S: 65), and that, in context, it is clear that Derrida is not chastising all feminists but only those who, like (traditional) men, believe "in the truth of woman, in woman-truth" (S: 63–65). A similar qualification should be applied to Robinson's observation that "Throughout *Spurs*, the feminist is linked with the 'dogmatic' philosopher; both readers of woman attempt to pin her down, to dis-cover her truth" (1991: 82). Again, a clarification is called for: it is only those feminists who endorse the assumptions of metaphysics that Derrida describes as "dogmatic."

Unlike critics of Derrida such as Meese and Robinson, I do not assume that Derrida's critique of "progressive," "reactive," or "dogmatic" feminism amounts to a rejection of all feminism.[14] I understand it rather as a critique of feminism that refuses to put in question its aspiration to become like men. While Derrida can call *Spurs* "an anti-feminist as well as anti-phallogocentric text—since precisely the symmetry of those two things is its central motif," he also goes on to affirm that "feminism is necessary.

Feminism has been necessary and is still necessary in certain situations" (1985a: 30). Derrida, on my reading, is not advocating the demise of feminism, any more than he is embracing feminism as an uncomplicated movement that always knows what it is doing and is in complete control of itself. He is claiming that "to close oneself in feminism is to reproduce the very thing one is struggling against" (1985a: 30)—namely, "phallogocentrism." Derrida is anti-feminist insofar as feminism refuses to remain self-critical, insofar as it refuses to learn from its mistakes and refuses to remain open. His critique of feminism is a critique of a feminism that tries to maintain itself as if it were impervious to the deconstruction of phallogocentrism. As the above quotation from "Choreographies" (C: 68) makes clear, he is not advocating feminism at all, but neither is he dismissing it.[15] On the contrary, he acknowledges, as we just saw, its necessity. Refusing to be an advocate for feminism, at least in a straightforward sense, does not, I suggest, necessarily mean that one is against it. It may mean that one sees its dangers; it may also mean, for Derrida, that he is conscious of his position as a man, and it may be much more helpful in the end for men to be cautious of embracing labels which do not fit very well, than for men to brandish the label of feminism without having thought through what it might mean for them to step into that role. "Feminism" has, after all, legitimated all sorts of texts by men, and it is not always easy to tell whether the term indicates a wish to sell books, ideas, and conferences rather than any fundamental rethinking of the position of women on the part of men.[16] The ambiguity Derrida enjoys, in maintaining his stance of "on the one hand . . . on the other hand" is, I suggest, both self-conscious and respectful of women—more responsible perhaps than Levinas, despite the fact that it is a responsibility that is learned in important respects from Levinas.[17] If Derrida has no respect for those whose work shows no respect for his, it is not because he is anti-feminist. It may be because it is hard to respect feminists—or anyone else—who treat him as the enemy. We need to ask ourselves not only about what Derrida has to offer feminism, but also what mechanisms are in play in the dismissal of "deconstruction." Whence do attacks on deconstruction gather their force, and what is their true target? Whose cathexes are at stake/in play here?

QUESTIONS OF STRATEGY AND STYLE

Irigaray's question is, "How can the double demand—for both equality and difference—be articulated?" (TS: 81; CS: 78) Aware of the difficulty of making more than one gesture at a time, Irigaray thinks that there can be "no clear univocal utterance. . . . It is still better to speak only in riddles, allusions, hints, parables. Even if asked to clarify a few points. Even if people plead that they just don't understand. After all, they have never understood" (SO: 143; SA: 178). Less polemically and more practically, she suggests that several different "paths" must be pursued in order to reopen "the figures of philosophical discourse—idea, substance, subject, transcendental subjectivity, absolute knowledge—in order to pry out of them what they have borrowed that is feminine" (TS: 74; CS: 72). In *This Sex Which Is Not One* Irigaray identifies four such paths: philosophical reinterpretation, psychoanalytic interpretation, mimicry, and strategies based on the recognition that "if women are such good mimics . . . *they also remain elsewhere*" (TS: 76; CS: 74).

The first path involves interrogating "*the conditions under which systematicity itself is possible*" (TS: 74; CS: 72), in other words, elucidating the supporting and mirroring role that the feminine has played throughout the history of philosophy as the excluded other that has nonetheless served as a source of sustenance and "nourishment" for the "speaking subject" (TS: 75; CS: 72). "For each philosopher," says Irigaray in a passage that underlines the similarities with Heidegger's epochal history of being that I sketched in chapter four, "beginning with those whose names define some age in the history of philosophy, we have to point out how the break with material contiguity is made, how the system is put together, how the specular economy works" (TS: 75; CS: 73). Articulating these "conditions" of discourse is also a matter of acknowledging the repression of the feminine.

The second approach that Irigaray outlines is psychoanalytic. Irigaray says,

> we need to pay attention to the way the unconscious works in each philosophy, and perhaps in philosophy in general. We need to listen (psycho)analytically to its procedures of repression, to the structuration of language that shores up its representations, separating the true from the false, the meaningful from the meaningless, and so forth (TS: 75; CS: 73).

The influence of Saussure's conception of linguistics can be discerned in Irigaray's call for "an examination of the *operation of the 'grammar'* of each figure of discourse, its syntactic laws or requirements, its imaginary configurations, its metaphoric networks" (TS: 75; CS: 73). Irigaray adds, crucially, that we also need to pay attention to what is not articulated in language "at the level of utterance: *its silences*" (TS: 75: CS: 73).[18] Irigaray sees the need to demonstrate how silences that mark the place of woman in the history of philosophy also support and enable its articulation. The excluded other acts as a supplement without which what is said would not be the same. What Levinas calls the saying in the said, and what Derrida sees as the structure of the supplement, find echoes in Irigaray's archeological retrieval of what it has meant to be a woman.

The problem is how to "introduce ourselves into" the "tightly-woven systematicity" (TS: 76; CS: 73) that language constitutes. One response is mimicry. Irigaray says,

> There is, in an initial phase, perhaps only one "path," the one historically assigned to the feminine: that of *mimicry*. One must assume the feminine role deliberately. Which means already to convert a form of subordination into an affirmation, and thus to begin to thwart it. Whereas a direct feminine challenge to this condition means demanding to speak as a (masculine) "subject," that is, it means to postulate a relation to the intelligible that would maintain sexual indifference (TS: 76; CS: 73–74).

Braidotti underscores the significance of Irigaray's use of mimicry as a strategy that undercuts, rather than reinforcing, metaphysical assumptions: "It is important to make a distinction between the inevitability of essentialism in the critique of metaphysics and the mimetic strategy that feminist theoreticians such as Irigaray adopt in order to work out and on sexual difference" (1989: 99). There are clearly resonances between Irigaray's suggestion of the strategic adoption of mimicry as a strategy, and Derrida's affirmative or positive deconstructive gesture. In both cases, women inhabit the position of the feminine while in the process of transforming it. Derrida says, "In a given situation, which is ours, which is the European phallogocentric structure,[19] the side of the woman is the side from which you start to dismantle the structure" (WB: 194). Just as Irigaray stipulates that mimicry is an initial phase, so Derrida recognizes that inhabiting the position of the feminine can be subversive only up to a certain point. He says, "you can use the force of woman to reverse, to undermine this first stage of opposition" (WB: 195), but adds that "the opposition between women and men stops being pertinent" (WB: 194) once the "feminine force" has achieved its work of reversal, or "once you have deconstructed this opposition" (WB: 195).[20]

Irigaray outlines a fourth response to "the position of exclusion" (TS: 88; CS: 86) from language in which, according to Lacan's linguistic reinterpretation of Freud, women find themselves. That is, to situate the *"elsewhere of female pleasure"* (TS: 77; CS: 74). Irigaray elaborates:

> That *"elsewhere of feminine pleasure"* can be found only at the price of *crossing back through the mirror that subtends all speculation.*[21] For this pleasure is not simply situated in a process of reflection or mimesis, nor on one side of this process or the other: neither on the near side, the empirical realm that is opaque to all language, nor on the far side, the self-sufficient infinite of the God of men. Instead, it refers all these categories and ruptures back to the necessities of the self-representation of phallic desire in discourse. A playful crossing, and an unsettling one, which would allow woman to rediscover the place of her "self-affection" (TS: 77; CS: 75).

What, then, is the relationship between the strategic stances adopted by Irigaray and Derrida? While Derrida refrains from direct criticism, some of his comments appear to be critical of Irigaray's approach. Derrida says, for example, "The specular reversal of masculine 'subjectivity,' even in its most self-critical form—that is, where it is nervously jealous both of itself and of its 'proper' objects—probably represents only one necessary phase. Yet it still belongs to the same program [the model of progress]" (C: 67). If this "specular reversal" refers to Irigaray, as I think it must, Derrida seems to be alleging that Irigaray's attempt to recast the idea of subject fails to effect a radical break with phallogocentrism, merely reinvoking it. One could attribute Derrida's apparent reluctance to grant the radicality of Irigaray's gesture to his conviction that "the hierarchy of dual oppositions [in this case male and female] always reestablishes itself" (PS: 42; PT: 57), or to his belief that one cannot "reproduce the Law in the face of the Law" (WB: 192). One could ask at what point such acknowledgments become a refusal to do anything that is not a repetition of the same, a refusal to acknowledge the possibility of rethinking the other as other. One could muster other Irigarayan responses to Derrida's suspicion that the specular reversal of masculine subjectivity remains at the first level of the deconstructive strategy, citing, for example, her observation: "To escape from a pure and simple reversal of the masculine position means in any case not to forget to laugh" (TS: 163; CS: 157).[22] Berg emphasizes the importance of laughter for Irigaray (1988: 69–70).[23] One of the most memorable moments for me, in which Irigaray uses humor to make her point, occurs in *This Sex Which Is Not One*, when Irigaray is commenting on Lacan's understanding of women and their pleasure. Irigaray says, "the right to experience pleasure is awarded to a statue" (TS: 90; CS: 89), and goes on to quote Lacan: "Just go look at Bernini's statue in Rome, you'll see right away that St. Theresa is coming, there's no doubt about it" (TS: 90–91; CS: 89). The series of questions with which Irigaray follows this quotation, which I imagine her articulating with her eyebrows raised in mock surprise, accomplishes more than some writers could in a book: "In Rome? So far away? To look? At a statue? Of a saint? Sculpted by a man? What pleasure are we talking about? Whose pleasure?" (TS: 91; CS: 89).

If we take to heart both the fact that Irigaray advocates that we operate on several different levels, and her specification of mimicry as only an "initial" phase, Derrida's comment that "specular reversal . . . probably represents only one necessary phase" can be read not as a criticism of Irigaray, but as a qualification that she herself might endorse. On such a reading the distance between the two would not seem so great as it might first appear. Irigaray does not assume it is easy to avoid the trap of merely reversing the balance of sexual power, exchanging the terms rather than fundamentally challenging the hierarchical model. She engages in "a rigorous interpretation of phallogocentrism" precisely in order to question "the symbolic itself" because she knows that "we do not escape so easily from reversal" (TS: 162; CS: 157).

Clearly Irigaray is indebted to Derrida and, equally clearly, she does not see her writing as having the same effect as Derrida's. Just as she draws on Heidegger's questioning of being and Levinas' radical rethinking of alterity while she also sees them as bolstering up a tradition that has eclipsed women, so too, for all the influence Derrida has on Irigaray, there is a sense in which Derrida's preoccupations betray the same masculine biases as his male predecessors. Irigaray registers this betrayal in her essay "Belief Itself," in a discussion that illustrates the impossibility of characterizing Derrida's influence on Irigaray in one or two summary statements, as if it could be isolated from the tradition(s) that both of them assume yet put into question. In "Belief Itself" Irigaray chooses to concentrate on Derrida's "discussion of the *fort-da* of little Ernst" (SG: 28; SP: 40) rather than "*Le facteur de la vérité*," which also appears in *The Post Card*, and which (given her interest in the question of sexual difference) would have been the more obvious choice since it addresses the question of the "Truth in (the) Place of Female Sexuality" (PC: 442–54; CP: 470–82).[24] However, if Derrida is right when he says that "All of Lacan's work supposes that one should take seriously the problematic of *Jenseneits* (*Beyond* . . .), the very problematic that for so many psychoanalysts appears mythological, poetic, speculative" (PC: 421; CP: 449), perhaps Irigaray's "Belief Itself" can be seen as an opening not only on to Derrida, but also to Lacan.[25] Irigaray writes,

> The son merely listens attentively to the father's game (or sometimes vice versa) . . . takes the measure of the father's game, intends to take him by surprise, take him by surprise in the figures of the game, their placings and enlacings. He is not encountering *her* but the father who encounters her, the father's link to her, his place in relation to her, his place as it issues from and with her. By this retroaction the son gives himself or gives himself back, with or without her, a *face* that can be present, rediscovered, behind the father's back (SG: 42; SP: 54).

Ostensibly a commentary on Derrida's *The Post Card* and, more specifically, on the essay "To Speculate—on 'Freud,'" Irigaray's essay incorporates a complex series of patrilineal allegiances and philosophical references. Figured in the passage above are various (metaphorical and sometimes reversible) father-son relationships: Socrates and Plato; Freud [the father of psychoanalysis] and Derrida; Freud (the father of Sophie and grandfather of her son) and little Ernst. If, at the most overt level, the "game" refers to little Ernst's casting away and drawing back of the cotton reel/spool, it also describes Freud's psychoanalytic game of interpreting his grandson's relationship to Sophie, and Derrida's philosophical game "that intends to take him [the father—Freud] by surprise." There are other philosophical fathers to which the passage refers us more obliquely—Heidegger and Levinas, for example, and, in turn, their Judeo-Greek forefathers. The reference to "placings and enlacings" (*emplacements et enlacements*) recalls, among other texts, Derrida's discussion of Heidegger's "The Origin of the Work of Art," in which the idea of laces plays a prominent role—an image on which Derrida also draws repeatedly in *The Post Card*. Irigaray's allusion to the gift calls to mind many of Derrida's texts, among them *Spurs*, and his second essay on Levinas "At This Very Moment," while the mention of the word *face* (in the context of the many references throughout the essay to the "face to face") evokes Levinas' own philosophy.[26]

I point to this multi-layered context in terms of which Irigaray's relation to Derrida is played out to signal the complexity of that relation.

Rather than drawing premature conclusions about Irigaray's criticisms of or dependence on Derrida, I have tried to spell out some of the multiple levels at which this relationship functions, before directly confronting Irigaray's relation to Derrida. Let me organize my remarks about this relation around Irigaray's "Le v(i)ol de la lettre," in *Parler n'est jamais neutre* (1985b: 149–68).

BETWEEN IRIGARAY AND DERRIDA

I think that whatever constitutes a refusal or an interrogation of Derrida in Irigaray's work is not opaque to Derrida's way of questioning; it is never simply a refutation or an attempt to block out Derrida's questions. It is always also a way of taking them seriously, and this will sometimes mean for Irigaray that the questions turn into something else, turn against themselves. For all that, the questions are taken no less seriously—perhaps they are sometimes taken more seriously than they take themselves, and perhaps this is sometimes Irigaray's point. Irigaray says, referring to the "between," "One might even say that the more one tries to appropriate it, through reproduction or repetition, for example, the more one is caught up in play (*est pris au jeu*), the more one puts oneself in play (*se prend au jeu*), the more one puts into play (*met en jeu*)" (VL: 167).[27] According to Irigaray, reading a text, for Derrida, is always an effect of difference (see VL: 149).

Rather than try to engage a summary of Derrida's major contribution to philosophy to set the scene for reading Irigaray's essay on his work (as if this contribution could be reduced to a series of propositions), let me confine my discussion of the Derridean corpus to a few guiding motifs that occur in those texts that form the basis of Irigaray's first essay on Derrida.[28] There are many commentaries available on the work of Derrida.[29] In order to avoid redundance, I will refer to Rodolphe Gasché's timely and authoritative reading of Derrida in *The Tain of the Mirror*. In keeping with its many other accomplishments, Gasché's interpretation of Derrida serves as a corrective to what Gasché calls "so-called deconstructionist criticism" (Gasché, 1986: 274). Its particular characterization of what Derrida is *not* doing also opens on to precisely what interests Irigaray's delimitation of the Derridean project of *différance*.

In the title *Of Grammatology* Derrida announces his intention to pursue a science of writing. Or, more accurately, it would be fair to assume that the author is promising such an inquiry, as long as the title is read according to the usual conventions in terms of which the tradition has understood phonetic writing. The graphematic series of the written phrase would be taken to represent phonemes; the written word would translate the spoken word, which in turn would echo the speaker's intentions. All this could be assumed as a matter of course—were it not for the fact that it is precisely this assumption that Derrida sets out to question under the heading *Of Grammatology*.

> Writing will be "phonetic," it will be the outside, the exterior representation of language and of this "thought-sound." It must necessarily operate from already constituted units of signification, in the formations of which it has played no part (OGr: 31; DG: 47).

It should therefore come as no surprise to find that even before the science of writing can get under way, its very possibility is brought into question by the author who nevertheless retains as the title of this project the science of writing—thereby announcing that which he already deems impossible. In the "Exergue"[30]—an inscription outside the text itself—Derrida says of grammatology "above all" that, "however fecund and necessary the undertaking might be . . . such a science of writing runs the risk of never being established as such and with that name" (OGr: 4; DG: 13). This cautionary note is not to be taken lightly. It is sounded in various registers throughout the book—indeed, it provides the structural key with which to decipher the book. Derrida immediately specifies the risk of which he warns in other ways—namely, his hesitation in endorsing the possibility of developing grammatology "as such"[31] or "with that name." There is the risk of "never being able to define the unity of its project or its object" and the risk of "not being able either to write its discourse on method or to describe the limits of its field" (OGr: 4; DG: 13–14). Such risks correspond to a willingness to bring into question the sufficiency of a scientific method that would take itself to be capable of grounding absolutely and adequately its founding propositions.[32] Derrida's stated "final intention" in *Of Grammatology* is a far cry from Husserl's apodicticity: it is "To make enigmatic what one thinks one understands by the words 'proximity,' 'immediacy,' 'presence' (the proximate [*proche*], the own [*propre*], and the pre- of presence)" (OGr: 70; DG: 103). The modesty of Derrida's expressly intended project should be compared to the extravagance of some of the claims made in the name of deconstruction—by those who see themselves as followers and by those who cast themselves as opponents of deconstruction.

Addressing the question of why he continues to use the term "writing" despite the fact that he is reformulating the "vulgar concept of writing," Derrida says that writing in the traditional sense—that is, opposed to, derivative from, and mutually exclusive of speech—

> could not have imposed itself historically except by the dissimulation of the arche-writing, by the desire for a speech displacing its other and its double and working to reduce its difference. If I persist in calling that difference writing, it is because, within the work of historical repression, writing was, by its situation, destined to signify the most formidable difference (OGr: 56; DG: 83).

The phrase the "vulgar concept of writing" clearly recalls Derrida's discussion of Heidegger's characterization in *Being and Time* of the "vulgar concept of time" (see OG: 32–33; OGe: 35). Heidegger rehabilitates our linear and scientifically based understanding of time through his elaboration of structures—such as that of "anticipatory resoluteness" and "being-towards-death"—which allow him to point to the fact that the present now-point always already assumes a past and is oriented toward a future. Heidegger's reconception of temporality can no more totally repudiate the common, traditional, or vulgar conception of time than Derrida's concept of arche-writing can divorce itself entirely from the classical notion of writing. Derrida's effort to recast writing, as he attests, "will be laborious and we know a priori that its effectiveness will never be pure and absolute" (OGr: 46; DG: 68). While Derrida has been misunderstood by some as putting writing before speech, his analysis of speech and writing is not one that puts texts first, as if the written text could be understood in opposition to speech, any more than presence and absence could be understood as polar opposites, as terms which do not inform one another, or any more than Derrida imagines he could deconstruct metaphysics by using any language other than that which metaphysics itself provides.

Explicating what Derrida means by *arche-writing* or general writing, Gasché reminds us, referring to *Of Grammatology*,[33] that if in one sense Derrida questions the traditional priority that philosophers have accorded to speech over writing, this questioning can never simply be a matter of merely reversing the hierarchy (1986: 271–73). As Gasché explains,

> All substitution of a graphocentrism for logocentrism is thoroughly excluded. The order of dependence between speech and writing cannot

> be argued. . . . To deconstruct the ethico-theoretical hierarchy of speech
> and writing . . . is to construct the signifying structure or system of referral
> that accounts for both exclusion and contamination (1986: 271–73).

"Arche-writing" is a name that Derrida gives to this referral system or "infrastructure" (Gasché 1986: 273). Arche-writing, "as a law," accounts for "the economy that organizes the various relations of speech and what is commonly called writing" (1986: 273). Once it becomes clear that Derrida is rethinking the boundary between speech and writing, the viability of interpretations that take him to be simply privileging writing over speech is put in question. What is at issue is not whether speech or writing is in some ultimate sense more foundational, but the very possibility of such foundational thinking. In question is the very meaning of assigning a privilege to one term of the opposition speech/writing—and, by implication, to a host of other related privileges inscribed in the metaphysical tradition, including subject/object, presence/absence, and author/text.

Since writing, in the sense of arche-writing, is a term employed in the articulation of a system in which speech is always already referred to writing through, for example, its metaphoric functioning, it can readily be seen, in Gasché's words, that it

> has little or nothing to do with the (anthropological, subjective, and so on)
> act of writing, with the psychological pleasures and displeasures to which
> it gives rise, with an instrument of notation or communication, or with an
> aesthetic and merely self-referential signifying practice (1986: 274).

Elaborating his point, Gasché continues, "Writing in Derrida's sense is not determined by what it is about, nor has it anything essentially in common with the signs present on the page, or with the (literary or philosophical) production of these signs. Neither is it the essence of the literal sign or of the act of its engendering" (1986: 274). Irigaray's response to assertions about what Derrida does *not* mean to address through his concept of arche-writing might be, "Why not?" Why does writing have nothing to do with pleasure? I hope I do not need to add that my formulation of Irigaray's position indicates a repudiation neither of Gasché nor of Derrida. Gasché's response to the particular issue of psychologism to which he is responding,[34] is not in question. I am merely using it as a textual occasion to point out what sets Irigaray's questions in motion.

Similarly, no one could read Derrida's texts on Freud and seriously maintain that they do not take account of the pleasure in writing. Irigaray's questions do not remain at the level of such empirical claims. Irigaray asks of Derrida's texts, just as Derrida asks of Levinas' texts, what they do and where they go—and where they do not go, despite themselves, despite their best intentions. This is not a matter of intentions. It is a matter of positioning, of Irigaray reading Derrida as a woman—and not merely as a woman, but as a woman who has understood the importance of his work and tried to go beyond it.

In order to see the purpose of and the path by which Irigaray could arrive at such questions, it is necessary to understand the pertinence of a basic opposition that Irigaray allows to act as an initial framework for her commentary, a framework that she will slowly submit to questioning. The opposition between the letter and the phoneme is a detour, one which Irigaray nevertheless must examine (VL: 149). The letter is distinct, one, unitary, whereas phonemes can only be articulated in relation to one another, as essentially plural. The letter "must be *one*, identical to itself, not identical to others" (VL: 150).[35] Non-unitary, unsayable except through supplementarity, phonemes preclude any attempt to reduce them to the singular (VL: 153, note 7). The deciphering of one letter of the alphabet as distinct from another depends on the literal spacing of the letters—the legibility of writing presupposes that each letter be distinguishable and separate from the next. The identity of letters requires the literal spacing of letters on the page, such that the blank intervals between letters are presupposed in order for the letters to appear as different from one another. Irigaray says, "The only imperative would be [the] non-ambiguity of the inscription" (VL: 150). The operation of such an imperative, which ensures the legibility of letters, involves and requires that letters maintain their distance from one another. The spaces that separate one letter from the next are intrinsic to their differentiation. The gaps or blanks between letters are not merely inserted after the fact, they are part of what makes it possible to distinguish one letter from another in the first place.[36] "But this spacing is not regulated by writing (*graphisme*) itself" (VL: 150–51). In addition, or as a presupposition of their spacing, letters depend on their visibility. They therefore function in service to the eye. "Without this servitude the letter says nothing" (VL: 151). If the letter is "*finite* form, *defined, one, unique, distinct* and *distant*" (VL: 160), it is nonetheless subordinate to a network of bodily and material coordination. What is written is "a function of the exigencies or the freedom of gesture, of the mobility of the body, of the submission of the inscriber to certain rhythms, of the field of vision" (VL: 151), "in the service of the gaze" (VL: 160), dependent on some form of support, requiring the pliability/supplication (*suppléance*) of matter (see VL: 151).

What might first appear to be a function that appeals only to the discontinuity between individual and discrete letters, at second glance occurs only through "contiguity" (see VL: 151). Ink must flow from a pen, and contact must be made with a material surface; fluidity and pliability are assumed. The letter cannot be ruptured from all processes of contiguity or from "différance" (VL: 152). Otherwise the letter would appear to be engendered from nowhere, mythically original, "delegated to *Nature* or to *logos*" (VL: 152). This "*without-origin*" of the letter credits it with the order of a first principle. The processes that govern the production of the letter are not arbitrary, they do not come from nowhere. They are culturally specific and rooted in a "social body" (VL: 152).

Like the mirror image, which "constitutes me as one, distinct" (VL: 153), but which "necessitates a surface-support" (VL: 153), the letter requires a "blank space" (VL: 151) for its inscription. The reflection that constitutes an image in a mirror immobilizes the gesture (see VL: 153), cutting itself off from the series of gestures that precede and follow it, and providing an image of unity where in fact there is none. The image resolves into a unity and condenses into one: the series of movements that lead up to and proceed in the wake of the illusory, momentary capturing of an instantaneous and whole presence (VL: 153). Creating a fiction of absolute presence and uniformity, the mirror image imposes a coherence that is nonetheless conditioned by "fragmentation" and "dispersal" (VL: 154). Similarly, the letter requires the distancing or spacing ensured by its material inscription. Its production is subject to the variations permissible by the medium (see VL: 152) that serves as its support, regulated by the indeterminacies of its production process, by the pliability of the material inscribed, by the efficiency of the implements used to produce a script. The tracing of the letter, if it is to acquire some permanence, if it is to constitute a mark, cannot be accomplished in thin air. It requires a medium, a support, a hand to do the tracing (or some mechanical substitute), an implement with which to write. The curve of the hand, the gesture, and the look give shape to the form of the letter, so that alphabetic writing is not literally graphic. Conventions such as tracing letters from left to right depend on the acculturation of the hand to this movement (see VL: 151).[37] What might first appear to be the result of purely formal requirements—that each letter be separable and distinct from the others—comes to be seen as subject to the technique of writing.

As Irigaray says, "The letter then is form, one, distinct, distant, inscribed on a support thanks to a technique, and it represents nothing *a priori* other than the reduction of the inscriber to her/his training (*dressage*) and to the stereotype of movement, to the attention of the gaze" (VL: 152).

The requirements of the written code are thoroughly bound up with the conventions of writing that characterize a particular culture, founded on the specific mechanics of imprinting letters on a page, for example. The production and technique of writing structures and organizes a space, so that the writing process can no longer be construed as "literal" (VL: 151). The rules of graphics that enable us to differentiate letters from one another extend beyond graphics itself; they are determined by the mechanics of production, not simply by the formal idea of identity and non-identity. Or rather, the identity or non-identity of the letter is never purely formal: "The mechanical and the formal remain inefficient without grounding/earth (*sans terre*), without a source of production" (VL: 152). Production, in its turn, is dependent on "labor and technique" (VL: 152).

Thus far, Irigaray follows Derrida. What she questions, however, is the source of the rupture between the two different categories of resources necessary for the production of a written code (see VL: 152). Phonetic articulation is "unsayable without supplementary traits, articulable by the implication or exclusion of certain differentiated traits" (VL: 156). The production of the phoneme is the result of a network or tissue of differences, without origin or end (see VL: 157). In Irigaray's view, there is, for Derrida, "*nothing outside the play of différance*" (VL: 157).

If we take seriously the suggestion that Irigaray's reworking of the concept of alterity is profoundly influenced by Levinas, we should not be surprised to find that one of the problems Irigaray has in reading Derrida is the erasure of the body. To the extent that Derrida inherits the terms of his discourse from Husserl and Heidegger, he might also be implicated, however unwittingly, in their difficulty in accounting for corporeality. Irigaray acknowledges the necessity of "*screens, instruments, tools, supports, even resistance,* for every reinscription of traces" (VL: 164), but thinks that Derrida somehow disposes "of *eyes*, of *hands*, or *mouths*, of *sex*, and those of *others*," as if they were "tools, instruments, supports" (VL: 164).

Writing is subject to the contours of the body, to the support of the materials on which inscriptions are inscribed, to the curvature of a hand, to the viability of the writing instruments developed for the function of inscription. Writing is subservient to a series of bodily and material manipulations, including the rhythmic motility of the gesture and the regime of the gaze—the distance separating each character of the alphabet, a spacing

251

that "is not regulated by writing (*graphisme*) itself" (VL: 150–51)—a series of blanks that make possible the act of distinguishing the form of one letter from the form of another. "Writing (*graphisme*) then would no longer be literal" (VL: 151). It is always an effect—of the pliability, flexibility, and reliability of the materials engaged in its production. The messages encoded in a series of conjoined letters are dependent on another order. Their articulation "supposes the training of gestures and the assistance of the *gaze*, the submission to the gaze which alone can rapidly *enclose* a written form, isolate it and recognize it" (VL: 150).

It is not that Derrida shows himself completely unaware of any of this. Indeed, the themes that Irigaray elaborates are drawn precisely from Derrida's own observations about the history and development of writing. Irigaray can only say what she says on the basis of Derrida's (non-)history of writing. One or two quotations will serve to make this point: Derrida speaks of the "Compromise . . . between the eye and the hand" (OGr: 289; DG: 409). He says that "our writing and our reading are still largely determined by the movement of the hand" (OGr: 288; DG: 408), and "the space of writing is thus not an originally *intelligible* space" (OGr: 289; DG: 409).[38] For Irigaray, notwithstanding his influence on her, Derrida is "always already caught . . . in the labyrinth of *mirrors*, in *veils*, in *apparitions (apparences)*, or *semblances/appearances (apparaître)*" (VL: 164). Because of this infinite play of reflections, she says "I teach you nothing" (VL: 164)—an assertion that acknowledges the depths of Derrida's analyses even if it signals Irigaray's unwillingless to completely situate or circumscribe her own concerns within the orbit of Derrida's designs on metaphysics. She accuses someone (Derrida?) of trickery, of cheating (see VL: 167). The accused accords, Irigaray notices, repetition a privilege (see VL: 168), as if one could not get away from what Levinas calls "the same." Yet Irigaray nonetheless establishes a certain parallelism between herself and Derrida, one which is "still susceptible to all kinds of analyses" (VL: 168).

It is probably no accident that Irigaray does not mention Derrida by his proper name in her text except in footnotes or in parentheses. She thereby effects a marginalization of the author whose tactics and strategies she nevertheless invokes and employs—establishing a symmetry, a space, an exchange between them. Playing Derrida at his own game, her reading of his work proceeds neither according to the rules of straightforward exegesis, nor in keeping with the conventions of hermeneutical interpretation. She provides no explicit enumeration of cumulative theses about Derrida that would clearly summarize his position. At times it is hard to distinguish Irigaray's voice from the one she comments on—again, this coincidence, this reluctance to attribute ideas in line with scholarly tradition is not incidental to her thinking. Rather, Irigaray prefers to approach Derrida (and others) more indirectly, obliquely, by subterfuge and play, by allowing her text to reiterate the very strategic maneuvers that characterize Derrida's text even as she works to undermine them, to bring them into question, to ask about what they exclude, and to demonstrate their limits.

The relationship between Derrida and Irigaray could never be read as pure or absolute—it is a relation that is precisely always already compromised in the sense that writing (in the traditional sense), Derrida wants to suggest, always already informs speech. By describing the exchange between Irigaray and Derrida in terms of a compromise, I mean to take account of Irigaray's proposal that sexual difference—and not just difference—is the epochal question. Can this difference of emphasis be explained in terms of politics? Or can it be explained in terms of Irigaray's "being"—in the sense of occupying the position of—a woman? Perhaps. To inhabit, no matter how interrogatively, the position of a woman shares some structural features of the relationship Derrida sets up between writing and arche-writing. Irigaray retains the term "woman" in much the same way that Derrida retains the term "writing": both terms commemorate a historical concept at the same time as unhinging the foundations of that concept, reelaborating what the conditions and possibilities of each concept might be or might become.

Deconstruction provides one way of articulating the shifting categories of feminist discourse. There are others that come from the discourse of feminism itself, and still others that come from the discourses of medicine and science. The impetus for deconstructing one of the oppositions that has been a central concern throughout this work, that of sex and gender, does not come from Derrida, even if he provides some tools for deconstructing it. It comes from a variety of sources, including texts that I have mentioned in the area of feminism and science—texts by Irigaray and Kristeva, texts by Anglo-American feminists. That is not to say that none of these texts bear the mark of deconstruction; some of them do so more vividly than others—above all, the texts of Irigaray.

I have suggested a reading of Irigaray that does not see her as committing a travesty against the majestic writings of a master even though her writing is a transgressive reading: it goes against the grain; she reads not just on the surface but under the surface, pulling texts apart by adding new tensions to them. If Irigaray wants in some sense to recuperate the letter, which has been stolen from the scene of writing—violated, even raped ("*Le v(i)ol de la lettre*")—this recuperative movement is not without ambiguity. Gesturing toward the materiality of parchment, ink, fluidity, blood, air, Irigaray's title recalls Derrida's reading of Lacan's "The Seminar on *The Purloined Letter*," "*Le facteur de la vérité*."[39] Thus, Irigaray returns to the letter, restitutes the purloined letter, returns Derrida to Lacan—a series of gestures that cannot be unfolded here, but which point in a direction that this work would have to go were it to go beyond itself. One of the ways in which Irigaray brings into question the authority of Derrida's interpretative strategies is by subjecting him to the discourse of psychoanalysis. But that is a subject that I will have to leave for another time.

My attempt has been to show how essentialism has become an obfuscating term that interferes with a responsible reading of Irigaray's texts. It has functioned as an excuse for a general dismissal of Irigaray's work that glosses over the specificity of a variety of alleged misrepresentations, and universalizes what often turn out to be unfounded allegations against so-called post-structuralist feminism. Feminists need to talk about and find ways of combating sexism, racism, heterosexism, and all the other "isms" for which the accusation of essentialism has been allowed to stand. To the extent that essentialism mystifies these urgent and pressing problems it covers over not only the importance of thinking through the question of sexual difference, but also the damaging and dehumanizing dynamics and the multiple faces of the imperialism of the same. These dynamics need to be confronted on their own terms—directly, specifically, forcefully, and articulately—not through the vague discourse of essentialism.

afterword

IRIGARAY, FREUD, LACAN

As THIS BOOK WAS NEARING COMPLETION, I WRESTLED repeatedly with the problem of how to deal with the question of psychoanalysis: given its importance for Irigaray's work, it did not seem possible to write a book on Irigaray without somehow addressing the issue. Yet I knew that if I began to confront the question seriously, not only would the discussion be impossible to confine to the limits of this study as presently conceived, but even if I found a way of reconceptualizing the present book, I might well discover that this process would detract from the philosophical import of Irigaray's work. I was reluctant to risk changing the focus so radically—and also reluctant to delay the project for what could turn into a number of years! I finally decided on the following compromise:[1] What follows is a brief attempt to point in the direction of one area that would have to be pursued in order to take Irigaray studies one step further. I make no claims for comprehensiveness —I simply want to make a few observations about Irigaray's use of psychoanalysis in her commentary on Derrida in "Belief Itself," which is played out partially in terms of her rereading of Freud and Lacan. Having paid attention to the philosophical heritage of Beauvoir, Hegel, Heidegger, Levinas, and Derrrida, through which Irigaray's critique of the tradition is filtered, let me use Irigaray's essay as a textual focus around which to thematize (albeit in the most cursory way) the impact of psychoanalysis on Irigaray's project.

The last few pages of Irigaray's "Belief Itself," as Irigaray confirms in a footnote (SG: 50; SP: 62), echo Heidegger, thereby reverberating within the "correspondence" Derrida observes between Freud and Heidegger, who, says Derrida,

> are preoccupied with each other, passing all their time in deciphering
> each other, in resembling each other, as one ends up by resembling that

which is excluded, or, in absolute mourning, whoever has died. They could not read each other—therefore they have spent all their time and exhausted all their forces in doing so (PC: 357; CP: 379–80).

Irigaray's evocation of Heidegger in the concluding pages of "Belief Itself" is no mere rhetorical flourish, but the last of a series of correspondences she establishes between her own text and Derrida's *The Post Card*. Throughout her essay, Irigaray engages with the terms in which Derrida's reading of Freud is set forth.[2] The parallels between Irigaray's essay and Derrida's *The Post Card* are too numerous to explain in detail here, but among the most striking I would include Irigaray's use of the image of the veil. Heidegger's understanding of truth as unconcealment or unveiledness is a recurrent trope for Derrida, and one that is played out in Irigaray's texts at many different levels.

Commenting on the use that Freud makes of Andersen's fairy tale in the *Interpretation of Dreams*, Derrida says, "If one takes into account the more than metaphoric equation between veil, text, and textile, Andersen's text has the text as its theme. Or more precisely the determination of the text as veil within the space of the truth, the reduction of the text to a movement of *aleitheia*" (PC: 418; CP: 446).[3] By casting part of her commentary in the form of a children's story, Irigaray recapitulates the structure that Derrida finds and thematizes in Freud's appeal to Andersen's fairy tale. Irigaray's process of interpretation is, she tells us, "at times . . . like a children's story" (SG: 25, SP: 37; and SG: 37, SP: 49).

Taking her cue from the "curtained cot (or veiled bed, *verhängten Bettchens*)" (SG: 29; SP: 41) through which little Ernst throws his cotton reel, Irigaray emphasizes the importance of the veil, while at the same time noticing how Freud neglects to thematize the role of the "more or less transparent veil" (SG: 30; SP: 42). The veil plays a crucial role in Irigaray's essay, not least in terms of the connection she establishes between the veil and the figure of the angel as messenger and mediator, an image on which Derrida also draws.[4] Angels, says Irigaray, "have been misunderstood, forgotten, as the nature of that first veil, except in the work of poets, perhaps, and in religious iconography" (SG: 35; SP: 47). "Guardians of free passage" (SG: 42; SP: 54), angels allow messages to be transmitted "from the beyond" (SG: 35; SP: 48).

Since, as Irigaray observes, "The mother's presence" in Freud's account of the *fort-da* game "presumes . . . a rather white and transparent screen: air, canvas, veil" (SG: 30; SP: 42), Freud's failure to dwell on the veil also signals his failure to reflect on the mother.[5] Irigaray writes:

> So Freud says nothing, knows nothing, wants to know nothing about what stands between him and him, between him and her, disappearing and reappearing in the scene with the reel, before Ernst notices himself in the mirror. The veil is necessary as a setting, a mediation for the performance of presence in absence, for the process of re-presentation in this particular scene, where for the first time the son plays symbolically with the mother, but it is then neglected, censored, repressed, forgotten by Freud. The father of psychoanalysis notes what it is that enables Ernst to confuse the other in himself, the other in the same . . . he takes note of it in his description, but then goes right on. . . .
>
> But he, after all, is not playing: he is framing a theory. This tale, in which the child's naïveté is useful as an objective, scientific guarantee, can be interpreted as he likes, thus standardizing, prescribing the desire of his descendants, indeed retroactively his own, and that of his ancestors. She must be thrown over there, put at a distance, beyond the horizon, so that she can come back to him, back inside him, so that he can take her back, over and over again, reassimilate her, and feel no sorrow (SG: 30–31; SP: 43).

Irigaray expresses Freud's neglect of the mother in a number of different ways, most notably in relation to Derrida's notion of the *poste restante* and Lacan's notion of the real. She refers to the postal principle that Derrida elaborates in *The Post Card*, a principle that, like the pleasure principle (and it is not incidental that the principles of Derrida and Freud share the initials "PP"),[6] includes as part of its structure deferral and delay. Irigaray introduces the idea of "A '*poste restante*' or P. O. box where messages for unknown persons with no fixed addresses are held, undeliverable by the usual, already coded, telecommanded, circuits" (SG: 25; SP: 37). Irigaray is drawing on the series of associations that Derrida develops in *The Post Card* in her use of the term "poste restante." As Alan Bass explains in a translator's note to "*Le facteur de la vérité*,"

> For Derrida, writing is always that which is an excess remainder, *un reste*. Further, in French, mail delivered to a post office box is called *poste restante*, making the dead letter office the ultimate *poste restante*, literally "remaining mail." Thus, Derrida is saying that Lacan's notion that the non-delivered letter, *la lettre en souffrance*, always

arrives at its destination overlooks the structural possibility that a letter can always remain in the dead letter office, and that without this possibility of deviation and remaining—the entire postal system—there would be no delivery of letters to any address at all (PC: 443).[7]

Irigaray's reference to the "poste restante"—the mail box in which excess mail remains undelivered and unaccounted for, and yet at the same time that which is assumed for the proper functioning of the mail system—also recalls Lacan's notion of the real. The "real, or what is perceived as such," says Lacan, "is what resists symbolisation absolutely. In the end, doesn't the feeling of the real reach its high point in the pressing manifestation of an unreal, hallucinatory reality?" (Sem I: 67).[8] Alan Sheridan stresses that the real is that which returns, that which is resistant to the symbolic—the "impossible."[9] Irigaray gathers up the impossible, unrepresentable remainder when she says, "So, at this poste restante, a woman's message came my way recently that could not be decoded by the usual interpretative methods. . . . Yet, this message is in my opinion the essential preliminary for any consideration of sexual difference" (SG: 25; SP: 37). The message Irigaray received, a message that, she reports, met with the resistance of another psychoanalyst, was as follows: "At the point in the mass when they, the (spiritual) father and son, are reciting together the ritual words of the consecration, saying, 'This is my body, this is my blood,' I bleed" (SG: 25–26; SP: 38). This message about belief, communion, and blood is undecipherable according to the normal channels of communication, in which, Irigaray says, "Everything is set up in such a way that she is lost at the poste restante, never arrives at the destination, never comes face to face with him" (SG: 34; SP: 46). Irigaray establishes a parallel between the woman who delivers a message that cannot be assimilated into the accepted psychoanalytic framework and Sophie—the excluded woman/mother/daughter in Freud's account of the fort-da game, whose death, as Derrida points out, forms the unthematized background to Freud's *Beyond the Pleasure Principle* (PC: 326–37; CP: 348–57):[10] "Are there not some obvious similarities between the two—notably Sophie, the Sunday[11] daughter, whose death is so hard for her father to accept?" (SG: 28; SP: 40). Irigaray thereby elicits certain parallels between the discourse of belief that surrounds the religious celebration of communion and that which sustains psychoanalysis. In both scenes women are excluded from representation, yet, without them, what is represented in the credo of faith, in psychoanalytic discourse, would not be organized in the same way. The mother, the woman, is forgotten, operating as a silent center around which the text works itself out.

Irigaray comments that belief "makes us forget the real" (SG: 26; SP: 38). It becomes clear as Irigaray's essay progresses that in this case belief makes us forget "that it is they, the wives and mothers, who are being offered up in communion here" (SG: 46; SP: 58). Faith, says Irigaray in a passage that also evokes Lacan, "aims to double its own reflection, to square or even cube all its numbers or letters and thereby make the other—with a capital O—the other of the same" (SG: 26; SP: 38–39).[12] Like Levinas, Irigaray wants to allow the other to be radically other, and not to see it merely as a reflection of the same.

The titles of both Derrida's essay, "To Speculate—on 'Freud,'" and Irigaray's, "Belief Itself," may be traced back to a particular passage in "Beyond the Pleasure Principle," in which Freud announces his hesitation about whether the hypotheses he advances in his attempt to go beyond the pleasure principle have scientific status (SE 18: 59).

It should be clear by now that neither Irigaray's nor Derrida's readings of Freud can be read as if they were innocent of the history and the questions to which both subject them: questions about the purity and clarity of assigning origins to any reading of any text (and, particularly, a text of Freud's that has accumulated such a wealth of interpretations already, not the least of which bear the mark of Lacan); questions about the privileging of certain conscious, fully present, and unveiled concepts in one's reading of a text above others—unconscious, absented, but beneath the surface;[13] questions about the authenticity (*Eigentlichkeit*) of the "as such," or the possibility of identifying the proper lines of inheritance that bind and unbind these texts to one another, insofar as they call upon the same proper names to establish or verify what is to be said about Freud (Heidegger's name springs to mind, for example).

"Therefore," says Irigaray, "I shall term the preliminary to the question of sexual difference: belief itself" (SG: 27; SP: 39). This "therefore" gathers up several "threads" (*fils*) (to use a word whose multiple resonances in French are lost neither on Derrida nor on Irigaray) that weave in and out of Irigaray's text.[14] The status of belief is up for question at several levels: for example, Freud's belief in his own hypotheses, his faith in the project of psychoanalysis, his belief in himself, and his questioning of the degree of scientific certainty ascertained by his method. An uncertain relationship obtains between Freud as the father of psychoanalysis and as the "subject" of his discourse—a relationship that is implicated in a complex network of allegiance. As one who speculates on the meaning, value, worth, and scientific validity of the writing up of his observations, Freud reflects on both the psychoanalytic procedure and the operation of writing. As the grandfather of little Ernst and as the father of Sophie (little Ernst's absent mother), Freud himself is the subject of his discourse. The themes of belief, faith, the scriptures, the devil, constantly recur throughout Derrida's reading of Freud's "Beyond the Pleasure Principle," and the fact that Irigaray reiterates these themes by calling her essay "Belief Itself" is in line with the repetition compulsion that Freud explores in his essay.[15]

By reading how the father of psychoanalysis writes his reflections on little Ernst's *fort-da* game according to the very same repetition-compulsion that characterizes child's play, Derrida capitalizes on the values with which Freud invests "what is purely speculative" (SE 18: 59). Drawing on the plural senses of the "speculative structure in general"—"specular reflection"; "production of surplus value, of calculations and bets on the Exchange"; "overflowing the (given) presence of the present, the given of the gift" (PC: 284; CP: 303–4)—Derrida has some allegations of his own about Freud:

> I am alleging that speculation is not only a mode of research named by Freud, not only the oblique object of his discourse, but also the operation of his writing, the scene (of that) which he makes by writing what he writes here, that which makes him do it, and that which he makes do, that which makes him write and that which he makes—or lets—write. To make to do, to make write, to let do, or to let write: the syntax of these operations is not given (PC: 284; CP: 304).

Speculating on the economy by which Freud repeatedly attempts to "rein" in (PC: 272; CP: 290),[16] to tie down, or to make systematic his thesis about the pleasure principle (although not always successfully), Derrida comments on Freud's "deliberate avoidance of philosophy, a rejection of the philosophical debt, genealogy, or descendance" (PC: 272; CP: 290), citing Nietzsche, "whose guesses and intuitions," according to Freud's own testimony, "often agree in the most astonishing way with the painfully laborious [*mühsamen*] findings of psychoanalysis," and who (for that very reason?) "was for a long time avoided" (PC: 263; CP: 281).[17] The "speculation" employed by Freud is, according to Derrida, "neither philosophical nor scientific in the classical sense" but is rather an approach that "supposes something which here is named Repression, to wit that which permits a pleasure to be lived and perceived as unpleasure, for example" (PC: 288; CP: 308). "Repression," says Derrida, "upsets the logic implicit in all philosophy: it makes it possible for a pleasure to be experienced—by the ego—as unpleasure" (PC: 289; CP: 309). The logic of philosophy is "the order of that which *represents* itself or *presents* itself clearly and easily in order to coordinate itself with the value of presence which governs everything that is *self-evident* in *experience*" (PC: 289; CP: 309). The relationship between the pleasure principle (PP) and the reality principle (PR) subverts the value of presence affirmed by the logos of classical philosophy. The relationship between the PP and the PR is not one that maintains them as ideals that oppose one another, but rather one in which they supplement one another. Derrida says, "Pure pleasure and pure reality are ideal limits, which is as much to say fictions" (PC: 284; CP: 304). Establishing a relationship of deferral, the reality principle intervenes on behalf of the pleasure principle, not in order to impose a "definitive inhibition" or "renunciation of pleasure, only a detour in order to defer enjoyment" (PC: 282; CP: 301). Pleasure is delegated to the reality principle by the pleasure principle. The reality principle thereby stands in for the pleasure principle, performing the role of a surrogate, ensuring the authority of pleasure. Derrida says:

> the pleasure principle . . . organizes everything, but can encounter . . . external obstacles. These obstacles do sometimes prevent it from coming to its conclusion or from triumphing, but do not put it into question *as* a principal *tendency* to pleasure, but on the contrary confirm it as soon as they are considered obstacles.
> . . . When the simple, direct, and imprudent affirmation of the pleasure principle puts the organism into danger, then the "ego's instincts of self-preservation" force the principle into retreat, not into disappearing by *simply* yielding its place, but into *leaving* the reality principle in its place as a delegate, its courier, its lieutenant, or its slave, its domestic in that it belongs to the same economy, the same house (PC: 282; CP: 301).

Little Ernst brings back to himself the spool or reel by means of the string to which it is attached (a tie which therefore never really allowed a definitive departure, so that any return is not so much a product of reattachment as it is a result of the refusal to let go properly in the first place). Freud's account of little Ernst's "game," which consists of throwing away and bringing back the "wooden reel," is familiar:

> What he did was to hold the reel by the string and very skillfully throw it over the edge of his curtained cot, so that it disappeared into it, at the

same time uttering his expressive "o-o-o-o." He then pulled the reel out of the cot again by the string and hailed its reappearance with a joyful "*da*" ["there"]. This then, was the complete game—disappearance and return. As a rule one only witnessed its first act, which was repeated untiringly as a game in itself, though there is no doubt that the greater pleasure was attached to the second act (SE 18: 15).

Freud thinks that the "long-drawn out 'o-o-o-o' . . . represented the German word '*fort*' ['gone']" (SE 18: 14–15). He attaches a footnote to his interpretation of the game played by little Ernst:

A further observation subsequently confirmed this interpretation fully. One day the child's mother had been away for several hours and on her return was met with the words "Baby o-o-o-o!" which was at first incomprehensible. It soon turned out, however, that during this long period of solitude the child had found a method of making *himself* disappear. He had discovered his reflection in a full-length mirror which did not quite reach to the ground, so that by crouching down he could make his mirror-image "gone" (SE 18: 15, note 1).

Lacan, commenting on Freud's interpretation of little Ernst's "fort-da" game—which is a source for Lacan's understanding of the acquisition of language at the symbolic level—highlights the themes of presence and absence, the idea of language as symbolization, and the sense in which "desire becomes human" (Sem I: 103)—which, for Lacan, means that the desire of the subject is intimately bound up with the desire of the other.[18]

Let me return to Derrida's commentary on Freud, which includes the following observations:

One provides oneself (and dispenses with) the head of what one needs by doing without it in order to have it. A capitalized pleasure: the child identifies himself with the mother since he disappears as she does, and makes her return with himself, by making himself return without making anything but himself, her in himself, return. . . . He makes himself disappear, he masters himself symbolically . . . he makes himself reappear henceforth without a mirror (PC: 319; CP: 340).

Derrida finds in Freud's description of the *fort-da* operation a repetition of the operation itself: "Just as Ernst, in recalling the object (mother, thing, whatever) to himself, immediately comes *himself* to recall *himself* in an immediately supplementary operation, so the speculating grandfather, in describing or recalling this or that, recalls *himself*" (PC: 320–21; CP: 342). Derrida bets on Freud (see CP: 410; PC: 384), repeatedly putting his money on an interpretation that emphasizes the extent to which "The writing of a *fort-da* is always a *fort-da*" (CP: 342; PC: 321), or, "the repetitive process is to be identified not only in the content . . . but already, or again, in Freud's writing, in the *démarche* of his text, in what he does as much as in what he says" (PC: 295; CP: 315–16).[19] Derrida specifies Freud's procedure more specifically:

> What repeats itself . . . is the speculator's indefatigable motion in order to reject, to set aside, to make disappear, to distance (*fort*), to defer everything that appears to put the PP into question. He observes every time that something does not suffice, that something must be put off until further on, until later. Then he makes the hypothesis of the beyond come back [*revenir*] only to dismiss it again. This hypothesis comes back [*revient*] only as that which has not truly come back [*revenu*], that which has only passed by in the specter of its presence (PC: 295; CP: 316).[20]

I will not stop to rehearse the various dismissals that Derrida summons in support of his case. Suffice it to note that he says that Freud

> does what he is describing, to wit, what Ernst is doing: *fort/da* with his spool [*bobine*]. And each time that one says *to do*, one must specify: *to allow* to do (*lassen*). Freud does not do *fort/da*, indefatigably, with the object that the PP is. He does it with himself, he recalls himself (PC: 320; CP: 341–42).

Freud, then, writes himself, writes his life, in recalling his grandson's game. "The speculator," says Derrida, "himself recalls himself. He describes what he is doing. Without doing so *explicitly*" (PC: 322; CP: 343).[21] In a key passage, Derrida interrogates the nature of this recalling— Freud's remembering himself through the writing of *Beyond the Pleasure Principle*:

> Under what headings can one say that in recalling what happens (on) to the subject (of) Ernst he is recalling himself, recalling that it happened

to him? Under several interlaced, serial headings, in the "same" chain of writing.

First, he recalls to himself that Ernst recalls (to himself) his mother: he recalls Sophie. He recalls to himself that Ernst recalls his daughter to himself in recalling his mother to himself. . . . The mother of the one is not only the daughter of the other, she is also his mother; the daughter of the one is not only the mother of the other, she is also his daughter, etc. Even at the moment when the scene, if this can be said, took place, and even before Freud undertook to relate it, he was in a situation to identify himself, as is all too readily said, with his grandson, and, playing both colors, to recall his mother in recalling his daughter . . . (PC: 323; CP: 344–45).

As if in response to this passage, Irigaray writes,

If we are to reframe the paternal scenario, see how it made its mark, play it backward, we cannot merely master the female whom the father was always seeking to take or take back in his threads, the female who, already, exceeded the father and whom he endlessly sought to bring back into his game. . . .

If we do not rethink and rebuild the whole scene of representation, the angels will never find a home, never stay anywhere. Guardians of free passage, they cannot be captured, domesticated, even if our purpose is to see ourselves in them (SG: 42; Sp: 54–55).

Irigaray warns that if we do not rethink and rebuild the scene of representation we risk the disappearance of angels. Rilkean figures, read through Heidegger, angels bring together in a disjunctive, impossible-to-think union the religious transcendence of spirituality with the material immanence of bodies. They are go-betweens, creating passages between the unseen and the seen. As the figure whose appearance and disappearance little Ernst seeks to control in his "first language game," the mother, says Irigaray, "subsists before language . . . and beyond language" (SG: 46; SP: 58). She "remains the elemental substrate of life, existing before all forms, all limit, all skin, and of heaven, visible beyond-horizon. Between these extremes stand the angels and the annunciation of the fulfillment of the flesh" (SG: 46; SP: 58).

notes

NOTES TO PREFACE

1. Recent discussions of the prominence of gender in feminism include Butler, 1990; De Lauretis, 1987; Flax, 1987; Scott, 1986; and Showalter, 1989.
2. I borrow this phrase from Whitford, 1991: 20, who applies it to another critic, because it serves well to make the point that I neither mean to ignore the usefulness of Showalter's analysis in other respects, nor to reduce the impact of her thought to a position she takes at one point in one of many texts.
3. In contrast to Showalter, Rosalind Delmar says that the focus on sexual difference and the "employment of psychoanalysis and critical theory to question the unity of the subject, to emphasize the fragmented subject, is potentially subversive of any view which asserts a 'central' organizing principle of social conflict" (1986: 28). Disagreement about the discourse of sexual difference is further complicated by the fact that some American theorists have adopted the term "gender" to refer to what British and French feminists call "sexual difference." On the confusion between the terms sexual difference and gender, see Elliot, 1991: 3–4.
4. The same disjunction is to be found in a phrase Schor uses in order to distinguish between Beauvoir's and Irigaray's conception of the subject, "For Irigaray . . . the main attribute of the subject is not activity but language" (1989: 44).
5. See, for example, Weedon's comments on feminist uses of psychoanalytic theory (1987: 71).
6. Tavor Bannet, 1989: 19–20.
7. I have in mind, for example, the position of those Schor describes as elaborating a "linguistic critique" of essentialism. For them, she says, "Within the symbolic order centered on the phallus there can be no immediate access to the body: the fine mesh of language screens off the body from any apprehension that is not already encultured" (1989: 41).
8. One of the earliest arguments against Irigaray's alleged essentialism is Plaza, 1978.
9. Segal, 1987: 132–34; and Moi, 1985: 139.
10. Fuss, 1989: xiii, and chap. 4, 55–72. Fuss makes some pertinent and valuable observations in relation to other critics of Irigaray, such as her comments on Moi (1989: 56), and on Plaza (1989: 67), but she still thinks that "Irigaray might rightly be accused . . . of a certain tendency to universalize and to homogenize, to subsume all women under the category of 'Woman'" (1989: 68). Fuss concludes, that "Irigaray works towards securing a woman's access to an essence of her own, without actually prescribing what that essence might be" (1989: 72).

Fuss' reading attests to the confusion that still surrounds the charge of essentialism. I want to suggest that to characterize Irigaray as aspiring to secure "a woman's access to an essence of her own" is to misrepresent her work. If Irigaray is read in the context of Heidegger's questioning of traditional concepts of essence, and Derrida's elaboration of Heidegger, the inadequacy of the idea that Irigaray would try to secure an essence for women, or the implication that she might conceivably prescribe such an essence, quickly emerges.

11. As Gatens says, "Critics of feminists of difference tend to divide the entire theoretical field of social enquiry into an exclusive disjunction: social theory is *either* environmentalist *or* it is essentialist. Therefore, and it follows quite logically from this premise, if feminist theories are not environmentalist then they must be essentialist" (1991a: 141).

12. This insight is by no means new. Showalter, for example, acknowledges that to talk about gender "is a constant reminder of the other categories of difference, such as race and class, that structure our lives and texts, just as theorizing gender emphasizes the parallels between feminist criticism and other forms of minority discourse" (1989: 3). Once Irigaray's questioning of sexual difference is understood not so much as a refusal to consider gender, as an insight that gender cannot be adequately analyzed without a confrontation with the nature of sexual difference, the distance between Showalter and Irigaray does not seem so great. Also see Kaplan, 1986: 148, whom Showalter quotes.

13. Whitford, 1991. Also see Grosz, who by emphasizing the importance of what she calls "*sexed corporeality*" (1993: 188), argues for a reading of Irigaray that seems to me consonant with my own. According to Grosz, Irigaray's "work is a facing up to the implications of" what Grosz identifies as "the crisis of reason," that is, "to know (as woman, as other) the knower (as man has been and woman is now becoming). Her work poses the question of the partiality, that is, the sexualization of all knowledges" (1993: 210).

14. In the introductory remarks to her book, Whitford says, "Although Irigaray's relation to Hegelian and post-Hegelian philosophy is undoubtedly one of the perspectives which would shed considerable light on her formulations of questions of desire, subjectivity, identity, and death, it is not the theme in this book. For in order to examine her from this perspective, it would be necessary to see her first as a philosopher, and this is the position that I want to establish here" (1991: 3). The present work builds upon the groundwork that Whitford has laid with her careful and cogent analysis. The appearance of Whitford's book enabled me to pursue my discussion of Irigaray's philosophical sources, without feeling a responsibility to cover every aspect of her work. Nonetheless, by reading her philosophical interventions both in terms of her inheritance of phenomenological and post-phenomenological analyses, and as a critique of that tradition, I hope to provide an overall picture of Irigaray's work.

15. I am grateful to Adelaide Russo, and particularly to Michelle Massé for discussions on the question of finding a voice.

16. See Kelly Oliver's discussion of the "importing" of "the French Feminists" (1993: 163–80).

17. Here I am echoing Whitford when she points to the problems associated with "Irigaray's stardom" (1991: 5). Whitford elaborates these difficulties when she

says of Irigaray's work, "Because of the power of her critique, she runs the risk of being taken for a guru, someone with special powers of insight, who can be expected to pronounce with authority on every social issue, from nuclear power to test-tube babies" (1991: 17).

18. See Whitford's comments on the relationship between Beauvoir's and Irigaray's work (IR: 24–25).

19. Nancy F. Cott expresses the sorts of tensions I have in mind when she says, "Feminism is nothing if not paradoxical. It aims for individual freedoms by mobilizing sex solidarity. It acknowledges diversity among women while positing that women recognize their unity. It requires gender consciousness for its basis, yet calls for the elimination of prescribed gender roles" (1986: 49).

20. For a more detailed account of Irigaray's use of psychoanalytic concepts, see Whitford, 1991. See also Hirsh (forthcoming, 1994).

21. If Irigaray had not written a book called *An Ethics of Sexual Difference*, I would have used that as my title!

NOTES TO CHAPTER ONE

1. For a more detailed analysis of the differences between feminists who focus upon sexual difference, and those who see sexual equality as more central, see Jaggar (1990: 239–54).

2. Also see Scott, 1988b: 167–77. For another useful discussion of the case of Sears against the EEOC that delineates the issues of sexual difference versus sexual equality see Catharine A. MacKinnon, "Legal Perspectives on Sexual Difference" (Rhode, 1990: 213–25). See also Frug, 1992: 12–18.

3. See, for example, Culler, 1982: 43–64; Felman, 1981; Fuss, 1988; Heilbrun, 1988; Jacobus, 1986; Kamuf, 1982, 1988; Kamuf and Miller, 1990; Miller, 1991; Okin, in Rhode, 1990: 145–59; Showalter, 1977, 1987; Spacks, 1975.

4. It has to be added that some of the ground that Jacobus assumes is in danger of being lost. As Faludi (1991) has documented, there is a backlash against the successes achieved by the feminist movement. In tandem with this backlash, often in the context of debates over political correctness, some campuses are witnessing increasingly visible opposition to women's studies and multicultural courses that try to give women and minorities the voices that they have long been denied. While Jacobus could assume in 1986 that the act of reading women's texts in feminist classrooms is uncontested, this is no longer something that can be taken for granted.

5. See Spacks, 1975.

6. This is Miller in dialogue with Kamuf (1982).

7. Susan Fraiman echoes Miller's call to refocus energies on "Women's Studies," rather than "Gender Studies," when she says, in the closing lines of an enlightening article, "Go and teach women's studies. Fight Gendrification!" "Against Gendrification: Agendas for Feminist Scholarship and Teaching in Women's Studies" (1990: 9). Showalter declares "premature" Jehlen's "call for radical comparativism" "since [in 1981] we had no body of criticism that explored the issues of gender in male authors as gynocriticism had done for

female authors" (1989: 5); see Jehlen, 1981. Showalter's warning can be placed alongside the caution that Fraiman and Miller exhort feminists to exercise about "gendrification." Also see Showalter, 1982.

8. Kamuf elaborates her position in the following questions: "If feminist theory lets itself be guided by questions such as what is women's language, literature, style or experience from where does it get its faith in the form of these questions to get at truth, if not from the same central store that supplies humanism with its faith in the universal truth of man? And what if notions such as 'getting-at-the-truth-of-the-object' represented a principal means by which the power of power structures are sustained and even extended?" (1982: 44); "Yet what is it about those structures [of power that have prevented knowledge of the feminine in the past] which could have succeeded until now in excluding such knowledge if it is not a similar appeal to 'we' that has had a similar faith in its own eventual constitution as a delimited and totalizable object?" (Kamuf, 1982: 45).

9. On the exclusionary practices of feminism, particularly with regard to race, see Spelman, 1988.

10. Cixous, 1981: 256.

11. Rhode formulates the same problem elsewhere: "What gives feminism its unique force is the claim to speak from women's experience. But that experience counsels sensitivity to its own diversity across such factors as time, culture, class, race, ethnicity, sexual orientation, and age" (Rhode, 1991: 334). Also see Alcoff, 1988: 405; and Butler, 1992: 15.

12. Kristeva, 1986. For an excellent and original interpretation of Kristeva's relation to Woolf, see Miglena I. Nikolchina, "Meaning and Matricide: Reading Woolf via Kristeva," Ph.D. diss., University of Western Ontario, London, Ontario, January, 1993.

13. In the foregoing sketch of feminism I have relied on Kristeva's categorization of three periods, but in discussing the debate over essentialism I am going beyond her specifications of the three phases.

14. See, for example, Riley, 1988.

15. Spivak affirms strategic essentialism in an interview conducted by Elizabeth Gross: "In fact I must say I am an essentialist from time to time. There is, for example, the strategic choice of a genitalist essentialism in anti-sexist work today. How it relates to all of this other work I am talking about—I don't know, but my search is not a search for coherence, so that is how I would answer that question about the discourse of the clitoris. . . . I think it's absolutely on target to take a stand against the discourses of essentialism, universalism as it comes in terms of the universal—of classical German philosophy or the universal as the white upper class male . . . [Spivak's ellipses] etc. But *strategically* we cannot. Even as we talk about *feminist* practice, or privileging practice over theory, we are universalizing—not only generalizing but universalizing. Since the moment of essentializing, universalizing [sic], saying yes to the onto-phenomenological question is irreducible, let us at least situate it at the moment; let us become vigilant about our own practice and use it as much as we can rather than make the totally counter-productive gesture of repudiating it. One thing that comes out is that you jettison your own purity as a theorist. . . . Whereas the great custodians of the anti-universal are obliged therefore simply to act in the interest

of a great narrative, the narrative of exploitation while they keep themselves clean by not committing themselves to anything. In fact they are actually run by a great narrative even as they are busy protecting their theoretical purity by repudiating essentialism" (1984/85: 183–84). A few years later Spivak says, "I have . . . reconsidered this argument about the strategic use of essentialism. . . . I would say that one of the reasons why the strategic use of essentialism has caught on within a personalist culture is that it gives a certain alibi to essentialism. The emphasis falls on being able to speak from one's own ground, rather than on what the word strategy implies, so I've reconsidered it. I think it's too risky a slogan in a personalist academic culture, within which it has been picked up and celebrated. Now I think my emphasis would be more on noting how we ourselves and others are what you call essentialist, without claiming a counter-essence disguised under the alibi of strategy. . . . It seems to me that vigilance, what I call building for difference, rather than keeping ourselves clean by being whatever it is to be an anti-essentialist, that has taken on much greater emphasis for me at this point" (1989: 127–28).

16. Spivak, 1989: 145, 147.
17. Spivak advises us "not to chat about essentialism" (1989: 147).
18. Schor asks the rhetorical question, "by defining essentialism as I just have have I not in turn essentialized it, since definitions are by definition, as it were, essentialist?" (1989: 40).
19. See Braidotti (1991).
20. See also Schor, 1985; Gallop, 1985; and Jardine, 1985.
21. Just as the political and theoretical heritage of French feminists informs their work, so does the climate in which American and English feminists write.
22. Irigaray says in an interview, "I don't particularly care for the term *feminism*. It is the word by which the social system designates the struggle of women. I am completely willing to abandon this word, namely because it is formed on the same model as the other great words of the culture that oppresses us. I prefer to say 'the struggles of women,' which reveals a plural and polymorphous character. But I think that when certain groups of women criticize and fight against feminism, they don't take into account the gesture they are making with regard to the dominant culture. After all, it is necessary to consider the way they attack us, and it is most generally under the label of feminism. In this case, it is necessary to claim the term back and then to refine it and say something else" (Baruch and Serrano, 1988: 150).
23. See Kaufmann-McCall, 1983: 282–93.
24. Baruch and Serrano, 1988: 151.
25. Gatens' citations are to Freud, SE: vol. VII, and Stoller, 1968. For a critique of Gatens see Plumwood, 1989: 2–11. See also Gatens 1989; Butler, YFS: 35–49.
26. Gatens (1991a) cites the following texts: Greer, 1971; Millett, 1971; Oakley, 1972; Chodorow, 1978; Dinnerstein 1977. Gilbert, 1980, and Jacobus, 1986, can be added to this list.
27. Stoller says, "We can say that the *core* gender identity remains unchanged throughout life; this is not to say that gender identity is not constantly developing and being modified, but only that at the core the awareness of being either a male or female remains constant . . . this core gender identity is produced, starting at

birth, by three components. The first of these is the contribution made by the *anatomy of the external genitalia.* By their 'natural' appearance, the external genitalia serve as a *sign* to parents that the ascription of one sex rather than the other at birth was correct. . . . The second component, the *infant-parent relationships,* is made up of the parents' expectations of the child's gender identity, their own gender identities, the child's identifications with both sexes, libidinal gratifications and frustrations between child and parents, and many other psychological aspects of preoedipal and oedipal development. The third component is the postulated *biological force*" (1968: vol. 1, 72–73). Insofar as Stoller acknowledges that there is a biological component to the formation of gender identity, his distinction between sex and gender is not absolute. He suggests that "the normal development of gender identity may be as follows: A sex-linked genetic biological tendency toward masculinity in males and femininity in females works silently but effectively from fetal existence on, being overlaid after birth by the effects of environment, the biological and environmental influences working more or less in harmony to produce a preponderance of masculinity in men and of femininity in women" (ibid., 74).

28. See Weedon, 1987.

29. Sigmund Freud, "The Psychogenesis of a Case of Homosexuality in a Woman" (SE 18: 145–72, esp. 170–71).

30. A variety of overlapping rationales are offered in support of the perceived need to revise or rethink a distinction that has played a central role in articulating feminist agendas. For a good discussion of the issue of sexual difference, in relation to the sex/gender distinction, see Gatens, 1991a. It is within the context of challenging metaphysical notions of identity that Butler casts doubt on the adequacy with which contemporary feminist theory delineates the sex/gender distinction (1990: 11). See also Harding, 1989; Fox Keller, 1989; Messer-Davidow, 1989; Delphy, 1993; and Haraway, 1991.

31. Butler says, "If the immutable character of sex is contested, perhaps this construct called 'sex' is as culturally constructed as gender" (1990: 7). Butler's book, *Bodies that Matter: On the Discursive Limits of Sex* (New York: Routledge, 1993), appeared just as the present work was going to press, and I did not have time to take account of it. Clearly it will be a crucial book, just as *Gender Trouble* has been determinative of major questions for feminist discourse in the last few years. Butler re-visits the questions she raises about sex in *Gender Trouble,* (see 1993: 6). As far as I can tell, having just dipped into the book, Butler's questioning seems to be in line with what I am arguing, namely, that even if "bodies" are constructed, there is still a sense in which we need to acknowledge sexed bodies as distinct from their performative genders; even if the sex/gender distinction is to be rethought, it cannot be altogether repudiated. Butler confirms this point in an interview when she says, "I have shifted. I think I overrode the category of Sex too quickly in *Gender Trouble.* I try to reconsider it in *Bodies That Matter,* and to emphasize the place of constraint in the very production of sex" (1994: 32–33).

32. Butler observes that "perhaps it [sex] was always already gender, with the consequence that the distinction between sex and gender turns out to be no distinction at all" (1990: 7). While I can see the force of this formulation in its context, and I do not want to underestimate the overall importance of Butler's

contribution, I wonder whether at times, for all the sophistication of her analysis, she does not elide sex into gender at the risk of rendering the body out of bounds. Butler is right to emphasize the fact that sex is always already "established as 'prediscursive,' prior to culture, a politically neutral surface *on which* culture acts" (ibid.)—but this should not be taken to mean that sex is empty of all meaning. Butler returns to these issues in her next chapter in the careful questions she asks: "Locating the mechanism whereby sex is transformed into gender is meant to establish not only the constructedness of gender, its unnatural and nonnecessary status, but the cultural universality of oppression in nonbiologistic terms. How is this mechanism formulated? Can it be found or merely imagined? Is the designation of its ostensible universality any less of a reification than the position that grounds universal oppression in biology?" (37). These questions derive their force, it seems to me, precisely from the need to avoid allowing the category of gender to entirely dissolve the particularity of bodies. Racism is one of the most dramatic problems implicated by the tendency to apply the category of gender as a universal. For a useful discussion of this problem, see Spelman, 1988.

33. Irigaray adds a footnote to this statement, referring readers to her essay "Why Define Sexed Rights" (JTN: 81–92; JT: 101–15) for her "much more radical" views. There we find her stipulating that she has "regularly worked with women or groups of women who belong to liberation movements, and in these I've observed problems or impasses that can't be resolved except through the establishment of an equitable legal system for both sexes" (JTN: 82; JT: 102). She adds that "the strategy of equality, when there is one, should always aim to get differences recognized. For example, having equal numbers of men and women in all sectors of social activity in order to get them to progress. Of course, on one level this is a totally desirable solution. But it's not enough . . . because the current social order, and that includes the order defining occupations, is not neutral when viewed in terms of the difference of the sexes" (JTN: 84; JT: 105).

    Contrary to popular opinion, my own view is that Kristeva does not deny, any more than Irigaray does, the need to continue the struggle for equal rights. She also asks whether that struggle goes far enough. It seems to me that Kristeva is right when she suggests that insofar as feminism must cast itself in opposition to the dominant culture, it will be shaped negatively according to what that culture denies women. She has been maligned for formulating the contradictory positions women occupy in a male-dominated culture (Kristeva, 1980: 137). For a critique of her position that deals specifically with this point, see Alcoff, 1988: 418.

34. Oliver puts forward the hypothesis that "some American feminists projected the charges of essentialism which were coming from black feminists onto The French Feminists. Overlooking their differences, and their theories of difference, some American feminists criticized The French Feminists for their essentialism and elitism, the very charges which were being brought against American feminists themselves. In an essentializing move, some American feminists reduced The French Feminists to one concept, feminine writing, and then projected all of the charges of excluding women onto their theories. Against the French feminists, American feminists could define themselves as nonessentializing, more inclusive, and more inaccessible to women" (Oliver, 1993: 168).

35. See Rhode, 1990; Harris, 1991; and Williams 1991.

36. Nell (now Onora O'Neill) distinguishes between formal and substantive equality of opportunity. Formal equality of opportunity, which represents the interpretation often given in the classical liberal tradition of political thought, is that in which "A and B can have equal opportunities with respect to *x* without being likely to enjoy *x*" (1980: 335). In the substantive interpretation of equality of opportunity, "women have an equal opportunity to enter law school only if they are admitted in proportions appropriate to the number who apply, and their applications are not being deterred or reduced by any policy of the school so that the pool of applicants contains all women who wish to go to that law school. . . . A strong commitment to substantive equality of opportunity demands that any under-representation of some group in some line of employment/income group/educational group be due solely to the unmanipulated choice of that group" (1980: 338).

NOTES TO CHAPTER TWO

1. I have not attempted anything like an exhaustive survey of the critical literature on Beauvoir. However, during the 1980s several journals devoted issues, either in part or in whole, to Beauvoir's work. A number of the articles deal with her relation to Sartre and existentialism. Among the most important is Le Doeuff, FS: 277–89. In the same issue of *Feminist Studies*, see Felstiner, FS: 247–76; Dijkstra, FS: 290–303; Fuchs, FS: 304–13. Also see Simons, 1990: 227–30; Card, 1990: 290–99; Dallery, 1990: 270–79; Frye, 1990: 300–304; Ferguson, 1990: 280–89; Jaggar and McBride, 1990: 249–69; Seigfried, 1990: 305–22; Young, 1990: 231–48. *Yale French Studies* 72 was devoted to Beauvoir. See especially Simons, YFS: 165–79; Portuges, YFS: 107–118; Butler, YFS: 35–49; Patterson, YFS: 87–106. *L'esprit créateur* 29 includes Suleiman, 1989: 42–51; Bair, 1989: 75–85; and Kaufmann, 1989: 21–32. Simons also documents the shortcomings of H. M. Parshley's translation of *The Second Sex* 1983: 559–564.
2. Exemplary in this respect is Whitford, 1991.
3. I use the word "successors" advisedly—despite the lack of direct dependence on Beauvoir's work on the part of French feminists, and despite the fact that in some cases they display overt hostility toward it. I am grateful to Toril Moi, who read an earlier draft of this chapter, and whose generous comments helped me clarify my thinking on this and other points. While I do not find myself always in agreement with Moi's position, her work on Beauvoir raises many of the issues with which I am concerned in this paper, including the role of Beauvoir as a writer. See, for example, Moi, 1990a and 1990b.
4. See, for example, Butler, YFS: 35; Butler, 1987: 128; Allen, 1989: 79; Kaufmann, YFS: 121; Moi, 1992; Spelman, 1988: 66; and Wittig, 1992: 10.
5. The context of this phrase will be important for this analysis. Beauvoir says, "What peculiarly signalizes the situation of woman is that she—a free and autonomous being like all human creatures—nevertheless finds herself living in a world where men compel her to assume the status of the Other. They propose to stabilize her as object and to doom her to immanence since her transcendence is to be overshadowed and forever transcended by another ego (*conscience*) which is essential and

sovereign. The drama of woman lies in this conflict between the fundamental aspirations of every subject (ego)—who always regards the self as the essential—and the compulsions of a situation in which she is the inessential" (SS: xxxiii; DS: 31).

6. O'Brien says, "If de Beauvoir is to be criticized, it is her model of a common, dualist but genderically differentiated consciousness which must be considered seriously, and her insistence that woman is primordially Other, an object and never a subject in her historical development: one lonely leg of a dualism which she somehow shares with men who have courageously and freely faced up to the risky job of mediating their two-legged existential fate" (1981: 68).

7. Jean-Paul Sartre says, "Human freedom precedes essence in man and makes it possible; the essence of the human being is suspended in his freedom. What we call freedom is impossible to distinguish from the being of 'human reality.' Man does not exist *first* in order to be free *subsequently*; there is no difference between the being of man and his being-free" (BN: 60; EN: 60).

8. Singer argues that "Beauvoir gives freedom what it lacked in the traditional existentialist account, which is to say that Beauvoir gives freedom a foundation, a context, a history, and something to do" (1993: 140). I am sympathetic with Singer's attempt to retrieve Beauvoir's "discourse of otherness" (1993: 132), and I think it provides an important corrective to this largely neglected aspect of *The Second Sex*. I suggest, however, that this strategy risks underplaying the extent to which Beauvoir remains convinced of the existentialist tenet that one can choose to overcome all obstacles.

9. O'Brien acknowledges the importance of Beauvoir's argument that "women have no history" (1981: 72), but does not connect this with her thematization of woman as other. Consequently, O'Brien does not see the full complexity of women's situation as Beauvoir presents it. She sees that, for Beauvoir, woman is torn "between a project to ensnare man in her immanence and a project to struggle out of his gaoler's grasp, his 'project' of perpetuating her convenient and useful immanence" (73), but she does not take account of the fact that women too, according to Beauvoir, find their role "convenient."

10. As we saw in the previous chapter the kind of rethinking of the sex/gender distinction I suggest calls into question the adequacy of the label "essentialism," at the same time requiring us to reexamine what we mean when we oppose gender to sex. In this respect, see Schor's discussion of the essentialism debate in relation to Beauvoir and Irigaray (1989: 50). I agree that "Irigaray's project is diametrically opposed to Beauvoir's but must be viewed as its necessary corollary" (45). If I were to situate my own task in relation to Schor's, I would say that my attempt is to show the details of this paradoxical relationship, which I think Schor describes correctly. I am emphasizing the need to think through the relationship between two aspects of Beauvoir's work, namely women's cultural conditioning as feminine, and women's otherness. By suggesting that both Beauvoir herself and many of her critics have understood the need to change women's situation better than they have understood women's otherness, I hope to explain how Irigaray's work can be both "diametrically opposed to" and a "necessary corollary of" Beauvoir's.

11. The inadequacy of Beauvoir's assessment of motherhood has often been remarked. Rich (1986) is among the more prominent feminists to have explored the complex experience that motherhood is; see esp. chap. 1, pp. 21–40. Also see

Ruddick, FS: 342–67; for a further development of her ideas see Ruddick, 1989. On the question of Beauvoir and motherhood see Patterson, YFS: 87–106; and Portuges, YFS: 107–18.

12. See, for example, Andrea Nye's discussion of oppression, and the difference between Marxist and existentialist responses to the problem (1988: 84–85).

13. Hegel discusses the feminine in the limited context of the role of the family in the ethical order, a discussion on which the next chapter focuses. See PhS: 267–78; PhG: 317–30. As Mills says, "In Hegel's analysis of the master-slave dialectic, there is no mention of woman: master and slave are both seen as males even though historically many slaves were women" (1987: 14). Mills claims that Hegel's "system does not permit woman to be viewed as fully human" (1987: 8). She argues that "in the same way that first nature is overreached by Spirit in Hegel's system of philosophy, woman is overreached by man: man's desire over-reaches woman's desire and the spheres of man's second nature overreach the sphere of first nature to which woman is confined" (1987: 14). O'Brien says of the master-slave dialectic, "Hegel's scenario remains a recognition and a struggle for recognition between two adult males. Master and slave are inaugurating human history and the transcendence of nature in conditions under which the institution of patriarchy is already established for all time, and from time out of mind. . . . Beauvoir's claim that the master and slave passages are applicable to men and women is, therefore, problematic" (1981: 70).

14. See, for example, Spelman, 1988 for a critique of Beauvoir's neglect of race, and for an informed and informative examination of an unacknowledged parochialism in *The Second Sex*.

15. Clearly Beauvoir's dependence on the Hegelian master-slave dialectic is only one dimension of the philosophical language that constrains her articulation of women's situations; another aspect is her adherence to existentialist ethics. This chapter examines the historical, philosophical, and conceptual limitations that imposed themselves on Beauvoir, and to which she succumbed. Despite the fact that it has long been known that Kojève and Sartre were major influences upon Beauvoir, there is still a considerable lack of clarity as to the exact nature of Kojève's Marxist-Hegelian influence. This may be due in part to Beauvoir's own insistence on the fact that the only important influence on *The Second Sex* was Sartre's philosophy. In a memorial essay, Simons writes of her first attempt to interview Beauvoir:

> I hesitantly posed my first question about the influence of the interpretations of Hegel by Kojève and Hyppolite on The Second Sex. Of course she had read them, she replied, but I must remember, she said leaning towards me in emphasis, that the only important influence on The Second Sex was Being and Nothingness by Jean-Paul Sartre.
>
> I was taken aback. Here was the forbidden name, the name that I had in angry reaction consigned to the footnotes in all my papers, moved back to center stage. Although I knew from her autobiographies that she saw Sartre as the real philosopher, I had hoped that as a feminist she would no longer see her philosophical work as merely derivative from Sartre's. I was unprepared for the forcefulness of her reply. It was impossible to see her in a passive role, as merely the follower of Sartre. Yet it was this very image of her work that she seemed to be defending so forcefully. Later I perceived her attitude as a defense of Sartre,

who was still under attack for his late support of the May 1968 uprising. The fate of her own work concerned her much less (YFS: 204).

16. See Suleiman, 1989, for a discussion of how Beauvoir saw herself in relation to her writing. Of particular interest are Suleiman's comments on Beauvoir's use of pronouns (1989: 44).

17. Moi distances herself from the critic who "obsessively returns to the question of femininity, or more specifically to what one might call the *personality topos,* passionately discussing Beauvoir's looks, character, private life or morality. The implication is that whatever a woman says, or writes, or thinks, is less important and less interesting than what she is" (1990a: 27). I hope that the extent to which my remarks are biographical will be taken neither as an obsession with the feminine, nor as an inappropriate digression into details about Beauvoir's personal life, but rather as an examination of her political attitudes, which, I would argue, is central to an understanding of her intellectual contribution to feminist theory.

18. The exemplary status with which Beauvoir was invested is noted, for example, by Appignanesi: "The aura of romance which surrounded Simone de Beauvoir's exemplary life did not diminish as I began to read her." (1988: 2) She develops this theme in chapter seven of her book, entitled "The Exemplary Life" (1988: 132–47).

19. Appignanesi evokes the legendary fascination Beauvoir's life held for feminists in the sixties, and the mythology of her relationship to Sartre (1988: 1–2). See also Okely, 1986: 1.

20. This sentiment is already expressed in *The Second Sex:* "Some of us have never had to sense in our femininity an inconvenience or an obstacle" (SS: xxxii; DS: 29). As late as 1982 Beauvoir corroborates, in an interview, her view that she "never suffered" from being female (Simons: 1992: 29).

21. See Beauvoir FOC: 199–200; FDC: 207–8. Evans quotes this passage (1983: 352).

22. In understanding "writer" as equivalent to "man" here, I am not assuming that writers are automatically considered male. I am simply pointing out that Beauvoir uses the terms "writer" and "women" so that one category excludes the other. To say that she was treated "both as a writer . . . and as a woman" implies that she understands the two terms here to be mutually exclusive. Many of Beauvoir's responses to Schwarzer support this reading. Schwarzer (1984) says, for example, "You have written and created 'as a man'. And at the same time, you have attempted to change the world." Beauvoir responds "Yes. And I believe that a two-pronged strategy of this kind is the only way. We mustn't refuse to take on qualities that are termed masculine! We must be ready to take the risk of involving ourselves in this male world which is, quite simply, the world itself to a large degree. Of course, this way a woman runs the risk of betraying other women, and of betraying feminism. She will think she has escaped. . . . But the other way, she runs the risk of suffocating in 'femininity'" (1984: 116). Given that Beauvoir understands risk as a crucial distinguishing factor between men and women (see discussion below), her use of the term "risk" here is particularly significant, as is her negative depiction of femininity. See also Heath, 1989: 9–10. I am grateful to Toril Moi for discussion of this point.

23. There is no question that Beauvoir herself acknowledges, after writing *The Second Sex*, that she lived a privileged life. For example, in a 1976 interview she says, "Quite early in my life I had accepted the male values, and was living accordingly. Of course, I was quite successful, and that reinforced in me the belief that man and woman could be equal if the woman wanted equality. In other words, I was an intellectual. I had the luck to come from a sector of society, the bourgeoisie, which could afford not only to send me to the best schools but also to allow me to play leisurely with ideas. Because of that I managed to enter the man's world without too much difficulty" (Gerassi, 1976: 79). The point I am arguing is that this privilege can also be found in the theoretical framework of Beauvoir's analysis.

24. The context in which this retraction appears amounts to a reassessment of Beauvoir's position vis-à-vis feminism since *The Second Sex*. At the same time, Beauvoir retracts her earlier view that "the state of women and society would evolve together" (ASD: 491; TCF: 504).

25. See Beauvoir's endorsement of Mitchell's (1972) analysis of socialism and feminism (ASD: 491–92; TCF: 505).

26. As several comments in her autobiograpical works reveal, Beauvoir was reluctant to engage in politics. Later in life she questions her judgment in this matter, saying at one point for example, "Nizan had been right in his contention that there is no way of avoiding political engagement; to abstain from politics is in itself a political attitude. I was gripped with remorse" (PL: 359; FA: 368). A few pages later Beauvoir says, retrospectively, "though public affairs interested me, I could not regard them as my personal concern" (PL: 367; FA: 376).

27. Le Doeuff comments, "The ethics underlying Beauvoir's thought are not hard to identify since she says herself that her point of view is that of existentialist morality. *The Second Sex* is also a labour of love, and as a wedding gift she brings a singular confirmation of the validity of Sartrism: your thought makes possible an understanding of women's condition, your philosophy sets me on the road to emancipation—your truth will make me free" (1991: 59).

28. Moi makes a similar point when she comments on the superiority Beauvoir displays as a writer (1990a: 67).

29. For further documentation of Beauvoir's shift vis-à-vis feminism see Felstiner, FS: 258–59.

30. Beauvoir also sees the necessity of going beyond her earlier insistence that it is not men that should be fought, but the system: "Of course one must fight men as well. After all, one is an accomplice, one still profits by the system, even if one hasn't created it oneself. The man of today didn't set up this patriarchal society but he profits from it, even if he is one of those who are critical of it. And he has made it very much a part of his own unconscious thinking" (Schwarzer, 1984: 34–35). Men, Beauvoir goes on to say, must be approached with "suspicion." But while she is prepared to acknowledge this at a theoretical level, she finds a way of sidestepping it at a personal level. Asked whether she has ever felt this suspicion of men, Beauvoir answers, "No. I have always got on very well with the men in my life." Beauvoir elaborates on why she thinks that she has managed to avoid many of the conditions which have helped to make women in general feel inferior when Alice Schwarzer asks her to comment on her statement in *The Second Sex* that she

found herself "in a position of great impartiality" with regard to the "problem of femininity." She says that of course she has not been able to escape her "female condition" completely—"I have the body of a woman." She goes on: "But clearly I have been very lucky. I have escaped many of the things that enslave a woman, such as motherhood and the duties of a housewife. And professionally as well— in my day there were fewer women who studied than nowadays. And, as the holder of a higher degree in philosophy, I was in a privileged position among women. In short, I made men recognise me: they were prepared to acknowledge in a friendly way a woman who had done as well as they had, because it was so exceptional. Now that many women undertake serious study, men are fearful for their jobs" (36–37). See also Beauvoir's comments about how she was misunderstood in *The Second Sex*, particularly in relation to the question of the sameness or differences of the sexes, and on the question of femininity (PL: 367–68; FA: 375–76). One might add that although it is certainly true that one needs to fight the manifestations of sexism in men's behavior, it is much less clear that one should "fight" men as such. In other words, to attack men for their sexism without acknowledging such behavior as a symptom, and not merely a cause of patriarchal structures is, I suggest, to leave the problem unaddressed at its most fundamental level. For more recent comments about Beauvoir's relation to feminism see the 1982 and 1985 interviews by Simons (1992). Of particular interest is Beauvoir's resistance to the idea that she experienced discrimination both as a student and as a writer whose association with Sartre was common knowledge (1992: 35–37).

31. The fuller description of existentialist ethics Beauvoir provides is as follows: "Every subject plays his part as such specifically through exploits or projects that serve as a mode of transcendence; he achieves liberty only through a continual reaching out toward other liberties. There is no justification for present existence other than its expansion into an indefinitely open future. Every time transcendence falls back into immanence, stagnation, there is a degradation of existence into the "*en-soi*"— the brutish life of subjection to given conditions—and of liberty into constraint and contingence. This downfall represents a moral fault if the subject consents to it; if it is inflicted upon him, it spells frustration and oppression. In both cases it is an absolute evil. Every individual concerned to justify his existence feels that existence involves an undefined need to transcend himself, to engage in freely chosen projects" (SS: xxxiii; DS: 31). Referring to this passage, Le Doeuff asks, "In stating that one is against the oppression of women because it puts them in a position where they commit a fault, is one not destined to remain indifferent to those aspects of oppression which do not resemble the fault of bad faith?" (1991: 59). See also how Le Doeuff develops her point under the heading "On the bad faith of the oppressed" (1991: 60–61).

32. Beauvoir's use of the concept *Mitsein* is significantly different from Heidegger's. Heidegger makes it clear that *Mitsein* is not so much "fellowship" or "friendliness" but rather the fact that there are always already others alongside me in the world. Heidegger says, "Dasein's . . . understanding of Being already implies the understanding of others. This understanding, like any understanding, is not an acquaintance derived from knowledge about them, but a primordially existential kind of Being, which, more than anything else, makes such knowledge possible.

Knowing oneself [*Sichkennen*] is grounded in Being-with, which understands primordially" (BT: 161; SZ: 123–24).

33. Kaufmann-McCall sets out to "develop" and "mediate between" two antagonistic claims (1979: 209). On the one hand, there is the claim that *The Second Sex* is a "pioneering and uniquely ambitious attempt to explore, within a philosophical framework, all aspects of woman's situation." On the other hand, there is the claim that Beauvoir "seems to be undermined by the pervasive influence in *The Second Sex* of Sartre and of Sartrean existentialism, a philosophy which, in the context of feminist theory, is perceived as ideologically sexist" (1979: 209). I think Kaufmann-McCall succeeds in unravelling the problematic relationship between these two claims. Kaufmann-McCall provides a very useful discussion of Beauvoir, and on the whole I agree with her interpretation of the relationship between Sartre and Beauvoir.

34. Lloyd sets out "to trace de Beauvoir's diagnosis of the condition of women back to its Hegelian origins" (1986: 87), and she has a helpful discussion of Hegel's master-slave dialectic (1986: 88–93). However, because she assumes that "de Beauvoir's application of Hegel's philosophy is taken not from the original version, but from Sartre's adaptation of it in *Being and Nothingness*" (1986: 93), Lloyd concentrates most of her attention on Sartre's (rather than Hegel's) discussion of the subject's relation with others (1986: 93–96).

Mackenzie acknowledges that Beauvoir's "dualistic phenomenomology . . . owes much to Hegel and Sartre" (1986: 146), but then goes on to devote her attention entirely to Hegel's impact on Beauvoir's thinking.

One notable exception to the general failure to distinguish between the influence of Sartre and Hegel on *The Second Sex* is a Ph.D. dissertation by Carol Craig, which unfortunately, to my knowledge, has not been published in any other form. Craig provides a rich discussion of Beauvoir's use of Hegel and Sartre, claiming to show, I think appropriately, that "Throughout *The Second Sex* de Beauvoir uses Hegelian and Sartrian concepts to analyze the male-female relationship. At times the use of these two theoretical perspectives is quite compatible. But there are several occasions when there is a tension, if not a basic incompatibility in such a use of Sartrian and Hegelian ideas" (1979: 206). Craig goes on to demonstrate this in terms of Beauvoir's "theory of conflict and resolution (1979: 206). Craig depends on Kojève's reading of Hegel, claiming quite correctly that Beauvoir would have been influenced by his 1930 lectures (1979: 15), and that since Kojève "has an existentialist tinge, he makes Hegel more compatible with de Beauvoir's ideas" (1970: 15). By focusing upon Hegel's explication of the master-slave dialectic, rather than Kojève's reading of Hegel, I hope to uncover the incompatibility between Beauvoir's aims, and her use of Hegel.

35. See PL: 456–70; FA: 470–84.

36. Reviewing Hyppolite (1974) and Kojève (1969), Henri Niel (1947) provides a sense of the atmosphere surrounding the revival of interest in Hegel that is represented by the publication of these two books.

37. Referring to Kojève's discussion of the master-slave dialectic, Poster observes, "Undoubtedly Kojève has here colored Hegel with his own Marxism" (1975: 14). He adds that "Kojève was able to put in relief those aspects of Hegel's thought that led to Marxism and existentialism" (1975: 16). While it is known that Kojève

had read Heidegger's *Being and Time* published in 1927 (Poster, 1975: 33), it is much less clear whether he had read Sartre's *Being and Nothingness*. There is disagreement as to how far Kojève's reading of Hegel influenced Sartre, or indeed whether Sartre influenced Kojève. According to Fry, Kojève lectured in Paris between 1933 and 1939, and "published his translation and commentary of chapter IV A of the *Phänomenologie* in the *Mesures* in 1939" (1988: 4). Fry says of Kojève's lectures on Hegel, "The version we possess today appeared in 1947— four years after the publication of *L'être et le néant*. If there seems to be a similarity between Sartre's position in *L'être et le néant* and Kojève's position in his *published* lectures, it is not necessarily the case that Sartre was influenced by Kojève. That the lectures were published, revised, after *L'être et le néant* and that Kojève was accused of existentializing Hegel are both sufficient conditions of the hypothesis that the influence ran in a counter-direction . . . it is not at all improbable that the editing of Kojève's lectures took a contemporary and popular position, namely *L'être et le néant*, into account. It is, for example, likely that the footnotes to Kojève's chapters were added during editing" (1988: 6). Fry adds, "It is not possible to exclude that *some* knowledge of Kojève's Hegel interpretation—the master/servant analysis, for example—may have filtered through to Sartre in the prevailing atmosphere in Paris" (1988: 6). For a discussion of the impact Kojève's influential reading of Hegel had on French philosophy in general, see Descombes, 1980: chap. 1.

38. See, for example, Irigaray's comments at E: 23, IR: 174; E: 17–18; IR: 169; and SO: 134–35, SA: 167.

39. See also Sartre's remark about Hegel's master-slave relation and bad faith (BN: 109; EN: 101).

40. For a discussion of Sartre's use of Hegel in the context of the other, see Schroeder, 1984: chap. 2, 58–122. Also see Theunissen, 1986: 199–254.

41. On the question of Sartre's influence on *The Second Sex* see Simons, 1992.

42. See Whitmarsh's discussion (1981: 31) of Beauvoir's view of her own philosophical ability and her use of Sartre's work. Also see Simons (1986: 167–69).

43. Craig (1979: appendix 3) discusses Beauvoir's contribution to existentialist ethics in *The Ethics of Ambiguity* (1948). Also see Craig on the relationship between Beauvoir's analysis of women and Sartre's analysis of oppression in *Anti-Semite and Jew* (1970). For a well-argued and detailed discussion of the relationship between Sartre's analysis of the Jews' situation and Beauvoir's account of women's situation, see Friedlander, 1986.

44. As Cottrell says, "The basic philosophical problem in existentialist ethics is in reconciling the view that we can and should choose to be free and autonomous beings with the equally important view that we are in some essential way responsible to others" (1976: 82–83). For detailed discussions of the problems in interpreting Sartre's philosophy of freedom, see Caws, 1979; Busch, 1990; Flynn, 1984.

45. See Collins and Pierce, 1980. For a more qualified view, see Burstow, 1992. Also see Le Doeuff, who discusses the sexist imagery of *Being and Nothingness* (1980: 281–84, and 1991: 70–74). Le Doeuff also comments on the achievement Beauvoir accomplished in tailoring existentialist philosophy to meet at least

some of the needs of feminist theory, given the drawbacks of her starting point. She says, "In *The Second Sex*, one finds none of the Sartrian incapacity to thematize oppression" (1980: 287). She adds, "Simone de Beauvoir made existentialism work 'beyond its means' because she got more out of it than might have been expected" (1980: 287). Le Doeuff restates her point in *Hipparchia's Choice* (1991: 60). For Le Doeuff, Beauvoir's horizons were limited because she retained certain assumptions which failed to break free of the liberalism she imagined she was going beyond (1980: 287).

46. In order to stress the importance of the constraints imposed on the individual by situation, Beauvoir refers again to the situation of women in a harem. See SS: xxxiii; DS: 30; and *The Ethics of Ambiguity*, 1948: 38. Beauvoir neglects the question of whether it is appropriate for her to legislate what counts as freedom for women of a different cultural heritage than her own.

47. This point is also made by Kaufmann, 1986: 211.

48. Le Doeuff comments that the "relation of Simone de Beauvoir's work to time can be rapidly outlined as follows: we do not really know how women's oppression came into being, but we can see something of how it is maintained and how it causes suffering; at any rate, it is gradually ceasing, somewhat at least, and it must stop completely" (1991: 92).

49. See Le Doeuff's discussion of the Hegelian key (1980: 285–86), and her later reworking of the same idea (1991: 117–18).

50. See Le Doeuff, 1980: 285.

51. Mills (1987) makes a similar point in her criticism of feminists such as O'Brien (1981) who have appropriated Hegel's master-slave dialectic in their analyses of reproductive consciousness. Mills says, "What these theorists miss is the crucial fact that for Hegel the process of mutual recognition requires *in the first place* that both subjects have the ability to recognize the Other as equal" (1987: 13).

52. O'Brien says, "Prestige is, of course, a created social value, and, indeed, this is what transcendence is; the ability to create value and to be recognized by others as so doing" (1981: 69).

53. Bernstein makes a related point when he says, "it is not adequate for each of us to simply risk our life with the other watching, for each of us could reasonably conclude from such demonstrations that the one risking his life was doing it strictly to impress the other, thus admitting that the onlooker was the sole arbiter of independence and hence only he truly possessed self-consciousness" (1984: 15–16).

54. Schroeder makes two relevant points. The first is the distinction he draws between "self-knowledge" and "the kind of person one can become and the kind of harmony with the world one can achieve." His claim is that in his discussion of the master-slave relation Hegel is concerned with the latter rather than the former. Schroeder goes on to argue that, unlike Sartre, Hegel is not concerned to prove the existence of the other. "Hegel simply takes the existence and presence of other living conscious beings for granted" (1984: 73–74).

55. Craig's discussion of freedom is useful (1979: 57 and 65).

56. Beauvoir gives no reference to the quotation from Hegel, but I take it that the quotation is a rendering of what Miller translates as "the other is the dependent consciousness whose essential nature is simply to live or to be for another" (PhS:

115; PhG: 146). If I am right in identifying this passage as the one Beauvoir has in mind, there is a discrepancy between Hyppolite's rendering of this passage, and Beauvoir's. Hyppolite's translation of Hegel reads, *"l'autre est la conscience dépendante qui a pour essence la vie ou l'être pour un autre,"* while Beauvoir quotes Hegel as saying, *"L'autre [conscience] est la conscience dépendante pour laquelle la réalité essentielle est la vie animale, c'est-à-dire l'être donné par une entité autre."* (The original text reads *"die andere das unselbständige, dem das Leben oder das Sein für ein Anderes, das Wesen ist."*) Despite the discrepancy, I think that Beauvoir's phrase is close enough to the original to assume that this is the passage she had in mind. We can assume that either Beauvoir is quoting from memory, or she is giving her own translation of Hegel, without referring to Hyppolite. Another possibility is that Beauvoir is quoting another edition, perhaps the edition to which Sartre referred. There is a difficulty in establishing exactly what edition that would have been, however, since Sartre refers to the "Edition Cosson" (BN: 321; EN: 282). Fry says, "Helmut Schneider, of the Hegel-Archiv, Bochum, assures me this is spurious and a misprint for 'Lasson'" (1988: 3, note 6).

57. This review is simply to orient the reader, and is not intended to be exhaustive. There are already many commentaries available on the master-slave dialectic and its role in Hegel's philosophy. In addition to Kojève's (1969) reading of Hegel, which displays both existentialist and Marxist influences, see also Hyppolite, (1974: 168–89); Hoffman, 1983: 83–109; Kelly, 1966 and 1969. While Hyppolite, Hoffman, and Kelly share Kojève's tendency to read the master-slave relation as one which has socio-historical implications, Hans-Georg Gadamer throws doubt on the validity of such interpretations (1976: 73). For another interpretation that stresses, like Gadamer, the importance of considering the master-slave relation in the context of Hegel's *Phenomenology of Spirit* as a whole, and for extensive bibliographic references to secondary work on Hegel, see Flay, 1984: 81–112 and 299–317.

58. See Gadamer, 1976: 69–70.

59. Craig makes the point nicely when she says, "An intriguing feature of de Beauvoir's work is that although she is committed to woman's emancipation she scarcely uses th[e] liberating aspect of the Hegelian master-slave dialectic. . . . It is partly in accepting so whole heartedly Hegel's notions of the preconditions of human development that de Beauvoir's theory goes astray" (1979: 24–25). Also see O'Brien: "De Beauvoir's claim that the master and slave passages are applicable to men and women is . . . problematic" (1981: 70). O'Brien adds, in a footnote, "The slave does not remain immured in animality, and Beauvoir's analogy must stop at half point" (1970: 214–15, note 7).

60. See, for example, Beauvoir's use of the term "enslavement" (SS: 713; DS 2: 478).

61. Sartre finds fault with Hegel's account on two grounds—"epistemological optimism" and "ontological optimism"—both of which Sartre associates with Hegel's alleged identification of being with knowledge (BN: 324; EN: 285). It is with the first charge that I shall be concerned here. By epistemological optimism, Sartre means that Hegel believes in absolute truth. He says that it seems to Hegel that "the truth of self-consciousness can appear; that is, that an objective agreement can be realized between consciousness—by authority of the Other's recognition of me and my recognition of the Other. This recognition can be simultaneous and reciprocal: 'I know that the Other knows me as himself'" (ibid.). While Sartre

thinks that Hegel's understanding of the self as dependent upon another in its very being is a "brilliant intuition" (BN: 321; EN: 282), he also thinks Hegel fails to draw the full consequences of his intuition (BN: 326; EN: 287). Putting too much hope in knowledge as the deliverer of truth, Hegel jeopardizes his initial understanding of the fact that "the Other's existence is necessary in order for me to be an object for myself" (BN: 326; EN: 287). According to Sartre, Hegel treats the being of life as if it were nothing more than knowledge of life. Sartre's argument seems to amount to no more than a restatement of the view that since in Hegel's philosophy the other is ultimately subsumed by the standpoint of absolute knowledge, any standpoint other than that, in this case, that of the slave, must be inessential and as such inconsequential.

62. O'Brien makes a similar point in a different context when she acknowledges that Beauvoir is "less aware of the difficulties of an analysis of human history which gives a negative value to the process of reproduction than Hegel himself was" (1981: 71).

63. Also see the following passages: PhS: 112, PhG: 142; PhS: 113–14, PhG: 144. Gadamer corroborates the importance of the reciprocal nature of the master-slave relation (1983: 94–95).

64. Sartre says, "If bad faith is possible, it is because it is an immediate, permanent threat to every project of the human being; it is because consciousness conceals in its being a permanent risk of bad faith. The origin of this risk is the fact that the nature of consciousness simultaneously is to be what it is not and not to be what it is" (BN: 116; EN: 107).

65. It is perhaps pertinent to recall at this point that the individual's confrontation with death has an important role in Sartre's differentiation of fear from anguish (see part 1, chap. 1, sec. 5 of Being and Nothingness, "The Origin of Negation") as "the recognition of a possibility as my possibility" (BN: 73; EN: 71). In order to understand more adequately the relation between Sartre's conceptions of freedom, death, and others, one would need to analyze in detail his account of bad faith in relation to part three of Being and Nothingness, on "Being for Others." Here Sartre includes a discussion not only of Hegel, but also of Husserl and Heidegger (BN chap. 1, sec. 3). On the complexity of the role of the other in Sartre's philosophy, its relation to Husserl's conception of others, Heidegger's Mitsein, and Hegel's notion of the other, see Theunissen, 1976.

66. We have already seen that Beauvoir saw the difficulties of the view that humans have absolute freedom before Sartre did.

67. O'Brien says that Beauvoir "does not analyse with sufficient rigor how much of 'immanence' is natural and how much historical. She assumes an immanence which rests, on the one hand, on an intransigent and unalterable biological function and, on the other hand, on certain transcendental assumptions about the nature of social life, such as the hypothesis that women are too weakened by childbirth to participate in production or to demonstrate inventiveness" (1981: 71). The same difficulty emerges in Beauvoir's reflections on The Second Sex in her autobiographical writings, for example see PL: 367; FA: 375–76.

68. Le Doeuff articulates the nexus of problems at stake here in slightly different terms when she identifies as "the fundamental thesis" of the The Second Sex the idea "that all women are from the outset constituted as inessential" (1991: 58),

and goes on to discuss the analogy Beauvoir draws between a "moral fault" and "oppression" (1991: 58). See also Le Doeuff, 1991: 92–99.

69. Beauvoir follows the Sartrian model that one is what one does, or that one is no more than one's acts or accomplishments. As Sartre says, "Man is nothing else but that which he makes of himself" (1947: 18; 1970: 22). Of course one can choose whether or not to accept the responsibility implied by this view. One can see that it would be difficult for women to develop and follow through fundamental projects, that is, life goals. If women are not in the habit of taking control of their lives, being reflective about their decisions, and facing up to their responsibilities as free human beings, it will be hard for them to develop such habits. As Morris observes in her discussion of Sartre's concept of bad faith, "To be able to reflect is a distinctively human activity, one that needs to be explained and one that requires practice to be performed well" (1980: 35).

70. Keefe also observes that "the question of women's complicity in their condition" is one "that Beauvoir is never clear on" (1983: 112).

71. There is, of course, considerable controversy as to whether or not women have always been subordinated to men. See, for example, Bachofen, 1967; and Engels; 1971. For a discussion that provides a good point of entry into this debate see Rich, 1986: chaps. 5 and 6, 84–127.

72. Woman is elevated, for example, as nature. See SS: 162–63; DS: 237.

73. Perhaps the duality that Beauvoir finds in the habitual representation of women as nature, as both that which is to be conquered and harnessed, and as the transcendent unknowable other, has its roots in Enlightenment ideas about nature. Jordanova takes up the question of how women were aligned with nature in eighteenth- and nineteenth-century thought. She shows that during the Enlightenment, the different meanings attached to the concept of nature corresponded to an ambiguity in the popular conception of women as nature. Nature, she argues although complex, can be characterized as "that realm on which mankind acts, not just to intervene in or manipulate directly, but also to understand and render it intelligible. This perception of nature includes people and the societies they construct. Such an interpretation of nature led to two distinct positions: nature could be taken to be that part of the world which human beings have understood, mastered and made their own. . . . But secondly, nature was also that which has not yet been penetrated (either literally or metaphorically), the wilderness and deserts, unmediated and dangerous nature. To these positions correspond two senses in which women are nature. According to the first, they, as repositories of natural laws, can be revealed and understood. . . . According to the second position it was woman's emotions and uncontrolled passions which gave her special qualities" (1980: 66).

74. The mysterious bodily processes of reproduction provide men with the perfect site of mystification—women's bodily functions retain a certain fascination, of which men can be afraid, from which they can be alienated, and even repulsed.

75. See Kojève, 1969: 19.

76. Gadamer discusses in detail the paradox to which I allude here. He says, "Only something which in spite of being negated is still there, in other words, only what negates itself, can by its existence confirm for the 'I' what the latter strives for in its desiring, namely, that it needs to acknowledge nothing other than itself. . . . That a

person demands recognition from another implies, to be sure, that the other is canceled, but on the other hand, what is demanded of the other implies to an equal extent that the other is recognized as free and hence implies just as much the return of the other to itself, to its free existence, as it implies the return of the first consciousness to itself" (1976: 62–64). Gadamer warns against focusing only on the master's dependency, arguing that the "essential point in Hegel's argument seems to me to be that it is aimed precisely at the master's coming to realize his inferiority and that it rejects the more obvious dialectic of dependency" (1976: 68).

77. I am grateful to Nancy Stepan for helping me to think about the relation between sex and gender, in a paper she presented at the Commonwealth Center for Cultural and Literary Change at the University of Virginia on February 11, 1991, and for alerting me to the work of Laqueur (1990).

78. O' Brien says of the master-slave dialectic, "Hegel's parable is very significant in the class struggle model of history, as Marx was able to see, but it said little about the history of generic struggle. In substituting the latter, de Beauvoir, who posits socialism as the condition of generic equality, loses sight of class distinctions" (1981: 70).

79. In answer to the question, "What should women do in order to liberate themselves without falling into the quest for power like men?" Irigaray responds, "Is it good that at certain moments certain women occupy certain positions? Surely, if they can use them in order to make things move. The problem is whether they can remain women and not become total men. I think that this is not easy" (Baruch and Serrano, 1988: 153).

80. Irigaray differentiates her position from Beauvoir's on the question of woman by making clear that she is no longer interested in construing woman as the other of man in a reversal that mimics Marx's overturning of Hegel, or Nietzsche's overturning of Plato (see JA: 108–9).

81. This last line refers to Beauvoir, 1965 and 1984a.

NOTES TO CHAPTER THREE

1. I would like to note that my reading of *Antigone* coincides on important points with that of Annie Pritchard (1992), whose article I read after completing this chapter. I agree, for example, that "moral agents are always *gendered subjects*" (1992: 77) and that this aspect of the play has not been fully considered by critics. As Pritchard says, "Hegel *does* think that Antigone's gender is important to the action of the play, but his reading simplifies important elements of the text" (1992: 77). Pritchard goes on to point out the extent to which central passages of the play, such as the ode to man, are gendered (1992: 86). I also agree with Pritchard's emphasis on Antigone's mirroring relationship with her mother (1992: 90).

2. See, for example, ML: 100–119, AM: 107–27; and TD: 112–23. Irigaray also comments on the separation of Kore-Persephone from her mother Demeter in Baruch and Serrano, 1988: 157, and discusses Clytemnestra in several contexts; see, for example, SG: 11–12; SP: 23–24. See also Burke's discussion of Irigaray on Ariadne (1987).

3. Irigaray's interest in the figure of Antigone is not limited to Sophocles' depiction of her. Asked what she proposes to teach in *This Sex Which Is Not One*, Irigaray

answers: "I shall once again take the figure of Antigone—in Sophocles, Hölderlin, Hegel, and Brecht—as my point of departure. I shall attempt to analyze what Antigone supports, shores up, in the operation of the law. How by confronting the discourse that lays down the law she makes manifest that subterranean supporting structure that she is preserving, that other 'face' of discourse that causes a crisis when it appears in broad daylight. Whence her being sent off to death, her 'burial' in oblivion, the repression—censure?—of the values that she represents for the City-State: the relation to the 'divine,' to the unconscious, to red blood (which has to nourish re-semblance, but without making any stain on it)" (TS: 167; CS: 161–62). This "oblivion," "repression," and "censure" take on a peculiar significance in the light of the circumstances of Irigaray's departure from the University of Vincennes, which she explains in a footnote. Irigaray was asked what she proposed to teach before the "restructuring" of the Department of Psychoanalysis of the University of Vincennes in 1974, and reports that a "commission of three members named by Jacques Lacan wrote me without further explanation that my project 'could not be accepted.' I who had been an instructor in the department since the founding of the University of Vincennes was thus suspended from my teaching" (TS: 167: CS: 161).

4. Segal points out that Sophocles' Antigone "refers to herself repeatedly as 'bride of Hades,' a term that makes the analogy with Persephone unmistakable, particularly as the association with Persephone was a regular feature of funerary practices and funerary epigrams for girls who died young" (1983: 167).

5. Antigone is also referred to in passing in "The Blind Spot of an Old Dream of Symmetry" (SO: 117–18; SA: 146–47); in *An Ethics of Sexual Difference* (esp. ES: 107–108, E: 105–106; and ES: 118–20, E: 114–16); and in *This Sex Which Is Not One* (TS: 167–68; CS: 161–62). Irigaray returns to the figure of Antigone in *Le temps de la différence* (TD: 81–100). See also *Sexes and Genealogies* (SG: 1–2 and 110–14; SP: 13–14 and 124–28).

6. See Freud, "Femininity," in *New Introductory Lectures on Psychoanalysis,* SE 22: 112–35. Despite the reservations Freud expresses early in this essay about the ease with which passivity can be equated with femininity, his later account of the girl's resolution of the castration complex and her entry into the Oedipal situation appears to assume she is destined for passivity. Freud's acknowledgment, in the opening pages of the essay, that it is "inadequate . . . to make masculine behaviour coincide with activity and feminine with passivity" (115), and his warning that "we must beware . . . of underestimating the influence of social customs, which . . . force women into passive situations" (116) are soon eclipsed by an assumption that seems to ignore his own advice. He assumes that in order to achieve "normal" femininity, the girl must renounce "a certain amount of activity. . . . Passivity now has the upperhand, and the girl's turning to her father is accomplished principally with the help of passive instinctual impulses" (128).

7. Irigaray, SO: 13–129; SA: 9–162. For a discussion of Irigaray's reading of Freud in *Speculum* see Gallop, 1982.

8. Eteocles breaks the agreement that he and Polynices had made on their joint succession to the throne following the death of Oedipus, to occupy the throne in alternate years. Polynices' attack upon Thebes is therefore designed to restore the rights that his brother violated.

9. The quotation is from Hegel, 1970: 175.
10. Hegel PhS: 263–99, PhG: 312–42; and PhS: 424–53, PhG: 490–522. While my discussion focuses on the *Phenomenology*, I will also refer to other works including Hegel's *Aesthetics: Lectures on Fine Art* (1974). Hegel's texts on tragedy have been collected together in *Hegel on Tragedy* (1962). This collection contains excerpts from a number of different works, including Hegel's consideration of tragedy not only in the context of the aesthetics, but also in the context of the history of philosophy (Hegel, 1955), his political philosophy (Hegel, 1952), and his philosophy of religion (Hegel, 1988).
11. Hegel gives a primary role to the conflict that he sees as characteristic of the "body politic" in his consideration of the dramatic composition of tragedy in the *Aesthetics*.
12. The quotation is from Hegel, (1970: 123).
13. On the role of the philosophical reader, or the "we" see Flay, 1984: 10 and 170.
14. Laqueur 1990: esp. 25–62.
15. On the untrained or unphilosophical eye see note 13, above. Mills notes that Hegel's "references to the *Antigone* are scattered throughout the *Phenomenology's* discussion of the ethical world and ethical action to support his claims regarding the relationship between male/human law and female/divine law" (1987: 24). While it is certainly true that Hegel's allusions to the play are "scattered" and that Antigone is rarely named, it is also the case that the entire section "The True Order: The Ethical World" is organized by Hegel's reading of Antigone, as Derrida acknowledges (G: 142; Gl: 161).
16. Using the famous imagery of the tree and the ship, Haemon warns his father, "A man, though wise, should never be ashamed of learning more, and must unbend his mind. Have you not seen the trees beside the torrent, the ones that bend them saving every leaf, while the resistant perish root and branch? And so the ship that will not slacken sail, the sheet drawn tight, unyielding, overturns. She ends the voyage with her keel on top. No, yield your wrath, allow a change of stand" (A: 710–19). Teiresias echoes Haemon's warning when he tells Creon to "Yield to the dead" (A: 1029).

    I have used Wyckoff's translation of *Antigone*, which I find most readable, but, in the process of writing this chapter, I have also often referred to *Sophocles: The Theban Plays*, trans. E. F. Watling (Harmondsworth, Middlesex: Penguin, 1986), and *Sophocles*, vol. 1, The Loeb Classical Library, trans. F. Storr (Cambridge, Mass.: Harvard University Press, 1977).
17. On the importance of Hegel's theory of tragedy for Hegel's philosophy as a whole see Russo (1936: 133).
18. I restrict my attention to Hegel's discussion of the family in the *Phenomenology of Spirit*; for feminist considerations of Hegel's treatment of women in *Hegel's Philosophy of Right*, and *Lectures on the Philosophy of World History* see Easton (1987) and Raven (1988).
19. In observing that the heroic characters in Sophocles' *Antigone* display "honorable guilt," and that nature "comes into collision with spirit through the universal forces of action," I am condensing several points that Hegel makes about the play in his *Aesthetics*. To comprehend tragic conflict of the type that *Antigone* is the supreme representation, we need to bear in mind Hegel's understanding of

pathos. He says, "we must above all reject the false idea that they have anything to do with guilt or innocence. The tragic heroes are just as much innocent as guilty. On the presupposition that a man is only guilty if alternatives are open to him and he decides arbitrarily on what he does, the Greek plastic figures are innocent: they act out of this character of theirs, on this 'pathos,' because this character, *this* 'pathos' is precisely what they are: their act is not preceded by either hesitation or choice. It is just the strength of the great characters that they do not choose but throughout, from start to finish, *are* what they will and accomplish. They are what they are, and never anything else, and this is their greatness" (AFA vol. 2: 1214). If at first Hegel's justification is obscure in claiming that "ethical consciousness is more complete, its guilt more inexcusable, if it knows *beforehand* the law and the power which it opposes" (PhS: 284; PhG: 336), it becomes less so when read against the background of Hegel's description of heroic figures and the way in which "It is the honor of these great characters to be culpable" (AFA, vol. 2: 1215). The task of heroic figures is to be completely what they are, nothing more, and nothing less.

   With regard to my claim that nature is in collision with Spirit in the universal forces of action, I have in mind Hegel's distinction between different types of dramatic conflict. Hegel distinguishes between three main types of collision (AFA, vol. 1: 206). While Hegel does not discuss Sophocles' *Antigone* in his consideration of situation and collision, it is clear that he identifies the play in the third category of collision, that is, the one that deals with the disruption of Spirit alone, which is bound up with human action proper. Having reached a point where he can deal with the "*resolution*" of the discord in collision, Hegel says that "this movement, taken as a whole, belongs no more to the province of the situation and its conflicts, but leads to the consideration of what we have described above as 'the action proper'" (AFA, vol 1: 217). Clearly, Hegel is referring back to the type of collision that characterizes the disruption of Spirit. Hegel considers three points that are essential to grasp in connection with action that is capable of artistic representation, the first of which he specifies as "the universal powers forming the essential content and end for which the action is done" (AFA, vol. 1: 219). Under the heading, "The Universal Powers over Action," Hegel names Sophocles' *Antigone* as the kind of tragedy in which "interest and aims . . . fight" each other, specifying that Creon's edict forbidding the right of burial to Polynices "contains an essential justification, provision for the welfare of the entire city. But Antigone is animated by an equally ethical power, her holy love for her brother, whom she cannot leave unburied, a prey of the birds. Not to fulfill the duty of burial would be against family piety, and therefore she transgresses Creon's command" (AFA, vol. 1: 221). Thus it is clear that Hegel sees the actions of Creon and Antigone as depicting the clash of spirit with itself, through the collision of universal forces.

20. As Dennis Schmidt says, "the key insight that tragedy discloses shows the transformation of this inner structure from its original role as the source of tension and diremption into its role as the source of harmony and reconciliation" (1988: 146).

21. For the allusions to the covert existence of the law on which Antigone acts, see Haemon's references to the "dark corners" (A: 692), in which he has heard people's

discontent over Creon's edict and the "undercover speech in town" (A: 700).

22. For a discussion of Spirit that relates Hegel's treatment of Antigone to the *Phenomenology* as a whole, see Flay, 1984: 163–82, and Taylor, 1975: 171–78.

23. Hegel's discussions of Greek tragedies are not merely examples. As Flay points out, "These plays themselves are a part of the very polis whose presuppositions they take up, an active yet reflective objectification of the explicit self-consciousness of the Greeks about their own presuppositions. . . . These art works of the Greeks are the ultimate form of immediate, true spirit. In these works which are themselves actions within the polis, not only are the individual acts and their presuppositions brought to objectivity for the spectacle or the seeing; they are also brought to objectivity as an absolute act of self-consciousness, both in respect to their creation and to their viewing. That is to say, the art works themselves are both an element of culture and an embodiment of that culture as a whole: the polis is self-conscious through them" (1984: 168–69). Also see Vernant, 1970.

24. Irigaray, IR: 198; SP: 13–14. Because it seems more accurate, I have used David Macey's translation of the essay, "The Necessity for Sexuate Rights," here, rather than Gillian Gill's. However, in general, I refer to the latter's translation of *Sexes et Parentés*.

25. Hegel elaborates the reasons why the death of an individual in his particularity bears no essential relation to his "work": "partly because, if his death was such a result, it is the natural negativity and movement of the individual as a [mere] existent, in which consciousness does not return into itself and become self-consciousness; or partly because, since the movement of what [merely] exists consists in its being superseded and becoming a being-for-itself, death is the side of diremption in which the attained being-for-self is something other than mere existent which began the movement" (PhS: 270–71; PhG: 322).

26. The exchange between Antigone and Creon provides a particularly clear example of the way in which Antigone considers herself to be acting under a different law from that which Creon invokes (A: 511–19). Creon: And you are not ashamed to think alone?

> Antigone: No, I am not ashamed. When was it shame to serve the children of my mother's womb?
> Creon: It was not your brother who died against him, then?
> Antigone: Full brother, on both sides, my parents' child.
> Creon: Your act of grace, in his regard, is crime.
> Antigone: The corpse below would never say it was.
> Creon: When you honor him and the criminal just alike?
> Antigone: It was a brother, not a slave, who died.
> Creon: Died to destroy this land the other guarded.
> Antigone: Death yearns for equal law for all the dead (A: 510–19).

27. Knox shows how Sophocles' language impresses upon his readers "Antigone's devotion to those of her own blood." He provides examples of "a host of phrases (many of them containing words which seem to be fresh coinages of Sophocles) which emphasize the physical intimacy, the near unity, of those born of the same mother" (1983: 79).

28. As Knox says, "it was of course the immemorial duty of the family and especially of the women to wash the corpse, to dress it for burial, and to sing in passionate, self-lacerating sorrow of their loss. At the funeral of one of its members the cohesion, exclusiveness, and age-old sanctity of the family was most strikingly displayed. Creon's decree strikes at the very heart of family loyalty" (1983: 87).

29. Knox comments that "in her devotion to family," Antigone "ignores completely the rights of the *polis*" (1983: 82). He adds, "Her loyalty is extreme and exclusive; far from admitting that the *polis* has any claims on her, she practically ignores its existence" (1983: 83).

30. The chasm that separates Antigone's thinking from Creon's is exhibited when Antigone says, "Nothing that you say fits with my thought. I pray it never will. Nor will you ever like to hear my words" (A: 409–501). Knox elaborates on the way in which Antigone remains steadfast in her decision to stand by Polynices throughout the play. "From this high resolve she never retreats. In the short glimpse we are given of her in the guard's account of her capture, the same defiant self-confidence is emphasized. Caught red-handed, she was 'not at all disturbed'. . . . Face to face with Creon she speaks just as boldly: 'I say I did it. I do not deny it' (A: 443). Creon's next question offers her an excuse, a way of retreat. 'Did you know my proclamation forbade it?' (A: 447). But she refuses to accept the offer. 'I knew. How could I fail to? It was public' (A: 448). The defense of her action which follows destroys forever any possibility of compromise, excuse, or pardon" (1983: 64–65). Knox adds that "Antigone shares with Electra the distinction of being the most intransigent of Sophoclean heroes. Ajax and Philoctetes at least discuss the possibility of surrender, Oedipus at Thebes and at Colonus makes minor concessions, but Antigone, like Electra, never for one second or in one detail wavers from her fixed resolve" (1983: 67).

31. Haemon's speech to his father (A: 683–723), which, significantly, comes shortly after Creon's statement that he "won't be called weaker than womankind" (A: 680), is organized around the theme that it is necessary for Creon to take into consideration points of view other than his own. He says "someone else might bring some further light" (A: 687); he refers to the talk in the town in support of Antigone (see note 11, above); and finally, he says, "it can be no dishonor to learn from others when they speak good sense" (A: 721–23).

32. Creon says of Antigone, "She is my sister's child, but were she child of closer kin than any at my hearth, she and her sister should not so escape their death and doom" (A: 486–89). See also A: 182–83. On Creon's resolute refusal to acknowledge the blood ties of the family, see Goheen, 1951: 88–90.

33. Creon says at the end of *Antigone*, after the chorus advises him to take heed of Teiresias' "terrible prophecies" (A: 1091), "I've come to fear it's best to hold the laws of old tradition to the end of life" (A: 1113–14). On the error of Creon's ways and its consequences, see also A: 1243, 1269–70, and 1349.

34. Hegel continues, "The self-certainty and self-assurance of a nation possesses the *truth* of its oath, which binds all into one, solely in the mute unconscious substance of all, in the waters of forgetfulness. Thus it is that the fulfillment of the Spirit in the upper world is transformed into its opposite, and it learns that its supreme right is a supreme wrong, that its victory is rather its own downfall. The dead, whose right is denied, knows therefore how to find instruments of

vengeance, which are equally effective and powerful as the power which has injured it" (PhS: 287; PhG: 337).

35. See A: 659–80.

36. I am not suggesting that, in Hegel's account, Antigone herself is conscious of the significance of her deed, but rather that, insofar as her act transforms nature's unconscious force into a human action, she makes it conscious. I am extrapolating from what Hegel says in paragraph 452: PhS: 270; PhG: 321. Derrida's comments on the meaning Hegel gives to the task of burial are helpful (G: 144; Gl: 163–64).

37. Hegel says, explaining the transition that Polynices makes from the family to the political realm, "He passes from the divine law, within whose sphere he lived, over to human law" (PhS: 275; PhG: 327).

38. Knox's discussion of the opposition between the family and the polis is illuminating. He reminds us that the rights of the family are more ancient than those of the polis, and how not only Sophocles, but also Aeschylus associates the male with the idea that the marriage tie takes precedence over blood-ties, while females are habitually represented as giving priority to blood loyalty (1983: 77–79)

39. See, for example, Richard Jebb's edition of Sophocles' *Antigone* (1928). In reference to lines 904–20 Elizabeth Wyckoff says in the notes to her translation, "Jebb (following and followed by many) brackets these lines, which are in all the MSS, and were known to Aristotle as Antigone's. I think he is wrong, but he should not be pilloried as a prudish Victorian for this. The positions of his note and appendix are well taken and held. Some sensible contemporaries (e.g. Fitts and Fitzgerald) are with him still. For those, like myself, who are sure the lines are Antigone's, there is drama in her abandoning her moralities and clinging to her irrational profundity of feeling for her lost and irreplaceable brother, devising legalistic arguments for her intellectual justification. Jebb finds the syntax of 909–12 strained past all bearing, but I believe Antigone's obscurity here a touch of realism parallel to the confused and contradictory negatives of her opening lines, which Jebb allows her" (A: 206). For further discussion of the issue, see, for example, Gellrich's perceptive discussion, 1988: 50–62. Hester also provides a review of the debate (1971: 177–78). Lesky, like Goethe, thinks Antigone's argument "that fate might have made good the loss of a husband and children, never of a brother" is "strange" (1978: 108); neither Goheen (1951: 78–79) nor Knox (1983: 76–206) ultimately think that there is any inconsistency in Antigone's position. Other critics who discuss the problem include Mills, 1987: 21–23, and Derrida, G: 145; Gl: 164, and 165; 186.

40. Knox makes the point that, after *Antigone* line 543, Antigone talks "as if Ismene had ceased to exist" (1983: 82).

41. Hegel says, "The objective reality of the relationship [between husband and wife] does not exist in them, but in the children, and by their witnessing the development in the children of an independent existence which they are unable to take back again; the independent existence of the children remains an alien reality, a reality all its own" (PhS: 273; PhG: 325). On Hegel's discussion of the family in *Hegel's Philosophy of Right,* see Irigaray's reflections in her essay "Love between Us," in *J'aime à toi,* pp. 39–63.

42. See Hegel, AFA, vol. 1: 564.

43. The fact that Hegel limits his consideration of the range of familial relationships

to only three, and disregards that between sisters, or relationships within the extended family is left unexplained. Derrida remarks that "His classification seems limited: he does not justify its historical, sociological, ethnological model, to wit the Western Greek family" (G: 147; Gl: 167).

44. Hegel says, "Antigone honours the bond of kinship, the gods of the underworld, while Creon honours Zeus alone, the dominating power over public life and social welfare" (AFA, vol. 2: 1213).

45. See Hegel, PhS: 275; PhG: 327.

46. Hegel says, "Every other relationship to him which does not remain one simply of love but is ethical, belongs to human law and has the negative significance of raising the individual above his confinement within the natural community to which he in his [natural] existence belongs" (PhS: 271; PhG: 323).

47. Mills says, "Curiously, Hegel fails to even mention Ismene" (1987: 30).

48. Ismene lacks the courage to join Antigone's act of defiance, but on hearing that Antigone has performed the burial on her own, she is willing to share her punishment. Antigone, however, will not hear of this. Knox's commentary on this aspect of the play is helpful. He makes the point that Antigone's plea to her sister is not mere rhetoric. Without her help Antigone is unable to lift the body of her brother, and therefore can only perform a "symbolic" burial of the corpse, covering it with a "film of dust" (1983: 64). Knox also offers as the reason for Antigone's haughty refusal of Ismene's belated support of her action the fact that "Antigone is resentful of the sister whose cowardice forced her to abandon her plan for a proper burial of the body, and furious at the thought that the glory for which she gives her life might be shared with an unworthy sister. For this glory is all she has. Like Achilles she has chosen a short life with glory. 'You chose to live, and I to die' (A: 555). And like Achilles the one thing she finds intolerable is that this glory, so dearly bought, should in any way be diminished" (1983: 65).

49. See Vickers, 1973. Also see A: 466 and 512.

50. Derrida, G: 165; Gl: 186.

51. Antigone refers to her suffering in the opening lines of the play (A: 1–5), and recalls them again before going on to specify her relationship to Polynices with reference to her mother. "Who lives in sorrows many as are mine how shall he not be glad to gain his death? And so, for me to meet this fate, no grief. But if I left that corpse, my mother's son, dead and unburied I'd have cause to grieve as now I grieve not" (A: 463–68). Antigone emphasizes the importance she attaches to the fact that Polynices shared her "mother's womb" (A: 511). Also see A: 858–71 and 585–601.

52. But Sophacles says the brothers are "one mother's sons" (A: 146), and "Sons of one man" (A: 145). See Segal on the Greek vocabulary for maternal and paternal kinship (1983: 172–73).

53. Ismene says in "Oedipus at Colonus" that Eteocles is younger than Polynices. See "Oedipus at Colonus," translated by Robert Fitzgerald, in Sophocles, 1954: 95. See note 51.

54. Irigaray also comments on the importance of the mother in "Each Sex Must Have Its Own Rights," when she says "Hegel explains that the daughter who remains faithful to the laws relating to her mother has to be cast out of the city, out of society. . . . The daughter is forbidden to respect the blood bonds with her mother" (SG: 1–2; SP: 14).

55. Segal says that "Creon confronts an opposing principle of an especially feminine kind, Antigone's 'reverence for those of the same womb,'" *homo splanchnous sebein* (511). On this basis Antigone defends herself against the male-oriented, civic ethic of the polis. She makes kinship a function of the female procreative power: she defines kinship in terms of the womb (*splanchna*). Thus at the end of her great speech on the unwritten laws she calls Polyneices 'the one (born) from my mother, dead' (*ton ex emēs/métros thanonta*) whom she, for that reason, will not leave 'a corpse unburied' (*anthapton . . . nekyn*, 466–67). As her defiance of Creon continues into the stichomythy, her word *homosplanchnos* some fifty lines later etymologically defines 'brother' as 'one of the same womb' (511). *Homosplanchnos* calls attention to the root meaning of the familiar word for 'brother,' *adelphos*, from *a-* ('same,' equivalent to *homo-*) and *delphys* ('womb,' equivalent to *splanchna*). In this view of kinship she reopens, on a personal level, the debate between Apollo and the Erinyes in Aeschylus' *Oresteia*; however, she gives the decisive tie of blood not to the father's seed, as Olympian Apollo and Olympian Athena do (*Eumenides* 657–66, 734–41), but to the mother's womb" (1983: 171–72).

56. See A: 869.

57. See note 19 above on the issue of guilt.

58. The passage Irigaray probably has in mind here is in paragraph 474, where Hegel says, "But if the universal thus easily knocks off the very tip of the pyramid and, indeed, carries off the victory over the rebellious principle of pure individuality, viz. the Family, it has thereby merely entered on a conflict with the divine law, a conflict of self-conscious Spirit with what is unconscious" (PhS: 286; PhG: 337).

59. Irigaray says, "What is the nature of the laws that Antigone respects? They are religious laws relating to the burial of her brother who has been killed in a war among men. These laws have to do with the cultural obligations owed to the mother's blood, the blood shared by the brothers and sisters in the family. The duty to this blood will be denied and outlawed as the culture becomes patriarchal. This tragic episode in life—and in war—between the genders represents the passage into patriarchy. The daughter is forbidden to respect the blood bonds with her mother" (SG: 2; SP: 14). See also Baruch and Serrano, 1988: 156–57.

60. As Derrida observes, "Intermittence—jerking rhythm—is an essential rule. If there were only war, the community's natural being-there would be destroyed" (G: 147; Gl: 166).

61. For further references to women as the weaker sex in *Antigone*, see A: 61–63, 484–85, 578–79, 740–41, 746, and 756. There is also an important association between youth and womanhood, which Hegel notices and develops, and on which I will comment later.

62. Creon not only makes repeated reference to Antigone's sex, as if he regards her refusal to obey him as a test of his male strength (see A: 484 and 525). His sensitivity to the fact that it is a woman who challenges his authority is highlighted when he insults his son Haemon by calling him "Weaker than a woman!" (A: 749) and a "woman's slave" (A: 756).

63. Hegel says that "Womankind—the everlasting irony [in the life] of the community—changes by intrigue the universal end of the government into a private end, transforms its universal activity into a work of some particular individual, and perverts the universal property of the state into a possession and

ornament of the Family. . . . In general, she maintains that it is the power of youth that really counts: the mother who bore him, that of the brother as being one in whom the sister finds man on a level of equality, that of the youth as being one through whom the daughter, freed from her dependence [on the family] obtains the enjoyment and dignity of wifehood. The community, however, can only maintain itself by suppressing this spirit of individualism, and, because it is an essential moment, all the same creates it and, moreover, creates it by its repressive attitude towards it as a hostile principle" (PhS: 288; PhG: 340–41).

64. Szondi argues that the conflict between nature and art is central not only to Hölderlin's and Schelling's conception of tragedy, but also to Hegel's, although Hegel gives it a different emphasis. Szondi says, "The conflict between inorganic law and living individuality, between the universal and the particular, is thus not illuminated: it is dynamically surpassed and absorbed into the heart of the notion of identity" (1986: 49–50).

65. Heidegger, 1987: 146–65; 1953: 112–26. Also see Ehrenberg, 1954: 61–66.

66. Flay says, the "overarching presupposition of unity is evidenced not only in the reflection that the polis is one, but even more concretely and reflexively embodied in the conservative view of the chorus in the plays to which Hegel directs us" (1984: 166–67). He adds that the chorus "as the unity of the polis is there to speak for the ethical substance" (169).

67. To follow up the theme of youth in *Antigone*, see A: 216, 681, 719, 726, 728, 735, and 1034.

68. Foucault says of sex, "one had to speak of it as of a thing to be not simply condemned or tolerated but managed, inserted into systems of utility, regulated for the greater good of all, made to function according to an optimum" (1984: 24). It is in the sense in which Foucault thinks of the discourse of sexuality as being produced in the age of repression that is analogous to the way in which Hegel sees the "spirit of individualism" as not only being subject to suppression, but also as being created by that suppression in the first place.

69. Gellrich comments that Antigone's "character disseminates in directions that are not contained with or controlled by the moral claim to which Hegel maintains she adheres in burying her brother" (1988: 53).

70. Consider how Hegel can maintain without contradiction both that Antigone embodies ethical consciousness par excellence, and that, since she violates the law of the state knowingly, her "guilt is more inexcusable" than it would have been had she buried her brother in ignorance of Creon's edict. How can Antigone's act of defiance be at one and the same time the supreme representation of ethical consciousness, in the Hegelian sense, and nevertheless implicate her as inexcusably guilty? We should not make the mistake of imposing on the figure of Antigone our contemporary idea of character. Recall that in his account of the concrete development of dramatic poetry, Hegel makes a point of differentiating between the "modern use of the term" character, and the "individual pathos" of the heroic figure. If we cannot make sense of the heroic figure of Greek tragedy by simply imputing to it modern notions of character, neither can we reduce it to merely abstract moral principles. Hegel says, "They occupy a vital central position between both, because they are firm figures who simply are what they are, without any inner conflict, without any hesitating

recognition of someone else's 'pathos', and therefore (the opposite of our contemporary 'irony') lofty, absolutely determined individuals, although this determinacy of theirs is based on and is representative of a particular ethical power" (AFA, vol. 2: 1209–10).

71. Knox shows that the terms in which Antigone speaks of her "loyalty to blood relationship" are "exactly the terms a citizen would use of his loyalty to the *polis*, in political terms, in fact. . . . This loyalty of hers is in fact a political loyalty not only because the particular circumstances force her to choose between family and *polis*, but also because historically the strong, indissoluble tie of blood relationship had in earlier times, through the *genē*, the 'clans,' been the dominating factor in the citizen's social and political environment. It was much older than the *polis*, and in democratic Athens still showed on every side signs of its continued power as a rival and even a potential danger to the newer civil institutions and forms of organization" (1983: 76).

72. Barber says that Hegel "restores Antigone and the female race to the bondage of history . . . harking back to the very physical nature that dialectics supersede" (1988: 12). Barber elaborates a few pages later: "Although everywhere else in his work both the youthful and the senatorial Hegel proclaim the dialectical preeminence of spirit over nature, with women, nature is given preeminence over spirit. When he remarks that the differences in the physical characteristics of the sexes has a rational basis that endow them with intellectual and ethical significance, Hegel blithely stands the dialectic on its head, giving it (as Marx was to do decades later) a material base. So that to maintain the special position of women, Hegel is forced into a kind of proto-materialism in which the dog of spirit gets wagged by the tail of nature" (1988: 17). See *The Philosophy of Right*, trans. and ed. T. M. Knox (Oxford: Clarendon Press, 1945), para. 165.

73. Reprinted in Benhabib, *Situating the Self: Gender, Community and Postmodernism in Contemporary Ethics* (New York: Routledge, 1992), pp. 242–59; see esp. 245.

74. On Antigone's wild nature, or her identification with untamable, unthinkable dimensions, see Segal, 1983: 170–71.

75. Hölderlin, 1988: 111. See Szondi's "The Notion of the Tragic in Schelling, Hölderlin, and Hegel" for a discussion of Hegel's understanding of tragic conflict as the contradiction of "inorganic law and living individuality" (Szondi 1986: 49–50). Szondi's essay shows the proximity between Hölderlin's understanding of tragedy in terms of the paradox that subsists in man's place in relation to nature, "a place which not only indicates that he is her servant, but which also reveals nature's dependence on man" (Szondi 1986: 46). For Hölderlin, as Szondi says, the dialectic of tragedy is one "in which the strong can appear by itself only as weakness and requires something weak in order that its strength may appear" (Szondi 1986: 47). We have seen how close this understanding of tragedy is to Hegel's own conception of it, as represented in his discussion of the *Antigone* in the *Phenomenology of Spirit*. Women, as the eternal irony of the community, constitute the weak link in the community. The strength of the community can only appear through its suppression of the spirit of individuality that women represent.

For an interesting discussion of Hölderlin's and Heidegger's understanding of Antigone and Oedipus, see Fynsk, 1986: 174–229.

76. Antigone is regarded by the chorus as "*autonomos*" (A: 821). Knox says this is "a

word which is generally applied to cities—'independent, living under their own laws'—but is here applied, in a bold figure of speech which contains the essence of the play's conflict, to an individual—she 'lives by her own law'" (1983: 66).

77. Irigaray rejects the assumption of the "patriarchal" society—that men are "civil" and women are "uncivil"—and emphasizes instead the ways in which patriarchal society is itself lacking in civility, enumerating the ways in which it pays no respect to women (TD: 85–92). It is noteworthy that the chorus says of Antigone, "The girl is bitter. She's her father's child" (A: 471), or, as Lacan says, "'She is *homos*.' We translate that as best we can by 'inflexible.' It literally means something uncivilized, something raw" (Lacan, 1992: 263).

78. See also SG: 5; SP: 17–18.

NOTES TO CHAPTER FOUR

1. On the ontological difference, see Heidegger, BT: 20–35; SZ: 1–15. Irigaray uses the Heideggerian phrase *"ontico-ontological difference"* in her essay "Any Theory of the 'Subject' Has Always Been Appropriated by the 'Masculine,'" where she calls for a "recasting" of the philosophical "economy" that it represents (SO: 145; SA: 181).

2. Another important question that arises for Irigaray in the orbit of the epochal question of sexual difference is, "How to say otherwise 'I love you'" (JA: 201).

3. See IR: 170, E: 18; and Jardine and Menke, 1991: 103. On the relation between morphology and the imaginary, see WE: 64–65. Also see Gatens, 1991: 147–49; Grosz, 1989: xix and 113–119; and Whitford, (1991: 58–59.

4. Heidegger, 1992; 1985b; 1982a; 1984b.

5. See Bernasconi, 1989b.

6. Levinas says in the introduction to *Existence and Existents*, "If at the beginning our reflections are in large measure inspired by the philosophy of Martin Heidegger, where we find the concept of ontology and of the relationship which man sustains with Being, they are also governed by a profound need to leave the climate of that philosophy, and by the conviction that we cannot leave it for a philosophy that would be pre-Heideggerian." (EE: 19; DE: 19).

7. Irigaray says, "In so far as Heidegger does not leave the 'earth,' he does not leave metaphysics" (OA: 10).

8. Schor is right when she observes that "the forgetting of fluids participates in the matricide that according to Irigaray's myth of origins founds Western culture: 'He begins to be in and thanks to fluids [OA: 36]'" (Schor: 1989 49). I am not suggesting that we can afford to neglect Irigaray's critical remarks about Heidegger, but that they need to be understood in the context of a deeper influence. It is partly because critics such as Schor have already begun to document the critical aspects of Irigaray's reading of Heidegger—although more detailed work remains to be done in this area—that I am emphasizing what I take to be Heidegger's profound importance for Irigaray. I hope that this preparatory work will set the context for a more thorough investigation not only of the relation between Irigaray and Heidegger, but also her reading of other philosophers. Let me also note here that I have tended to focus on Irigaray's more "philosophical" texts rather than her more "lyrical" texts—not that any such

distinction can or should be strictly maintained, of course—for example, I have not dealt in much detail with *Elemental Passions*, but I hope that my attempt to establish the philosophical import of Irigaray's project will open on to an appreciation of her other work too.

9. As Whitford says, "Western feminism in all its forms is an inheritor of the Enlightenment and its contradictions" (1991: 38).

10. Rhode makes a similar point: "To those concerned with sexual equality, no issue has been more critical than sexual difference. Nor has any issue remained more divisive or elusive. . . . The law's traditional response to such gender inequalities has focused on issues of gender differences. Analysis has proceeded in largely Aristotelian terms: the sexes should receive similar treatment to the extent they are similarly situated, and different treatment to the extent they are different in some ways relevant to important social goals. In theory, this approach has bordered on tautology. In practice, it has yielded results that are both overlooked and overvalued. On some issues courts have transformed biological differences into cultural imperatives. On other questions women's special circumstances have remained unacknowledged and unaddressed. By taking difference as a given, traditional approaches deflect attention from broader issues surrounding its social construction and consequences" (1990: 197).

11. See also section 14, where Heidegger says, "In ontology . . . an attempt has been made to start with spatiality and then to Interpret the Being of the 'world' as *res extensa*. In Descartes we find the most extreme tendency towards such an ontology of the 'world,' with, indeed, a counter-orientation towards the *res cogitans*—which does not coincide with Dasein either ontically or ontologically" (BT: 95: SZ: 66).

12. I will comment on Descartes' proof for the existence of God in the next chapter, in the context of Levinas' appropriation of the idea of perfection, which, in Descartes' mind, is inseparable from the concept of God. Levinas draws on the idea of the Cartesian God's perfection in his understanding of the infinite alterity of the Other.

13. Heidegger says, "Those entities which serve phenomenologically as our preliminary theme—in this case, those which are used or which are to be found in the course of production—become accessible when we put ourselves with them in some such way. Taken strictly, this talk about 'putting ourselves into such a position' [*Sichversetzen*] is misleading; for the kind of Being which belongs to such concernful dealings is not one into which we need to put ourselves first. This is the way in which everyday Dasein always *is*. . . . " (BT: 96; SZ: 68). For further discussion of Heidegger's discussion of everydayness, see Haar, 1993a.

14. See Sartre, BN: 119–23; EN: 111–14. Also see Heidegger, who says, for example, that the world "has already been disclosed beforehand whenever what is ready-to-hand within-the-world is accessible for circumspective concern" (BT: 106: SZ: 76).

15. Other examples Heidegger gives include, "when I open the door . . . I use the latch" (BT: 96; SZ: 67).

16. Heidegger says, "In conspicuousness, obtrusiveness, and obstinacy, that which is ready-to-hand loses its readiness-to-hand in a certain way" (BT: 104; SZ: 74).

17. For Heidegger's distinction between "readiness-to-hand" (*Zuhandenheit*) and "presence-at-hand" (*Vorhandenheit*), see BT 95–107; SZ 67–76.

18. "Existentiales" are distinct from "Categories," a term Heidegger reserves for designating the structure of "entities whose character is not that of Dasein," in other words, entities that are "present-at-hand" (BT: 71; SZ: 45).

19. Also see Eisenstein and Jardine, 1985; Rhode, 1990; Jaggar, 1990; and Cornell, 1991.

20. MacKinnon, 1987: 35.

21. See also Irigaray's "Women on the Market" (TS: 170–91; CS: 167–85), and "Commodities among Themselves" (TS: 192–97; CS: 189–93).

22. The question of technology is at issue for Heidegger even when his ostensible subject lies elsewhere. As Reiner Schürmann points out, Heidegger's reading of Nietzsche is "*formally* about Nietzsche, but *materially* about technology" (1987: 182).

23. While Plato (1970) argues that women could be philosopher-kings in the ideal city he describes in the *Republic*, his reasons, as Julia Annas persuasively argues, can hardly be considered feminist. Rather, what he has in mind is the good of the state as a whole, and not women's rights, desires, or potentialities (see Annas, 1979: 15–33). For further discussion of Plato's views on women, see Dickason, 1980: 45–53.

24. Gatens acknowledges the problem I am addressing here when she argues "that it is a primary weakness of much feminist theory that it engages with philosophy or theory only at the socio-political level. Such engagement implicitly assumes that metaphysics, theories of human nature and epistemology are sex-neutral. On the contrary . . . they often provide the theoretical underpinning for the biases which become visible at the socio-political level" (1991b: 2).

25. Unlike philosophy, Irigaray thinks that feminism should neither offer a "univocal utterance," nor restrict itself to the measured, logical, rational tones of universality. She says, "It is still better to speak only in riddles, allusions, hints, parables" (SO: 143; SA: 178).

26. Aristotle, while he pays attention to the question of sexual differences, does so only in order to define woman as deficient in comparison with man. In terms of Caroline Whitbeck's useful classification, Aristotle's view of women amounts to construing woman as "partial man" (Whitbeck, 1980: 54–57). Not only is woman judged inferior in terms of her physiology—she is an "impotent male" because she contributes only the material and not the formal cause in reproduction—she also has an inferior capacity for deliberating, and is dubbed "irrational." See Aristotle's *Metaphysics* and *Nicomachean Ethics* (see, Aristotle,1980a and 1975), and, for a discussion of Aristotle's position on women, see Allen, 1979. While Aristotle, along with many other male philosophers, may appear to take seriously the question of sexual difference, in fact he seems to have prejudged the outcome of his inquiry so that his empirical investigations conform to his presupposition that women are weaker than and inferior to men, and that they can only be understand as falling short of the standard set by men, as lesser men. Hence no real confrontation with the question of sexual difference takes place—women are merely considered inferior versions of men.

27. Irigaray makes many observations consonant with this statement in her discussion of Freud, in "The Blind Spot of an Old Dream of Symmetry"—for example, in reference to the "active/passive polarity in the Freudian sexual economy" (SO: 91;

SA: 111), she says, "Of course, it has not escaped us that fundamental concepts of classical philosophy are being resorted to here" (SO: 93: SA: 113).

28. I am understanding "culture" here in the sense that Sherry B. Ortner articulates it in her well known article "Is Female to Male as Nature Is to Culture?" She says, "Every culture, or, generically, 'culture,' is engaged in the process of generating and sustaining systems of meaningful forms (symbols, artifacts etc.) by means of which humanity transcends the given of natural existence, bends them to its purposes, controls them in its interest. We may broadly equate culture with the notion of human consciousness (i.e., systems of thought and technology), by means of which humanity attempts to assert control over nature.

   "Now the categories 'nature' and 'culture' are of course conceptual categories— one can find no boundary out in the actual world between the two states or realms of being. . . . Culture (i.e., every culture) at some level of awareness asserts itself to be not only distinct from but superior to nature, and that sense of distinctiveness and superiority rests precisely on the ability to transform—to 'socialize' and 'culturalize'—nature" (Ortner, 1993: 63).

29. Irigaray says that if the aim of women "were simply to reverse the order of things, even supposing this to be possible, history would repeat itself in the long run, would revert to sameness: to phallocratism. It would leave room neither for women's sexuality, nor for women's imaginary, nor for women's language to take (their) place" (TS: 33; CS: 32). Also see SO: 134; SA: 167, where she distances herself from the construction of the subject according to the master-slave model, which takes "the form of rivalry within the hom(m)ologous, of a death struggle between two consciousnesses" (SO: 134; SA: 167).

30. Irigaray reflects on the malaise of post-Chernobyl Europe, in "A Chance for Life: Limits to the Concept of the Neuter and the Universal in Science and Other Disciplines" (SG: 185–206; SP: 199–222). This essay, which I first heard presented at the Institute of Contemporary Arts, London, England (1990), represents one of Irigaray's most direct articulations of the character of the technological age, and the urgency of thinking through the assumptions we make in a technological world. Also see SG: 5, SP: 17–18; and SG: 107–8, SP: 122.

31. On the idea of the end of philosophy see Sallis, 1986.

32. Heidegger says, in "What are Poets For?" ("Wozu Dichter?"): "The fact that we today, in all seriousness, discern in the results and the viewpoint of atomic physics possibilities of demonstrating human freedom and of establishing a new value theory, is a sign of the predominance of technological ideas whose development has long since been removed beyond the realm of the individual's personal views and opinions" (PLT: 112; H: 267).

33. I am, of course, providing only a very cursory reading of one among many ways of articulating the Heideggerian problem. For further discussion of Heidegger's understanding of the essence of technology and its place in Heidegger's philosophy, see Haar, 1993b. Among good general discussions of Heidegger's work, two standard works include Marx, 1971, and Pöggeler, 1989. More recent discussions include Bernasconi, 1985 and 1993, and Schürmann, 1987; on the question of time, see Krell, 1986, and Wood, 1989.

34. See, for example, Heidegger's comments in "The End of Philosophy and the Task of Thinking" on cybernetics, which, he says "transforms language into an

exchange of news. The arts become regulated-regulating instruments of information" (BW: 376; SD: 64).

35. Heidegger, TB: 1–24; SD: 1–25.

36. Heidegger introduces the term "Ereignis, the event of Appropriation" to name "time and Being . . . in their belonging together" (TB: 19; SD: 20), and he goes on to acknowledge his earlier neglect of the primordial status of space: "Since time as well as Being can only be thought from Appropriation as the gifts of Appropriation, the relation of space to Appropriation must also be considered in an analogous way. We can admittedly succeed in this only when we have previously gained insight into the origin of space in the properties peculiar to site and have thought them adequately. . . . The attempt in *Being and Time*, section 70, to derive human spatiality from temporality is untenable" (TB: 23; SD: 24).

37. See also Heidegger's use of the terms *Ereignis* and *Ge-Stell* in "The Way to Language" (1982c: 125–36; 1959: 256–68).

38. I develop some of these points in chapter six, in my discussion of Derrida's commentary on Heidegger's "The Origin of the Work of Art," in "Restitutions" (see 1987b). For further discussion of "The Origin of the Work of Art," see McCumber, 1989: 124–42; Sallis, 1990: 168–89; and Taminiaux, 1993.

39. For an analysis of the concept of "*Ereignis*" in Heidegger's philosophy, see Dastur, 1993.

40. Heidegger, "Building Dwelling Thinking" (PLT: 145–61, esp. p. 157); "Bauen Wohnen Denken" (VA: 139–56, esp. p. 152). To follow up the problem of place, see Casey, 1983. See also Casey, 1987.

41. See also, for example, Heidegger, 1982c: 127; 1985a: 246.

42. See Derrida's discussion of the linear representation of time with reference to Aristotle (OG: 57–62; OGe: 66–72).

43. Irigaray uses the phrase "L'espace-temps" elsewhere too, thereby reversing Heidegger's "time-space." See, for example, SO: 145, SA: 181; and SG: 25, SP: 37: 25.

44. "*Ousia* and *Grammē*: A Note on a Note from *Being and Time*," in *Margins of Philosophy* (Derrida, 1982: 31–67); "*Ousia et Grammē*: Note sur une note de *Sein und Zeit*," *Marges de la philosophie* (Paris: Minuit, 1972), pp. 33–7, first published in *L'endurance de la pensée: Pour saluer Jean Beaufret* (Plon, 1968).

45. Cf. Nye, 1989: 49.

46. Heidegger makes clear that he regards *Being and Time* as preparatory when he says, for example, "the book merely leads us to the threshold of the question, not yet into the question itself" (1981: 21).

47. Heidegger also refers to the notion of the "clearing" in his discussion of the work of art, describing the open place in which the work of art stands forth (OWA: 61; H: 49).

48. When Irigaray says of woman that "insofar as she is a container, she is never a closed one" (ES: 51; E: 55), it is this statement by Aristotle, perhaps, that she has in mind.

49. Irigaray is quoting Aristotle's Physics, Book 4, chap. 1. 209a. I prefer to use the Loeb edition, rather than the Oxford edition to which Carolyn Burke and Gillian C. Gill refer in translating *Éthique de la différence sexuelle*.

50. Irigarary is quoting P: Book 4. chap. 4. 211b

51. I do not agree with the suggestion that in her discussion of the "maternal-feminine as a metaphor of *place* in the traditional sexual configuration . . . Irigaray wants to . . . bring about a new ethics which would valorize and universalize the feminine, the place" (Lindsay, 1989: 24). Her point is not to "universalize the feminine" but to point to its absence in the philosophical texts that have defined the Western tradition.

52. This chapter of *Éthique de la différence sexuelle* appears in English as "Sorcerer Love: A Reading of Plato's Symposium, Diotima's Speech," trans. Eleanor H. Kuykendall, *Hypatia* 3 (3) (Winter 1989): 32–44.

53. See Kristeva's reading of the *Symposium* (1987: 59–82) which has some interesting parallels to Irigaray's discussion. Also see Nikolchina, 1993: 182–93.

54. Cf. Plato's view of poets, who are vessels of divine inspiration (1970: Book 10).

55. Irigaray quotes Plato at SL: 34; E: 30.

56. Diotima's account of love's parentage is also, perhaps, what Nietzsche had in mind in the first section of *Ecce Homo*, "Why I Am So Wise" (1969: 222–35, esp. 222–3), which Derrida recalls under the heading "Logic of the Living Feminine," in the essay "Otobiographies: The Teaching of Nietzsche and the Politics of the Proper Name," trans. Avital Ronell (1985b: 3–38). Derrida acknowledges that Nietzsche speaks of his mother and father "symbolically, by way of a riddle; in other words, in the form of a proverbial legend" (1985b: 16), and refers to his own earlier reflections in *Glas*: "Elsewhere, I have related this elementary kinship structure (of a dead or rather an absent father, already absent to himself, and of the mother living above and after all, living on long enough to bury the one she has brought into the world, an ageless virgin inaccessible to all ages) to a logic of the death knell [*glas*] and of *obsequence*. There are examples of this logic in some of the best families, for example, the family of Christ (with whom Dionysus stands face to face, but as his specular double)" (1985b: 18). Although the similarities are unmistakable, Derrida does not include among his exemplary families the family of Eros as depicted in Diotima's speech—perhaps because it is a source that Nietzsche overturns, or reverses, in his retelling of it. According to the words of Diotima, "On a given day, now [Love] flourishes and lives, when things go well with him, and again he dies, but through the nature of his sire revives again. Yet his gain forever slips away from him, so that eros never is without resources, nor is ever rich" (SL: 34; E: 30). Plato, then, has Diotima tell us that love revives, not through his mother, but through his father, whereas for Nietzsche it is the opposite. "I am," says Nietzsche at the beginning of his pseudo-autobiographical reflections, "to express it in the form of a riddle, already dead as my father, while as my mother I am still living and becoming old. This dual descent, as it were, both from the highest and the lowest rung on the ladder of life, at the same time a *decadent* and a *beginning*—this, if anything, explains that neutrality, that freedom from all partiality in relation to the total problem of life, that perhaps distinguishes me" (1969: 222).

There are further parallels between Nietzsche's explanation of what distinguishes him from the rest of humanity, and the lineage of eros according to Diotima. For example, Nietzsche remarks upon the combination of his "extreme poverty" of health and "exuberance of spirit" (1969: 222), and upon his "access to apparently separate worlds" (1969: 225). Let me mention one further series of echoes that may have informed Irigaray's text. Derrida comments on "the alliance that Nietzsche follows in turning his signature into riddles," namely the "demonic neutrality (*neutralité démonique*) of midday delivered from the negative and from the dialectic" (1985b: 17). The "neutrality" resembles too closely the "*fécondité médiumnique, démonique*" (SL: 38; E: 32) of which Irigaray speaks to be merely coincidental.

57. Irigaray is quoting from Plato, 1975: 206.
58. Plato, 1977: 157d.
59. Nye, 1989: 46–55.
60. On the question of whether or not Diotima is a fictional figure, Taylor, says "I cannot agree with many modern scholars in regarding Diotima of Mantinea as a fictitious personage" (1963: 224), and then goes on to say "we shall not go wrong by treating the 'speech of Diotima' as a speech of Socrates" (225).
61. Eryximachus proposes that "the flute-girl who came in just now be dismissed: let her pipe to herself or, if she likes, to the women-folk within, but let us seek our entertainment today in conversation" (Plato, 1975: 176e).
62. For a more detailed discussion of the feminine in Nietzsche see Graybeal, 1990.
63. See ML: 4, AM: 10; ML: 83, AM: 89–90; ML: 108, AM: 116; ML: 115, AM: 122; ML: 116, AM: 124; ML: 118, AM; 126.
64. See ML: 4, AM: 10; ML: 82, AM: 89.
65. See ML: 83, AM: 89; ML: 86, AM: 92; ML: 104, AM: 112; ML: 106, AM: 113.
66. See ML: 79, AM: 85; ML: 83, AM: 89; ML: 87, AM: 93; ML: 96, AM: 103; ML: 111, AM: 118; ML: 118, AM: 126.
67. See ML: 108, AM: 116; ML: 86, AM: 92.
68. See ML: 85, AM: 92; ML: 86, AM: 92; ML: 92, AM: 98; ML: 106, AM: 113; ML: 111, AM: 119; ML: 118, AM: 126.

NOTES TO CHAPTER FIVE

1. Whitford acknowledges a similar point when she distinguishes between three different senses of Irigaray's conception of the female imaginary: "there is the position of the female in the male imaginary; there are the scraps or debris of what might be an alternative imaginary (a fragmented female imaginary); and there is the anticipation of a more fully deployed female imaginary which might exist in creative intercourse with the male" (1991: 67–68).

2. Irigaray comments on her use of the terms "sex" and "gender" in a footnote: "If we are going to reconsider the question of culture and its systems of representation on the basis of sexualized bodies as places where different subjectivities are located we need to take issue with the economy of grammatical gender. Hence the necessity to separate the two notions of *gender* and *sex* in order to try to dialecticize a point that Hegel never differentiated. Thus, the word *sex* is used in regard to male and female persons and not just to male and female genital organs" (SG: 128; SP: 142). Gillian C. Gill clarifies Irigaray's point in a translator's note: "Traditionally, the region mapped by the English words *gender* and *sex* does not correspond to that of the French words *genre* and *sexe*. Most notoriously, *le sexe*, which in modern usage has come to mean 'the sexual organs' as well as 'sex,' is a common colloquial word for penis. The inapplicability of the

singular noun *le sexe*, with its highly phallic connotations, has been one of Irigaray's most crucial points as a feminist theorist. Hence her need to footnote a change in her use of the words *le sexe* and *le genre*, a change that in fact moves French closer to English usage" (SG: 128).

3. See Levinas, 1986: 347; 1982, 190. For a discussion of this point see Bernasconi, 1988: 14, 1993: 216–18.

4. See JTN: 17–19, and 23–28. Also see "When the Gods Are Born," in ML: 123–90; AM: 131–204.

5. In a number of different contexts, Irigaray makes clear that it is not so much subjectivity *per se* of which she is critical but rather the metaphysical presuppositions in which the discourse of subjectivity is implicated—what she calls the "logic of the subject" (TS: 98; CS: 96). She says, for example, "the issue is not one of elaborating a new theory of which women would be the *subject* or the *object*, but of jamming the theoretical machinery itself, of suspending its pretension to the production of a truth and of a meaning that are excessively univocal. Which presupposes that women do not aspire to be men's equals in knowledge. That they do not claim to be rivaling men in constructing a logic of the feminine that would still take onto-theo-logic as its model, but that they are rather attempting to wrest this question away from the economy of the logos" (TS: 78; CS: 75–76). Irigaray adds that women have never "taken part" in "the social order" as "subjects" (TS: 84; CS: 81), and goes on to ask, "What would become of the symbolic process that governs society . . . if women, who have been only objects of consumption or exchange, necessarily aphasic, were to become 'speaking subjects' as well? Not of course, in compliance with the masculine, or more precisely the phallocratic, 'model'" (TS: 85; CS: 81–82). [While I have changed the sentence structure slightly, by omitting some intervening clauses, I think this quotation is consonant with Irigaray's meaning].

6. Silverman uses this statement as an indication of Irigaray's willingness to dispense with subjectivity.

7. Grosz agrees that Irigaray "is interested in developing accounts of subjectivity and knowledge that acknowledge the existence of two sexes, two bodies, two forms of desire and two ways of knowing" (1990b: 169). Whitford also argues that Irigaray does not advocate abandoning subjectivity (1991: 38, and 135).

8. Irigaray draws an analogy between racism and sexism for example, calling sexism "the most unconscious form of racism" (JTN: 120; JT: 144).

9. Irigaray calls sexual difference "the most radical difference and the one most necessary to the life and culture of the human species" (EP: 3).

10. Discussions of Levinas' impact on Irigaray tend to be limited to brief references, or confined to parts of chapters or articles. Grosz includes a short but useful discussion of Levinas in her chapter on "Luce Irigaray and the Ethics of Alterity" (1989: 141–46 and 155–58).

11. For more comprehensive accounts of Levinas' philosophy than I can provide here see Peperzak, 1992; Bernasconi and Critchley, 1991; Bernasconi and Wood, 1988; Bernasconi, 1989a; Burggraeve 1985. The most comprehensive bibliography is Burggraeve, 1986.

12. Levinas adds, "My admiration for Heidegger is above all an admiration for *Sein und Zeit*. I always try to relive the ambiance of those readings when 1933 was still

unthinkable" (EI: 38; EeI: 34). Levinas calls Heidegger's philosophy "a great event of our century" (EI: 42; EeI: 40), and regards as an "essential contribution" his "new way of reading the history of philosophy," a way which is "direct," a way of "conversing with philosophers and asking for absolutely current teachings from the great classics . . . in this hermeneutic one does not manipulate outworn things, one brings back the unthought to thought and saying" (EI: 43–44; EeI: 40–41). For further discussion of Heidegger's importance for Levinas see the entire section of the interview devoted to Heidegger (EI: 37–44; EeI: 33–41). Also see Levinas' comments in "Ethics of the Infinite" (1984: 51–52).

13. Levinas says, "I think that one cannot seriously philosophize today without traversing the Heideggerian path in some form or other. *Being and Time*, which is much more significant and profound than any of Heidegger's later works, represents the fruition and flowering of Husserlian phenomenology. The most far-reaching potentialities of the phenomenological method were exploited by Heidegger in this early work and particularly in his phenomenological analysis of 'anguish' as the fundamental mood of our existence. Heidegger brilliantly described how this existential mood or *Stimmung* revealed the way in which we were attuned to Being. Human moods, such as guilt, fear, anxiety, joy or dread, are no longer considered as mere physiological sensations or psychological emotions, but are now recognized as the ontological ways in which we feel and find our being-in-the-world, our being-there as *Befindlichkeit*" (1984: 51). Elsewhere, reiterating the importance of Heidegger's analyses of *Befindlichkeit* and anxiety, Levinas goes on to say, "*Sein und Zeit* has remained the very model of ontology. The Heideggerian notions of finitude, being-there, being-toward-death, etc., remain fundamental. Even if one frees oneself from the systematic rigors of this thought, one remains marked by the very style of *Sein and Zeit*'s analyses, by the 'cardinal points' to which the 'existential analytic' refers" (EI: 40; EeI: 37).

14. Derrida's parenthetical observation gives a sense of the difficulty one has in trying to sort out Levinas' philosophical allegiances: "It could no doubt be demonstrated that Levinas, uncomfortably situated in the difference between Husserl and Heidegger—and, indeed, by virtue of the history of his thought—always criticizes the one in a style and according to a scheme borrowed from the other, and finishes by sending them off into the wings together as partners in the 'play of the same'" (WD: 98; ED: 145). That Derrida might be accused of the same ploy, enlisting Heidegger's help against Levinas and Levinas' against Heidegger, compounds the difficulty of situating Derrida's own work in relation to both Levinas and Heidegger.

15. Having commented on Levinas' early Heideggerian critique of Husserl, Derrida traces Levinas' turn away from Heidegger and toward Husserl (WD; ED). In his 1930 book *The Theory of Intuition in Husserl's Phenomenology*, as Derrida rehearses, Levinas rejects Husserl's theoretism in favor of a Heideggerian position. But in 1947 with the publication of *Time and the Other* and *Existence and Existents*, Levinas distances himself not only from Husserl but also from Heidegger, placing them both within the tradition with which he wants to break—that is the tradition which adheres to an Eleatic notion of being.

16. Among the disappointments Heidegger's later philosophy holds for Levinas is "the disappearance in it of phenomenology properly speaking" (EI: 42; EeI: 39). That

Levinas can choose to criticize Heidegger for not being enough of a phenomenologist, while simultaneously maintaining that phenomenology enacts the very neutralization against which Levinas warns, presents an irony that is not lost on Derrida. Even if, in Derrida's words, phenomenology "gives the most subtle and modern form to this historical, political and authoritarian neutralization," its subtlety does not mitigate its culpability (WD: 96; ED: 144). Perhaps it only increases the urgency with which Levinas seeks to remind his readers that neutrality still operates as a guiding force, however well-hidden it might be.

17. Levinas says, "I learned very early, perhaps even before 1933 and certainly after Hitler's huge success at the time of his election to the Reichstag, of Heidegger's sympathy toward National Socialism. It was the late Alexandre Koyré who mentioned it to me for the first time on his return from a trip to Germany. I could not doubt the news, but took it with stupor and disappointment, and also with the faint hope that it expressed only the temporary lapse of a great speculative mind into practical banality" (AC: 485).

18. See Levinas' 1990 prefatory note to "Reflections on the Philosophy of Hitlerism" (RP: 63). For a recent discussion of the question of Heidegger's politics see Lacoue-Labarthe, 1990.

19. See EE: 19; DE: 19.

20. In explicating this paradoxical weighty freedom Levinas introduces the idea of the "there is" (il y a) a term with which Levinas evokes the "anonymity" (TO: 47; TA: 26) of "existing without existents" (TO: 46; TA: 25), drawing on Blanchot's depiction of the ego's enchainment to itself (Blanchot, 1942). Levinas refers to Blanchot at TO: 56; TA: 37. Levinas also attributes to Blanchot the related theme of the impossibility of escape that is represented by the "phenomenon of impersonal being" or the "there is" (EI: 48; EeI: 45). Blanchot explores the same phenomenon under the rubric of "neutrality," and in terms of the notion of "disaster."

21. For further discussion of "sensible transcendental," see Whitford, 1991: 144.

22. The term "third party" appears frequently in Levinas' work. It is a reference to society in general, as Levinas makes clear when he uses as its equivalent the phrase "the whole of humanity" (TI: 213; TeI: 188). In *Otherwise than Being* Levinas says, "The third party is other than the neighbor, but also another neighbor, and also a neighbor of the other, and not simply his fellow. What then are the other and the third party for another? What have they done to one another? Which passes before the other? The other stands in a relationship with the third party, for whom I cannot entirely answer, even if I alone answer, before any question, for my neighbor. . . . The third party introduces a contradiction in the saying whose signification before the other until then went in one direction. . . . The relationship with the third party is an incessant correction of the asymmetry of proximity in which the face is looked at" (OB: 157–58; AE: 200–201).

23. Levinas says, "The work of ontology consists in apprehending the individual (which alone exists) not in its individuality but in its generality" (TI: 44; TeI: 14).

24. See, for example, Levinas' recognition of "a sense somewhere else than in ontology," which is to "subordinate ontology to this signification beyond essence" (OB: 64; AE: 80).

25. On the question of the end of philosophy in Levinas, Heidegger, and Derrida, see Bernasconi, 1986; 1993: 190.

26. For further discussion of the "end of philosophy" see the final section of *Totality and Infinity* (TI: 298; TeI: 274–75).

27. The "straightforwardness" of the face to face, Levinas says, "preserves the discontinuity of relationship, resists fusion. . . . Discourse is a rupture and commencement, breaking of rhythm which enraptures and transports the interlocutors—prose" (TI: 203; TeI: 177).

28. In *Otherwise than Being*, Levinas will speak, not so much of separation, but of the trace of separation. See OB: 79; AE: 100.

29. For a discussion of the contrast between the Levinasian conception of ethics and the Christian ethic, see Llewelyn, 1991: 14–26.

30. Levinas emphasizes the dimension of transcendence as characteristic of the ethical relation in "Transcendance et hauteur," which provides a useful if condensed summary of Levinas' *Totality and Infinity*. In the discussion that follows Levinas' explication of the book's main theses, Levinas says, in response to a comment by Minkowski, "I would say that transcendence remains essential to what I wanted to say. I regret not having succeeded in clarifying this notion. In my opinion, transcendence is only possible when the Other is not initially the fellow human being or the neighbour; but when the Other is distant, when it is other, when it is the one with whom initially I have nothing in common. . . . Transcendence is only possible with the Other, with respect to whom we are absolutely different, without this difference depending on some quality. Transcendence seemed to me to be the point of departure for our concrete relations with the Other" (TH: 107–8).

31. I develop this point below, under the heading "Inequality, Asymmetry and Singularity."

32. Levinas uses the phrase "despite oneself" frequently in *Otherwise than Being*.

33. "I am not afraid of the word God, which appears quite often in my essays," says Levinas in EI: 111; EeI: 105. See also Levinas' discussion of the "impossibility of escaping God" (OB: 128; AE: 165).

34. To be concerned to prove that God exists is to remain caught up in showing "the prestige of the totality and of efficacity, to which a philosophy of being would unfailingly return, and from which come the popular certainties" (OB: 94; AE: 120). See the discussion that follows, OB: 94–97; AE: 120–124. Also see OB: 121; AE: 155.

35. See also *Ethics and Infinity*, where Levinas says, "In the access to the face there is certainly also an access to the idea of God" (EI: 92; EeI: 97).

36. As Robbins says, Levinas insists upon the distinction between his philosophical and non-philosophical works (1991: 103). The quotation from Levinas that Robbins summons in support of her observation serve well to make the point: "I always make a clear distinction in what I write, between philosophical and confessional texts. I do not deny that they may ultimately have a common source of inspiration. I simply state that it is necessary to draw a line of demarcation between them as distinct methods of exegesis, as separate languages. I would never, for example, introduce a talmudic or biblical verse into one of my philosophical texts, to try to prove or justify a phenomenological argument," (DC: 54; quoted by Robbins, 1991: 166).

37. See, for example, Levinas' explanation of the sense he wants to give to the term expulsion: "There is an expulsion outside of being, it is in itself, before I set

myself up. I am assigned without recourse, without fatherland" (OB: 103; AE: 131). Whatever the philosophical import of such a claim, one cannot help but read into the words "without fatherland" an unambiguous reference to Jewish history. The fact that Levinas dedicates *Otherwise than Being* to "the memory of those who were closest among the six million assassinated by the National Socialists, and of the millions on millions of all confessions and all nations, victims of the same hatred of the other man, the same anti-semitism" removes any doubt that Levinas' Judaism, and in particular the experience of World War II, informs his philosophical position.

38. Derrida is quoting TI: 293; TeI: 269. In *Otherwise than Being*, Levinas, apparently distancing himself from the formulation "the good beyond being," says "'Goes beyond'—that is already to make a concession to ontological and theoretical language, as though the beyond were still a term, an entity, a mode of being, or the negative counterpart of all that. An approach is not a representation" (OB: 97; AE: 124). By preferring the word "approach" to the formulation of going beyond, Levinas builds upon his earlier discussion of proximity, where he suggested that perhaps the contact or contiguity between neighbors cannot be understood on the basis of a purely geometrical space (see OB: 81; AE: 103).

39. Levinas claims, "The saying is a way of greeting the Other, but to greet the Other is already to answer for him" (EI: 88; EeI: 93).

40. See, for example, TI: 33–35, TeI: 3–5; and TI: 62, TeI: 33.

41. The claims of formal logic, dominant in philosophy, are not adequate to the distinction between need and desire according to Levinas. He says, "The distinction between need and Desire can not be reflected in formal logic, where desire is always forced into the forms of need. From this purely formal necessity comes the force of Parmenidean philosophy. But the order of Desire, the relationship between strangers who are not wanting to one another—desire in its positivity—is affirmed across the idea of creation *ex nihilo*" (TI: 104; TeI: 77–78).

42. See also Levinas' observation "The other metaphysically desired is not 'other' like the bread I eat, the land in which I dwell, the landscape I contemplate, like, sometimes, myself, this 'I,' that 'other.' I can 'feed' on these realities and to a very great extent satisfy myself, as though I had simply been lacking them" (TI: 33; TeI: 3).

43. Levinas says, "Knowledge has always been interpreted as assimilation. Even the most surprising discoveries end by being absorbed, comprehended, with all that there is of 'prehending' in 'comprehending.' The most audacious and remote knowledge does not put us in communion with the truly other; it does not take the place of sociality; it is still and always a solitude" (EI: 60; EeI: 61–62).

44. Levinas says, "All enjoyment is a way of being, but also a sensation—that is, light and knowledge. It is absorption of the object, but also distance with regard to it. . . . The subject separates from itself. Light is a prerequisite for such a possibility" (TO: 63; TA: 46).

45. There is a great deal more to be said about this "distance" or duality that characterizes Levinasian subjectivity. For the sake of clarity I do not develop many important themes in Levinas' work that are only indirectly related to the

theme of ethics, such as that of solitude, the weight or materiality of existence, and the "there is."

46. Levinas says, "The world offers the subject participation in existing in the form of enjoyment, and consequently permits it to exist at a distance from itself. . . . In the perspective that opens upon the tool, beginning with the modern tool—the machine—one is much more struck by its function which consists in suppressing work, than by its instrumental function, which Heidegger exclusively considered.

"In work—meaning, in effort, in its pain and sorrow—the subject finds the weight of existence which involves the very freedom of the existent (trans. modified)" (TO: 67–68; TA: 51–54).

47. When Levinas repeats a similar criticism in 1960, he does so without any qualifying statement, distancing himself more decisively from Heidegger: "As material or gear the objects of everyday use are subordinated to enjoyment—the lighter to the cigarette one smokes, the fork to the food, the cup to the lips. Things refer to my enjoyment. This is an observation as commonplace as could be, which the analyses of *Zeughaftigkeit* do not succeed in effacing" (TI: 133; TeI: 106).

48. See TO: 44–57; TA: 24–38, EE: 57–101; DE: 92–174.

49. Levinas says, in a note at the end of the section entitled "Enjoyment" in *Otherwise than Being*, "In *Totality and Infinity*, the sensible was interpreted in the sense of consumption and enjoyment" (OB: 191; AE: 94, note 8 to chap. 8).

50. Happiness outweighs any anxiety about what the future will bring for Levinas (TI: 149; TeI: 123).

51. As in consumption, a negation of alterity occurs for Levinas in coming to know something. Levinas says that in knowledge, one is in "a relation with what one equals and includes, with that whose alterity one suspends, with what becomes immanent, because it is to my measure and to my scale" (EI: 60; EeI: 61).

52. "Violence and Metaphysics: An Essay on the Thought of Emmanuel Levinas"; "Violence et métaphysique: Essai sur la pensée d'Emmanuel Levinas" (Derrida, 1978: 79–153; ED: 117–228). This is Derrida's first essay on Levinas.

53. The phrase "no man's land" is in English in the original.

54. For a more detailed discussion of the concept of the face to face in Levinas' work, particularly in relation to what Levinas calls the "first word" of the face—"you shall not commit murder" (TI: 199; TeI: 173)—see Robbins, 1993.

55. See Levinas' discussion of language as representation and as giving (TI: 168–74; TeI: 142–49).

56. See, for example, *Time and the Other*, where, in the context of his discussion of death, Levinas asks another stream of questions which concern the possibility of maintaining a relationship with alterity, culminating in the question, "How can a being enter into relation with the other without allowing its very self to be crushed by the other?" (TO: 77; TA: 65). He repeats this question toward the end of *Time and the Other*, "How, in the alterity of a you, can I remain I, without being absorbed or losing myself in that you?" (TO: 91; TA: 85). As we shall see in more detail, the answer he gives is, "Through paternity" (TO: 91; TA: 85).

57. Levinas says, the "hither side" of the "who" (as distinct from the "who" understood as "what") "would remain a modality of being, a way of withdrawing, of excepting oneself, of drawing back without disappearing, of drawing back into the night of a oneself" (OB: 28; AE: 35).

58. I am drawing largely on Levinas' discussion of equality and inequality in *Totality and Infinity*, where the problem is approached with reference to the face-to-face relation. In *Otherwise than Being*, the face to face is no longer the locus for his discussion. It is consciousness itself that Levinas explicates in terms of equality, maintaining that his own account of "oneself" as a "hypostasis" exhibits an inequality with itself. See, for example, OB: 107; AE: 136.

59. See Llewelyn, 1988: 275.

60. See Levinas' comments on equality and inequality in relation to infinity: "Absolute knowledge, such as it has been sought, promised or recommended by philosophy, is a thought of the Equal. . . . On the other hand, the idea of the Infinite implies a thought of the Unequal" (EI: 91; EeI: 96). Levinas uses the word "proximity" occasionally in his early work (see, for example, TO: 94; TA: 89) but it is not until *Otherwise than Being* that it becomes a key term.

61. Levinas says, "The equality of all is borne by my inequality, the surplus of my duties over my rights. The forgetting of self moves justice. It is not without importance to know if the egalitarian and just State in which man is fulfilled (and which is to be set up, and especially to be maintained) proceeds from a war of all against all, or from the irreducible responsibility of the one for all, and if it can do without friendships and faces" (OB: 159–60; AE: 203).

62. Another difference between the relation of eros and that of the face to face, is that in the latter relation there is no return to self. See, for example, OB: 138, AE: 175; and OB: 141, AE: 179. Whereas in eros, the lover not only loves the beloved, but also loves the love received in turn, or loves being in love.

63. Levinas says that in *Otherwise than Being* "the proximity of the Other is presented as the fact that the Other is not simply close to me in space, or close like a parent, but he approaches me essentially insofar as I feel myself—insofar as I am— responsible for him" (EI: 96; EeI: 103).

64. On the meaning of proximity, see, in particular, OB: 100; AE: 126–27.

65. In *Otherwise than Being*, Levinas, in his attempt to be ever more precise in for- mulating the infinite obligation of the face to face, and to distinguish it from the bland duty of moral principles, distances himself from the terms he uses in *Totality and Infinity*. Thus, in *Otherwise than Being*, we find the idea of being committed is not far enough removed from the language of traditional moral- ity. Levinas says: "The for-the-other involved in saying must not be treated in terms of consciousness of . . . thematizing intentionality, nor in terms of com- mitment. The signifyingness of saying does not refer to commitment; for commitment presupposes saying" (OB: 50–51; AE: 65). Also see *Otherwise than Being*, Chapter 5 esp. OB: 136–40; AE: 174–79, where Levinas makes it clear that one's responsibility for the other is not such that it can be represented as something one could recall. It should be emphasized that Levinas is not object- ing to the idea of commitment as such. Levinas objects to understanding commitment as freedom, as if to commit oneself were simply to agree to a con- tract which one freely chooses. His point is that one finds oneself always already committed.

66. Levinas refers to Dostoyevsky to make the point that the face-to-face relation should not be understood as reciprocal: "Each of us is guilty before everyone for everyone, and I more than the others" (from *Brothers Karamazov*, Book VI, 11a;

quoted in OB: 186; AE: 186). Also see his comment "I can substitute myself for everyone, but no one can substitute himself for me" (EI: 101; EeI: 108).

67. Levinas says, "We think, as Europeans, that when one does something spontaneously, it is worth much more than when it is commanded. In reality in *Otherwise than Being*, it turns out that free action for the Other is not at all pure choice, that it is commanded, that it begins with an obligation, that it begins with obsession" (1989b: 111).

68. See Levinas' observation in 1982 that, in *Existence and Existents* and *Time and the Other*, "the ideas to which I hold today are still sought" (EI: 51; EeI: 49). As a rule (the reference to sensibility quoted earlier is an exception), Levinas does not differentiate his position in *Otherwise than Being* from his earlier works, and I take this to support my view that there is no substantial redefinition of his project, no significant "break" in his corpus. This is not to deny, of course, the novelty of his later work. Important developments in his work are indicated by his decision to reformulate older ideas.

69. Levinas says, "One of the fundamental themes of *Totality and Infinity* . . . is that the intersubjective relation is a non-symmetrical relation. In this sense, I am responsible for the Other without waiting for his reciprocity, were I to die for it. Reciprocity is *his* affair" (EI: 98; EeI: 105).

70. Levinas says, "The interpersonal relation I establish with the Other, I must also establish with other men; there is thus a necessity to moderate this privilege of the Other; from whence comes justice. Justice, exercised through institutions, which are inevitable, must always be held in check by the initial interpersonal relation" (EI: 90; EeI: 95).

71. See Levinas' discussion of Descartes in *Ethics and Infinity* (EI: 91–92; EeI: 97).

72. Levinas continues, "The discussion thus remains ontological, as though the comprehension of being ordered all thought and thinking itself. By the very fact of formulating statements, is not the universality of the thematized, that is, of being, confirmed by the project of the present discussion, which ventures to question this universality? Does this discourse remain then coherent and philosophical? These are familiar objections!

But does the coherence that would be lacking in this discussion consist in the immobility of the instant of truth, in its possibility of synchrony? The objection would then presuppose what is in question: the reference of all signification to essence. But our whole purpose was to ask if subjectivity, despite its foreignness to the said, is not stated by an abuse of language through which in the indiscretion of the said everything is shown" (OB: 155–56; AE; 198). In his discussion of "Skepticism and Reason" Levinas comments further on the capacity of Western philosophy to "affirm itself to be coherent and one" (OB: 169; AE: 215).

73. See Levinas' note 1 to chap. 4, OB: 193; AE: 125. Also see OB: xli; AE: ix–x.

74. Compare Levinas' approach to the other to his characterization of Sartre's, who, however much he tried to depart from traditional interpretations of alterity, remained, in Levinas' view, subservient to them. Levinas says, "I was extremely interested in Sartre's phenomenological analysis of the 'other,' though I always regretted that he interpreted it as a threat and a degradation, an interpretation that also found expression in his fear of the God question" (DC: 16).

75. See, for example, Levinas, 1969: 33; DL: 55–56.

76. Paul Davies presented a nuanced reading of Levinas' concept of the caress at the Collegium Phaenomenologicum in Perugia, Italy, 1990.

77. See the final pages of *Otherwise than Being*, where Levinas explicitly distinguishes the acknowledgment of a "difference between oneself and the others" (OB: 177; AE: 223) from eros. Eros, which is "complacent," is to be distinguished from the "non-erotic openness" (OB: 177; AE: 224) that Levinas has in mind.

78. Derrida's second essay on Levinas, which I discuss in chapter six, deals with the theme of the feminine (see Derrida, 1991).

79. Also see Levinas' articulation of the face to face in *Existence and Existents*. Here too Levinas does not yet see the need to separate definitively the face to face—which he again refers to in terms of the widow and orphan—from eros (EE: 95; DE: 162–63).

80. See, for example, Jeremiah 7:6 and 22:3. For further references, see TO: 83 (translator's note 64).

81. In a note to "Violence and Metaphysics," Derrida comments on the rich poetry of Levinas' writing: "in *Totality and Infinity* the thematic development is neither purely descriptive nor purely deductive. It proceeds with the infinite insistence of waves on a beach: return and repetition, always, of the same wave against the same shore, in which, however, as each return recapitulates itself, it also infinitely renews and enriches itself. Because of all these challenges to the commentator and the critic, *Totality and Infinity* is a work of art and not a treatise" (WD: 312, note 7; ED: 124).

82. Blanchot comments on the "strange structure" which Levinas captures sight of in the idea of a transcendent immanence. He says, "In his own unique way, Jean Wahl used to say that the greatest transcendence, the transcendence of transcendence, is ultimately the immanence, or the perpetual referral, of the one to the other. Transcendence within immanence: Levinas is the first to devote himself to this strange structure (sensibility, subjectivity) and not to let himself be satisfied by the shock value of such contrarieties" (1986: 48; Laruelle, 1980: 85).

83. Just as Levinas seeks to overcome Hegel's dialectical system, so Irigaray "refuses the opposition of immediate/mediate as it is developed in the Hegelian system" (SG: 127, note 1; SP: 141).

84. See also OB: 204; AE: 160.

85. On the relation between justice and responsibility, Levinas says, "In no way is justice a degradation of obsession, a degeneration of the for-the-other, a diminution, a limitation of anarchic responsibility, a neutralization of the glory of the Infinite, a degeneration that would be produced in the measure that for empirical reasons the initial duo would become a trio. But the contemporaneousness of the multiple is tied about the diachrony of two: justice remains justice only, in a society where there is no distinction between those close and those far off, but in which there is the impossibility of passing by the closest" (OB: 159; AE: 203).

86. As we saw at the beginning of this chapter, Irigaray's call is for a "cultural transformation, the nature of which we can barely conceive" (JTN: 21; JT: 25).

87. Léon Bloy, *Lettres à sa fiancée* (Paris, Editions Stock, 1947).

88. See, for example, OB: 135–36, AE: 173; and OB: 166, AE: 211.
89. As Levinas says in *Existence and Existents*,

> There is a duality in existence, an essential lack of simplicity. . . . Existence casts a shadow, which pursues it tirelessly. . . . Little John the simpleton, simple or innocent, in the Russian folktale, tossed the lunch, which he was to carry to his father at work in the field, to his shadow, so as to slip away from it; but after he had dropped everything his shadow, like a last and unalienable possession, still clings to him.
>
> Existence drags behind it a weight—if only itself—which complicates the trip it takes" (EE: 28; DE 37–38).

90. Derrida remarks, in the final footnote to "Violence and Metaphysics" and in passing that "*Totality and Infinity* pushes the respect for dissymetry so far that it seems to us impossible, essentially impossible, that it could have been written by a woman. Its philosophical subject is man (vir)" (WD: 320, ED: 228). Derrida declines to deal with eros in "Violence and Metaphysics" because it follows the same structure as the rest of the book, however much it renews it. "Is not this principled impossibility for a book to have been written by a woman unique in the history of metaphysical writing? Levinas acknowledges elsewhere that femininity is an 'ontological category.' Should this remark be placed in relation to the essential virility of metaphysical language? But perhaps metaphysical desire is essentially virile, even in what is called woman. It appears that this is what Freud (who would have misconstrued sexuality as the 'relationship with what is absolutely other'), thought, not of desire, certainly, but of libido" (WD: 321; ED: 228). Derrida does not elaborate on these enigmatic notes until he writes "At This Very Moment in This Text Here I Am."
91. Irigaray, 1984: 173–99.
92. Diotima's understanding of love is taken up in phrases such as: "a birth that will never take place . . . the call to birth . . . Bringing me back to life" (FC: 232–33; E: 174–75) and "a birth still in the future . . . a birth that has never taken place" (FC: 233; E: 175). See also, for example, FC: 231, E: 173; FC: 234, E: 176; and FC: 244, E: 187.
93. The words *aimée* and *amante*, both feminine, are rendered in this translation as "beloved" and "loved one," translations which are intended to capture a passive and an active sense, respectively. The word *amant* (masculine) is translated as lover. As translator Carolyn Burke points out, the "full engagement with the masculine *amant* cannot be rendered grammatically in English due to lack of gender" (FC: 256). This engagement with the masculine is, however, of central importance to the motif which Irigaray's reading of Levinas emphasizes above all.
94. Similar formulations recur throughout Irigaray's work. See, for example, SG: 108–9; SP: 122–24.
95. See, especially, "Divine Women," SG: 57–72; SP: 69–85. See also Stockton, 1992.
96. Also see FC: 242; E: 184.
97. For a discussion of the contestation between ethics and ontology that is played out between Levinas and Heidegger, see Bernasconi, 1987, and Greisch, 1987.
98. For more detailed analyses of Heidegger's relation to Levinas see Bouckaert, 1970, Keyes, 1972, Hederman, 1980, O'Connor, 1980, and Manning 1993.
99. In his essay, "The Origins of Heidegger's Thought," Sallis points out that if truth remains an issue of *Dasein's* self-disclosure in *Being and Time*, "Heidegger comes

in the later work to dissociate truth from Dasein's self-understanding. . . . The happening of truth is set at a distance from self-understanding" (1978: 54). Sallis develops his point in relation to Heidegger's "The Origin of the Work of Art" (Heidegger, 1975b). See Sallis, 1978: 54–56. The point is not that there is a complete change of direction in Heidegger's thinking, but that there is a development of the same concerns that reveals the continuity between the project of *Being and Time* and the paths Heidegger pursued in his later work. Since Levinas focuses on the Heidegger of *Being and Time*, he does not acknowledge this change in Heidegger's thinking.

NOTES TO CHAPTER SIX

1. The phrase, "*il n'y a pas de hors-texte*," means literally—as Spivak notes in parentheses "there is no outside-text." See Gasché's discussion (1986: 279–83) of the confusion that has arisen about this claim—confusion, I would add, that has arisen in part because readers have failed to take note of Spivak's parenthetical clarification and her superb preface to *Of Grammatology*.
2. In a conversation I had with Rodolphe Gasché after he heard an earlier version of chapter one, its Heideggerian motif became clearer to me than it had been while I was writing it. Jill Robbins, also at the State University of New York at Buffalo, has commented on this aspect of the book.
3. Gadamer, in his essay "The Nature of Things and the Language of Things" (1960), asks whether the "battle cry" of phenomenology is "dubious" (1977: 74), for "even Husserl understood the idea of the thing-in-itself in terms of the idea of the progress of our knowledge, which has its ultimate demonstration in scientific investigation" (1977: 73).
4. In "Choreographies," Christie McDonald appends a long footnote to one of Derrida's responses, directing the reader to three texts (C: 72–73). The first text is "At This Very Moment in This Work Here I Am"—Derrida's second article on Levinas—and the other two essays are by Levinas; "Judaism and the Feminine Element" and "And God Created Woman," both of which are discussed by Derrida in "At This Very Moment in This Work Here I Am." Levinas' "And God Created Woman," is a Talmudic reading which comments on various rabbinical interpretations of the account found in Genesis, chapter two, of how God created the world.
5. Derrida points to the "constant oscillation between the letter and the spirit of Husserlianism" (WD: 86; ED: 129) in Levinas' philosophy. I am suggesting that he finds a similar pattern in Levinas' treatment of sexual difference, even if Derrida himself does not state it in these terms. David Boothroyd has commented on the relevance of Derrida's distinction between spirit and letter to Levinas' discussion of Heidegger (1988: 15–16).
6. On the theme of the gift, see also WB: 199–200.
7. For a discussion of Levinas' treatment of the feminine in the context of his Judaism, see Chalier, 1991. See also Chalier, 1982.
8. Levinas says that "the social governs the erotic" (AG: 168; EC: 133), a belief that, since, as we know, Levinas equates woman with eros (using the terms "feminine"

and "erotic" almost interchangeably), amounts to saying that woman represents desire (in the general, as well as the specifically sexual sense) and man represents the law.

9. It is noteworthy that Derrida distinguishes between two different senses of neutralization in "Women in the Beehive," a distinction that represents a refinement of his earlier position as articulated in "Choreographies." He says, referring to his discussion in "*Geschlecht*," "Heidegger's discourse is not simple, nor simply beyond classical thought on this subject; certainly this motif on neutralization in his discourse could also reconstruct phallocentrism. There is a certain neutralization which can reconstruct the phallocentric privilege. But there is another neutralization which can simply neutralize the sexual opposition, and not sexual difference, liberating the field of sexuality for a very *different* sexuality, a more multiple one. At that point there would be no more sexes . . . there would be one sex for each time. One sex for each gift. A sexual difference for each gift" (WB: 199).

10. Also see Derrida's comment: "To desexualise the link to the wholly-other (or equally well, the unconscious as a certain philosophical interpretation of psychoanalysis tends to do today), to make sexuality secondary with respect to a wholly-other that in itself would not be sexually marked ("beneath erotic alterity, the alterity of the one for the other; responsibility before eros: [AE: 113n; OB: 192 n. 27]), is always to make sexual difference secondary *as* femininity" (AV: 43; EM: 55).

11. Schapiro, 1968: 203–9.

12. For a more detailed discussion of Derrida's "*Geschlecht,*" see Armour, 1993: 286–92. See also Derrida, 1977.

13. Derrida asks his questioner (who begins with a reference to the maverick dance of the feminist Emma Goldman), "Was the matrix of what was to be the future of feminism already there at the end of the last century?" and he continues to ask questions of the same order, such as "whether a program, or locus of begetting, was not already in place in the nineteenth century for all those configurations to which the feminist struggle of the second half of the twentieth century was to commit itself and then to develop" (C: 67).

14. For an interpretation of Derrida that acknowledges that he does recognize that there is more than one type of feminist, see Findlay, 1989. Findlay argues, however, that in Derrida's "figuration" of the "difference between feminine figures" there lies an incipient "homophobia" (1989: 63).

15. Derrida makes the point less ambiguously in a later interview: "I would say that for me deconstruction is *certainly* not feminist. . . . If there is one thing that it must not come to, it's feminism. . . . Feminism is a form—no doubt a necessary form at a certain moment—but a form of phallogocentrism among many others" (1985a: 30).

16. On male philosophers' use of the trope of woman, see Robinson, 1991: 80–81, Braidotti, 1987: 236–38, Jardine and Smith, 1987, Radhakrishnan, 1989: 196, and Whitford 1991: 30.

17. While there is no doubt that some of Derrida's comments about feminists appear polemical when read in isolation, I read his criticisms not as a dismissal of feminism as a whole but only of those versions of feminism that refuse to

question their own relation to the discourse of equal rights. On this point, if not on others, Irigaray would agree with him.

18. For a more detailed account of Irigaray's psychoanalysis of the philosophers, see Whitford, 1991.

19. Derrida recognizes the cultural and historical specificity of the relations between "Man" and "Woman" in Western countries: that it is "not an eternal and universal situation" and that it could change (WB: 195).

20. My reading of Irigaray's relation to Derrida on this point differs from Whitford, who says that they agree "that the transcendental subject, traditionally thought to be non-gendered, is in fact gendered male. At that point, they part company. Irigaray, focusing on sexual difference, privileges the subordinate term, and argues for women's accession to subjectivity, while Derrida sees this demand as phallocentric" (1991: 128). I have suggested that, while Derrida is critical of feminism insofar as it restricts itself to such demands, he also affirms their necessity as a first step—a step that must be repeated "interminably" since metaphysics tends to reassert itself. The need to reverse metaphysical hierarchies is therefore an ever-present need, but it is not the only gesture we can make. It is also important to be vigilant about the possibility—perhaps necessity—of such reversals becoming dogmatic, reinscribing patriarchy, reinventing the law. When Whitford says that "deconstruction avoids addressing its own implication in violence, by simply locating the violence elsewhere" (1991: 131), she does not take account of the sense in which Derrida acknowledges that even deconstruction cannot avoid the law—cannot avoid violence.

21. Whitford observes (about *Speculum*, but her remark refers equally to *This Sex Which Is Not One*) that when Irigaray "examines the idea of the mirror, she is clearly addressing Lacan's theory of the imaginary and the role of the mirror in the construction of subjectivity" (1991: 65). Also see Grosz, 1990b: 173.

22. Also see Irigaray's comments on laughter in "The Female Gender" (SG: 115; SP: 130).

23. Berg (referring to WD: 256) also points out that Derrida is not averse to laughter: "A discourse which takes itself seriously, which believes in its own legitimacy, is what Derrida means by logocentric" (1988: 70).

24. At the end of the chapter it will become clear that there is a sense in which Irigaray's earlier essay on Derrida, "*Le v(i)ol de la lettre*," had already taken account of "*Le facteur de la vérité*."

25. It is worth noting that Derrida makes a point of calling attention to "the discussions of fetishism and feminine sexuality in *Spurs*, *Glas*, or *The Postcard*, specifically in *Le facteur de la vérité*" (C: 70). "*Le facteur de la vérité*" is the text in which Derrida discusses Lacan's "The Purloined Letter" (Lacan, 1991). Derrida observes that this "'Seminar' belongs to an investigation of the 'repetition compulsion' (*Wiederholungszwang*) which, in the group of texts from 1919 to 1920 (*Beyond the Pleasure Principle*, *Das Unheimliche*) transforms, at least in principle (see *The Double Session*, notes 52 and 67), the relation of psychoanalysis to literary fiction" (PC: 421; CP: 449).

26. The allusions to Levinas are also unmistakable in several other formulations, for example, in Irigaray's invocation of an infinite debt and her account of the

"dwelling place" (SG: 33; SP: 44), which are reminiscent of Levinas' descriptions in "Living from . . . Enjoyment" (TI: 110–14; TeI: 82–86) and "Habitation and the Feminine" (TI: 154–56; TeI: 127–29).

27. By employing a variety of associations, Irigaray evokes several different senses of the word *jeu*: "being taken in by play," "freeing oneself up in play," and "putting oneself at risk," suggesting at the same time that the very idea of playing with words is at stake. I am grateful to Adelaide Russo for her help with translating these phrases, and throughout this section.

28. See Derrida, 1976; 1978; 1981a. See also "Différance" in Derrida, 1982b.

29. Culler (1982) introduces Derrida to literary readers, while Llewelyn (1986) and Gasché (1986) provide a more philosophical orientation. Also see Critchley, 1992, for a discussion of Derrida's relation to Levinas.

30. The "exergue" is the space or inscription on a coin. It derives from the Greek "*ex-ergon*," outside the work. On the "exergue" see Alan Bass' translator's note 1 to Derrida, 1982b: 209.

31. Derrida remarks on the impossibility of presenting the other "as such" (OGr: 47; DG: 24).

32. Derrida says, "There cannot be a science of différance itself in its operation, as it is impossible to have a science of the origin of presence itself, that is to say of a certain nonorigin" (OGr: 63; DG: 92).

33. Gasché has in mind the following passage by Derrida: "Writing is the dissimulation of the natural, primary, and immediate presence of sense to the soul within the logos. Its violence befalls the soul as unconsciousness. Deconstructing this tradition will therefore not consist of reversing it, of making writing innocent. Rather of showing why the violence of writing does not *befall* an innocent language. There is an or[i]ginary violence of writing because language is first, in a sense I shall gradually reveal, writing. 'Usurpation' has always already begun. The sense of the right side appears in a mythological effect of return" (OGr: 37; DG: 55).

34. This is a point that Gasché emphasized in a conversation I had with him about the target of his account of Derrida's concept of writing.

35. Compare Derrida's observation that "Letters, which have no meaning by themselves, signify only the elementary phonic signifiers that make sense only when they are put together according to certain rules" (OGr: 299; DG: 423).

36. See Derrida's discussion of Mallarmé, where he attends to the blank whiteness of the page (1981a: 195–98; 222–25).

37. Compare what Derrida says, OGr: 288–89; DG: 408–9.

38. Many other quotations could be marshalled in support of the convergence between Derrida and Irigaray. Compare, for example, their references to Hegel's *Aufhebung*, VL: 149; and OGr: 25, DG: 40.

39. See PC: 413–96; CP: 441–524.

NOTES TO AFTERWORD

1. I want to thank in particular Michelle Massé and Margaret Whitford for constructive advice about how to solve this problem.

2. For example, the opening lines of Irigaray's essay on the subject of time evoke

Derrida's references to time (PC: 301, CP: 322; and PC: 358–59, CP 381–82).

3. See Derrida's discussion of the function of Hans Andersen's fairy tale "The Emperor's New Clothes" in Freud's *Interpretation of Dreams* (PC: 416–19; CP: 445–48).

4. See, for example, PC: 43–44, CP: 50; and PC: 255, CP: 272. As Bass notes in the glossary to *The Post Card*, if the Greek *angelos* means messenger, it is also related to the idea of a mail courier or "*facteur*," which means both postman and factor.

5. See also Irigaray's observation that "What Ernst wants is to master presence-absence with the help of a more or less white, more or less transparent veil" (SG: 30; SP: 42).

6. See discussion of the PP below, as well as note 21.

7. Also see Alan Bass' note on "restance," which is of particular interest because it comments on the significance of the "middle voice" (PC: 261, note 5).

8. Jardine says that "In Lacanian literature, the 'Real' designates that which is categorically unrepresentable, nonhuman, at the limits of the known; it is emptiness, the scream, the zero point of death, the proximity of jouissance" (1985: 122–23), and Rose explains the real in terms of its relation to the imaginary and the symbolic (1983: 31).

9. Sheridan says, "The 'real' emerges as a third term, linked to the symbolic and the imaginary: it stands for what is neither symbolic nor imaginary, and remains foreclosed from the analytic experience, which is an experience of speech. What is prior to the assumption of the symbolic, the real in its 'raw' state (in the case of the subject for instance, the organism and its biological needs), may only be supposed, it is an algebraic x. This Lacanian concept of the 'real' is not to be confused with reality, which is perfectly knowable: the subject of desire knows no more than that, since for it reality is entirely phantasmatic." (1985: ix–x).

10. Freud's footnote that records that the death of Sophie occurs when little Ernst is "five and three-quarters" (SE 18: 16) is the occasion for a long discussion by Derrida about the fact that Sophie dies in 1920, "the very year in which her father publishes *Beyond*" (PC: 328; CP: 349).

11. Sophie's parents call her "the Sunday child." Derrida notices the relation between this name and "the strange and artificial composition of *Beyond* . . . in *seven* chapters" (PC: 329; CP: 350). Also see PC: 386; CP: 412.

12. Implicit in Irigaray's claim that faith makes the other "the other of the same" is the challenge to Lacan that Whitford articulates when she says, "The term itself, the 'other of the other,' is a direct challenge to Lacan's lapidary pronouncement: 'there is no Other of the Other' [Lacan 1985: 311; 1966: 813]" (Whitford, 1991: 104). Irigaray often objects that Lacan reduces "the other to the Other of the Same" (TS: 98–99; CS: 96).

13. Irigaray says, "Belief is safe only if that in which or in whom the assembly communes or communicates is subject to concealment" (SG: 27; SP: 39).

14. Irigaray says, for example, "All the threads and all the sons (*tous les fils et les fils*) come and go between these two places of the invisible [the presence of God and the mother's presence], those two hidden presences, between which everything is played out, in which everything meets" (SG: 32; SP: 44). Irigaray's use of the word *fils* indirectly refers to Derrida, who says that Freud, as the "speculating grandfather . . . recalls *himself*. And thereby . . . enters into a contract with himself in order to hold onto all the strings/sons [*fils*] of the descendance. . . . The net [*filet*] is in place,

and one pulls on a string [*fil*] only by getting one's hand, foot, or the rest, caught. It is a lasso or a lace" (PC: 321; CP: 342). In a note, Derrida adds: "Concerning the double stricture of the *lace* in relation to the *fort-da*, I must refer to Glas (Paris: Galilee, 1974) and 'Restitutions—de la vérité en pointure,' *La vérité en peinture* (Paris: Flammarion, 1978).

15. See, for example, PC: 275, CP: 294; PC: 380–81, CP: 405–7; PC: 269–71, CP: 287–89.

16. The quotation is from Freud, SE 20: 57.

17. The quotation is from Freud, SE 20: 60.

18. See Lacan, 1985: 2.

19. *Démarche*, means procedure, but broken up into its parts: *dé* (a privative prefix, like the English "dis" in "distance," carrying a sense of separation) and *marcher* (to walk or to work), it recalls the idea of the step (*pas*), which also is a way of stating the negative. Derrida plays on the idea of the steps that Freud takes throughout his essay, pointing out how he steps forward only to draw back every time he tries to go beyond the pleasure principle. See, for example, his observation, "We have not advanced one step, only steps for nothing on the path of the manifest investigations. It repeats itself in place. And yet . . . reproductivity itself will have begun to work without saying anything" (PC: 296; CP: 317).

20. "PP" is an abbreviation for "Pleasure Principle." As Alan Bass, the translator of *The Post Card* notes, "In French the pronunciation of PP is *pépé*, which is also the affectionate term for grandfather. Derrida will play upon this double meaning throughout" (PC: 287, translator's note 18). Freud is, of course—in addition to being the observer of and "speculator" on little Ernst—his grandfather, a relation that Derrida, as one might expect, makes much of. Bass adds in his glossary that PP is also the abbreviation for "Plato's Pharmacy" (PC: xxv), an earlier essay of Derrida's in *Dissemination* to which he often refers in *The Post Card*. PP is also an abbreviation for the "Postal Principle" that organizes *The Post Card* "as differantial relay" (PC: 54).

21. Derrida goes on, "He recalls *himself*. Who and what? Who? himself, of course. But we cannot know if this 'himself' can say 'myself'. . . . The *fort-da* already would suffice to deprive us of any certainty on this subject. This is why, if a recourse, and a massive recourse, to the autobiographical is necessary here, the recourse must be of a new kind. This text is autobiographical, but in a completely different way than has been believed up to now. . . . *Beyond* . . . therefore, is not an *example* of what is allegedly already known under the name of autobiography. It writes autobiography . . ." (PC: 322; CP: 343).

bibliography

For a comprehensive bibliography of Irigaray's work and secondary sources of her work as of 1991, see Whitford (1991).

Alcoff, Linda. (1988) "Cultural Feminism versus Post-Structuralism: The Identity Crisis in Feminist Theory." *Signs* 13 (3): 405–436.

Al-Hibri, Azizah Y., and Margaret Simons, eds. (1990) *Hypatia Reborn: Essays in Feminist Philosophy*. Bloomington and Indianapolis: Indiana University Press. [The essays on Beauvoir are reprinted from a special issue of *Women's Studies International Forum* 8 (3) (1985), which featured *Hypatia: A Journal of Feminist Philosophy*, and published selected papers from the program of a conference held at the University of Pennsylvania in 1984, "*After The Second Sex*: A New Beginning."]

Allen, Christine Garside. (1979) "Can a Woman Be Good in the Same Way as a Man?" In *Woman in Western Thought*, ed. Martha Lee Osborne. New York, Random House.

Allen, Jeffner. (1989) "An Introduction to Patriarchal Existentialism: A Proposal for a Way out of Existential Patriarchy." In *The Thinking Muse: Feminism and Modern French Philosophy*, ed. Jeffner Allen and Iris Marion Young. Bloomington and Indianapolis: Indiana University Press.

Annas, Julia. (1979) "Plato's *Republic* and Feminism." In *Woman in Western Thought*, ed. Martha L. Osborne. New York: Random House.

Appignanesi, Lisa. (1988) *Simone de Beauvoir*. London: Penguin.

Aristotle, *Metaphysics* 1–9 (1980a). Translated by Hugh Tredennick, The Loeb Classical Library. Cambridge, Mass.: Harvard University Press.

Aristotle. (1975) *Nicomachean Ethics*. Translated by H. Rackham, The Loeb Classical Library. Cambridge, Mass.: Harvard University Press.

Aristotle. (1980b) *Physics* Books I–IV, vol. 4. Translated by Philip H. Wicksteed and F. M. Cornford, The Loeb Classical Library. Cambridge, Mass.: Harvard University Press.

Armour, Ellen T. (1993) "Deconstruction and Feminist Theology: Toward Forging an Alliance with Derrida and Irigaray." Ph.D. diss., Graduate Department of Religion, Vanderbilt University.

Bachofen, J. J. (1967) *Myth, Religion, and Mother Right*. Translated by Ralph Manheim. Princeton, N.J.: Princeton University Press.

Bair, Deirdre. (1989) "Simone de Beauvoir: Reflections on a Work in Progress." *L'esprit créateur* 29 (4) (Winter): 75–85.

Barber, Benjamin. (1988) "Spirit Phoenix and History's Owl or the Incoherence of Dialectics in Hegel's Account of Women." *Political Theory* 16 (1) February: 5–28.

Baruch, Elaine Hoffman, and Lucienne J. Serrano, eds. (1988) *Women Analyze Women*. New York: New York University Press. Originally published in *Women Writers Talking*, ed. Janet Todd (New York: Holmes and Meier, 1983), pp. 231–45.

Beauvoir, Simone de. (1948) *The Ethics of Ambiguity*. Translated by Bernard Frechtman. Ontario: Citadel Press. *Pour une morale de l'ambiguité* (Paris: Gallimard, 1947).

———. (1954) *The Second Sex*. Translated by H. M. Parshley. New York: Knopf; *Le deuxième Sexe*, 2 vols., Paris: Gallimard (1949).

———. (1965) *A Very Easy Death*. Translated by Patrick O'Brian. New York: Pantheon Books. *Une Mort Très Douce* (Paris: Gallimard, 1964).

———. (1984a) *Adieux: A Farewell to Sartre*. Translated by Patrick O'Brian, Harmondsworth, Middlesex: Penguin; *Le céremonie des adieux*, (Paris: Gallimard, 1981).

———. (1984b) *All Said and Done*. Translated by Patrick O'Brian, Harmondsworth, Middlesex: Penguin. *Tout compte faite* (Paris: Gallimard, 1972).

———. (1984c) *The Prime of Life*. Translated by Peter Green. Harmondsworth, Middlesex: Penguin. *La force de l'âge* (Paris: Gallimard, 1960).

———. (1985) *The Force of Circumstance*. Translated by Richard Howard. Harmondsworth, Middlesex: Penguin. *La force des choses* (Paris: Gallimard, 1963).

Benhabib, Seyla. (1991) "On Hegel, Women and Irony." In *Feminist Interpretations and Political Theory*, ed. Mary Lyndon Shanley and Carole Pateman. Oxford: Polity Press in association with Basil Blackwell. Reprinted in Benhabib, *Situating the Self: Gender, Community and Postmodernism in Contemporary Ethics* (New York: Routledge, 1992).

Berg, Elizabeth. (1982) "The Third Woman." *Diacritics* 12 (Summer): 11–20.

Berg, Maggie. (1988) "Escaping the Cave: Luce Irigaray and Her Feminist Critics." *Literature and Ethics: Essays Presented to A. E. Malloch*, ed. Gary Wihl and David Williams. Kingston and Montreal: McGill-Queen's University Press.

Bernasconi, Robert. (1985) *The Question of Language in Heidegger's History of Being*. New Jersey: Humanities.

———. (1986) "Levinas and Derrida: The Question of the Closure of Metaphysics." *Face to Face with Levinas*, ed. Richard Cohen. Albany: State University of New York Press.

———. (1987) "Fundamental Ontology, Metontology, and the Ethics of Ethics." *Irish Philosophical Journal* 4 (1 and 2): 76–93.

———. (1988) "The Trace of Levinas in Derrida." *Derrida and Différance*, ed. David Wood and Robert Bernasconi. Evanston, Ill.: Northwestern University Press.

———. (1989a) "Rereading *Totality and Infinity*." In *The Question of the Other: Essays in Contemporary Continental Philosophy*, ed. Arleen Dallery and Charles Scott. Albany: State University of New York Press.

———. (1989b) "Seeing Double: *Destruktion* and Deconstruction." In *Dialogue and Deconstruction*, ed. Diane Michelfelder and Richard Palmer. Albany: State University of New York Press.

———. (1993) *Heidegger in Question: The Art of Existing*. New Jersey: Humanities Press.

Bernasconi, Robert, and Simon Critchley. (1991) *Rereading Levinas*. Bloomington, Ind.: Indiana University Press.

Bernasconi, Robert, and David Wood. (1988) *The Provocation of Levinas*, London: Routledge and Kegan Paul.

Bernstein, J. M. (1984) "From Self-Consciousness to Community: Act and Recognition in the Master-Slave Relationship." *The State and Civil Society: Studies in Hegel's Political Philosophy*, ed. Z. A. Pelczynski. Cambridge: Cambridge University Press.

Blanchot, Maurice. (1942) *Aminadab*, Paris: Gallimard.

———. (1986) "Our Clandestine Companion." Translated by David Allison. In *Face to Face with Levinas,* ed. Richard Cohen. Albany: State University of New York Press; "Notre compagne clandestine," in Laruelle (1980).

Bleier, Ruth. (1991) "Science and Gender." In *A Feminist Reader in Knowledge*, ed. S. Gunew. New York: Routledge.

Boothroyd, David. (1988) "Responding to Levinas." In *The Provocation of Levinas: Rethinking the Other*, ed. Robert Bernasconi and David Wood. London: Routledge.

Bouckaert, Luk. (1970) "Ontology and Ethics: Reflections on Levinas's Critique of Heidegger." *International Philosophical Quarterly* 10 (3): 402–19.

Bowlby, Rachel. (1988) "Flight Reservations." *Oxford Literary Review* 10 (1–2): 61–72.

Braidotti, Rosi. (1987) "Envy: or With My Brains and Your Looks." In Jardine and Smith (1987).

———. (1989) "The Politics of Ontological Difference." In *Between Feminism and Psychoanalysis*, ed. Teresa Brennan. New York: Routledge.

———. (1991) *Patterns of Dissonance*. New York: Routledge.

Burggraeve, Roger. (1985) *From Self-Development to Solidarity. An Ethical Reading of Human Desire in Its Socio-Political Relevance according to Emmanuel Levinas.* Translated by C. Vanhove-Romanik. Leuven: The Center for Metaphysics and Philosophy of God.

———. (1986) *Emmanuel Levinas: Une bibliogaphie primaire et secondaire (1926–1985)*. Leuven: The Center for Metaphysics and Philosophy of God.

Burke, Carolyn (1987). "Romancing the Philosophers: Luce Irigaray." *The Minnesota Review* 29: 103–114.

Burstow, Bonnie. (1992) "How Sexist Is Sartre?" *Philosophy and Literature* 16 (1) (April): 32–48.

Busch, Thomas W. (1990) *The Power of Consciousness and the Force of Circumstance*. Bloomington and Indianapolis: Indiana University Press.

Butler, Judith. (1986) "Sex and Gender in Simone de Beauvoir's *Second Sex*." *Yale French Studies* 72: 35–49.

———. (1987) "Variations on Sex and Gender: Beauvoir, Wittig and Foucault." In *Feminism as Critique*, ed. Seyla Benhabib and Drucilla Cornell. Minneapolis: University of Minnesota Press.

———. (1990) *Gender Trouble: Feminism and the Subversion of Identity*. New York: Routledge.

———. (1992) "Contingent Foundations: Feminism and the Question of 'Postmodernism.'" *Feminists Theorize the Political*, ed. Judith Butler and Joan W. Scott. New York: Routledge.

———. (1993) *Bodies that Matter: On the Discursive Limits of Sex*, New York: Routledge.

———. (1994) "Gender as Performance: An Interview with Judith Butler," *Radical Philosophy* 67, Summer.

Card, Claudia. (1990) "Lesbian Attitudes and *The Second Sex*." In Al-Hibri and Simons, pp. 290–99.

Casey, Edward. (1983) "Keeping the Past in Mind." *Review of Metaphysics* 37 (September): 77–95.

———. (1987) *Remembering: A Phenomenological Study*. Bloomington: Indiana University Press.

Caws, Peter (1979) *Sartre*. London: Routledge.

Chalier, Catherine (1982) *Figures du féminin: Lecture d'Emmanuel Levinas*. Paris: La Nuit surveillée.

———. (1991) "Ethics and the Feminine." In Bernasconi and Critchley, pp. 119–29.

Chodorow, Nancy. (1978) *The Reproduction of Mothering*. Berkeley: University of California Press.

Christian, Barbara. (1989) "The Race for Theory." *Gender & Theory: Dialogues on Feminist Criticism*, ed. Linda Kauffman. Oxford: Basil Blackwell.

Cixous, Hélène. (1981) "The Laugh of the Medusa." In *New French Feminisms*, ed. Elaine Marks and Isabelle de Courtivron. Brighton, Sussex: Harvester Press. Revised from "Le rire de la méduse." *L'arc* (1975).

Clément, Catherine. (1987) "Peelings of the Real." In *Critical Essays on Simone de Beauvoir*, ed. Elaine Marks. Boston: G. K. Hall & Co.

Collins, Margery, and Christine Pierce. (1980) "Sexism in Sartre's Psychoanalysis." In *Women in Philosophy*, ed. Carol Gould and Marx Wartofsky. New York: G. P. Putnam and Sons.

Cornell, Drucilla. (1991) *Beyond Accommodation: Ethical Feminism, Deconstruction, and The Law*. New York: Routledge.

Cott, Nancy F. (1986) "Feminist Theory and Feminist Movements: The Past before Us," ed. Juliet Mitchell and Ann Oakley. Oxford: Basil Blackwell.

Cottrell, Robert D. (1976) *Simone de Beauvoir*. New York: Frederick Ungar Publishing Company.

Craig, Carol. (1979) "*The Second Sex* in the Light of the Hegelian Master-Slave Dialectic and Sartrian Existentialism." Ph.D. diss., University of Edinburgh, microfilm.

Critchley, Simon. (1992) *The Ethics of Deconstruction*. Oxford: Basil Blackwell.

Culler, Jonathan. (1982) *On Deconstruction: Theory and Criticism after Structuralism*. Ithaca, N. Y.: Cornell University Press.

Dallery, Arleen. (1990) "Sexual Embodiment: Beauvoir and French Feminism (*écriture féminine*)." In Al-Hibri and Simons, pp. 270–79.

Dastur, Françoise. (1993) "Language and *Ereignis*." In *Reading Heidegger: Commemorations*, ed. John Sallis. Bloomington and Indianapolis, Indiana University Press.

De Lauretis, Teresa. (1987) *Technologies of Gender*. Bloomington: Indiana University Press.

———. (1990) "Upping the Anti (sic) in Feminist Theory." In *Conflicts in Feminism*, ed. Marianne Hirsch and Evelyn Fox Keller. New York: Routledge.

Delmar, Rosalind. (1986) "What Is Feminism?" In *What Is Feminism*, ed. Juliet Mitchell and Ann Oakley. Oxford: Basil Blackwell.

Delphy, Christine. (1993) "Rethinking Sex and Gender." In *Women's Studies International Forum*, 16 (1): 1–9.

Derrida, Jacques. (1976) *Of Grammatology*. Translated by Gayatri Chakravorty Spivak. Baltimore and London: The Johns Hopkins University Press. *De la grammatologie* (Paris: Minuit, 1967).

———. (1977) "*Geschlecht* II: Heidegger's Hand." Translated by John P. Leavey. In *Deconstruction and Philosophy: The Texts of Jacques Derrida*. Chicago: University of Chicago Press. "Le main de Heidegger (1984–85)," In *Psyché: Inventions de l'autre*. (Galilée, 1987).

———. (1978) *Writing and Difference*. Translated by Alan Bass. Chicago: University of Chicago Press. *L'écriture et la différence* (Paris: Seuil, 1967).

————. (1979) *Spurs: Nietzsche's Styles*. Translated by Barbara Harlow. Chicago: University of Chicago Press. Bilingual edition. *Eperons: Les Styles de Nietzsche* (Paris: Flammarion, 1978).

————. (1981a) *Dissemination*. Translated, with an introduction and additional notes, by Barbara Johnson. Chicago: University of Chicago Press. *La Dissémination* (Paris: Seuil, 1972).

————. (1981b) *Positions*. Translated by Alan Bass. Chicago: University of Chicago Press. *Positions* (Paris: Minuit, 1971).

————. (1982a) "Choreographies." Interview with Christie V. McDonald. *Diacritics* 12: 66–76. Also published in the reedition of *The Ear of the Other: Otobiography, Transference, Translation*, ed. Christie McDonald (Lincoln: University of Nebraska Press, 1988).

————. (1982b) *Margins of Philosophy*. Translated by Alan Bass. Chicago: University of Chicago Press: *Marges de la philosophie* (Paris: Minuit, 1972).

————. (1983) "*Geschlecht*: Sexual difference, ontological difference." *Research in Phenomenology* 13: 65–83. "Geschlecht: différence sexuelle, différence ontologique," in *Martin Heidegger*, ed. Michel Haar (Paris: L'Herne, 1983).

————. (1985a) "Deconstruction in America: An Interview with Jacques Derrida," James Creech, Peggy Kamuf and Jane Todd." *Critical Exchange* 17 (Winter): 1–33.

————. (1985b) *The Ear of the Other: Otobiography, Transference, Translation: Texts and Discussions with Jacques Derrida*. Translated by Peggy Kamuf. New York: Schocken Books: *L'Oreille de l'autre: otobiographies, transferts, traductions: textes et débats avec Jacques Derrida* (Montreal: VLB, 1982).

————. (1986) *Glas*. Translated by John P. Leavey, Jr., and Richard Rand. Lincoln: University of Nebraska Press. *Glas* (Paris: Editions Galilée, 1974).

————. (1987a) *The Post Card: From Socrates to Freud and Beyond*. Translated by Alan Bass. Chicago: University of Chicago Press. *La Carte postale: de Socrate à Freud et au-delà* (Paris: Aubier-Flammarion, 1980).

————. (1987b) "Restitutions." In *The Truth in Painting*. Translated by G. Bennington and I. McLeod. Chicago: University of Chicago Press. "Restitutions de la Vérité en Pointure." In *La Vérité en peinture*. (Paris: Flammarion, 1978).

————. (1987c) "Women in the Beehive: A Seminar with Jacques Derrida." In *Men in Feminism*, ed. Alice Jardine and Paul Smith. London: Methuen.

————. (1991) "At This Very Moment in This Work Here I Am." Translated by R. Berezdevin. In *Re-Reading Levinas*, ed. R. Bernasconi and Simon Critchley. Bloomington: Indiana University Press. "En ce moment même dans cet ouvrage me voici," in *Textes pour Emmanuel Levinas*, ed. Françoise Laruelle (Paris: Jean-Michel Place, 1980).

Descartes, René. (1979) "Meditations on First Philosophy." In *The Philosophical Works of Descartes*. Vol. 1. Translated by Elizabeth S. Haldane and G. R. T. Ross. Cambridge: Cambridge University Press.

Descombes, Vincent. (1980) *Modern French Philosophy*. Translated by L. Scott-Fox and J.M. Harding. Cambridge: Cambridge University Press.

Dickason, Anne. (1980) "Anatomy and Destiny: The Role of Biology in Plato's Views of Women." In *Women and Philosophy: Toward a Theory of Liberation*, ed. Carol C. Gould and Marx W. Wartofsky. New York: G. P. Putnam's Sons.

Dijkstra, Sandra. (1980) "Simone de Beauvoir and Betty Freidan: The Politics of Omission." FS: 290–303.

Dinnerstein, Dorothy. (1977) *The Mermaid and the Minotaur*. New York: Harper & Row.

Easton, Susan M. (1987) "Hegel and Feminism." In *Hegel and Modern Philosophy*, ed. David Lamb. New York: Croom Helm, in association with Methuen.

Ehrenberg, Victor. (1954) *Sophocles and Pericles*. Oxford: Basil Blackwell.

Eisenstein, Hester, and Alice Jardine. (1985) *The Future of Difference*. New Brunswick: Rutgers University Press.

Elliot, Patricia. (1991) *From Mastery to Analysis: Theories of Gender in Psychoanalytic Feminism*. Ithaca and London: Cornell University Press.

Engels, Frederick. (1971) *The Origin of the Family, Private Property and the State*. New York: International Publishers.

Evans, Mary. (1983) "Simone de Beauvoir: Dilemmas of a Feminist Radical." In *Feminist Theories: Three Centuries of Women's Intellectual Traditions*, ed. Dale Spender. London: Women's Press.

Faludi, Susan. (1991) *Backlash: The Undeclared War against American Women*. New York: Crown Publishers.

Felman, Shoshana. (1981) "Re-reading Femininity." *Yale French Studies* (62): 19–44.

Felstiner, Mary Lowenthal. (1980) "Seeing *The Second Sex* through the Second Wave." *Feminist Studies* 6 (2) (Summer): 247–76.

Féral, Josette. (1978) "Antigone or the *Irony of the Tribe*." *Diacritics* (September): 2–14.

Ferguson, Ann. (1990) "Lesbian Identity: Beauvoir and History." In Al-Hibri and Simons, pp. 280–89.

Findlay, Heather. (1989) "Is there a Lesbian in this Text? Derrida, Wittig, and the Politics of the Three Women." In *Coming to Terms: Feminism, Theory, Politics*, ed. Elizabeth Weed. New York: Routledge.

Flax, Jane. (1987) "Postmodernism and Gender Relations in Feminist Theory." *Signs* 12 (4): 621–43.

Flay, Joseph C. (1984) *Hegel's Quest for Certainty*. Albany: State University of New York.

Flynn, Thomas R. (1984) *Sartre and Marxist Existentialism: The Test Case of Collective Responsibility*. Chicago and London: University of Chicago Press.

Foucault, Michel. (1984) *History of Sexuality*, Vol. 1. Translated by Robert Hurley. Harmondsworth, Middlesex: Penguin. *Histoire de la sexualité 1: La volonté de savoir* (Paris: Gallimard, 1978).

Fox Keller, Evelyn. (1989) "The Gender/Science System: or, Is Sex to Gender as Nature Is to Science?" In *Feminism & Science*, ed. N. Tuana. Bloomington: Indiana University Press. Originally published in *Hypatia* 2 (3) (Fall).

Fraiman, Susan. (1990) "Against Gendrification: Agendas for Feminist Scholarship and Teaching in Women's Studies." *Iris* (Spring/Summer): 5–9.

Freud, Sigmund. (1951–73) *The Standard Edition of the Complete Psychological Works of Sigmund Freud*. Translated by James Strachey. Edited by James Strachey in collaboration with Anna Freud. London: The Hogarth Press and the Institute of Psycho-analysis.

Friedlander, Judith. (1986) "The Anti-Semite and the Second Sex: A Cultural Reading of Sartre and Beauvoir." In *Women in Culture and Politics: A Century of Change*, ed. Judith Friedlander et. al. Bloomington: Indiana University Press.

Frug, Mary Joe. (1992) *Postmodern Legal Feminism*. New York: Routledge.

Fry, Christopher M. (1988) *Sartre and Hegel: The Variations of an Enigma in "L'Etre et le Néant."* Bonn: Bouvier.

Frye, Marilyn. (1990) "History and Responsibility." In Al-Hibri and Simons, pp. 300–304.

Fuchs, Jo-Ann P. (1980) "Female Eroticism in *The Second Sex.*" *Feminist Studies* 6 (2) (Summer): 304–13. Reprinted in a revised version under the name of Jo-Ann Pilardi, as "Female Eroticism in the Works of Simone de Beauvoir," in *The Thinking Muse*, ed. Jeffner Allen and Iris Marion Young (Bloomington: Indiana University Press, 1989).

Fuss, Diana (1988) "Reading Like a Feminist." *Differences* 1 (2): 77–92.

———. (1989) *Essentially Speaking: Feminism, Nature & Difference.* New York: Routledge.

Fynsk, Christopher. (1986) *Heidegger: Thought and Historicity.* Ithaca: Cornell University Press.

Gadamer, Hans-Georg. (1976) *Hegel's Dialectic: Five Hermeneutical Studies.* Translated by P. Christopher Smith. New Haven: Yale University Press.

———. (1977) *Philosophical Hermeneutics.* Translated by David E. Linge. Berkeley: University of California Press.

Gallop, Jane. (1982) *The Daughter's Seduction: Feminism and Psychoanalysis.* Ithaca: Cornell University Press.

———. (1985) *Reading Lacan.* Ithaca: Cornell University Press.

Gasché, Rodolphe. (1986) *The Tain of the Mirror: Derrida and the Philosophy of Reflection.* Cambridge, Mass.: Harvard University Press.

Gatens, Moira. (1989) "Sex/Gender Distinction: A Reply to Plumwood." *Radical Philosophy* 53 (Autumn): 54–55.

———. (1991a) "A Critique of the Sex/Gender Distinction." In *A Reader in Feminist Knowledge*, ed. Sneja Gunew. London: Routledge. Originally published in *Beyond Marxism? Interventions after Marx*, ed. J. Allen and P. Patton (NSW: Intervention Publications, 1983).

———. (1991b) *Feminism and Philosophy: Perspectives on Difference and Equality.* Bloomington: Indiana University Press.

Gates, Henry Louis. (1988) "Significant Others." *Contemporary Literature* 29 (4): 606–22.

Gellrich, Michelle. (1988) *Tragedy and Theory: The Problem of Conflict since Aristotle.* Princeton: Princeton University Press.

Gerassi, John. (1976) Interview with Beauvoir, "*The Second Sex* 25 Years Later." *Society* 13 (2) (Jan/Feb): 79–85.

Gilbert, Sandra. (1980) "Costumes of the Mind: Transvestism as Metaphor in Modern Literature." *Critical Inquiry* 7 (2) (Winter): 391–417.

Goheen, R. F. (1951) *The Imagery of Sophocles' Antigone.* Princeton: Princeton University Press.

Graybeal, Jean. (1990) *Language and the "Feminine" in Nietzsche and Heidegger.* Bloomington and Indianapolis: Indiana University Press.

Greer, Germaine. (1971) *The Female Eunuch.* London: Paladin. 1971.

Greisch, Jean. (1987) "Ethics and Ontology: Some Hypocritical Reflections." *Irish Philosophical Journal* 4 (1 & 2): 64–75.

Grosz, Elizabeth. (1989) *Sexual Subversions: Three French Feminists.* Sydney: Allen & Unwin.

———. (1990a) "Conclusion: A Note on Essentialism and Difference." Feminist Knowledge: Critique and Construct, ed. Sneja Gunew. London: Routledge, pp. 332–44.

————. (1990b) *Jacques Lacan: A Feminist Introduction*. London: Routledge.

————. (1993) "Bodies and Knowledge: Feminism and the Crisis of Reason." In *Feminist Epistemologies*, ed. Linda Alcoff and Elizabeth Potter. New York: Routledge, pp. 187–210.

Haar, Michel. (1993a) "The Enigma of Everydayness." In *Reading Heidegger: Commemorations*, ed. John Sallis. Bloomington and Indianapolis: Indiana University Press.

————. (1993b) *The Song of the Earth: Heidegger and the Grounds of the History of Being*. Translated by Reginald Lily. Bloomington and Indianapolis: Indiana University Press. Originally published as *Le chant de la terre* (Paris: l'Herne, 1985).

Harding, Sandra. (1986) *The Science Question in Feminism*. Ithaca: Cornell University Press.

————. (1989) "The Instability of the Analytical Categories of Feminist Theory." In *Feminist Theory in Practice and Process*, ed. Michelle Malson. Chicago: Chicago University Press. Originally published in *Signs* 11 (4) (Summer 1986): 645–66.

Haraway, Donna. (1989) *Primate Visions: Gender, Race and Nature in the World of Modern Science*. New York: Routledge, 1989.

————. (1991) *Simians, Cyborgs, and Women: the Reinvention of Nature*. New York: Routledge.

Harris, Angela P. (1991) "Race and Essentialism in Feminist Legal Theory." In *Feminist Legal Theory*, ed. Katharine T. Bartlett and Rosanne Kennedy. Boulder: Westview Press.

Heath, Jane. (1989) *Simone de Beauvoir*. New York: Harvester Wheatsheaf.

Hederman, Mark Patrick. (1980) "De l'interdiction a l'écoute." In *Heidegger et le question de dieu*, ed. Richard Kearney and J. S. O'Leary. Grasset: Paris.

Hegel, Georg W. F. (1952) *Hegel's Philosophy of Right*. Translated by T. Knox. Oxford: Clarendon Press.

————. (1955) *Hegel's Lectures on the History of Philosophy*. Vol. 1. Edited and translated by E. S. Haldane. London: Routledge & Kegan Paul.

————. (1962) *Hegel on Tragedy*, ed. Anne and Henry Paolucci. New York: Doubleday.

————. (1970) *Philosophy of Nature*. Vol. 3. Edited and translated by M. J. Petry. London: Allen & Unwin.

————. (1974) *Aesthetics: Lectures on Fine Art*. 3 vols. Translated by T. M. Knox. Oxford: Clarendon Press.

————. (1975) *Lectures on the Philosophy of World History*. Translated by H. B. Nisbet. Cambridge: University Press.

————. (1988) *Lectures on the Philosophy of Religion*. Edited by Peter C. Hodgson. Translated by R.F. Brown et.al. Berkeley: University of California Press.

————. (1979) *Phenomenology of Spirit*. Translated by A. V. Miller. Oxford: Clarendon Press. *Phänomenologie des Geistes*, ed. J. Hoffmeister (Hamburg: Felix Meiner, 1952).

Heidegger, Martin (1957a) *Holzwege*. Frankfurt: Vittorio Klostermann.

————. (1957b) *Identität und Differenz*. Pfullingen: Günther Neske.

————. (1959) *Unterwegs zur Sprache*. Pfullingen: Günther Neske, pp. 241–68.

————. (1969) "Time and Being." In *On Time and Being*. Translated by Joan Stambaugh. New York: Harper & Row. "Zeit und Sein," in *Zur Sache des Denkens* (Tübingen: Max Niemeyer, 1969).

———. (1974) "The Principle of Identity" in *Identity and Difference*. Translated by Joan Stambaugh. New York: Harper & Row. (includes the German text *"Der Satz der Identität"*).

———. (1975a) "Building Dwelling Thinking." In *Poetry, Language, Thought*. Translated by Albert Hofstadter. New York: Harper & Row. "Bauen Wohnen Denken," *Vorträge und Aufsätze* (Pfullingen: Günther Neske, 1978).

———. (1975b) "The Origin of the Work of Art." In *Poetry, Language, Thought*. Translated by A. Hofstadter. New York: Harper & Row. *Der Ursprung des Kunstwerkes* (Stuttgart: Reclam, 1982).

———. (1975c) "The Way Back into the Ground of Metaphysics." Translated by Walter Kaufmann. *Existentialism from Dostoevsky to Sartre*, ed. Walter Kaufmann. New York: New American Library.

———. (1977) "The Question concerning Technology." In *The Question concerning Technology and Other Essays*, New York: Harper & Row. "Die Frage nach der Technik," in *Vorträge und Aufsätze* (Pfullingen: Günther Neske, 1978).

———. (1978) "The End of Philosophy and the Task of Thinking." In *Martin Heidegger: Basic Writings*, ed. D. F. Krell. London: Routledge & Kegan Paul. *Zur Sache des Denkens* (Tübingen: Max Niemeyer, 1969).

———. (1980) *Being and Time*. Translated by John Macquarrie and Edward Robinson. Oxford: Basil Blackwell. *Sein und Zeit* (Tübingen: Max Niemeyer, 1984).

———. (1981) *Nietzsche*. Vol. 1: "The Will to Power as Art." Translated by David Farrell Krell. London: Routledge & Kegan Paul. *Nietzsche*, Erster Band (Pfulingen: Günther Neske, 1961).

———. (1982a) *Basic Problems of Phenomenology*. Translated by A. Hofstadter. Bloomington: Indiana University Press. *Die Grundprobleme der Phänomenologie* (Frankfurt: Vittorio Klostermann, 1978).

———. (1982b) *Nietzsche*. Vol. 4: "Nihilism." Translated by Frank A. Capuzzi, ed. David Farrel Krell. London: Harper & Row.

———. (1982c) "The Way to Language." In *On the Way to Language*. Translated by Peter D. Hertz. New York: Harper & Row. "Der Weg zur Sprache," in *Gesamtausgabe* Vol. 12, (Frankfurt: Vittorio Klostermann, 1985a).

———. (1984a) *Early Greek Thinking: The Dawn of Western Philosophy*. Translated by David Farrell Krell and Frank A. Capuzzi. San Francisco: Harper & Row.

———. (1984b) *The Metaphysical Foundations of Logic*. Translated by M. Heim. Bloomington: Indiana University Press. *Metaphysische Anfangsgrunde der Logik im Ausgang von Leibniz* (Frankfurt: Vittorio Klostermann, 1978).

———. (1985b) *History of the Concept of Time*. Translated by T. Kisiel. Bloomington: Indiana University Press. *Prolegomena zur Geschichte des Zeitbegriffs*, (Frankfurt: Vittorio Klostermann, 1979).

———. (1987) *Introduction to Metaphysics*. Translated by Ralph Manheim. New Haven: Yale University Press. *Einführung in die Metaphysik* (Tübingen: Niemeyer, 1953).

———. (1992) *The Concept of Time*. Translated by William McNeill. Oxford: Basil Blackwell. *Der Befriff der Zeit: Vortrag vor der Marburger Theologenschaft Juli 1924* (Max Niemeyer: Tübingen, 1989).

Heilbrun, Carolyn.(1988) *Writing a Woman's Life*. New York: Ballantine Books.

Hester, D. A. (1971) "Sophocles the Unphilosophical: A Study in the *Antigone*." Mnemosyne, (4th series) 24 (1): 177–78.

Hirsch, Marianne, and Evelyn Fox Keller. (1990) *Conflicts in Feminism*. New York: Routledge.

Hirsh, Elizabeth. (forthcoming, 1994) "Back in Analysis: How To Do Things with Irigaray." In *Engaging with Irigaray*, ed. Carolyn Burke, Naomi Schor, and Margaret Whitford. New York: Columbia University Press.

Hoffman, Piotr. (1983) "Hegel on the Life and Death Struggle." In *The Human Self and the Life and Death Struggle*. Gainsville: University Presses of Florida.

Hölderlin, Friedrich. (1988) "Remarks on Antigone." In *Essays and Letters on Theory*, ed. T. Pfau. Albany: State University of New York Press.

Holtby, Winifred. (1978) *Virginia Woolf: A Critical Memoir*. Chicago: Academy Press Limited.

hooks, bell. (1990) "Feminism: A Transformational Politic." In *Theoretical Perspectives on Sexual Difference*, ed. Deborah L. Rhode. New Haven: Yale University Press.

———. (1991) "Sisterhood: Political Solidarity between Women." In *A Reader in Feminist Knowledge*, ed. Sneja Gunew.

Husserl, Edmund. (1977) *Cartesian Meditations: An Introduction to Phenomenology*. Translated by Dorion Cairns. The Hague: Martinus Nijhoff.

Hyppolite, Jean. (1974) *Genesis and Structure in Hegel's Phenomenology of Spirit*. Translated by Samuel Cherniak and John Heckman. Evanston: Northwestern University Press. *Genèse et structure de la* Phénoménologie de l'Esprit *de Hegel*, (Paris: Aubier, Editions Montaigne, 1946).

Irigaray, Luce. (1977) Interview by Diana Adlam and Couze Venn, "Women's Exile." Translated by Couze Venn. *Ideology and Consciousness* (1): 62–76.

———. (1983) *L'oubli de l'air*. Paris: Minuit. 1983.

———. (1985a) *This Sex Which Is Not One*. Translated by Catherine Porter with Carolyn Burke. New York: Cornell University Press. *Ce sexe qui n'en est pas un* (Paris: Minuit, 1977).

———. (1985b) "Le v(i)ol de la lettre." In *Parler n'est jamais neutre*, Paris: Minuit.

———. (1985c) *Speculum of the Other Woman*. Translated by Gillian C. Gill. Ithaca: Cornell University Press. *Speculum de l'autre femme* (Paris: Editions Minuit, 1974).

———. (1986) "The Fecundity of the Caress." Translated by C. Burke. In *Face to Face with Levinas*, ed. R. Cohen. Albany: State University of New York. "Fécondité de la caresse: lecture de Levinas, *Totalité et infini*, section IV, B 'Phénoménologie de l'éros,'" in *Éthique de la différence sexuelle* (Paris: Minuit, 1984). Originally published in *Exercices de la patience* 5 (Spring 1983): 119–37.

———. (1989a) *Le temps de la différence*. Paris: Librairie Générale Française.

———. (1989b) "Sorcerer Love: A Reading of Plato's Symposium, Diotima's Speech." Translated by Eleanor H. Kuykendall. *Hypatia* 3 (3) (Winter): 32–44. Also translated in Irigaray, 1993a.

———. (1991a) *The Irigaray Reader*, ed. M. Whitford. Oxford: Basil Blackwell.

———. (1991b) *Marine Lover of Friedrich Nietzsche*. Translated by Gillian Gill. New York: Columbia University Press. *Amante marine. De Friedrich Nietzsche* (Paris: Minuit, 1980).

———. (1991c) "Questions to Emmanuel Levinas." Translated by Margaret Whitford. In *Re-Reading Levinas*, ed. R. Bernasconi and S. Critchley. Bloomington: Indiana University Press.

————. (1992a) *Elemental Passions*. Translated by Joanne Collie and Judith Still. New York: Routledge. *Passions élémentaires* (Paris: Minuit, 1982).

————. (1992b) *J'aime à toi: esquisse d'une félicité dan l'histoire*. Paris: Grasset.

————. (1993a) *An Ethics of Sexual Difference*. Translated by Carolyn Burke and Gillian Gill. Ithaca: Cornell University Press. *Éthique de la différence sexuelle* (Paris: Minuit, 1984).

————. (1993b) *Je, Tu, Nous: Toward a Culture of Difference*. Translated by Alison Martin. London: Routledge. *Je, tu, nous* (Grasset & Fasquelle, 1990).

————. (1993c) *Sexes and Genealogies*. Translated by Gillian C. Gill. New York: Columbia Press. *Sexes et Parentés* (Paris: Minuit, 1987).

Jacobus, Mary (1986) *Reading Woman: Essays in Feminist Criticism*. New York: Routledge.

Jaggar, Alison M. (1983) *Feminist Politics and Human Nature*. Brighton, Sussex: Harvester Press.

————. (1990) "Sexual Difference and Sexual Equality." In *Theoretical Perspectives on Sexual Difference*, ed. Deborah L. Rhode. New Haven: Yale University Press.

Jaggar, Alison, and William McBride. (1990) "Reproduction as Male Ideology." In Al-Hibri and Simons, pp. 249–69.

Jardine, Alice A. (1985) *Gynesis: Configurations of Woman and Modernity*. Ithaca: Cornell University Press.

Jardine, Alice A., and Anne M. Menke. (1991) *Shifting Scenes: Interviews on Women, Writing, and Politics in Post-68 France*. New York: Columbia University Press.

Jardine, Alice, and Paul Smith. (1987) *Men in Feminism*. New York: Methuen.

Jehlen, Myra. (1981) "Archimedes and the Paradox of Feminist Criticism." *Signs* 6 (4) (Summer): 575–601.

Jordanova, L. J. (1980) "Natural Facts: A historical perspective on science and sexuality." In *Nature, Culture and Gender*, ed. Carol MacCormack and Marilyn Strathern. Cambridge: Cambridge University Press.

Kamuf, Peggy. (1980) "Writing like a Woman." In *Women and Language in Literature and Society*, ed. S. McConnell-Ginet, R. Borker, and Nelly Furman. New York: Praeger.

————. (1982) "Replacing Feminist Criticism." *Diacritics* 12 (2) (Summer): 42–47.

————. (1988) *Signature Pieces: On the Institution of Authorship*. Ithaca: Cornell University Press.

Kamuf, Peggy, and Nancy K. Miller. (1990) "Parisian Letter: Between Feminism and Deconstruction." In Hirsch and Fox Keller, pp. 121–30.

Kaplan, E. Ann. (1983) "Is the Gaze Male?" In *Powers of Desire*, ed. Ann Snitow, Christine Stansell, and Sharon Thompson. New York: Monthly Review Press.

Kaplan, Cora. (1986) *Sea Changes: Culture and Feminism*. London: Verso.

Kaufmann, Dorothy. (1986) "Simone de Beauvoir: Questions of Difference and Generation." *Yale French Studies* (72): 121–31.

————. (1989) "Autobiographical Intersexts: Les mots de deux enfants rangés." *L'esprit créateur* 29 (4) (Winter): 21–32.

Kaufmann-McCall, Dorothy. (1979) "Simone de Beauvoir, *The Second Sex*, and Jean-Paul Sartre." *Signs: Journal of Women in Culture and Society* 5 (2): 209–23.

Kaufmann-McCall, Dorothy. (1983) "Politics of Difference: The Women's Movement in France from May 1968 to Mitterand." *Signs*, 9 (2): 282–93.

Keefe, Terry. (1983) *Simone de Beauvoir: A Study of Her Writings*. London: Harrap.

Kelly, George Armstrong. (1966) "Notes on Hegel's 'Lordship and Bondage,'" *The Review of Metaphysics* (June): 780–802. Reprinted in *Hegel: A Collection of Critical Essays*, ed. Alisdair McIntyre (Notre Dame: University of Notre Dame, 1976).

———. (1969) *Idealism, Politics and History*. Cambridge: Cambridge University Press.

Keyes, C. D. (1972) "An Evaluation of Levinas' Critique of Heidegger." *Research in Phenomenology* 2: 121–42.

Knox, Bernard. (1983) *The Heroic Temper: Studies in Sophoclean Tragedy*. Berkeley: University of California Press.

Kojève, Alexandre. (1969) *Introduction to the Reading of Hegel*. Translated by James H. Nichols, Jr. New York: Basic Books. *Introduction à la lecture de Hegel* (Paris: Gallimard, 1947).

Krell, David. (1986) *Intimations of Mortality: Time, Truth, and Finitude in Heidegger's Thinking of Being*. University Park: Pennsylvania State University Press.

Kristeva, Julia. (1980) "Woman Can Never Be Defined." In *New French Feminisms*, ed. E. Marks and I. de Courtivron. Brighton Sussex: Harvester Press.

———. (1986) "Women's Time." Translated by Seán Hand. In *The Kristeva Reader*, ed. Toril Moi. Oxford: Basil Blackwell. "Les temps des femmes," 33/34 *Cahiers de recherche de sciences des textes et documents* 5 (Winter 1979): 5–19. Previously translated by Alice Jardine and Harry Blake in *Signs: Journal of Women in Culture and Society* 7 (1) (Autumn 1981): 13–35. Reprinted in *Feminist Theory: A Critique of Ideology*, ed. N. O. Keohane et. al. (Brighton, Sussex: Harvester Press, 1982).

———. (1987) *Tales of Love*. Translated by Leon S. Roudiez. New York: Columbia University Press. *Histories d'amour* (Denoël, 1983).

Lacan, Jacques. (1985), *Écrits: A Selection*. Translated by Alan Sheridan. London: Tavistock Publications. *Écrits*. (Paris: Seuil, 1966).

———. (1986) *The Four Fundamental Concepts of Psycho-Analysis*, ed. Jacques-Alain Miller, translated by Alan Sheridan. Harmondsworth, Middlesex: Penguin. *Le Séminaire de Jacques Lacan*, Livre XI, Les quatre concepts fondamentaux de la psychanalyse 1964, ed. Jacques-Alain Miller (Paris: Seuil, 1973).

———. (1991a) "The Purloined Letter." *The Seminar of Jacques Lacan*, ed. Jacques-Alain Miller, Book II, The Ego in Freud's Theory and in the Technique of Psychoanalysis, ed. Jacques-Alain Miller, translated by Sylvana Tomaselli. New York: W. W. Norton. "La lettre volée," *Le séminaire de Jacques Lacan*, Livre II, Le moi dans la théorie de Freud et dans la technique de la psychanalyse 1954–1955, ed. Jacques-Alain Miller (Paris: Seuil, 1978).

———. (1991b) *The Seminar of Jacques Lacan*, Book I, Freud's Papers on Technique, ed. Jacques Alain-Miller, translated by John Forrester. New York: W. W. Norton: *Le séminaire de Jacques Lacan*, Livre I, Les écrits techniques de Freud 1953–1954, ed. Jacques-Alain Miller (Paris: Seuil, 1975).

———. (1992) *The Seminar of Jacques Lacan*, Book VII, ed. Jacques-Alain Miller. New York: W. W. Norton.

Lacoue-Labarthe, Philippe. (1990) *Heidegger, Art and Politics: The Fiction of the Political*. Translated by Chris Turner. Oxford: Basil Blackwell.

Laqueur, Thomas. (1990) *Making Sex: Body and Gender from the Greeks to Freud*. Cambridge, Mass.: Harvard University Press.

Laruelle, François, ed. (1980) *Textes pour Emmanuel Levinas*. Paris: Jean-Michel Place.

Le Doeuff, Michèle. (1980) "Simone de Beauvoir and Existentialism." *Feminist Studies* 6 (2) Summer: 277–89.

———. (1991) *Hipparchia's Choice: An Essay concerning Women, Philosophy, etc.* Translated by Trista Selous. Oxford: Basil Blackwell. *L'Etude et le rouet*, (Paris: Seuil, 1989).

Lesky, Albin. (1978) *Greek Tragedy.* Translated by H. A. Frankfort. New York: Barnes & Noble Books.

Levinas, Emmanuel. (1962) "Transcendance et hauteur." *Bulletin de la Société française de Philosophie* 7: 89–113.

———. (1969) "Judaism and the feminine element." Translated by E. Wyschogrod. *Judaism* 18 (1): 30–38. Originally published as "Le judaïsme et le féminin," in *L'Age Nouveau* (1960). Reprinted in Levinas, *Difficile liberté: essais sur le Judaïsme* (Paris: Albin Michel, 1963).

———. (1973) *The Theory of Intuition in Husserl's Phenomenology.* Translated by André Orianne. Evanston: Northwestern University Press. *Thèorie de l'intuition dans la phénoménologie de Husserl* (Paris: Vrin, 1984).

———. (1966) "The Trace of the Other." Translated by Alphonso Lingis. In *Deconstruction in Context*, ed. Mark C. Taylor. Chicago and London: University of Chicago Press, 1986. "La trace de l'autre," in *En découvrant l'existence avec Husserl et Heidegger* (Paris: Vrin, 1982). Originally published in *Tijdschrift voor Filosofie* (1963).

———. (1978a) *Existence and Existents.* Translated by Alphonso Lingis. The Hague: Martinus Nijhoff. *De l'existence à l'existant* (Paris: Vrin, 1984).

———. (1978b) "Signature." Translated by Adriaan Peperzak. *Research in Phenomenology* 8: 175–89. Reprinted in *Difficult Freedom: Essays on Judaism*, translated by Seán Hand (Baltimore: Johns Hopkins University Press, 1990). *Difficile liberté* (Paris: Albin Michel, 1976).

———. (1979) *Totality and Infinity: An Essay on Exteriority.* Translated by Alphonso Lingis, The Hague: Martinus Nijhoff. *Totalité et infini: essai sur l'extériorité* (La Haye: Martinus Nijhoff, 1980).

———. (1981) *Otherwise Than Being or Beyond Essence.* Translated by Alphonso Lingis. The Hague: Martinus Nijhoff. *Autrement qu'être ou au-delà l'essence*, 2nd edition (La Haye: Martinus Nijhoff, 1978).

———. (1982) *En découvrant l'existence avec Husserl et Heidegger.* Paris: Vrin.

———. (1984) "Ethics of the Infinite." *Dialogues with Contemporary Continental Thinkers.* Presented by Richard Kearney. Manchester: Manchester University Press. Reprinted in *Face to Face with Levinas*, ed. Richard A. Cohen (Albany: State University of New York Press, 1986).

———. (1985) *Ethics and Infinity: Conversations with Philippe Nemo.* Translated by Richard Cohen. Pittsburgh: Duquesne University Press. *Éthique et infini: dialogues avec Philippe Nemo* (Paris: Arthème Fayard et Radio France, 1982).

———. (1987) *Time and the Other.* Translated by R. Cohen. Pittsburgh: Duquesne University Press. *Temps et l'autre* (St. Clement: Fata Morgana, 1979). Originally published in Jean Wahl's *Le Choix, Le Monde, L'Existence* (Grenoble-Paris: Arthaud, 1947).

———. (1989a) "As If Consenting to Horror." Translated by Paula Wissig. *Critical Inquiry* 15 (2) (Winter): 485–88. "*Comme consentement à l'horrible.*" In *Le Nouvel Observateur* 22–28 Janvier (1988).

————. (1989b) "Interview with Edith Wyschogrod: December 31, 1982." *Philosophy & Theology* 4 (2) (Winter 1989): 105–18.

————. (1990a) "And God Created Woman." In *Nine Talmudic Readings*. Translated by Annette Aronowicz. Bloomington: Indiana University Press. "Et Dieu créa la femme," in *Du sacré au saint, cinq nouvelles lectures talmudiques* (Paris: Minuit, 1977).

————. (1990b) *Nine Talmudic Readings*. Translated by Annete Aronowicz. Bloomington: Indiana University Press. *Quatre lectures talmudiques* (Paris: Minuit, 1968); and *Du sacré au saint: cinq nouvelles lectures talmudiques* (Paris: Minuit, 1977).

————. (1990c) "Reflections on the Philosophy of Hitlerism." Translated by Seán Hand. *Critical Inquiry* 17 (1) (Autumn): 62–71: "Quelques réflexions sur la philosophie de L'Hitlérism," Esprit 2 (26) 1934: 199–208. Also published in *Emmanuel Lévinas,* ed. Catherine Chalier and Miguel Abensour (Paris: L'Herne, 1991).

Lindsay, Cecile. (1989) "L'Un e(s)t l'Autre: The Future of Differences in French Feminism." *L'esprit créateur* 29 (3) (Fall): 21–35.

Llewelyn, John. (1986) *Derrida on the Threshold of Sense*. London: Macmillan.

————. (1988) "Jewgreek or Greekjew." *The Collegium Phaenomenologicum: The First Ten Years*, ed. John C. Sallis, Giuseppina Moneta, and Jacques Taminiaux. Boston: Kluwer Academic Publishers.

————. (1991) *The Middle Voice of Ecological Conscience: A Chiasmic Reading of Responsibility in the Neighborhood of Levinas, Heidegger and Others*. New York: St. Martin's Press.

Lloyd, Geneveive. (1986) *The Man of Reason: "Male" and "Female" in Western Philosophy*. Minneapolis: University of Minnesota Press.

Mackenzie, Catriona. (1986) "Simone de Beauvoir: Philosophy and/or the Body." In *Feminist Challenges*, ed. Carole Pateman and Elizabeth Gross. Boston: Northeastern University Press.

MacKinnon, Catharine A. (1987) *Feminism Unmodified: Discourses on Life and Law*. Cambridge, Mass.: Harvard University Press.

Manning, Robert John Sheffler. (1993) *Interpreting Otherwise than Heidegger: Emmanuel Levinas's Ethics as First Philosophy*. Pittsburg: Duquesne University Press.

Marx, Werner. (1971) *Heidegger and the Tradition*. Translated by Theodore Kisiel and Murray Greene. Evanston: Northwestern University Press.

McCumber, John. (1989) *Poetic Interaction: Language, Freedom, Reason*. Chicago: University of Chicago Press.

Meese, Elizabeth A. (1990) *(Ex)Tensions: Re-figuring Feminist Criticism*. Urbana and Chicago: University of Illinois Press.

Merleau-Ponty, Maurice. (1964) *Sense and Non-Sense*. Translated by Hubert L. Dreyfus and Patricia Allen Dreyfus. Evanston: Northwestern University Press.

Messer-Davidow, Ellen. (1989) "The Philosophical Bases of Feminist Literary Criticisms." In *Gender & Theory: Dialogues on Feminist Criticism*, ed. L. Kauffman. Oxford: Basil Blackwell.

Miller, Nancy. (1982) "The Text's Heroine: A Feminist Critic and Her Fictions." *Diacritics*, 12 (2) (Summer): 48–53.

————. (1991) *Getting Personal: Feminist Occasions and Other Autobiographical Acts*. New York: Routledge.

Millett, Kate. (1971) *Sexual Politics*. London: Abacus, 1971.

Millot, Catherine. (1990) "The Feminine Superego," in *The Woman in Question: m/f*, ed. Parveen Adams and Elizabeth Cowie. Cambridge, Mass.: MIT Press.
Mills, Patricia Jagentowitz. (1987) *Woman, Nature and Psyche*. New Haven: Yale University Press.
Mitchell, Julliet. (1972) *Woman's Estate*. New York: Pantheon Books.
Moi, Toril. (1985) *Sexual/Textual Politics: Feminist Literary Theory*. London: Methuen.
———. (1990a) *Feminist Theory & Simone de Beauvoir*, Oxford: Basil Blackwell.
———. (1990b) "Simone de Beauvoir: The Making of an Intellectual Woman." *The Yale Journal of Criticism* 4 (1): 1–23.
———. (1992) "Ambiguity and Alienation in *The Second Sex*," *Boundary 2* 19 (2): 96–112.
Moore, Suzanne. (1988) "Getting a Bit of the Other." In *Male Order: Unwrapping Masculinity*, ed. Rowena Chapman and Jonathan Rutherford. London: Lawrence & Wishart.
Morris, Phyllis Sutton. (1980) "Self-deception: Sartre's resolution of the Paradox." In *Jean-Paul Sartre: Contemporary Approaches to His Philosophy*, ed. Hugh J. Silverman and Frederick A. Elliston. Pittsburgh: Duquesne University Press.
Niel, Henri. (1947) "L'Interprétation de Hegel." In *Critique* 3 (18) (November):426–37.
Nell, Onora. (1980) "How Do We Know Opportunities Are Equal?" In *Women and Philosophy: Toward a Theory of Liberation*, ed. Carol C. Gould and Marx W. Wartofsky. New York: G. P. Putnam's Sons.
Nietzsche, Friedrich. (1969) *On the Genealogy of Morals and Ecce Homo*. Translated by Walter Kaufmann and R. J. Hollingdale, ed. Walter Kaufmann. New York: Random House.
Nikolchina, Miglena I. (1993) "Meaning and Matricide: Reading Woolf via Kristeva." Ph.D. diss., University of Western Ontario, London, Ontario.
Nye, Andrea. (1988) *Feminist Theory and the Philosophies of Man*. London: Croom Helm.
———. (1989) "The Hidden Host: Irigaray and Diotima at Plato's Symposium." *Hypatia* 3 (3) (Winter): 45–61.
Oakley, Ann. (1972) *Sex, Gender and Society*. New York: Harper & Row.
O'Brien, Mary. (1981) *The Politics of Reproduction*. Boston: Routledge & Kegan Paul.
O'Connor, Noreen. (1980) "Being and the Good: Heidegger and Levinas." *Philosophical Studies*, 27: 212–20.
Okely, Judith. (1986) *Simone de Beauvoir*. London: Virago.
Okin, Susan Moller. (1990) "Thinking Like a Woman." In *Theoretical Perspectives on Sexual Difference*, ed. Deborah L. Rhode. New Haven: Yale University Press.
Oliver, Kelly. (1993) *Reading Kristeva: Unraveling the Double-bind*. Bloomington and Indianapolis: Indiana University Press.
Ortner, Sherry B. (1993) "Is Female to Male as Nature Is to Culture?" In *Women and Values: Readings in Recent Feminist Philosophy*, ed. Marilyn Pearsall. Belmont, Calif.: Wadsworth. Reprinted from *Woman, Culture, and Society*, ed. Michelle Zimbalist Rosaldo and Louise Lamphere (Stanford University Press, 1974).
Patterson, Yolanda. (1986) "Simone de Beauvoir and the Demystification of Motherhood." YFS: 87–106.
Peperzak, Adriaan. (1992) *To the Other: An Introduction to the Philosophy of Emmanuel Levinas*. West Lafayette: Purdue University Press.
Plato. (1970) *Republic* Book II. The Loeb Classical Library, translated by Paul Shorey. Plato VI. Cambridge, Mass.: Harvard University Press.

————. (1975) *Symposium*. The Loeb Classical Library, translated by W. R. M. Lamb. Plato III. Cambridge, Mass.: Harvard University Press.

————. (1977) *Theaetetus*. The Loeb Classical Library, translated by Harold North Fowler. Plato VII. Cambridge, Mass.: Harvard University Press.

Plaza, Monique. (1978) "'Phallomorphic Power' and the Psychology of 'Woman.'" Translated by Miriam David and Jill Hodges, *Ideology and Consciousness* 4 (Autumn): 4–36.

Plumwood, Val. (1989) "Do We Need a Sex/Gender Distinction?" *Radical Philosophy* 51 (Spring): 2–11.

Pöggeler, Otto. (1989) *Martin Heidegger's Path of Thinking*. Translated by Daniel Magurshank and Sigmund Barber. Atlantic Highlands, N. J.: Humanities Press International.

Poovey, Mary. (1988) "Feminism and Deconstruction." *Feminist Studies* 14 (1) (Spring): 51–65.

Portuges, Catherine. (1986) "Attachment and Separation in *The Memoirs of a Dutiful Daughter*." *Yale French Studies* 72: 107–118.

Poster, Mark. (1975) *Existential Marxism in Postwar France: From Sartre to Althusser*. New Jersey: Princeton University Press.

Pritchard, Annie. (1992) "Antigone's Mirrors: Reflections on Moral Madness." *Hypatia: A Journal of Feminist Philosophy* 7 (3) (Summer): 77–93.

Radhakrishnan, R. (1989) "Feminist Historiography and Post-Structuralist Thought: Intersections and Departures." In *The Difference Within: Feminism and Critical Theory*, ed. Elizabeth Meese and Alice Parker. Amsterdam and Philadelphia: John Benjamins Publishing Company.

Raven, Heidi. (1988) "Has Hegel Anything to Say to Feminists?" *The Owl of Minerva* 19 (2): 149–68.

Rhode, Deborah L., ed. (1990) *Theoretical Perspectives on Sexual Difference*. New Haven, Yale University Press.

Rhode, Deborah L. (1991) "Feminist Critical Theories." In *Feminist Legal Theory: Readings in Law and Gender*, ed. Katharine T. Bartlett and Rosanne Kennedy. Boulder: Westview Press.

Rich, Adrienne. (1986) *Of Woman Born: Motherhood as Experience and Institution*. New York: W. W. Norton and Company.

Riley, Denise. (1988) *Am I That Name?: Feminism and the Category of 'Women' in History*. New York: Macmillan.

Robbins, Jill. (1991) *Prodigal Son/Elder Brother: Interpretation and Alterity in Augustine, Petrarch, Kafka, Levinas*. Chicago: University of Chicago Press.

————. (1993) "*Visage, Figure*: Speech and Murder in Levinas' *Totality and Infinity*." In *Critical Encounters: Reference and Responsibility in Deconstructive Writing*, ed. Cathy Caruth and Deborah Esch. New Brunswick, N.J.: Rutgers University Press, 1994.

Robinson, Sally. (1991) *Gender and Self-Representation in Contemporary Women's Fiction*. Albany: State University of New York Press.

Rose, Jacqueline. (1983) Introduction II, *Feminine Sexuality: Jacques Lacan and the école freudienne*, ed. Juliet Mitchell and Jacqueline Rose, translated by Jacqueline Rose. New York: W. W. Norton and Company.

Rubin, Gayle. (1975) "The Traffic in Women: Notes on the 'Political Economy' of Sex." In *Toward an Anthropology of Women*, ed. R. R. Reiter. New York: Monthly Review Press.

Ruddick, Sara. (1980) "Maternal Thinking." *Feminist Studies* 6 (2) (Summer): 342–67.
———. (1989) *Maternal Thinking: Toward a Politics of Peace*, Boston: Beacon Press.
Russo, Salvatore. (1936) "Hegel's Theory of Tragedy." *Open Court* (50): 133–44.
Sallis, John. (1978) "The Origin of Heidegger's Thought." In *Radical Phenomenology: Essays in Honor of Martin Heidegger,* ed. John Sallis. Atlantic Highlands, N.J.: Humanities Press.
———. (1986) *Delimitations: Phenomenology and the End of Metaphysics*. Bloomington and Indianapolis: Indiana University Press.
———. (1990) *Echoes: After Heidegger*, Bloomington: Indiana University Press.
Sartre, Jean-Paul. (1947) *Existentialism*. Translated by Bernard Frechtman. New York: Philosophical Library. *L'existentialisme est un humanisme* (Paris: Editions Nagel, 1970).
———. (1956) *Being and Nothingness*. Translated by Hazel Barnes. New York: Washington Square Press. *L'être et le néant* (Paris: Gallimard, 1943).
———. (1970) *Anti-Semite and Jew*. Translated by George Becker. New York: Schocken Books. *Reflexions sur la question juive* (Paris: Gallimard, 1954).
Sayers, Janet. (1986) *Sexual Contradictions: Psychology, Psychoanalysis, and Feminism*. London: Tavistock.
Schapiro, Meyer. (1968) "The Still Life as a Personal Object—A Note on Heidegger and Van Gogh." In *The Reach of Mind: Essays in Memory of Kurt Goldstein*. New York: Springer.
Schmidt, Dennis. (1988) *The Ubiquity of the Finite: Hegel, Heidegger, and the Entitlements of Philosophy*. Cambridge, Mass.: MIT Press.
Schor, Naomi. (1985) *Breaking the Chain: Women, Theory, and French Realist Fiction*. New York: Columbia University Press.
———. (1989) "This Essentialism Which Is Not One: Coming to Grips with Irigaray." *Differences* 1 (2) (Summer): 38–58.
Schroeder, William Ralph. (1984) *Sartre and His Predecessors*. London: Routledge.
Schürmann, Reiner. (1987) *Heidegger on Being and Acting: From Principles to Anarchy*. Translated by Christine-Marie Gros. Bloomington: Indiana University Press.
Schwarzer, Alice. (1984) *After the Second Sex: Conversations with Simone de Beauvoir*. Translated by Marianne Howarth. New York: Pantheon Books.
Scott, Joan W. (1986) "Gender as a Useful Category of Historical Analysis." *American Historical Review* 91 (3–4) (November): 1053–75.
———. (1988a) "Deconstructing Equality-versus-Difference: Or, the Uses of Poststructuralist Theory for Feminism." *Feminist Studies* 14 (1) (Spring): 33–50.
———. (1988b) *Gender and the Politics of History*. New York: Columbia University Press.
Segal, Charles. (1983) "*Antigone*: Death and Love, Hades and Dionysus." In *Oxford Readings in Greek Tragedy*, ed. Erich Segal. Oxford: Oxford University Press. Previously published in Charles Segal, *Tragedy and Civilization: An Interpretation of Sophocles* (Cambridge: Harvard University Press, 1981).
Segal, Lynne. (1987) *Is the Future Female? Troubled Thoughts on Contemporary Feminism*. London: Virago.
Seigfried, Charlene Haddock. (1990) "*Second Sex*: Second Thoughts." In Al-Hibri and Simons.
Showalter, Elaine. (1977) *A Literature of Their Own: British Women Novelists from Brontë to Lessing*. Princeton University Press.

———. (1982) "Comments on Jehlen's 'Archimedes and the Paradox of Feminist Criticism,'" *Signs* 8 (1) (Autumn): 160–64.

———. (1987) "Critical Cross-Dressing; Male Feminists and the Woman of the Year." In *Men in Feminism*, ed. Alice Jardine and Paul Smith. New York: Methuen.

———. (1989) "The Rise of Gender." In *Speaking of Gender*, ed. Elaine Showalter. New York: Routledge.

Silverman, Kaja. (1988) *The Acoustic Mirror: The Female Voice in Psychoanalysis and Cinema*. Bloomington and Indianapolis: Indiana University Press.

Simons, Margaret. (1983) "The Silencing of Simone de Beauvoir: Guess What's Missing from *The Second Sex*." *Women's Studies International Forum* 6 (5): 559–64.

———. (1986) "Beauvoir and Sartre: The Philosophical Relationship." *Yale French Studies* 72: 165–79.

———. (1990) "Introduction" to Beauvoir articles in Al-Hibri and Simons.

———. (1992) "Two Interviews with Simone De Beauvoir." In *Revaluing French Feminism: Critical Essays on Difference, Agency, & Culture*, ed. Nancy Fraser and Sandra Lee Bartky. Bloomington: Indiana University Press. Reprinted from *Hypatia* 3 (3) (Winter 1989): 11–27.

Singer, Linda. (1993) "Interpretation and Retrieval: Rereading Beauvoir." In *Erotic Welfare: Sexual Theory and Politics in the Age of the Epidemic*. New York: Routledge. Reprinted from *Women's Studies International Forum* 8 (3) (1985): 231–38, originally published in Al-Hibri and Simons, 1990.

Sophocles. (1928) *Antigone*, ed. Richard Jebb. Cambridge: Cambridge University Press.

———. (1954) "Antigone." Translated by Elizabeth Wyckoff. In *Sophocles I*, ed. David Grene and Richmond Lattimore. *The Complete Greek Tragedies*. Chicago: University of Chicago Press.

———. (1986) *Sophocles: The Theban Plays*. Translated by E. F. Watling. Harmondsworth, Middlesex: Penguin.

———. (1977) *Sophocles*. Vol. 1. The Loeb Classical Library, translated by F. Storr. Cambridge, Mass.: Harvard University Press.

Spacks, Patricia Ann Meyer. (1975) *The Female Imagination*. New York: Knopf.

Spelman, Elizabeth V. (1988) *Inessential Woman: Problems of Exclusion in Feminist Thought*. Boston: Beacon Press.

Spivak, Gayatri Chakravorty. (1989) "In a Word. Interview." *Differences* 1 (2) (Summer): 124–54. Reprinted in Gayatri Chakravorty Spivak, *Outside in the Teaching Machine*. (New York: Routledge, 1993).

———. (1984/5) "Criticism, Feminism and the Institution: An Interview with Gayatri Chakravorty Spivak," conducted by Elizabeth Gross. *Thesis Eleven* 10/11: 175–87.

Stanton, Domna. (1989) "Difference on Trial: A Critique of the Maternal Metaphor in Cixous, Irigaray and Kristeva." In *The Thinking Muse: Feminism and Modern French Philosophy*, ed. Jeffner Allen and Iris Marion Young. Bloomington: Indiana University Press. Also published in *Poetics of Gender*, ed. Nancy K. Miller (New York: Columbia University Press, 1986).

Stockton, Kathryn Bond. (1992) "Bodies and God: Poststructuralist Feminists Return to the Fold of Spiritual Materialism." *Boundary 2* 19 (2) (Summer): 113–49.

Stoller, Robert. (1968) *Sex and Gender*, 2 vols. New York: Jason Aronson.

Suleiman, Susan Rubin. (1989) "Simone de Beauvoir and the Writing Self." In *L'esprit créateur* 29 (4) (Winter): 42–51.

Szondi, Peter. (1986) "The Notion of the Tragic in Schelling, Hölderlin, and Hegel." In *On Textual Understanding and Other Essays*. Translated by Harvey Mendelsohn. Theory and History of Literature, vol. 15. Minneapolis: University of Minnesota Press.

Taminiaux, Jacques. (1978) "Heidegger and Husserl's *Logical Investigations*: In Remembrance of Heidegger's Last Seminar (Zähringen, 1973)," translated by Jeffrey Stevens. *Radical Phenomenology: Essays in Honor of Martin Heidegger*, ed. John Sallis. Atlantic Highlands, N.J.: Humanities Press.

———. (1993) "The Origin of 'The Origin of the Work of Art,'" In *Reading Heidegger: Commemorations*, ed. John Sallis. Bloomington and Indianapolis: Indiana University Press.

Tavor Bannet, Eve. (1989) *Structuralism and the Logic of Dissent: Barthes, Derrida, Foucault, Lacan*. Urbana and Chicago: University of Illinois Press.

Taylor, A. E. (1963) *Plato: The Man and His Work*. London: Methuen.

Taylor, Charles. (1975) *Hegel*. Cambridge: Cambridge University Press.

Theunissen, Michael. (1986) *The Other: Studies in the Social Ontology of Husserl, Heidegger, Sartre, and Buber*. Translated by Christopher McCann. Cambridge, Mass.: MIT Press.

Tuana, Nancy. (1990) "Re-fusing Nature/Nurture." In *Hypatia Reborn*, Bloomington: Indiana University Press.

Vernant, Jean-Pierre. (1970) "Greek Tragedy: Problems of Interpretation." In *The Languages of Criticism: The Structuralist Controversy*, ed. Richard Macksey and Eugenio Donato. Baltimore: Johns Hopkins University Press.

Vickers, Brian. (1973) *Towards Greek Tragedy: Drama, Myth, Society*. London: Longman. 1973.

Weedon, Chris. (1987) *Feminist Practice & Poststructuralist Theory*. Oxford: Basil Blackwell.

Whitbeck, Caroline. (1980) "Theories of Sex Difference." In *Women and Philosophy: Toward a Theory of Liberation*, ed. Carol C. Gould and Marx W. Wartofsky. New York: G. P. Putnam's Sons.

Whitford, Margaret. (1991) *Luce Irigaray: Philosophy in the Feminine*. London and New York: Routledge.

Whitmarsh, Anne. (1981) *Simone de Beauvoir and the Limits of Commitment*. Cambridge: Cambridge University Press.

Williams, Patricia J. (1991) "On Being the Object of Property." *Feminist Legal Theory*, ed. Katharine T. Bartlett and Rosanne Kennedy. Boulder: Westview Press.

Wittig, Monique. (1992) *The Straight Mind and Other Essays*. Boston: Beacon Press.

Wood, David. (1989) *The Deconstruction of Time*. Atlantic Highlands, N.J.: Humanities Press.

Woolf, Virginia (1981) *A Room of One's Own*. San Diego: Harcourt Brace Jovanovich.

Young, Iris Marion. (1985) "Humanism, Gynocentrism and Feminist Politics." In *Women's Studies International Forum* 8 (3): 231–48.

———. (1990) "Humanism, Gynocentrism and Feminist Politics." In Al-Hibri and Simons.

Zuckert, Catherine. (1991) "The Politics of Derridean Deconstruction." *Polity* 23 (3) (Spring): 335–56.

Index

99, 102; loyalty and politics, 99,
294 n.71
Body: and Antigone's duty to Polynices,
93; and essentialism, 11, 23, 25;
female, 83, 105, 108; Hegelian,
85–86, 83, 120; lived, 129;
maternal, 108, 152; and
nature/culture distinction, 43,
122; and place of women, 158;
and psychoanalysis, 258; and
science, 43; and women's writing,
27–31; and writing, 249, 251
Bowlby, Rachel, 36
Braidotti, Rosi, 36, 138, 241
Brother: irreplaceability of, 97–104
Burial: Polynices', by Antigone, 97,
103, 107; rites, 99, 289 n.28
Butler, Judith, 43, 175, 270 n.31,
270–71 n.32

Caress, 200, 203
Cartesian dualism, 133; Heidegger's
overcoming of, 187
Chicago, Judy, 23
Chodorow, Nancy, 39
Christian, Barbara, 11
Cixous, Hélène, 10, 29
Class: and feminism, 6–7, 8, 33, 45, 76
Clement, Catherine, 79
Cogito ergo sum: Descartes', 134
Community: in relation to family,
90–91; law of, 88; irony of,
108–12
Complicity: of feminism, 79; and
oppression, 68; of women, 14,
53, 68
Consciousness: ethical, 107;
dependent, 67, 70; in relation to
self–consciousness, 61, 70
Corporeality (see also Body): 85, 251
Cott, Nancy F., 267 n.19
Cottrell, Robert, 279 n.44
Craig, Carol, 278 n.34, 281 n.59
Creon: downfall of, 120; and Antigone,
292 n.55, 293 n.62; edict of,
banning Polynices' burial, 87,
99, 105, 116–18, 292 n.70; and

Haemon, 286 n.16, 287 n.21, 289
n.31; on family ties, 289 n.32;
interpretation of the law, 86,
93–94, 102, 125, 288 n.26, 289
n.33, 291 n.44; and nature,
113–14; and women, 110–11
Culture (see also nature/culture
distinction): 77–78, 298 n.28;
role of, in Beauvoir, 48–49;
women's exclusion from, 143

Dasein (or human being as being-
there), and Being-in-the-world,
134–35, 138, 186; and disclosure,
312 n.99; existential status of,
136, 237; overcoming of
Cartesian tradition, 133–35;
Levinas' critique of, 210, 223
Death: role of, in master-slave dialectic,
63–65, 67, 71, 73; and the right
to burial, 98
De Beauvoir. See Beauvoir
Deconstruction, 129, 241–42, 246
De Lauretis, Teresa, 20
Delmar, Rosalind, 265 n.3
Derrida, 16, 88, 225–54; on Antigone,
96, 104, 291 n.43, 292 n.60; and
feminism, 19, 237–9, 314 n.20;
on Freud, 255–64; influence of,
10; influence of, on Irigaray, 35,
224; and language, 2; on Levinas
and the feminine, 200, 213,
232–5; on Levinas' conception
of same and other, 18, 174, 190,
197, 208, 211; on Levinas' break
with Parmenides, 200, 203, 209;
on Levinas and Plato, 184; and
metaphysics, 144, 189; multiple
sexualities, 44; Ousia and
Grammē, 148–49; Spurs, 165,
237–38
Descartes, Renée (see also Cartesian
dualism; Cogito ergo sum):
133–34, 183, 195, 227, 230
Descombes, Vincent, 279 n.37
Desire: in the master-slave dialectic,
64; in distinction from need, 160,

60, 70; and sense-certainty, 154;
on the tragic hero, 286–87 n.19;
Heidegger, Martin (*see also* Being;
Dasein, Ontological difference;
Technology): 127–64, 167; *Being
and Time* (*Sein und Zeit*), 128–29,
133, 138, 147, 149, 151, 177–78,
223, 227, 247, 303 n.12, 303
n.13; and the continental
tradition, 10, 35, 226, 228–31,
244, 251, 255; and existentialism,
56; history of Being, 240; and
language, 3; and Levinas, 177,
179, 181, 186, 201, 210, 223;
"Origin of the Work of Art,"
235; and the question of Being,
15–16, 243
Heraclitus (*see also* Presocratics): 130,
154
Heterosexuality, compulsory: 126
History, 194; of feminism, 78
Hölderlin, Friedrich, 124, 285 n.3,
294–95 n.75
Holtby, Winifred, 31
Homosexuality, 218
hooks, bell, 7, 11
Husserl, Edmund, 177–78, 227–28,
230, 251
Hyppolite, Jean, 274 n.15, 278 n.36,
281 n.56

Idealism, 179–80
Identity, 251
Imaginary, 173, 301–302 n.1
Immanence, women's: 75, 277 n.31
Incest taboo, 99
Individuality: in relation to Antigone,
95, 107; and death, 96 law of, 89
Inequality, 183, 191–92
Infinity, 183
Ingratitude, radical: 232–34
Instant, 210
Intentionality, 206
Intermediary, 159, 161
Irony: in Hegel, 108–12, 114–16, 292
n.63; of women, 88
Ismene, 99, 102–4, 291 n.47, 48

Jacobus, Mary, 26, 267 n.4
Jaggar, Alison, 35, 267 n.1
Jardine, Alice, 36, 76
Jebb, Richard, 290 n.39
Jehlens, Myra, 267 n.7
Jocasta, 99, 100, 104, 106, 117
Jordanova, L. J., 283 n.73

Kamuf, Peggy, 12, 26–30, 46, 268 n.8
Kant, Immanuel, 129
Kaufmann, Dorothy (*see also*
Kaufmann–McCall): 52
Kaufmann–McCall, Dorothy, 38, 55,
278 n.33
Keefe, Terry, 283 n.70
Kierkegaard, Soren, 56
Knox, Bernard, 117, 288–89 nn.27,
28, 29, 30. 290 n.38, 290 n.40,
291 n.48. 294 n.71, 295 n.76
Kojève, Alexander, 47, 56–57, 274 n.15,
278 n.34, 278–79 nn. 36, 37.
Kore–Persephone, 80–81, 284 n.2
Kristeva, Julia, 10, 27, 32, 34–35, 253,
268 n.13, 271 n.33

Labdacus, house of, 106
Labor: and the master-slave dialectic,
64–65
Lacan, Jacques, 1–3, 35, 37, 40,
242–44, 254, 255–64, 295 n.77
Language, 189–90, 241, 264; and
metaphysics, 165; and
psychoanalysis, 1–2; and the
symbolic, 262; women's exclusion
from, 30; women's relation to,
29–30
Laqueur, Thomas, 84, 119
Le Doeuff, Michèle, 60, 272 n.1, 276
n.27, 277 n.31, 279–80 n.45, 280
n.48, 282–83 n.68
Lesky, Albin, 290 n.39
Levinas, Emmanuel (*see also* Eros;
Ethics; Face to Face; Fecundity,
Other; Ethics; Responsibility)
170–224; and the continental
tradition, 10, 129, 131, 226, 228;
and the face, 244, 255; on the

O'Neill, Onora. See Nell, Onora
Ontological difference (*see also* Being: as distinct from beings): 16, 127, 167, 295 n.1
Ontology: and ethics, 177, 181, 209, 222; fundamental, 150, 223
Oppression, 14; in Beauvoir, 50–51, 59, 66, 72, 75; and complicity, 68
Other (*see also* Alterity; Beauvoir: concept of other; Face to face; Hegel: concept of the other): *Autrui/autre,* 192; and desire, 262; in existentialism, 67; as face to face, 181, 189; in Irigaray, 76, 78, 189; and Lacan 259; in Levinas, 18, 177, 182, 223, 259; and woman, 166, 233
Otherness, 169, 220; and history, 176; and knowledge, 185; and sameness, 171, 173; women's, 234

Parmenides (*see also* Presocratics): 130, 184, 208–12; Levinas' break with, 201–203, 220; on the other/same, 173
Paternity, 191
Patriarchy, 29–30, 174
Passivity, 197–98
Persephone (*see also* Kore-Persephone): 285 n.4
Phallogocentrism, 241–43
Phenomenology, 11, 35, 177, 187
Physis: in relation to *nomos,* 120
Place, 130, 137, 147, 158, 164, 300 n.51; in Aristotle, 155–56; and women, 152, 171, 235, 237
Plaza, Monique, 265 n.8
Pleasure, 242–43; and writing, 248; principle, 257, 261
Plato, 15, 130, 196; and the Good beyond being, 140, 184, 210; in relation to Socrates, 162, 244; *Symposium,* 130, 159–63
Polis: Antigone's relation to, 82, 103, 117; and family, 85; and nature, 115; women's relation to, 88

Polynices: Antigone's relation to, 82, 96, 101, 104, 106, 291 n.51, 292 n.55; burial of, 82, 87, 97, 99, 116, 118, 125, 292 n.59; death of, 86, 109, 113; and Eteocles, 285 n.8, 291 n.53; and Ismene, 102; and family of Oedipus, 100; treachery of, 93
Poste restante, 257–58
Poster, Mark, 278 n.37
Postmodernity: discourse of, 139
Poststructuralism, 2–3
Poovey, Mary, 4
Poster, Mark, 56
Presence, 246–47, 250
Present-at-hand (*Vorhanden*), 153–54
Pre-Socratics, 16, 130, 163–64
Pritchard, Annie, 284 n.1
Proximity, 193
Psychoanalysis, 1–2, 11, 35, 40, 240, 254–55

Queneau, Raymond, 56–57

Race, 6, 11–12, 45, 268 n.9, 274 n.14
Rachel, 216
Racism, 33

Ready-to-hand (*Zuhanden*) 136
Real, 257–59
Reality Principle, 261
Rebecca, 199, 216
Recognition: in Beauvoir's use of the master-slave dialectic, 61, 71; and Hegel's master-slave dialectic, 63–66, 70
Repetition-compulsion, 260
Representation: women's relation to, 171
Repression, 260
Reproduction, 44, 60
Responsibility: in Derrida, 235; and the face to face, 223; in Levinas, 198, 208
Rhode, Deborah, 30, 268 n.11, 296 n.10

Sophocles, 80, 97, 115, 285 n.3
Space/time, 146, 148
Spacks, Patricia Meyer, 27–29
Spelman, 268 n.9, 274 n.14
Spirit (Geist), 87, 89, 92
Spivak, 21, 33, 268–69 n.15, 269 n.17
Stanton, Domna, 4
Stoller, Robert, 39–41, 269–70 n.27
Subject, 168, 185, 197; death of, 29; and desire, 262; feminine and masculine, 75; in Freud, 259; and freedom, 61
Subjectivity, 37, 76, 139, 193–94, 242, 302 n.5, 302 n.7; and the feminine, 219, 240; and infinity, 182; in Levinas, 179, 188; and masculinity, 175; and metaphysics, 176; and otherness, 69
Substitution, 194, 198
Suleiman, Susan, 275 n.15
Symbolic, 177, 262
Szondi, Peter, 87, 293 n.64, 294 n.75

Taminiaux, Jacques, 228, 230
Tavor Bannet, Eve, 2
Technology, 139, 143–46, 298 n.30, 298 n.32, 298 n.33
Temporality, 149
Text, 312 n.1
Teiresias, 286 n.16
Thales, 130
Thebes, 93, 116, 286 n.8
There is (il y a), 187, 304 n.20
Theunissen, Michael, 279 n.40
Third party, 181, 192–93, 196, 206, 304 n.22
Time, 147, 164; and being, 138, 150, 153
Trace, 236

Tragedy, 288 n.23
Transcendence, 60, 72, 191; and existentialism, 58; in Beauvoir, 277 n.31; in Levinas, 305 n.30; and love, 205, 215; and the master-slave dialectic, 72; and self, 55; and situation, 48, 75
Tuana, Nancy, 122–24

Universality, 189, 194–95; in relation to Antigone, 105; and Being, 138; and ethics, 183; and Hegel, 89, 94; and Levinas, 182
Usefulness, 235–36

Van Gogh, Vincent, 235–36
Veil, 165, 252, 256

Whitbeck, Caroline, 297 n.26
Whitford, Margaret, 9, 265 n.2, 264 n.14, 266–67 n.17, 314 n.20
Weedon, 265 n.5
Woman: as container, 156–57; and nature, 66, 121; as other, 166–67; and politics, 118; as threat to unity, 111; and war, 111; and writing, 27–28, 253
Woolf, Virginia, 14, 27, 30–31
Writing, 246–53; and Beauvoir, 275 n. 22; and women, 26–29, 275 n.22
Wyckoff, Elizabeth, 290 n.39

Young, Iris Marion, 4

Zeno, 155
Zeus, 102, 291 n.44
Zuckert, Catherine, 2–3